Palgrave Studies in Creativity and Culture

Series Editors
Vlad Petre Glaveanu
Department of Psychology and Counselling
Dublin City University
Dublin, Ireland

Brady Wagoner
Communication and Psychology
Aalborg University
Aalborg, Denmark

Both creativity and culture are areas that have experienced a rapid growth in interest in recent years. Moreover, there is a growing interest today in understanding creativity as a socio-cultural phenomenon and culture as a transformative, dynamic process. Creativity has traditionally been considered an exceptional quality that only a few people (truly) possess, a cognitive or personality trait 'residing' inside the mind of the creative individual. Conversely, culture has often been seen as 'outside' the person and described as a set of 'things' such as norms, beliefs, values, objects, and so on. The current literature shows a trend towards a different understanding, which recognises the psycho-socio-cultural nature of creative expression and the creative quality of appropriating and participating in culture. Our new, interdisciplinary series Palgrave Studies in Creativity and Culture intends to advance our knowledge of both creativity and cultural studies from the forefront of theory and research within the emerging cultural psychology of creativity, and the intersection between psychology, anthropology, sociology, education, business, and cultural studies. Palgrave Studies in Creativity and Culture is accepting proposals for monographs, Palgrave Pivots and edited collections that bring together creativity and culture. The series has a broader focus than simply the cultural approach to creativity, and is unified by a basic set of premises about creativity and cultural phenomena.

Phillip McIntyre • Susan Kerrigan
Janet Fulton • Evelyn King
Claire Williams

Creativity and Creative Industries in Regional Australia

Interconnected Networks, Shared Knowledge and Choice Making Agents

palgrave
macmillan

Phillip McIntyre
Newcastle, NSW, Australia

Susan Kerrigan
Bolwarra Heights NSW, NSW, Australia

Janet Fulton
Whitebridge NSW, NSW, Australia

Evelyn King
Maitland NSW, NSW, Australia

Claire Williams
Newcastle NSW, NSW, Australia

ISSN 2755-4503 ISSN 2755-4511 (electronic)
Palgrave Studies in Creativity and Culture
ISBN 978-3-031-45974-0 ISBN 978-3-031-45972-6 (eBook)
https://doi.org/10.1007/978-3-031-45972-6

This Palgrave Macmillan imprint is published by the registered company Springer Nature Switzerland AG.
The registered company address is: Gewerbestrasse 11, 6330 Cham, Switzerland

Paper in this product is recyclable.

To Kevin Coffey, who knew how to build a strong community and infuse it with love, spirit and courage.

Preface

In this book we take a long hard look at the Hunter Valley in New South Wales (NSW) in Australia, a collection of towns and cities, an economic powerhouse of a region and one that is crucial to the country and continent it is located in. The creative industries here, as you'll discover in this book, form in every way imaginable one part of the global creative industries. As one of our participants claimed, the only way to be truly global is to be local first. His "little wireless program"—his words—is recorded in the upper reaches of the valley, in the ABC studios in Muswellbrook, and it not only has guests from all over the world but also has a highly rated national and international reach via broadcast, podcast and streaming. His story, which is much more complex than this, is only one of the many that you'll encounter in this book.

The overall aim of *Creativity and Creative Industries in Regional Australia: Interconnected Networks, Shared Knowledge and Choice Making Agents* is to trace the lived experience of working creatively in the regions, framed against the broader scholarly ideas about creativity and creative industries. It connects the lives, faces, relationships and talent that exist in the creative industries in the Hunter Region to the larger state, national and global networks that typify the creative industries in Australia and, we suspect, elsewhere. It explores the workings of the creative (eco)system they exist within. We peer beneath the broader aspects of the creative economy to allow real-life narratives to emerge while exploring how people organize themselves into generalized and often supportive structures, find adaptable business models, smooth out operational challenges and express their creative impulses in ways that potentially earn them a living.

In looking at the sets of interconnected networks that creative people, that is, choice making agents, engage with and the shared knowledges that exist within, this book provides a big picture view of the creative industries as they exist in regional Australia. At the same time, the book also marries these stories with a detailed statistical analysis. This comprehensive account sets out the rich and diverse composition of the 10,000 workers in gainful employment in the creative industries sectors of Australia's Hunter Region. The core of this creative workforce is composed of musicians, writers, publishers, advertisers, designers, artists, performers, presenters, journalists, filmmakers, photographers, storytellers, electronic gamers and architects, to name just a few of the occupations you will encounter, and they contribute $1 billion annually to the regional economy, an economy that is bigger than a number of Australian states and territories. This regional economy is located in the Hunter Valley of NSW, which is 160 kilometers (100 miles) north of Sydney. In 2017, the population of the region was more than 675,000, and these residents live in rural and semi-rural areas, and the various towns and cities that exist across 11 local government areas in the valley. The qualitative detail of this account is then provided by a little over 100 in-depth qualitative interviews with creative industries professionals, allowing the book to delve deeply into the personal working lives of a cross-section of regional creative workers. The book gives a broad set of insights into their training, business experience and personal journeys illustrating how people go about being creative, the challenges they meet and opportunities they encounter working in a dynamic set of creative industries.

In the book, we tell stories of more than one hundred "creatives", about their experiences and perceptions of the creative industries and themselves as creative workers—people who have transformed their art, creativity and passion into a way of life and a way to fund that way of life. And for each paid professional in the Hunter, as the book reveals, there is a thick layer of amateurs, interns and volunteers, together delivering cultural products and creative services to a surprisingly vast array of local and global businesses and audiences. To better understand each creative worker, their experiences are framed by the historical context of the sectors they work in, the common business models these sectors employ, as well as the operational methods and contemporary economic structures they are part of. These help to explain how these creative workers earn a living within the Hunter. In this way, the people behind the broader data come to life. Each chapter attempts to distill key ideas around which we can grasp the reality of work for each creative tribe.

This book thus details the lived experience of many of the creative workers who reside in this regional context while, at the same time, operating as part of the global creative industries. These industries are composed of four basic sectors—the arts, design, the media and information technology—and operate, as we argue in the book, as a creative system in action, one which is increasingly affected by the inspirations, competition and affordances provided by the digital age and increasingly dynamic global markets.

Newcastle, NSW, Australia — Philip McIntyre
Bolwarra Heights, NSW, Australia — Susan Kerrigan
Whitebridge, NSW, Australia — Janet Fulton
Maitland, NSW, Australia — Evelyn King
Newcastle, NSW, Australia — Claire Williams

Acknowledgments

It is worth noting that we have drawn on the following resources to complete this book:

ARC LP130100348, McIntyre, P., Balnaves, M., Kerrigan, S., King, E., & Williams, C. *Creativity and cultural production in the Hunter: An applied ethnographic study of new entrepreneurial systems in the creative industries*, 2013–2017.

ARC LP160101724, Cunningham, S., Hearn, G., McIntyre, P., Wikstrom, P., & Kerrigan, S. *Australian cultural & creative activity: A population & hotspot analysis*, 2016–2020.

McIntyre, P., Balnaves, M., Kerrigan, S., King, E., & Williams, C. (2019). *Creativity and cultural production in the Hunter: An applied ethnographic study of new entrepreneurial systems in the creative industries*. Australian Research Council. https://hciss.newcastle.edu.au/hci/final-report/

McIntyre, P., & Sheather, G. (2013). The Newcastle music industry: an ethnographic study of a regional creative system in action. *International Journal of Music Business Research (special issue on the Australian Music Economy)*, *2*(2), 36–60.

Phillip

Working with this team, on this book, at this time, has been a real pleasure. Susan, Janet, Evelyn, Claire and I have traveled a long path together from the project's inception through to the delivery of this book. I would like to acknowledge and thank Professor Mark Balnaves for shepherding this project through its funding phase, his delight at its success and all he contributed in that process. His insights and persistence were only outshone by his erudition and his good humor. I would also like to thank Distinguished Professor Stuart Cunningham for seeing what was possible with a project like this and taking us on that journey with him as we expanded the scope of the research onto the national stage. I would like to acknowledge the time and effort put into the project by both of our partners, the Newcastle Business Improvement Association and Technica CPT, who not only put their money behind the project but also took on the mantle of co-researchers with considerable aplomb. I would like to thank our publishers, Palgrave Macmillan, for also having faith in this project and, as always, bringing to it the level of professionalism they have always displayed. I want to thank every single soul from the Hunter Valley, from the river's headwaters right down to the port and beyond, who gave of their time and collective wisdom to make all of this possible. I want to thank my family for all the love they have given me as the time has crept on and I needed their re-energizing. Julie, there is very little to say other than "You are one of life's miracles and I'm extremely grateful you chose me to spend your life with."

Susan

I am enormously proud of the research presented here that confirms regional dwellers are locally and globally creative. These stories of regional creatives echo my lived experience. I was born in the Hunter Valley, educated here, started my creative career here and later returned to teach creative practice at the regional university. I am enduringly grateful to Phillip who invited me to join the team in 2012, and whose passion for explaining how we are creative has underpinned all facets of this research.

To Mark Balnaves, thanks for your contribution in the early days, and to Evelyn and Claire, for your enthusiasm for the Hunter's creatives. It was infectious, and many of the stories are here because of your contacts and networks. To Janet, it has been a pleasure to work with you again on our third research book. I do hope there will be more! This fine piece of research will be acknowledged as such by Swinburne University of Technology, who have employed me to continue my research into creative practice, and I am very grateful for that opportunity. Lastly to my family, David and our daughters, Alice and Rose—who we raised in the Hunter because we believed it would give them all they needed—thank you for your patience and support as I continue to explain how important creativity is to our lives.

Janet

Many, many thanks to Phillip, Susan, Evelyn and Claire for inviting me to be a part of this book. It is wonderful to write about this part of the world that we live in, about people who love the Hunter as much as I do.

I'd also like to thank the Royal Melbourne Institute of Technology (RMIT University), Australia, for giving me an academic home where I can continue to pursue my love of research and to those colleagues who have supported me over the last several years. And I would also like to give special thanks to Phillip and Susan: Phillip for imbuing me with a love of research over many years of mentorship and Susan for being my academic rock. You are both dear friends who I admire enormously.

And, last but definitely not least, thanks to my family for their ongoing love and support: Jade and Brendan; Pete and Demelza; and my grandbabies, Asha and Will.

Evelyn

To hear and share the stories of regional creatives and to understand more of the challenges they met in their quest to follow their passion and make a living was enlightening and inspirational. In my workplace, outside academia, I have seen many efforts that were designed to encourage business growth for artists, performers, designers and the whole pantheon of creative endeavor. Indeed, I learned much about the way the words "business" and "creative" are perceived by many to be inimical concepts. It seems that if people truly listened to the creative community, those efforts may have brought greater success in building sustainable jobs. Perhaps through the findings of this work, a marathon of listening, other such efforts may be more effective. I am grateful for the opportunity to hear those voices. And for the patience of my family during my distraction.

Claire

Working on this project with the team has been enormously rewarding and enjoyable. It has given me an opportunity to look in a different way at the work of people, many of whom I have engaged with professionally throughout my career as a creative industries practitioner, educator and arts manager in the Hunter Region and elsewhere. Thanks to the people we interviewed and to the countless others they represent—the writers, performers, artists, filmmakers, architects, designers, makers and others—whose contributions (so often undervalued) make our world more beautiful and more meaningful.

Contents

About the Authors

Phillip McIntyre is a Professor in the School of Humanities, Creative Industries and Social Sciences at the University of Newcastle, Australia. A communication and media scholar, his research focuses on creativity and innovation.

Susan Kerrigan is a Professor and Chair of the Department of Film, Games and Animation at Swinburne University of Technology, Australia. An expert in the fields of creative practice and screen production, her research highlights creative agents and how their practices produce creative products that are culturally consumed.

Janet Fulton is an Adjunct Associate Professor at RMIT University. Her research interests include creativity and cultural production, journalism, journalism education, media entrepreneurship and work-integrated learning.

Evelyn King worked in schools and academia before tackling PR at the Australian Museum. She has experience in cultural and heritage tourism, economic development, smart city initiatives, renewable energy and business start-ups.

Claire Williams is a writer and editor. Formerly Faculty Director, Creative Industries, at Hunter TAFE, she has also taught Communications, Information Studies and HR at tertiary level. She is also an actor and theater director working in stage and film.

List of Figures

List of Tables

1

Introduction

The Hunter Valley in Australia is a place historically defined, post-European arrival, by agriculture, coal and heavy industry. Vineyards and beach culture now also feature strongly in its story. It is, in some ways, reminiscent of the Ruhr Valley in Germany; the Midlands in the UK centered on Birmingham, Manchester and Liverpool; and possibly the North East corner of the USA, more specifically Cleveland, Pittsburgh or Philadelphia. All of these localities share the fact that in order to be global they were all firstly, and still are, local. This is what identifies them as localities. The region that is the focus of this book is a locality that is, like all other current localities similar to it, inextricably embroiled in the global, as will become evident further into the book. It is also, in many other ways, unlike any of these localities mentioned above in that the Hunter Valley fits in an odd place as far as state and federal bodies in Australia are concerned. It is, depending on the aims of the funding body and various policymakers, sometimes defined as "metropolitan" and at other times defined as "regional". It has also been described as 'a State within a State' (HIP, 2023, p. 6) and is seen as a national economic powerhouse since it has 'significantly more people and greater economic output than Tasmania, the Australian Capital Territory or the Northern Territory' (HIP, 2023, p. 6). It is 'Australia's largest regional economy,

The original version of the chapter has been revised. A correction to this chapter can be found at https://doi.org/10.1007/978-3-031-45972-6_17

P. McIntyre et al., *Creativity and Creative Industries in Regional Australia*, Palgrave Studies in Creativity and Culture, https://doi.org/10.1007/978-3-031-45972-6_1

with a gross regional product of over $47 billion pa and a population of nearly 775,000 (2021, ABS Estimated Resident Population) … It includes Greater Newcastle—the seventh largest urban area in Australia' (HIP, 2023, p. 2).

> It is a vibrant and diverse center with a focus on technology, research, knowledge sharing, industry and innovation. It has a dynamic start-up sector and many global companies across industries including aerospace, advanced manufacturing, mining and defence. It is also a rapidly growing center for renewable energy. The region is situated on Australia's main east coast transport corridor. It has sophisticated infrastructure, international gateways including an airport and deep sea port, its own media outlets and university … The Hunter combines an innovative economic and business environment with a high standard of living, proximity to Australia's largest city, Sydney and easy connections to Australia's other capital cities. (HIP, 2023, p. 2)

It is also a place where the creative industries flourish. Creative professionals in this region perform, sing, design, write, paint, record and film just as they do right across the globe. Many of them undertake business globally and quite a number have global reputations. In this book we tell the stories of these "creatives"; stories which are about their experiences and their perceptions of the creative industries and themselves as creative workers; how they have transformed their art, creativity and passion into a way of life and developed a way to fund it. The core of this creative workforce is composed of musicians, writers, publishers, advertisers, designers, artists, performers, presenters, filmmakers, photographers, storytellers, electronic gamers and architects. And for each paid professional in the Hunter, there is a thick layer of amateurs, interns and volunteers and support workers, that comprises a complex creative system in action—a term some would prefer to call a creative ecosystem—delivering cultural products and services to a surprisingly vast array of local and global businesses and audiences.

At the same time, we place these personal narratives against the broad and often global social and cultural structures each of these workers, freelancers and business people encounters in their daily creative practice. In doing this, we provide a big picture view of creativity and the creative industries as we set out a comprehensive review of the relevant literature, before giving a detailed statistical analysis of the creative industries and explaining the extensive ethnographic work the authors undertook for this project. We give a thorough account of that research explaining the rich and diverse composition of the 10,000 workers in gainful employment in the creative industries sectors. It's noteworthy that these creative operatives contribute $1 billion annually to the gross regional domestic product of Australia's Hunter region. The detail of this account was provided by a little over 100 in-depth qualitative interviews with creative industries workers, observations of their practices and working conditions, as well an artifact analysis, all of which has allowed us to delve deeply into the creative processes and personal working lives of a cross-section of these creative individuals, and the broader structures that provide the affordances typical of the creative industries worldwide. This regional project then took a nationally focused turn. With a number of other colleagues, we expanded the research to cover a variety of different regions across the country from metropolitan centers to regional hubs. While we give some detail of this work in our final chapter, this book concentrates on the initial study, the one that started it all for us.

The overall purpose for undertaking the work for *Creativity and Creative Industries in Regional Australia: Interconnected Networks, Shared Knowledge and Choice Making Agents* is thus not only to trace the lived experiences of working creatively but also to frame this against the broader scholarly ideas about creativity and the creative industries, in particular the systems model of creativity. In doing this, we connect the lives, faces, relationships and talent that exist in the creative industries in the Hunter region to the larger state, national and globally interconnected networks they exist within, as well as the shared knowledge that typifies each domain of creativity seen within creative industries right across the globe. We peer beneath the broader aspects of the creative industries to allow real-life narratives to emerge while exploring how people, those choice making agents existing within the creative ecosystem, organize themselves into generalized and often supportive structures, find adaptable business models, smooth out operational challenges and express their creative impulses in ways that potentially earn them a living. However, rather than this process being framed mainly by processes of economic efficiency and organization, we take the view, along with Gregory Hywood, that 'creativity has been the engine of growth' (2004, p. 13) for these industries. For us, it sits at the heart of the matter. It is the reason we took on this study and why we have written this book.

Our previous work on creative systems in action (McIntyre et al., 2016), drawing as it does on the systems model of creativity (Csikszentmihalyi, 1988, 1999, 2014), can be applied very well here. This will become more evident as the book progresses but for now we can say that:

> Systems, like ecosystems and ecologies, are characterized by multiple components that interact in densely interrelated networks. They are 'chaotic, highly nonlinear and essentially impossible to explain and predict from mechanisms and laws' (Sawyer, 2010, p. 368) and they are difficult to either understand or explain via a reductionist approach. Sawyer further argues that, like their biological cousins, 'social systems are complex systems that share many systemic properties with other complex systems, including the human mind' (ibid.). For example, an acceptance of complexity, rather than simplicity, is a prerequisite to understanding them. Along with complexity, systems exhibit multifactorial properties, as well as interconnectedness, non-linearity, dynamism, adaptability, scalability, emergence, self-organization and complementarity (McIntyre & Thompson, 2021, p. 17).

To reiterate, ecosystems, ecologies or (eco)systems, are all systems by any other name and thus share the characteristics of all systems. The model we are drawing on, the systems model of creativity, is made up of three major components which can be briefly set out in the following way. Creative activity or objects emerge for the interaction of a domain of knowledge, that is, shared knowledge that typifies a field. A field can be seen as a set of interconnected networks that operate at various scales across the creative system. Each of these is necessary but not sufficient in and of themselves for creativity to emerge, as is the third major component of the system, that is, the choice making agent. To abbreviate and repeat, domains are systems of shared knowledge, fields are structured as interconnected networks while agents have agency in this system, that is, they have the ability to make choices conditioned by the structures they interact with. We explain these ideas more fully in the next chapter, but what is important for us right now, though, is the major assumption that can be seen underpinning our ideas. This idea is that the context or the sociocultural situation in which creativity and innovation occurs, and is carefully nurtured, is as equally important to its emergence as is individual action. Novel and valued things, creative things, do not emerge in isolation from the world around them. All action is contextually dependent. We cannot emphasize this enough.

For our purposes, a context can be seen as the spatial, temporal and discursive spaces that are interconnected or woven together with other connected spaces or structures that precede or follow the object of our attention and also operate hierarchically in scale both above and below it. These contextual interconnections have an effect on the object that is located in that context. Giving a succinct account of many of the contextual events that eventually provide the setting for the operations of the creative industries, Dayan Thussu wrote:

> In the 1980s and 1990s fundamental ideological changes in the global political arena led to the creation of pro-market international trade regimes which had a huge impact on international communication. The processes of liberalization, deregulation and privatization in the communication and media industries, combined with new digital information and communication technologies have enabled a quantum leap in international communication. The resulting globalization of telecommunications, computer and media industries has enabled more information to travel more swiftly around a digitally linked globe than ever before in human history. (2019, p. 75)

As Handke and Towse also explained, digitization had a considerable impact on the creative industries transforming 'the way creative works are generated, disseminated and used. Digitization has also enabled the development of new types of creative goods and services' (2013, p. 1). Thussu contends that with the advent of digital distribution, a wide variety of revenue earning opportunities became available 'as the media and telecommunications sectors intersect globally. The expanding bandwidth, coupled with the rapid globalization of fixed and mobile networks, as well as the digitization of content and growing use of personal computers worldwide' (2006, p. 99) has helped a multitude of businesses capitalize on emerging markets and experiment with new commercial products and business models. The political, social, cultural, ethical, legal and environmental transformations have taken place on a scale not seen since the industrial revolution. In an edition of the *Communication Research and Practice* journal Servaes writes:

> The 1990s, with the fall of the Berlin Wall and the explosive growth of the World Wide Web as preludes, have been marked by the collapse of the physical, virtual and institutional barriers that have kept people apart. The ever closer trade relationships among nation-states, the growing power of transnational corporations, information and communication technologies (ICTs), internet, and discussions on e-governance, the emergence of global health and environmental issues, and a common style of consumption of material and cultural products have all helped to bring about what is described as 'globalization' of our world or the world becoming a 'global village.' However, globalization is not a product of the 1990s, or even the twentieth century, as many historians will explain (see, for instance, Hopkins, 2002). Therefore, Held, McGrew, Goldblatt and Perraton (1999, p. 414) conclude that "globalization is neither a wholly novel, nor primarily modern, social phenomenon. Its form has changed over time and across the key domains of human interaction, from the political to the ecological". (2015, p. 242)

This idea is reinforced by Timothy Havens and Amanda Lotz. They suggest that globalization 'involves a variety of complex and sometimes contradictory social and economic developments that have been taking place for centuries' (2016, p. 221). However, they observe that given the fundamentally global character of the internet, the practices and forms of globalization 'may change profoundly as digitization continues to change the media industries' (2016, p. 221). And it is not just the media industries that are being subject to disruption in this process. On the *Der Speigel International* website Schulz asserts that:

> The technological advances made in the last decade have been breathtaking, but it is likely still just the beginning ... We are witnessing nothing less than a societal transformation that ultimately nobody will be able to avoid. It is the kind of sea change that can only be compared with 19th century industrialization, but it is happening much faster this time. Just as the change from hand work to mass production dramatically changed our society over 100 years ago, the digital revolution isn't just altering specific sectors of the economy, it is changing the way we think and live. (2015, online)

At the same time as globalization and digitization have been primary drivers for recent developments in the creative industries, and elsewhere, one specific ideology, neoliberalism, also came to dominate in the political and economic sphere. As David Harvey suggested in his book *A brief history of neoliberalism*, this ideology has now become 'so embedded in common sense as to be taken for granted and not open to question' (2007, p. 5); the conceptual apparatus of neoliberalism took the best that liberalism had to offer in terms of individual liberty but then pragmatically narrowed its focus down to the primacy of "the market" which then became its central tenet.

Rosamund Davies and Gauti Sigthorsson wrote that 'the influence of neoliberalism on government policy [was an] important factor in changing organizational structures, mainly through the privatization of state-owned institutions and businesses and the relaxation of state-control through deregulation' (2013, p. 47). This situation had the effect of hollowing out mid-sized companies leaving an "ecology" of multinational corporations engaged in vertical disintegration outsourcing a lot of work to SMEs, a highly casualized workforce or an increasing pool of contractors and freelancers (Hesmondhalgh & Baker, 2011). For the creative industries, this situation gave rise to 'a handful of high-profile global players, stars and multinational companies, dependent on vast shoals of project-based micro enterprises' (Evans quoted in Davies & Sigthorsson, 2013, p. 49). This structural phenomenon has been dubbed the 'whales and plankton' ecology of the creative industries (Davies & Sigthorsson, 2013) and it is now a hallmark of these industries, as well as many others.

It is against this political, technological and economic context, related as it is to neoliberalism, globalization and digitization, that the idea of the creative industries became increasingly important (Gross, 2020). The changes these contextual factors have wrought are of deep concern to many who have come to depend on the creative industries to mediate their world through a variety of audio, visual and text based cultural forms. These mediations exist in a set of structural conditions that include international legal frameworks, industrial settings, trade agreements, public and private sector investment, including the second and third legs of the triple bottom line (Elkington, 1999), as well as a veritable host of sociocultural, environmental, economic, political and technological contextual entanglements that typify the many urban and regional spaces that creative industries operate in.

Urban agglomerations, cities, don't exist in isolation, just as regions too do not exist in isolation. They are, at one and the same time, spatial and temporal, that is, they are both historically and geographically located. As Fernand Braudel (1990) pointed out, the geography of a locality or region, the space it exists in, affects its patterns of settlement and has some effect on the systems of trade, culture and politics that develop there. These localities are also embedded in time with personal, local, regional, national and global histories being disseminated across them on an almost daily basis. These histories are also embedded in the actions taken by individuals and institutions that reside in these spaces. The way linked villages, towns and cities come to define themselves and are defined further afield is dependent in many senses on the geographical and historical interactions being enacted there. Hinterlands feed cities and cities depend on their hinterlands for survival as they both interact with larger cities and states. Smaller towns draw trade, wealth, knowledge and ideas from their larger urban cousins and the urban areas are sustained by migrations of people and goods to and from them. As Braudel thoughtfully puts it:

> Every urban settlement is bound to live by maintaining a balance between what it receives (or takes) and what it gives (or returns). The balance has perpetually to be adjusted, the point of equilibrium is never fixed. And the particular way a town draws on the outside world while modifying itself internally, the better to attach itself to its surroundings and dominate them, is never simple. (1990, p. 189)

These systemic contexts are thus crucial to 'explaining the system' (Braudel, 1990, pp. 161–162). As Braudel points out, cities and towns exist in 'circles of influence' (1990, p. 185). Similarly, cities operate within 'zones of urban attraction' (Braudel, 1990, p. 259). The multi-faceted influence of a regional capital, 'political and cultural in the broadest sense of both terms' (Braudel, 1990, p. 259), tends to exceed its designated city limits. This system is thus scalable, interconnected and interdependent.

As an example of all of this, the Hunter region in New South Wales (NSW), Australia, is a contested space operating as a system of many interactions and identities. It is not 'just there to be described' (McManus et al., 2000, p. 3). This can be seen in the 'emergence of the Hunter Region as a cultural bounding of physical space that has, itself, changed over billions of years' (McManus et al., 2000, p. 3).

Somewhere 'between 20,000 and 45,000 years ago the first people began to arrive in this ancient landscape, moving across the alluvial plains, through the dense rainforest, into the gullies and mountains, following the rivers and creeks' (Dunn, 2020, pp. 11–12). These first peoples, known later as Aboriginals by the Europeans, 'came to know the valley over generations, managing the land to take advantage of the abundant resources' (Dunn, 2020, p. 12). With an increasingly deep relationship 'to the land and Country came both physical and spiritual knowledge of the Hunter Valley. As well as trade items, stories and ceremony moved back and forth across the landscape' (Dunn, 2020, p. 15). While there were certainly virtual boundaries erected between social groups like the Wonnarua, Worimi, Awabakal and others, 'historical accounts for the first years of contact suggest a complex web of connections through trade, marriage and religion' (Dunn, 2020, p. 14). Layered on top of this ongoing system of Indigenous occupation in the valley, the Europeans formed their own boundaries:

> There is the water catchment regional boundary, the political regional boundary, the regional economy and the Hunter Region of every individual's geographical imagination. For some people, the Hunter Region is centered on Newcastle, for others it is focused on the vineyards or the coalfields, while for other people the Hunter Region is an area somewhere north of

the Central Coast. For other people it is not Sydney! (McManus et al., 2000, p. 3)

Within this contested space, the urban agglomeration connected to its rural hinterland and centered on Newcastle, has moved from thousands of years of Indigenous occupation, to very recently being a convict settlement to a coal town, to a steel city and now a post-industrial city intent on reinventing itself as a smart or creative city. In this regard, Marcus Westbury's book, *Creating Cities*, is a useful one in that it partially sees the world in systemic terms. Westbury identifies the connectivity those in Newcastle now experience. For him, every action that is taken in individual creative projects:

> is a microcosm of a wider network. Each is distinctive. Most of them are very much from and of Newcastle; they literally could not have happened anywhere else. Yet virtually all of them are connected. They are part of global movements, networks, dialogues and markets. (2015, p. 155)

We can see in Westbury's account an emphasis on interconnected systems of the type described by Manuel Castells in his book *The Rise of the Networked Society* (2010). Westbury's description also points to the diffuse nature of networked power that is typically seen in systems of the type described by Michel Foucault (quoted in Jordan & Weedon, 1995, p. 479) where he de-emphasized the notion of power hierarchies in favor of diffuse networks with nodes of varying influence. Westbury goes on, with an almost anti-Romantic point of view, to echo the research literature on creativity, which we will explore more fully shortly, suggesting that:

> Perhaps the most damaging myth of all is the idea that artists or creatives or whatever you want to call them are somehow special. That people who do things are some kind of "other" force that butts up against the status quo with special insights and talents and visions. I don't actually think that's true. It is the very ordinariness of action and imagination that I find reassuring. It is the diversity of people and places it comes from that I find solace in. It is the realization that the propensity for imagination and action is a force like any other. It responds to invitations and opportunities, to

collaborations and connections, and often lies dormant within communities and individuals. (2015, p. 156)

It is against this backdrop that we developed our research. The stories we ourselves are about to tell in this book about creativity and the creative industries, the interconnected networks, shared knowledge and choice making agents who reside there, are the result of a multi-year applied ethnographic study of key collaborative groups across all the major creative sectors in the Hunter Valley in NSW. We believe we have developed invaluable baseline data for the creative industries in the region. Policymakers, businesses, not-for-profits and all those working in, and dealing with these increasingly significant industries, either educationally, economically or culturally, will now know what they are, how they work, why they're important, and what's been happening with them. In this project, we've plotted these industries' approach to creativity and cultural production in the Hunter Region and, as a consequence, we believe it provides useful and detailed insights into the dynamic systems these industries are part of.

In an area as geographically, socially and industrially diverse as the Hunter Region, with its urban concentrations of more than 350,000 people, and with rural and tourism centers, and waterfront villages, there is a wide band of skills and market experience evident in the valley. Mining, defense, shipping, health, manufacturing, power generation, viticulture, education, agriculture and professional services are all evident in the region's profile but steel and aluminum production, shipbuilding, manufacturing and even coal production have all decreased their contribution in recent years. Alongside these significant and mature generators of jobs and related businesses, there is an identifiable and potentially strong economic sector now commonly referred to as the creative industries. At the heart of these industries, as suggested above by Gregory Hywood (2004) and used as the adjective within the term *creative industries*, lies creativity.

We take our cue here from the research literature into creativity (for summaries see, for example, Alexander, 2003; Kaufman & Sternberg, 2019; Pope, 2005; Sawyer, 2012). We don't see creativity as many Western common-sense understandings would have it. For us, creativity is defined in line with the literature, that is, as the bringing into being of novel objects, processes and ideas that are valued in at least one social setting (Hennessey, 2017; Hennessey & Amabile, 2010). On the other hand, drawing on Raymond Williams' formative ideas, culture for us is seen as 'the convergence between an anthropological and sociological sense of culture as a distinct "whole way of life"' (1981, p. 13) and the 'more specialized if also more common sense of culture as "artistic and intellectual activities"... broadly defined to include all the "signifying practices"' (1981, p. 13) of, in this case, the creative industries.

We also use the concept of the creative industries as an umbrella term covering sectors that are all connected by three defining features. Firstly, they 'all require some input of *human creativity*; second, they are *vehicles for symbolic messages*, that is, they are carriers of *meaning*; and third, they contain, at least potentially, some *intellectual property* that belongs to an individual or group' [italics in original] (Davies & Sigthorsson, 2013, p. 1). The creative industries are thus those industries, that is, loosely coupled systems of production, which use signifying practices to intentionally bring meaning into being via audio, visual and text based artifacts in order to create value. That value may be social, cultural, symbolic or economic. Innovation, for us, is similarly defined (McIntyre, 2011). It is, in line with Everett Rogers' thinking:

> an idea, practice, or object that is perceived as new by an individual or other unit of adoption. It matters little, so far as human behavior is concerned, whether or not an idea is "objectively" new as measured by the lapse of time since its first use or discovery. (2003, p. 12)

If it is entrepreneurial activity that 'takes creativity or innovation to enter and compete in an existing market, to change or even create a new market' (EC, 2003, p. 5) we can say that entrepreneurship itself 'deals with the process of developing new business ventures and/or promoting growth and innovation in existing firms' (Mazzarol, 2011, p. i).

All of this occurs within a system of production. Systems, whether they are also labeled ecosystems (Lawlor, 2014) or ecologies (Mayanja et al., 2019), are "wholes", that is, complete entities whose 'primary properties derive from the interactions of their parts' (Skyttner, 2006, p. 38).

At the same time, it is also true that 'a system in one perspective is a subsystem in another. But the system view always treats systems as integrated wholes of their subsidiary components' (Laszlo, 1972, p. 14). They are thus scalable: one system sitting inside another, sitting inside another and so on. Apart from this scalability, complex systems, as mentioned above, also share other similar characteristics. To repeat, these include interdependence, networks, self-organization, complementarity, scalability, non-linear dynamics and emergence. We can then say that social and cultural systems, sometimes referred to as ecosystems, (eco)systems or ecologies, are self-organized as interconnected networks built on shared knowledge and are populated by choice making agents.

In order to study those systems, or (eco)systems, we employed a largely qualitative methodology (Fetterman, 2011) based in anthropology, ethnography, supported by some initial quantitative work. As researcher Susannah Priest asserts, groups like the creative industries 'must be understood as whole systems, not isolated parts' (1996, p. 25) and, on this basis, research was undertaken to detail the creative activities of different participants and institutions, their entrepreneurial activities and the networks and knowledges involved in the creative industries in the Hunter region. This process involved a number of practical methods.

The first action taken in this research process was a literature review. We will detail this more fully in Chap. 2. A descriptive quantitative approach was then undertaken to support the more extensive qualitative aspects of the study. This quantitative aspect involved two measures and is set out in some detail in Chap. 4. Measure 1 of the statistical analysis involved a search of 2011 Census data using the ANZSCO 6 Digit Occupation Codes as listed in the final report from the Creative Industries Innovation Centre, *Valuing Australia's creative industries* (CIIC, 2013, pp. 24–25). This list of occupations was applied to the 11 local government areas (LGAs) of the Hunter Region. Measure 2 involved the use of the Creative Trident Methodology, explained more fully in Chap. 4, where data was drawn from both the 2011 and 2016 Census. Unlike Measure 1, this data was based on SA4 geographical areas. The collected data for Measure 2 was then used to calculate the specialist, support and embedded workers, their earning and average annual income. The later national study, derived from the Hunter study we are detailing here, and elaborated on more fully in the final chapter, used the same methodology as its basis but also drew on the 2020 ABS Census data.

The specific qualitative methods, which afforded the collection of the majority of the material we draw on for this book, included ongoing desktop research, 115 recorded in-depth semi-structured interviews with key informants, and participant observation over a four-year period in the field. Artifact analysis was also used. The initial data revealed in this ongoing and recursive research process informed, firstly, a creative industries forum conducted mid-way through the research process which was later complemented with a focus group of key informants from the Upper Hunter. The Miles and Huberman framework (Punch, 2014; Robson & McCartan, 2016) for qualitative data analysis (QDA) was then applied to the collected data which resulted in the "thick description" most ethnography entails (Denscombe, 2017; Geertz, 1973, pp. 5–6 & 9–10). As such, the conduct of this research followed the key methods and principles of ethnography. An outline of the results can be seen below but is revealed far more fully in Chaps. 5–14. These chapters examine each of the creative industries sectors separately, that is, music, performing arts, architecture, visual arts, fashion, advertising, PR and design, publishing, radio, film and television, and electronic games and interactive content.

We can say briefly here that the statistical analysis revealed that the Gross Regional Product (GRP) for the Hunter Region sat at $48.351 billion at the time of the study making it a bigger contributor to the national economy than some states and territories. Those employed in the creative industries, by our statistical Measure 1, which is elaborated on more fully shortly, constituted 2% of the working population in the region. They were conservatively estimated to contribute close to $1 billion to the Hunter GRP. The urban center of the Hunter Region, Newcastle, had the largest share of creative industries operatives as would be expected. Its nearest urban agglomeration, Lake Macquarie, had nearly as many as the regional capital and of the rural and semi-rural areas Maitland had the largest share, then Port Stephens. The Dungog LGA had the lowest number of creative industries residents with the Upper Hunter contributing less than 100 operatives to the overall total of 6535.

The data from the 2011 Census showed, by this measure, that the Advertising and Design sector in the Hunter constituted by far the largest sector in the creative industries in this region. This was followed by the Electronic Games and Interactive Content sector, with Architecture approximately a quarter of that of Advertising and Design. Together these three sectors represented 75% of the total creative industries occupations in the region. The lowest was the Film sector, followed by Radio, Fashion, Television and then the Performing Arts.

Measure 2 revealed that the number of people employed in the creative industries in the region rose from 2011 to 2016. Share of total workforce increased with a cumulative annual growth rate of 2% compared with a growth in the general workforce of 0.6%. The percentage of specialist and support workers dropped marginally with growth in employment for embedded creatives. Notably, there was an increase in income levels across the board for the creative industries. However, it is in the support sector where incomes rose the most, followed closely by those working as embedded personnel. Embedded creatives have the highest level of weekly income (McIntyre et al., 2019). These trends remain relatively close to the statistical information revealed later by the 2020 Census (Cunningham et al., 2022).

From the qualitative analysis we found that the creative industries sectors of music, performing arts, architecture, visual arts, fashion, advertising, PR and design, publishing, radio, film and television, and electronic games and interactive content, all constituted important parts of a diverse and continually dynamic creative system in action. This creative system focused on profiting from and valorizing the signifying practices used to produce, disseminate and consume the symbolic messages being produced. While we saw that the siloed structures of production that typify traditional economies are mutating rapidly, our research supported the idea that industries, of all types, are increasingly being seen as loosely coupled systems of production and yet many still appeared to apply nineteenth-century concepts of what an industry is to what this twenty-first-century phenomenon is now. Many were also still tending to see creative industries and "the creatives" that work within them using their own specific sectoral lens while a number of culturally specific beliefs and assumptions also played a major part in actions taken by institutions and individuals. It was also the case that the social and cultural value of these industries did not always equate to financial value.

The entrepreneurial ecosystems we uncovered were all seen to be adapting to pressures of globalization and digitization with many, however, employing extensions of more traditional business models. It was also the case that some sectors in the creative industries were mature while others could be seen as emerging, noting that if emergent sectors, such as games and interactive software, were to be encouraged and financed adequately, they could stimulate activity in nearly all of the other sectors. The project also found very little clustering in the way it had been envisaged by Michael Porter (1990) and it was obvious the internet had provided a way for many to bypass this clustering effect although traditional face-to-face activity was still vital to success for many. There is also a variety of collaborative activities occurring for creative practitioners in the region. These are often a function of the type of cultural production being engaged in, for example, film, television, radio, music and design activities all rely on collaboration to do what they do. There are also a number of efforts on the part of support organizations to foster collaboration and the setting up of production hubs, both local government and privately operated, have stimulated various forms of collaboration within certain creative industries sectors.

Other forms of infrastructure necessary to the creative industries are substantial in this region. It is both physical and digital. Production hubs, studios, theaters, museums and galleries, retail outlets, warehouses and office space as well as standard electricity, road and air transport infrastructure are all still highly important. However, there was not a single SME, organization or individual found in the ethnographic study who had not come to rely on the internet and its necessary software, hardware and telecommunications infrastructure to carry out their current social, cultural and financial activities. The promise of the National Broadband Network (NBN) has become substantial.

Many sectors rely on amateurs and pro-amateurs (pro-ams) to support industrial structures and the gift economy is enormous in comparison to what the ABS Census statistics were revealing. New occupations such as social media manager, transmedia storyteller, technopreneur or digital strategist are emerging at an exponential rate. Many operatives work cross-sectorally in order to gain an income, that is, multiple tasks equal one income. There is also a great deal of mobility between professions.

Operatives in the creative industries have to be T-shaped, that is, specialized vertically as well as multi-skilled horizontally. There is a rapidly growing trend toward outsourcing, freelancing and the casualization of the workforce which is having an effect on those who are members of this creative industries precariat.

There is also a "creative drain" of sector operatives who typically move away from the Hunter for approximately a decade and acquire international-level skills. However, many return to the Hunter to have a family and take advantage of the lifestyle opportunities, returning their hard-earned acquired skills as a gift to the regional community. Others completely new to the region also arrive in the Hunter, bringing a high level of expertise with them that is fed into the sectors they go on to work in, as they escape the financial and real estate pressures of the larger urban areas in the nation's capital cities. We observed in these migratory patterns a positive net inflow of skilled operatives for the Hunter Region.

While the hinterland was highly active itself and also fed into what the urban center was producing, we did find that regional understandings and actions tended to be focused at the urban center of the region, consisting of Maitland, Lake Macquarie and Newcastle LGAs, within what is a highly scalable regional system. At the same time, nearly all the operatives we encountered in the creative industries, by necessity, were "glocally" oriented, that is, they are locally embedded but globally active. As such, globalization, digitization and neoliberalism provide the broad context of play for the creative industries where they are subject to the same social, technological, economic, environmental, political, legal and ethical (STEEPLE) contextual factors that all other industries are. We cannot emphasize that enough.

All of this points to the existence of a creative system in action or, to put this in what is thought to be a more palatable form, a creative ecosystem or (eco)system, at work.[1] This (eco)system, a creative system in action, is made up of specialist, support and embedded persons, that is, those members of the creative industries who are counted elsewhere in

[1] Given all systems, whether they are labeled as systems, ecosystems or ecologies, share the same characteristics, which is what makes them systems, we often use these terms as though they are interchangeable. The use of the brackets in the term (eco)system is an attempt on our part to highlight this situation.

other industries such as in education, retail or manufacturing. This perspective recognizes that any industry must be a loosely coupled system of production where one organizing structure bleeds into the others that feed into it. For example, those working at Musos Corner in Newcastle West and at Eckersley's in Hamilton, nominally part of the retail industry, see themselves as integral parts of, respectively, the music industries and art worlds. Looking at creative activity in this way also affords the possibility of seeing pro-ams, as well as the all-important amateurs, volunteers and audiences, as comprising a crucial set of contributors to this entrepreneurial ecosystem. It is this system of the field, the social organization comprised of interconnected networks that coalesce around certain domains of shared knowledge, both combined with choice making agents, which produces novel objects and processes that have economic, social, cultural and symbolic value for both the economy and the broader social and cultural world it exists in.

References

Alexander, V. (2003). *Sociology of the arts: Exploring fine and popular forms.* Blackwell.

Braudel, F. (1990). *The identity of France: Vol. 1. History and environment.* Harper & Row.

Castells, M. (2010). *The rise of the network society* (2nd ed.). Wiley-Blackwell.

CIIC. (2013). *Valuing Australia's creative industries: Final report.* Prepared by SGS Economics and Planning for the Creative Industries Innovation Centre. Retrieved March 21, 2023, from https://sgsep.com.au/assets/main/Valuing-Australias-Creative-Industries-Final-Report-December-2013_Email.pdf

Csikszentmihalyi, M. (1988). Society, culture and person: A systems view of creativity. In R. Sternberg (Ed.), *The Nature of creativity: Contemporary psychological perspectives* (pp. 325–329). Cambridge University Press.

Csikszentmihalyi, M. (1999). Implications of a systems perspective for the study of creativity. In R. Sternberg (Ed.), *Handbook of creativity* (pp. 313–335). Cambridge University Press.

Csikszentmihalyi, M. (2014). *The systems model of creativity.* Springer.

Cunningham, S., McCutcheon, M., Ryan, M., Kerrigan, S., McIntyre, P., & Hearn, G. (2022). *Creative hotspots in the regions: Key thematic insights and findings from across Australia*. Australian Research Council/Digital Media Research Centre. QUT.

Davies, R., & Sigthorsson, G. (2013). Introducing the creative industries: From theory to practice.

Denscombe, M. (2017). *The good research guide for small-scale research projects* (6th ed.). Open University Press.

Dunn, M. (2020). *The convict valley: The bloody struggle on Australia's early frontier*. Allen & Unwin.

EC. (2003). *Green paper: Entrepreneurship in Europe*. European Commission. Commission of the European Communities. Retrieved March 21, 2023, from https://ec.europa.eu/invest-in-research/pdf/download_en/entrepreneurship_europe.pdf

Elkington, J. (1999). *Cannibals with forks: Triple bottom line of 21st century business*. Capstone Publishing.

Fetterman, D. (2011). Ethnography. In M. Lewis-Beck, A. E. Bryman, & T. Futing Liao (Eds.), *The Sage encyclopedia of social science research methods* (pp. 329–332). Sage.

Geertz, C. (1973). *The interpretation of cultures*. Basic Books.

Gross, J. (2020). The birth of the creative industries revisited: An oral history of the 1998 DCMS mapping document. .

Handke, C., & Towse, R. (2013). Introduction. In R. Towse & C. Handke (Eds.), *Handbook on the digital creative economy*. Edward Elgar.

Harvey, D. (2007). *A brief history of neoliberalism*. Oxford University Press.

Havens, T., & Lotz, A. (2016). *Understanding media industries* (2nd ed.). Oxford University Press.

Held, D., McGrew, A., Goldblatt, D., & Perraton, J. (1999). *Global transformations: Politics, economics, culture*. Polity Press.

Hennessey, B. (2017). Taking a systems view of creativity: On the right path toward understanding. *The Journal of Creative Behavior, 51*(4), 341–344. https://doi.org/10.1002/jocb.196

Hennessey, B., & Amabile, T. (2010). Creativity. *Annual Review of Psychology, 61*, 569–598. https://doi.org/10.1146/annurev.psych.093008.100416

Hesmondhalgh, D., & Baker, S. (2011). *Creative labor: Media work in three cultural industries*. Routledge.

HIP. (2023). *2023 Hunter investment prospectus*. Hunter Business Publications Pty Ltd.

Hopkins, A. (Ed.). (2002). *Globalization in world history*. Norton.

Hywood, G. (2004, July 29). Australians beware: We have not yet won the economic war. *The Age*. Retrieved July 15, 2017, from https://www.theage.com.au/national/australians-beware-we-have-not-yet-won-the-economic-war-20040729-gdycmz.html
Jordan, G., & Weedon, C. (1995). *Cultural politics: Class, gender, race and the postmodern world*. Blackwell.
Kaufman, J., & Sternberg, R. (Eds.). (2019). *The Cambridge handbook of creativity*. Cambridge University Press.
Laszlo, E. (1972). *The systems view of the world: The natural philosophy of the new developments in the sciences*. George Braziller.
Lawlor, A. (2014). *Innovation ecosystems: Empowering entrepreneurs and powering economies*. The Economist Intelligence Unit [for Barclays].
Mayanja, S., Ntayi, J., Munene, J., Kagaari, J., & Waswa, B. (2019). Ecologies of innovation among small and medium enterprises in Uganda as a mediator of entrepreneurial networking and opportunity exploitation. *Cogent Business & Management, 6*(1). https://doi.org/10.1080/23311975.2019.1641256
Mazzarol, T. (2011). *Entrepreneurship and innovation*. Tilde University Press.
McIntyre, P. (2011, July 6–8). *Bringing novelty into being: Exploring the relationship between "creativity" and "innovation"*. ANZCA 2011—Communication on the Edge: Shifting Boundaries and Identities, The University of Waikato. Retrieved from http://www.anzca.net/conferences/anzca11-proceedings.html
McIntyre, P., Balnaves, M., Kerrigan, S., King, E., & Williams, C. (2019). *Creativity and cultural production in the Hunter: An applied ethnographic study of new entrepreneurial systems in the creative industries*. Australian Research Council.
McIntyre, P., Fulton, J., & Paton, E. (2016). *The creative system in action: Understanding cultural production and practice*. Palgrave McMillan.
McIntyre, P., & Thompson, P. (2021). *Paul McCartney and his creative practice: The Beatles and beyond*. Palgrave Macmillan.
McManus, P., O'Neill, P., & Loughran, R. (Eds.). (2000). *Journeys: The making of the Hunter Region*. Allen & Unwin.
Pope, R. (2005). *Creativity: Theory, history, practice*. Routledge.
Porter, M. (1990). *The competitive advantage of nations*. Free Press.
Priest, S. (1996). *Doing media research: An introduction*. Sage.
Punch, K. (2014). *Introduction to social research: Quantitative and qualitative approaches* (3rd ed.). Sage.
Robson, C., & McCartan, K. (2016). *Real world research*. Wiley.
Rogers, E. (2003). *Diffusion of innovation* (5th ed.). The Free Press.

Sawyer, K. (2010). Individual and group creativity. In J. Kaufman & R. Sternberg (Eds.), *The Cambridge handbook of creativity* (pp. 366–380). Cambridge University Press.

Sawyer, K. (2012). *Explaining creativity: The science of human innovation* (2nd ed.). Oxford University Press.

Schulz, T. (2015, March 4). Tomorrowland: How Silicon Valley shapes our future. *Speigel Online: International.* Retrieved April 21, 2015, from http://www.spiegel.de/international/germany/spiegel-cover-story-how-silicon-valley-shapes-our-future-a-1021557.html

Servaes, J. (2015). Studying the global from within the local. *Communication Research and Practice, 1*(3), 242–250. https://doi.org/10.1080/22041451.2015.1079155

Skyttner, L. (2006). *General systems theory: Problems, perspectives, practice* (2nd ed.). World Scientific.

Thussu, D. (2006). *International communication: Continuity and change* (2nd ed.). Hodder Arnold.

Thussu, D. (2019). *International communication: Continuity and change* (3rd ed.). Hodder Arnold.

Westbury, M. (2015). *Creating cities.* Niche Press.

Williams, R. (1981). *Culture.* Fontana.

2

Creativity and the Creative Industries: History and Context

Culture Industry to Cultural Industries

One can see from the research literature into creative industries that there is a significant crossover between the idea of creative, cultural and copyright industries (Hartley, 2005, pp. 30–31). As Terry Flew writes in his book *The creative industries: Culture and policy*, terminology describing these industries 'changes across countries, with some referring to the cultural industries, the copyright industries, the digital content industries, and even the cultural and creative industries or—as in China—the cultural creative industries' (2012, p. 4). Despite the arguments over terminology that appear in the literature, the idea that there is a relationship between culture and economics has a long history and it starts, for our purposes, with the notion of the *culture industry* and its pluralized form the *cultural industries*. The members of the Frankfurt School:

> were the first social theorists to see the importance of what they called the "culture industry". [For them] mass culture and communications stand in the center of leisure activity, are important agents of socialization and mediators of political reality, and should be seen as primary institutions of

P. McIntyre et al., *Creativity and Creative Industries in Regional Australia*, Palgrave Studies in Creativity and Culture, https://doi.org/10.1007/978-3-031-45972-6_2

contemporary societies with a variety of economic, political, cultural, and social effects. (Holt & Perren, 2009, p. 95)

The term *culture industry* was employed by these researchers, in particular Theodor Adorno and Max Horkheimer, to identify the processes of industrialization of culture 'and the commercial imperatives that drove the system' (Holt & Perren, 2009, p. 95) which, employing a set of assumptions common to the period (Petrie, 1991), were anathema to them. Writing in the 1930s and 1940s, Adorno, a middle-class German intellectual and also a classical pianist, was appalled by popular music, radio and Hollywood films, remembering that popular music was at this time predominantly jazz. These popular cultural forms were what constituted the culture industry and were seen as trivial, base and meretricious by Adorno and Horkheimer. They set the culture industry apart from, and opposed to, high culture, fine art and all those forms thought not to be contaminated by a connection to commercial imperatives. These supposed higher forms of culture were not included in the culture industry. They were thought to be above that. In this case, it shouldn't be forgotten that the introduction of this term was designed as a pejorative and was employed to shock (Hesmondhalgh, 2019).

A number of French sociologists, in particular Bernard Miege, preferred to use the plural term *cultural industries* instead of the singular. They argued the latter usage 'suggested a "unified field" where all the different forms of cultural production that coexist in modern life are assumed to obey the same logic. [Miege and his compatriots] were concerned instead to show how complex the cultural industries are' (Hesmondhalgh, 2019, p. 29). For Hesmondhalgh, adopting Miege's notion of the cultural industries, these industries must include broadcasting, film industries, the content aspects of the internet industry, music industries (including recording, publishing and live performance), print and electronic publishing, video and computer games, and advertising and marketing (2019, p. 15). As you can see, the so-called high cultural forms like fine art are not included in Hesmondhalgh's list and he does acknowledge that amalgamating this list of industries under the term cultural industries has some definitional difficulties attached to it. In terms of the adjectival prefix, culture, Raymond Williams, for one, asserted that:

> There is some practical convergence between (i) the anthropological and sociological senses of culture as a distinct "whole way of life"… and (ii) the more specialized if also more common sense of culture as 'artistic and intellectual activities', though these, because of the emphasis on a general signifying system, are now much more broadly defined to include not only the traditional arts and forms of intellectual production but also all the "signifying practices"—from language through the arts and philosophy to journalism, fashion and advertising—which now constitute this complex and necessarily extended field. (1981, p. 13)

With this as a starting point, Hesmondhalgh recognized that if culture is defined using the broad anthropological understanding, that is, the idea of culture as "a whole way of life":

> it is possible to argue that all industries are cultural industries in that they are involved in the production and consumption of culture—for by this definition, the clothes we wear, the furniture in our houses and workplaces, the cars, buses and trains we use for transport, the food and drink we consume, are all part of our culture and they are nearly all produced industrially, often in order to make profit. (2019, p. 14)

The way to differentiate industries that contribute to culture and those that are "cultural" is to identify whether or not they produce material that is, following Williams, centered on signifying systems and signifying practices, that is, those that intentionally concentrate on making meaning. This contraction allows for the fact that:

> All cultural artifacts can be viewed as texts in the very broad sense that they are open to interpretation. Cars, for example, signify: they have meanings. Every car involves significant design and marketing inputs. However, if we over-extend the use of the term "texts", we lose sight of crucial distinctions. The *primary* aim of cars as a category is not to provide a set of meanings to customers, or to look nice, but to provide transport [italics in original]. (Hesmondhalgh, 2019, p. 14)

Hesmondhalgh also has a desire to not simply be pessimistic about the actions of the cultural industries. For many, the industrialization of culture is seen as an appalling development. As we saw above, this was certainly the case for Theodor Adorno. What do we make of an industry where the products it makes have the specific function 'of providing ideological legitimation of the existing capitalist societies and of integrating individuals into the framework of mass culture and society' (Hesmondhalgh, 2019, p. 14)? Rather than seeing all culture industries negatively, as Adorno did, Hesmondhalgh argues instead that we must recognize that the realm of these industries is a contested and ambivalent one. Rather than be overly concerned about the extent to which cultural industries serve the interests of the powerful, where 'contents and audiences are commodified, real diversity decreases, opposition and alternative voices are marginalized, public interest in communication is subordinated to private interests [and] access to the benefits of communication are unequally distributed' (McQuail & Deuze, 2020, p. 128), Hesmondhalgh (2019) argues that there are also, at exactly the same time, reasons to celebrate the cultural industries and the social and cultural benefits their various representations have circulated. The cultural industries actually produce exciting new directions and innovations in culture. For Hesmondhalgh, recognizing this doesn't call for complacency, but rather creates an awareness that there are always struggles to be observed around whose ideas become dominant and whose become subordinated and which of these can be seen most prominently within the innovative creations of the cultural industries.

As an extension of the term cultural industries, the more recent development of the notion of *creative industries* has taken hold (Cunningham, 2012). Developing out of a policy problem, the idea of the creative industries was taken to be, certainly by the Department of Culture, Media and Sport (DCMS) in the United Kingdom, 'those industries which have their origin in individual creativity, skill and talent which have a potential for job and wealth creation through the generation and exploitation of intellectual property' (DCMS, 2001). It is to an understanding of the idea of *creativity* we'll turn to now before returning to the term *creative industries*, giving it a fuller critique.

Creativity

Keith Sawyer argues that rational explanations of creativity require us 'to look critically at our own cultural assumptions about how creativity works, and scientific studies of creativity fail to support our most cherished beliefs about creativity' (2006, p. 33). Research in the broader interdisciplinary domain of creativity and cultural production, based primarily in psychology (for reviews see Bergquist, 1999; Kaufman & Sternberg, 2019; Lebuda & Glaveanu, 2019; Rothenberg & Hausman, 1976; Runco & Pritzker, 1999; Sawyer, 2012; Sternberg, 1999; Weisberg, 2006), as well as sociology (e.g., Alexander, 2003; Becker, 1982; Bourdieu, 1993, 1996; Wolff, 1993; Zolberg, 1990), philosophy (e.g., Paul & Kaufman, 2014), literary theory (e.g., Pope, 2005), and media, communication and cultural studies (e.g., McIntyre, 2012; McIntyre et al., 2016; Negus & Pickering, 2004) and others such as education (e.g., Bailin, 1988; McWilliam, 2009), has steadily worked toward the idea that a confluence of multiple factors, including biological, psychological, cultural and social factors, all need to be in place in order for creativity to occur (see, for example, Csikszentmihalyi, 1988, 1997, 1999, 2014; Dacey & Lennon, 1998; Gardner, 1993; Glaveanu, 2014).

It's important to note here, before we proceed further with examining the literature on creativity, that *innovation,* creativity's sister concept, also has a deep literature to draw on. What's crucial to understand is that this parallels the literature on creativity, to the point that the concepts of *creativity* and *innovation* appear to be deeply entwined (McIntyre, 2011).

As a term, *innovation* can be traced back to the Latin *innovare*, a noun of action or doing. It is defined in this sense as the action of innovating or the action of altering what is already established 'by the introduction of new elements or forms' (OED, n.d.-b, online). As Benoit Godin notes in his book *Innovation contested: The idea of innovation over the centuries* (2015), the concept of innovation is of Greek origin and it first appears in official English usage in the mid-1500s with the admonition not to innovate coming from Edward VI as the novel and unorthodox was not to be trusted. While this sense that innovation is an agent of change, for good or ill, has been a fundamental characteristic or component of most views of innovation since then, the definitions one finds in the literature have been added to, modified and changed in the ongoing usage of the term (e.g. see Dodgson & Gann, 2010, p. 14; Drucker, 1991, p. 11; Hofer & Polt, 1998, p. 6) where the general conclusion, so far, is that innovation is a net good and as Tidd et al. indicate, results from a systemic process (1997, pp. 29–30). However, it was in 1939 that a now relatively common meaning, that is, 'the action of introducing a new product into the market; a product newly brought on to the market' (OED, n.d.-b, online), first appears, and which forms the basis of understanding of the term for certain communities of scholars. At this time, economist Joseph Schumpeter writes in *Business cycles* that 'we will simply define innovation as the setting up of a new production function ... innovation combines factors in a new way, or that it consists in carrying out new combinations' (1939, p. 89). Hofer and Polt (1998) point out that the latter evolutionary economic school has tended to examine the way innovation acts in dynamic and systemic ways and how this phenomenon occurs and diffuses over time. This way of thinking suggests the system of innovation can be described as the recursive succession of invention, innovation and diffusion (Hofer & Polt, 1998). The latter stage of this iterative process, the diffusion of innovation, was taken up in the work of Everett Rogers. At the point that he was developing his thinking on the diffusion of innovation, a certain relativism was, of necessity, becoming apparent in understandings of innovation. He, for example, declared that:

> an innovation is an idea, practice, or object that is perceived as new by an individual or other unit of adoption. It matters little, so far as human behavior is concerned, whether or not an idea is "objectively" new as measured by the lapse of time since its first use or discovery. (2003, p. 12)

In raising the question of the relative nature of novelty, this literature on innovation has come quite close to recent definitions of creativity. While the term *creativity* has had a differing, much older but related history to that of the concept of *innovation* (Godin, 2015; Rothenberg & Hausman, 1976), perceptions of it appear to have recently arrived at the same basic conclusion that has been applied to innovation, that is, that it is systemic (McIntyre, 2011).

In exploring these ideas about creativity more fully we can see that:

> European conceptions of creativity have changed over the centuries. And once you leave Europe, you'll find an even wider range of conceptions of creativity cross culturally … The scientific explanation of creativity has found that many of our beliefs about creativity are inaccurate or misleading. That's why I call them creativity myths (Weisberg, 1988). These creativity myths are so widely believed that they sometimes seem obvious, common sense. (Sawyer, 2006, p. 18)

In the West, creativity is commonly seen by many to emanate from a 'divine agent' (OED, n.d.-a, online) and it refers to an activity thought 'to bring into being, cause to exist; esp. to produce where nothing was before, "to form out of nothing"' (OED, n.d.-a, online). This biblical sense of creativity helped set the stage for inspirationist approaches to perceiving creativity. These were taken up by the Romantics who rapidly anthropocentrized the supposedly divine nature of creativity. This development can also be partly traced back to Kantian thought on aesthetics and further uses from there (Petrie, 1991). They resulted in the idea that creative individuals possess a gift or talent that is beyond the grasp of mere mortals since 'according to the romantic, intuitive talent is innate, a gift that can be squandered but cannot be acquired—or taught' (Boden, 2004, p. 15). Both positions, the inspirational and the romantic, lead eventually to the stereotypical view of the quasi-neurotic artist (Freud, 1976). However, given the research into the phenomenon of genius and its relationship to creativity (e.g., Howe, 1999; Weisberg, 1993), these are conceptions of creative people, and from there creative activity, that are difficult to sustain (Gardner, 1993). As Keith Sawyer suggests, and as was mentioned above, we need to 'look critically at our own cultural assumptions about how creativity works' (2006, p. 33). Margaret Boden also asserts that the inspirational and romantic views common to the West:

> are believed by many to be literally true. But they are rarely critically examined. They are not theories, so much as myths: imaginative constructions,

> whose function is to express the values, assuage the fears, and endorse the practices of the community that celebrates them. (2004, p. 14)

Working away from these romantic and inspirationist myths there have also been a number of levels and differentiations being applied to the perceived differences between "ordinary" creativity and what is seen as "extraordinary" creativity. Some of the terms used to account for these differences include: 'big "C" versus little c; paradigm shifting versus garden variety; eminent versus everyday' (Schiffer, 1998, online).

Looking at the same set of differentiations, Margaret Boden (1994) applied a further set of names to the same phenomena. She called these *P & H creativity*. For Boden, P (or psychological) creativity is valuable if that person hasn't had that idea before. It is irrelevant to the individual if other people have had the idea and how many times they've had the idea. H (or historical) creativity, on the other hand, possesses value if it is both P creative and no one in human history has ever had the idea before. Most importantly she states that 'there can be no psychological explanation of this historical category. But all H-creative ideas, by definition, are P-creative too' (1994, p. 77). In making these declarations, Boden highlights the similarities that exist between all ways of being creative, the ordinary and the extraordinary. Furthermore, creativity can be seen to be a contextually dependent process. As Csikszentmihalyi argues, 'it is impossible to tell whether or not an object or an idea is creative by simply looking at it. Without historical context, one lacks the reference points necessary to determine if the product is in fact an adaptive innovation' (1988, p. 327).

While these are useful additions to our understanding, there is a further critical and related addition to the definition of creativity that must be accounted for. This is the notion of social validation since acts of creativity, like acts of innovation, are only creative within a specific sociocultural framework. Morris Stein published an article called 'Creativity and Culture' in *The Journal of Psychology* in the early 1950s. In this article he worked his way through a definition of creativity that was phrased as follows: 'The creative work is a novel work that is accepted as tenable or useful or satisfying by a group in some point in time' (1953, p. 311). In an echo of Rogers' definition of innovation cited above, this fundamental operation of value distinction within a society makes creativity itself culturally relative, 'since what is valued by one person or social group may or may not be valued—praised, preserved, promoted—by another' (Boden, 1994, p. 77). These conceptions have thus moved quite some way from what Simonton calls 'psychologically reductionist' accounts:

> Psychologists have tended to view creativity as an individual level phenomenon. That is, they have tended to concentrate on the cognitive processes, personality traits, and developmental antecedents associated with individual creators. This focus follows naturally from the very nature of psychology as a scientific enterprise dedicated to understanding individual mind and behavior. Yet this tradition of "psychological reductionism" has also inspired an antithetical conception of creativity as an exclusively societal-level event. In the extreme form, that is a complete "sociocultural reductionism", the individual becomes a mere epiphenomenon without any causal significance whatsoever. (2003, p. 304)

Looking across this research literature from psychology we can see that the psychodynamic school, seen in works by Sigmund Freud and others (see Sternberg, 1999), has centered its exploration of creativity on the tensions thought to exist between conscious and unconscious drives. These ideas led to a number of speculative and commercially successful applications of associated concepts of creativity based on the idea that "creative" thinking is somehow different to "ordinary" thinking. However, the validity of the ideas being sold, such as lateral thinking, divergent and convergent thinking, brainstorming and so on, has been subject to minimal empirical scrutiny (Sternberg, 1999, pp. 5–6). The positivist turn in psychology then produced psychometric approaches, which attempted to measure aspects of creativity quantitatively (Sawyer, 2012). The problematics of these attempts led, in part, to the development of cognitive approaches to the study of creativity. This approach sought an explanation of this basic human phenomenon by grappling with the cognitive processes thought to underpin creativity (Zolberg, 1990). Following this approach, B.F. Skinner, and the group that became known as the behaviorists, saw creativity as a cognitive behavior pattern, largely unconscious to the individual (Bergquist, 1999). Weisberg (1993), on the other hand, proposed and sought empirical evidence for the idea that ordinary cognitive processes applicable in everyday situations held the most appropriate solution to understanding creativity. The social-personality approaches that developed alongside the cognitive school suggested that personality variables, motivation and the sociocultural environment a creative individual existed in were also sources of creativity (Amabile, 1983, 1996; Sternberg, 1999). Finally, neuropsychology, with an insistence on a monist version of the alleged brain/mind duality, began explaining aspects of creativity in terms of the relationships between neurochemical processes and certain cognitive states. It focused some attention on the connection between the action of neurotransmitters, such as dopamine and serotonin, and how these are related to creative activity (e.g., Greenfield, 2008).

On their own, each of these schools of thought provides an explanation for creativity that is primarily focused on individual and isolated aspects of the phenomenon. In Simonton's (2003) terms, as suggested above, they are mostly psychologically reductionist. As such, the individual factors they look at can be seen as necessary but most certainly not sufficient to explain creativity. To assist in bringing these areas of thought together, Beth Hennessy and Teresa Amabile conducted a review of the psychological literature on creativity in 2010. They came to the conclusion that (Fig. 2.1):

> more progress will be made when more researchers recognize that creativity arises through a system of interrelated forces operating at multiple levels, often requiring interdisciplinary investigation. [The figure] presents a simplified schematic of the major levels at which these forces operate. The model is simplified because, as noted, existing research does cross levels. And, in fact, the "whole" of the creative process must be viewed as much more than a simple sum of its parts. (2010, p. 571)

Added to these appraisals, it should be noted that psychology, as a discipline, tends to view creativity as an activity just as pertinent to science, business and engineering as it is to art and cultural production. Sociology, surprisingly, tends to see things more narrowly. This discipline has tended to focus its work into creativity on a subset, that is artistic

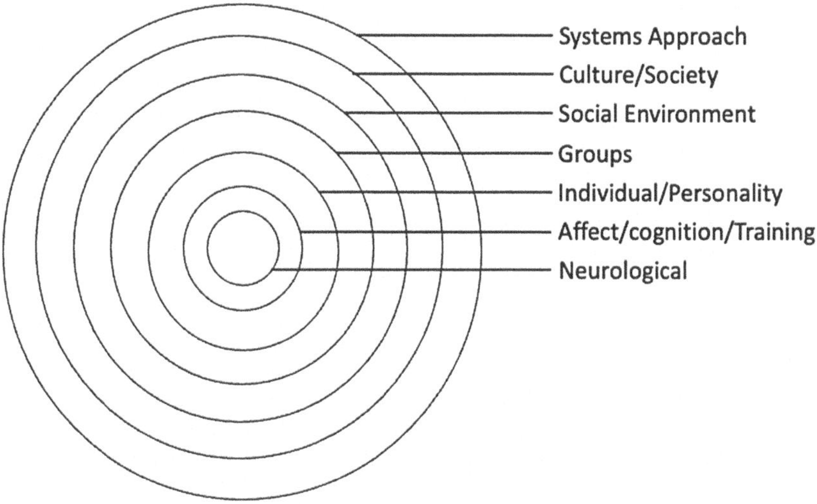

Fig. 2.1 The increasingly large concentric circles in this simplified schematic represent the major levels at which creativity forces operate. (Original in Hennessey & Amabile, 2010, p. 571)

activity, where there is also a tendency to conceive of art as a collective practice. For example, Howard Becker's (1982) development of the concept of Art Worlds supplied a fresh counter to psychologically reductionist perspectives. Becker refutes the notion that individuals alone are totally responsible for art works and supplies evidence to suggest that artistic output is dependent on a network of cooperating individuals. Similarly, Richard Peterson produced evidence that there are a series of what he calls *constraints* that have an effect on the form and content of cultural production. For him, these constraints are primarily social in character. He lists them as law, technology, industry structure, organizational structure, markets and occupational careers (1985, p. 64). He argues that 'the nature and content of symbolic products are shaped by the social, legal and economic milieu in which they are created, edited, manufactured, marketed, purchased and evaluated' (1985, p. 46) in an increasingly complex network of influence (1985, p. 45). Janet Wolff (1993), in her work on the social production of art, also contended that creative work must be seen as a collective enterprise. She argued, in an expanded precursor to Peterson, that individuals, as decisive agents, are highly dependent on the structures that both enable and constrain their activity. She asserts, in a manner similar to empirical sociologist Pierre Bourdieu, that 'structures enable human practices, by providing the conditions of action and offering choices of action' (1993, p. 24). Bourdieu (1993, 1996), also principally concerned with the way agency and structure interact in the process of bringing new cultural products into being, presented a complex view of cultural production. It can be summarized in part as:

> The interplay between a field of works which presents possibilities of action to an individual who possesses the necessary habitus, partially composed of personal levels of social, cultural, symbolic and economic capital that then inclines them to act and react within particular structured and dynamic spaces called fields. These fields are arenas of production and circulation of goods, ideas and knowledges. They are populated by other agents who compete using various levels of the forms of capital pertinent to that field. Bourdieu suggests that it is the interplay between these various spheres of cultural production that makes practice possible. (McIntyre, 2009, p. 161)

Bourdieu added to these ideas in his book *Rules of art*, here paraphrased by Inglis and Hughson:

> For the most part, individuals are not fully aware that everything they do is expressive of the habitus they have been socialized into. Instead, the habitus disguises itself by making people see the world in common-sense ways, and these ways do not allow actors to turn their critical reflection upon the habitus. People just experience things "as they are" … This commonsensical view of the world is what Bourdieu (1977, p. 80, 164) calls *doxa*, the unexamined ways of acting that are at the root of each group's mode of being in the world [italics in original]. (2003, p. 167)

For Bourdieu 'what people call "creation" is the conjunction of socially constituted habitus and a certain position (status), either already constituted or possible in the division of labor of cultural production' (Bourdieu in Zolberg, 1990, p. 125). He went further to state that:

> The heritage accumulated by collective work presents itself to each agent as a space of possibles, that is, as an ensemble of probable *constraints* which are the condition and counterpart of a set of *possible uses*. Those who think in simple alternatives need to be reminded that in these matters absolute freedom, exalted by the defenders of creative spontaneity belongs only to the naïve and ignorant [italics in original]. (1996, p. 235)

By seeing creativity as an interactive and dynamic process rather than one based on a set of romantic or inspirationist assumptions, Bourdieu provides a far less Ptolemaic, or person centered, and much more Copernican, or holistic and systemic, view of creativity than some of the earlier individually focused and psychologically reductionist accounts. Returning to the psychology perspective, in seeking to broaden the horizon of psychologists, Lebuda and Glaveanu (2019) claimed that the social context is deeply entwined with the personal in all manner of ways. As Beth Hennessey asserted, 'at long last, psychologists are beginning to apply a sociological perspective to the study of creativity; and they have also come to finally appreciate and benefit from the important work being done by sociologists' (2017, p. 343).

With these developments firmly in mind, and after scouring for commonalities in the literature on creativity, one could argue that:

> Creativity is a productive activity whereby objects, processes and ideas are generated from antecedent conditions through the agency of someone, whose knowledge to do so comes from somewhere and the resultant novel variation is seen as a valued addition to the store of knowledge in at least one social setting. (McIntyre, 2008, p. 1)

This definition, though more detailed, accords with what Beth Hennessy and Teresa Amabile identified in their review of the literature in 2010. As they state, most researchers around the world now 'agree that creativity involves the development of a novel product, idea, or problem solution that is of value to the individual and/or the larger social group' (2010, p. 572). Erica McWilliam from the Creative Industries Faculty at QUT and long-term contributor to the Centre for Creative Industries and Innovation (CCII) located there, summarizes this movement of thought well: 'recent scholarship has sought to unhook creativity from "artiness", individual genius and idiosyncrasy' (2009, p. 282).

This second generation thinking on creativity, in research terms at least, has suggested that the phenomenon of creativity comes about through a multifaceted interactive process and is centered in the confluence of a number of factors (Amabile, 1983, 1996; Csikszentmihalyi, 1988, 1997, 1999, 2014; Dacey & Lennon, 1998; Feldman et al., 1994; Glaveanu, 2014; Gruber, 1988; Montuori & Purser, 1995; Simonton, 2003; Sternberg & Lubart, 1991; Weisberg, 1993). Each of these so-called confluence approaches includes, to some varying degree, social, cultural and psychological factors that need to be in place for creativity to occur.

For example, John Dacey and Kathleen Lennon proposed what they called a biopsychosocial model of creativity that depends on an interplay of biological, psychological and social factors. In fact, they argue for an interactive causative process that operates across biological, cognitive, personality, microsocietal and macrosocietal factors. The basic premise of this approach:

> reveals a five-layer system of causation in which each layer interacts with and bidirectionally affects the other four. A sixth variable, time, runs across the whole, such that whatever the state of the interactions were at one time, they might well have changed at a later time. (1998, p. 124)

As a further example, Vlad Glaveanu argued that creativity can be conceived of as being distributed across a set of multiple factors and:

> emerges as a form of action engaged in by various actors (individual or groups), in relation to multiple audiences (again individuals or groups), exploiting the affordances of the culture (symbolic and material) world and leading to the generation of artifacts (appreciated as new and useful by self and/or others). (2014, p. 27)

He went on to present what he called a framework for distributed creativity that sets these ideas out in graphic form. He asserted that all of these factors presented in the framework are relational in nature and that there is an interplay between what he called the five As: 'actors, audiences, actions, artifact and affordances' (2014, p. 29). In this case, the essence of distributed creativity is that it is simultaneously social, material and temporal, is dynamic in nature, and is 'at once patterned and flexible, constrained by the past and fundamentally open to the future' (2014, p. 29).

Like the developments in the study of innovation (e.g., Drucker, 1991; Godin, 2015; McIntyre, 2011; Rogers, 2003), we can see that there has been a steady progression toward the idea that creativity comes about through the actions of a multi-factorial system at work. Assertions have also been made that creativity results from the dynamic operation of 'a system composed of three elements: a culture that contains symbolic rules, a person who brings novelty into the domain, and a field of experts who recognize and validate the innovation' (Csikszentmihalyi, 1997, p. 6) (Fig. 2.2).

While this model typifies creativity as an emergent property of the dynamic interaction of an interconnected social, cultural and psychological system in action, it is important to realize that each component in this non-linear system is integral to it with one being no more important or less necessary than the other. As Csikszentmihalyi also points out, 'it should be clear that time plays an important role in the creative process' (1988, p. 332). In summary 'each of the three main systems—person, field and domain—affects the others and is affected by them in turn' (Csikszentmihalyi, 1988, p. 329). Each component is a necessary factor in creativity but not sufficient, in and of itself, to produce novelty. It is, from this perspective, a creative system in action (McIntyre, 2013; McIntyre et al., 2016) that produces novel and valued things. These creative systems in action, must inevitably be fluid, open, dynamic and spatiotemporally dependent, as most active systems are. In this case, the creative system in action must:

> include a structured knowledge system manifest in all the collected works pertinent to that symbol system. This is called a domain. It also consists of a field, that is, a structured social organization that operates using domain knowledge in a process of coopetition. This field is populated by all those who can act upon and effect the symbol system, that is, those with varying expertise including other produsers, gatekeepers, cultural intermediaries

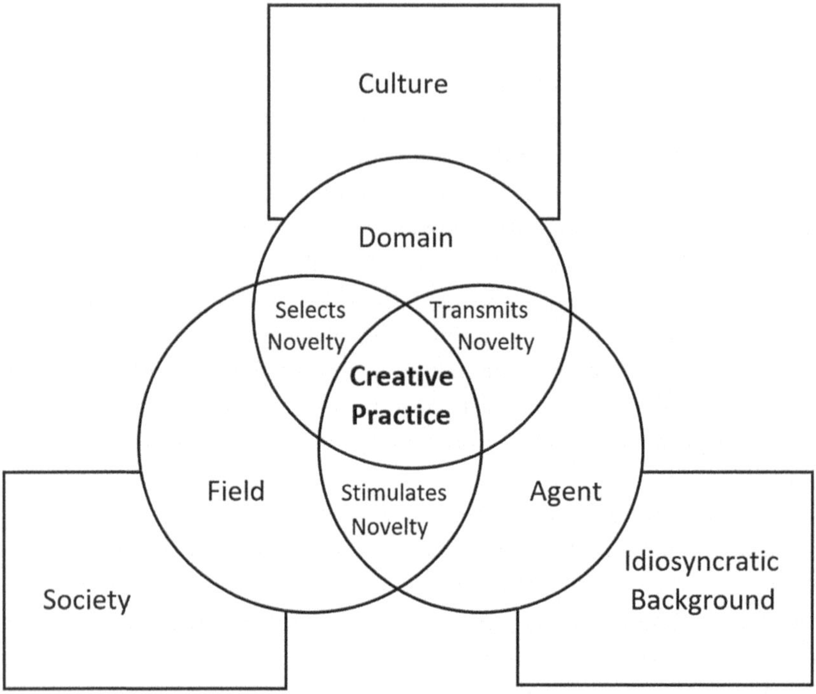

Fig. 2.2 Systems model of creativity reconceptualized by Kerrigan (2013, p. 114)

> and audiences. The third subsystem we will call an agent. This agent is an active choice making entity which may be scaled outward from individuals to dyads, groups and other collective entities such as institutions who make "changes to the stored information that pre-exists them" (Csikszentmihalyi, 1988: 329). These agents necessarily have a unique but shared background and bring their distinctive characteristics to bear on the entire system. (McIntyre, 2022, pp. 8–9)

As Beth Hennessy remarked in 2017, 'as early as the late 1960s, Barron was already writing about an "ecology of creativity", a perspective operationalizing creativity as the confluence of social and psychological processes' (2017, p. 342). She recognized Csikszentmihalyi as a 'pioneer in the effort to conceptualize and investigate creativity as the product of social and cultural influences as well as cognitive and psychological factors' (2017, p. 342) before going on to assert:

> While psychologists have tended to view creative breakthroughs as stemming from the talents and efforts of idealized lone "geniuses", creative behavior never occurs in isolation ... There have long been at least a few voices calling for the reconceptualization of creativity from a systems perspective. But in 2010 when we published our review, this perspective was largely overshadowed by a decontextualized, even reductionist, approach. Researchers and theorists were doing all that they could to break down questions of creativity into the absolutely smallest components they could control and measure. An exploration of the most recent literature reveals that this situation may, in fact, be changing. A growing number of publications are now reflecting a systems perspective. (2017, p. 342)

Hennessey went on to suggest:

> Entire volumes of journals have recently been devoted to the interface between creativity and culture, with much of this work having been carried out in workplace settings ... And McIntyre (2013) offers a comprehensive review of research and theorizing leading to an emerging view of creativity as a system in action. (2017, p. 343)

General systems thinking had discerned earlier that there are 'systems of organized complexity wherever we look. Man [sic] is one such system, and so are his societies and his environment' (Laszlo, 1972, p. 12). But there is a caveat. As Capra and Luisi explain:

> Human social systems exist not only in the physical domain but also in a symbolic social domain. While behavior in the physical domain is governed by the "laws of nature", behavior in the social domain is governed by rules generated by the social system itself. (2014, pp. 136–137)

In this case, we can't say with confidence that human systems operate by a predictable set of universally applicable formal laws as the material world has appeared to do. This of course includes creative systems. Since we can say these are largely self-referential systems, we can also assume they do behave as most other systems would. As in all systems, it is increasingly difficult to understand complex entities, like the social world, just by considering the individual parts or even by assuming one perspective such as a structuralist account or a phenomenological explanation. As sociologist Pierre Bourdieu (1993) has suggested, a meaningful grasp of reality needs to consider the complex relationships that exist between objective structures and subjective experiences of individual agents. We can no longer conceive of things as isolated atomistic events (Laszlo, 1972, p. 13).

While social systems exist in real time and real space they are premised on the experiences of the conceptual and the symbolic. Identities are built around sharing the ideas embedded in the symbolic domain of culture and communication and this identification creates the boundaries of the social system while allowing the system to organize itself around those shared cultural and social identities. Social systems are thus autopoietic or self-organized culturally as networks of communication (Luhmann 1990). Remembering Raymond Williams' formulation (1981) from above, that culture equals a whole way of life plus the intellectual activities and artifacts that typify particular societies, we can see that:

> Culture arises from a complex, highly nonlinear dynamic. It is created by a social network involving multiple feedback loops through which values, beliefs and rules of conduct are continually communicated, modified, and sustained. It emerges from a network of communication among individuals; and as it emerges, it produces constraints on their actions. In other words, the social structures, or rules of behavior, that constrain the actions of individuals are produced and continually reinforced by their own network of communication. The social network also produces a shared body of knowledge—including information, ideas and skills—that shapes the culture's distinctive way of life in addition to its values and beliefs. Moreover, the culture's values and beliefs affect its body of knowledge. (Capra & Luisi, 2014, p. 310)

In summing up these ideas, Keith Sawyer pointed out that 'many social systems are complex systems that share many systemic properties with other complex systems, including the human mind' (2019, p. 570).

Furthermore, one cannot fully understand complex entities by simply considering their individual parts:

> This raises the possibility that complex social systems generate novelty (cf. the concept of "distributed creativity": Sawyer & De Zutter, 2009). If so, a complete scientific explanation of creativity would have to include detailed accounts, at one and the same time, of both psychological and sociocultural mechanisms. (Sawyer, 2019, p. 570)

With this review of the research into creativity in place, it's now time to see how the notion of creativity has been dealt with in the literature on creative industries.

Creativity and the Creative Industries

Armed with all of the foregoing literature, we can now make some comparisons of this body of research with the literature coming from the creative industries. In doing so, we can not only observe the correspondences and disjunctures in the movements of thought to be found in both, but also see why the DCMS definition cited above is problematic. These are the questions we are trying to answer in this section: Are the narrative trajectories or the basic movements of thought about creativity similar for those researching creativity in comparison with those investigating creative industries? How do those researching the creative industries understand creativity?

What is first revealed in answering these questions is that the term *creativity* appears to have been conceived differently, at different times, by the various researchers who pursue the study of creative, cultural or copyright industries. For example, David Hesmondhalgh, who favors the term cultural industries, has argued persuasively that 'if I am right in focusing attention on the role of the cultural industries as systems for the management of symbolic creativity then a key issue here will be the relationship between symbol creators and cultural industry organizations' (2011, p. 69). In concluding his exceptional work, largely from a political economist's perspective, Hesmondhalgh argues, via Bill Ryan, that 'if the "fundamentally irrational" process of symbolic creativity "conflicts with the calculating, accumulative logic of modern capitalism" (Ryan 1992, p. 104), this helps to explain the very tangled and contradictory dynamics we have observed' (2011, p. 306) in the cultural industries. However, Ryan characterized creativity as a process that 'presumes the free flight of the imagination unbounded by non-artistic considerations' (1992, p. 154). If creativity is *not* fundamentally irrational, as many of those researching creativity now accept (those noted above), then this creates a problem for Ryan's overall critique. Despite this, it is clear that 'however dubious the romantic conceptions of opposing creativity or art to commerce may be, it has had the long term effect of generating very important tensions between creativity and commerce, which are vital to understanding the cultural industries' (Hesmondhalgh, 2011, p. 20). Hesmondhalgh justifiably reinforces this idea by also stating that 'it is impossible to understand the distinctive nature of cultural production without an understanding of the commerce/creativity dialectic' (2011, pp. 20–21). This is of course pragmatically important as this dialectic is often treated by those working within many forms of cultural production as though it was an absolute and concrete entity, rather than a discursive construct, as Hesmondhalgh points out. It therefore needs to be taken seriously. As Thomas' dictum states, 'if men [sic] define situations as real, they are real in their consequences' (Thomas & Thomas, 1928, p. 572). Once a person takes on the belief and acts as though it is real then 'gradually a whole life policy and the personality of the individual himself [sic]' (Thomas, 1967, p. 42) becomes premised on the belief system and they act according to that belief system.

Despite these critiques of the doxa of Romantic art, and the distinctions between art and commerce that reside within them, they appear to have been also accepted uncritically by Richard Caves (2000). Caves tends to see creativity through the narrow prism of artistic activity. However, as we have seen from the above, much of the research literature on creativity does recognize that creativity is a basic human attribute just as applicable to science, engineering and mathematics as it is to painting, sculpture, movie-making and music production (e.g., Florida, 2002; Simonton, 2004; Weisberg, 2006). This is what Richard Florida (2002) was pointing to when he saw that the future of cities around the planet depended on their capacity to attract the creative people necessary to sustain and motivate economic activity. He implicitly recognized that creativity is not simply the same thing as artistic activity since creative industries depend on all sorts of creative activity in order to function. Stuart Cunningham (2012) hints at this problematic in his elucidation of Howkins' broad definition of creative industries. The problem in defining creativity as simply the function of arts and culture and excluding the creative aspects of other activities such as information technology, engineering, business or science, perpetuates, to use Cunningham's phrase, 'the arts-science divide that has bedeviled the West' (2012, p. 208). This is a divide that is premised on the binaries developed by the revolution in thinking that was Romanticism and, as Peter Watson suggested, these 'constitute the modern incoherence' (2005, p. 610). This incoherence is not part of Eastern thinking where they appear not to be 'hung up on associated artistic bohemian values' (O'Connor & Gu, 2012, p. 202). It is, instead, a belief that is largely peculiar to the West and, one could claim therefore, not a universal way to understand the phenomenon of creativity (Niu & Sternberg, 2006). As Eisenberger and Shannock argue: 'Romanticism's emphasis on self-determination has had a strong influence on Western culture's view of intrinsic motivation and creativity' (2003, p. 122). The problem here is that, to repeat it from above, a rational explanation of creativity 'requires us to look critically at our own cultural model about how creativity works' (Sawyer, 2006, p. 33) and furthermore, research studies into this phenomenon 'fail to support our most cherished beliefs about creativity' (Sawyer, 2006, p. 33).

Terry Flew (2012) presents an overview of the origin of creative industries' policy, the models that have been employed to illustrate it, the changes in terminology, the nature of creative work, how the market for creative industries operates, the effect globalization has on cities and the creative spaces that exist there, and what there is of public policy focused at these industries. Importantly for us, his book also very briefly outlines some of the various assumptions made about creativity. He explores the work of Raymond Williams (1958), and Davis and Scase (2000). The latter see the creative process as having three important characteristics, that is, autonomy, non-conformity and indeterminacy (in Flew, 2012, p. 103). However, the idea of autonomy appears to be one aligned with a desire for an absence of constraint (Hume, 1952) and, if so, is linked to the foundational characteristics of what Praz et al. (1970) and Petrie (1991) call the Romantic agony. Davis and Scase (2000) appear to have made the same cultural assumptions as those Sawyer points out above. The evidence suggests that creation, even of the paradigm shifting sort, is reliant on a certain amount of conformity as it 'is usually less radical a departure from the existing framework than we tend to believe' (Bailin, 1988, p. 89). Sharon Bailin asserts:

> There is not a real discontinuity between achieving highly within the rules of a discipline and achieving highly when it entails going beyond or changing some rules. The latter is, rather, an extension of the former. It would be incorrect to view any discipline or creative activity as taking place within rigid boundaries and being totally delimited and defined by rules. Instead, the possibilities for what can be achieved are really open-ended. Furthermore, one never breaks down all the rules, since to do so would be to abandon the discipline. (1988, p. 96)

John Hartley, editor of the influential compendium *Creative Industries* and for many years one of the principal researchers at the ARC Centre of Excellence for Creative Industries and Innovation at the Queensland University of Technology (QUT), has advocated for a general paradigm shift in thinking about creativity. He asserts that the objective now is to 'understand creative innovation as a general cultural attribute rather than one restricted only to accredited experts such as artists, and thus to theorize creativity as a form of emergence for dynamic systems' (2012, p. 199). This shift in thinking certainly parallels the development in the more general research literature on creativity, summarized briefly above. It also parallels the conclusion coming from much of the specific research literature on creativity within psychology (Hennessey, 2017; Hennessey & Amabile, 2010). Hennessey and Amabile claim that more researchers in psychology are beginning to recognize 'that creativity arises through a system of interrelated forces operating at multiple levels, often requiring interdisciplinary investigation ... in fact, the "whole" of the creative process must be viewed as much more than a simple sum of its parts' (2010, p. 571).

In tracing this shift in thinking about creativity, Brian Moeran and Ana Alacovska, editors of *Creative Industries: Critical Readings Vols 1–4* (2012), which is a collection of much of the important writing on the creative industries, placed a set of varied entries about the concept of creativity in their compendium. These entries parallel some of the developments in thinking from the research literature on creativity mentioned above. Leaving aside the rhetoric of the fourth entry, the first that concerns us here, from Olsen (1954), relies on seeing creativity as primarily person-centered and cognitive, the second, from Negus and Pickering (2004), moves beyond this to question many of the cultural assumptions that underpin thinking about creativity in the West, and the third, from Peter Tschmuck, author of *Creativity and Innovation in the Music Industry* (2006), accepts that creativity is a systemic process. Confluence models of creativity start to appear in the narrative of Hartley et al. The authors declare, referencing Mockros and Csikszentmihalyi (1999), that:

> The key point to note therefore is that creativity is part of a complex dynamic system of feedback, one in which novel ideas and acts may result in creativity—but only in the context of an interaction with a symbolic system inherited from previous generations and with a social system qualified to evaluate and accept novelty. (Hartley et al., 2013, p. 67)

The authors then mention one of the more interesting ideas about Western understandings of creativity. While there is an emphasis on innovation, newness, originality or most often novelty in many common Western perceptions of creativity (Niu & Sternberg, 2006), this cultural assumption, what Hartley et al. argue is primarily derived from an ideological base, neglects the fact that tradition and convention are just as essential to creativity as novelty is. As Negus and Pickering have asserted, creativity 'builds on one or more existing cultural traditions ... In this sense creative talent requires a tradition so that it can learn how to go further within it or beyond it' (2004, p. 91). For Robert Weisberg, one of the central protagonists in many of the debates on creativity that occur within psychology, 'true originality evolves as the individual goes beyond what others had done before' (1988, p. 173). If this is the case, as Bailin (1988), Weisberg (1988), and Negus and Pickering (2004) have all argued, 'commitment, training, discipline and access to the traditions and conventions of the domain of knowledge are just as critical to creativity as rule-breaking and unconventional behavior' (McIntyre, 2011, p. 246).

Hartley et al. highlight another key debate about creativity that has circulated in the literature, particularly that coming from sociology. They present a seeming paradox suggesting that 'much value creation in the creative industries is due to "mundane" or "humdrum" labor, the work of accountants, lawyers and a range of technical staff located on the boundary where commerce meets art' (2013, p. 68). As sociologist Howard Becker (1982) clearly points out in his book *Art Worlds*, attributing creativity only to those things that are done by those whose work is designated as a core activity, as opposed to a non-core activity done by humdrum or mundane workers, is highly problematic. The temptation is to put the core activity at the center of creative action. But once we move past having individual creators at the center of creative action, Hartley et al.'s supposed paradox ceases to be a paradox. To accomplish this shift, one must accept the idea of creativity as an emergent property of a system at work. A system, not individuals alone, produces creativity and that system has many causal factors involved, including a field of active contributors, some of whom would be seen in the earlier discourse as merely humdrum workers. This necessary shift in thinking would go some way to resolving the issues raised by authors such as Dawson and Holmes when they argue in their book *Working in the Global Film and Television Industries: Creativity, Systems, Space, Patronage*, in a manner similar to Howard Becker, that:

> The practice of drawing sharp distinctions between above-the-line and below-the-line workers needs to be interrogated and that we need other ways to understand creativity in an industry with a complex social division of labor involving large numbers of people working cooperatively. (2012, p. 14)

As they conclude, 'creativity, then, is not a quality possessed by individuals but a characteristic determined by the social nature of production' (2012, p. 15). One may not necessarily agree with their use of the word "determined" however. Creativity, as sociologists Pierre Bourdieu (1996) and Janet Wolff (1993) have at various times asserted, is not some metaphysical process that operates beyond the action of external conditions but is deeply entwined with the structures it emerges from. As such, creativity is circumscribed, not determined, by those structures that provide the conditions for its possible emergence. If this is the case, it is also misleading to only call these structural factors "constraints" (e.g., Peterson, 1985) since they do both; they enable and constrain at one and the same time. They provide the conditions which give rise to the possibility of action, decision-making and choice-making that is the hallmark of creativity.

The Creative Industries

With the above as background, we can now ask: what is the problem with the DCMS definition of the creative industries? To familiarize ourselves with that definition again, Stuart Cunningham states that the most common definition used to identify creative industries includes 'those industries which have their origin in individual creativity, skill and talent which have a potential for job and wealth creation through the generation and exploitation of intellectual property' (2011, p. 1). Since the term and this definition primarily arose out of a policy desire (Gross, 2020; Hesmondhalgh, 2007; O'Connor, 2012), it has come to represent a 'seemingly heterogeneous set of industries possessing an underlying commonalty around creativity as a primary driver' (Flew, 2012, p. 83). To put the problem simply, if creativity is not solely artistic activity, which is demonstrably true from a research point of view, then we can't say creativity is a distinguishing factor of the creative industries since *all* industries are, by definition, creative. *All* industries have their origins in some form of creativity, skill and talent and *all* are engaged in the pursuit of wealth creation. However, not all are doing this via the exploitation of intellectual property. But here resides another problem; the notion of intellectual property does not just refer to copyright but also to patents. Many industries have built their wealth creation on patents but do not reside within our common-sense understanding of creative industries.

Those industries built on patents include the pharmaceutical industries, biotechnology industries, the electronics industry, financial services in their use of business methods patents, and petroleum and refining industries, to name just a few. Notwithstanding John Howkins' claim in *Creative economy* (2001) that many of these must be included, none of these industries could be seen, from a common sense framework, as creative industries. The DCMS definition is therefore far too loose to suffice. So how do we move closer to delineating the creative industries?

Davies and Sigthorsson write that the notion of the creative industries operates as an umbrella term that covers a wide set of sectors which are all connected by three defining features. Firstly, they 'all require some input of *human creativity*; second, they are *vehicles for symbolic messages*, that is, they are carriers of *meaning*; and third, they contain, at least potentially, some *intellectual property* that belongs to an individual or group' [italics in original] (2013, p. 1). Points one and three are problematic, as discussed immediately above, but it is the second of these features that is most significant. Symbolic creativity is of a different order to other forms of creativity. Not all industries have as their primary function the task of intentionally generating meaning and for Davies and Sigthorsson 'a tremendous range of economic activity arises from the creation of *pleasure* and *meaning*' [italics in original] (2013, p. 1). David Hesmondhalgh, a strident critic of the term creative industries, also prefers the term *symbolic creativity* using it to move well beyond a romantic emphasis on artistic activity and all that entails. He suggests that:

> The invention and/or performance of stories, songs, images, poems, jokes and so on, in no matter what technological form, involves a particular type of creativity—the manipulation of symbols for the purposes of entertainment, information and perhaps even enlightenment. (2019, p. 9)

The idea that creative industries are engaged in the creation of symbolic meaning attempts to give some solidity to the production, management, circulation and selling of, as Raymond Williams (1981) puts it, signifying practices. There are a number of creative sectors that do this.

The UK Creative Industries Mapping Document 2001 (Varbanova, 2001) lists advertising, architecture, the art and antiques market, crafts, design, designer fashion, film and video, interactive leisure software, music, the performing arts, publishing, software and computer services, television and radio. On the other hand, a recent report to the NSW Department of State and Regional Development 'breaks down the creative industry into the following sectors: advertising, architecture, design, visual arts, music, performing arts, publishing, film, television, radio, electronic games' (NSW SRD, 2009, p. 7). Others list similar sectors such as advertising, architecture, design, art, craft, fashion, performing arts, publishing, music, performing arts, film, TV and radio, software and video games (e.g., Howkins, 2001). This diverse group of sectors is commensurate with the above definition—they 'all require some input of *human creativity*; second, they are *vehicles for symbolic messages*, that is, they are carriers of *meaning*; and third, they contain, at least potentially, some *intellectual property* that belongs to an individual or group' [italics in original] (Davies & Sigthorsson, 2013, p. 1). For many of these industries copyright is paramount. For the World Intellectual Property Organization (WIPO) the core copyright industries include: press and literature; music, theatrical productions and opera; motion picture and video; radio and television; photography; software, databases and computer games; visual and graphic arts; and advertising services (PWC, 2020, p. 33). No matter which creative industries' model is used (DCMS, NESTA, KEA, etc.) and no matter which report on the creative industries is accessed, these lists and models most often include design, the arts, information technology and the media industries as broad subdivisions within the creative industries (Flew, 2012, p. 84). We could map out a version of these lists which would look like the following (Fig. 2.3):

While this structure is not intended to be comprehensive, all-encompassing or definitive, it is worth noting here that this hierarchical representation could have another layer scaled down to sectors that subsist under these others. For example, under publishing we could include books, magazines, print, zines, blogs, etc. and then at a lower scale list the occupations that are associated with each of them such as journalist, editor, publisher, printer and so on. Graphic design might include UX design, animation, illustration and the many other hybrids that are proliferating in this area. Visual arts might include painting, sculpture, photography and so on. Advertising and marketing might also include

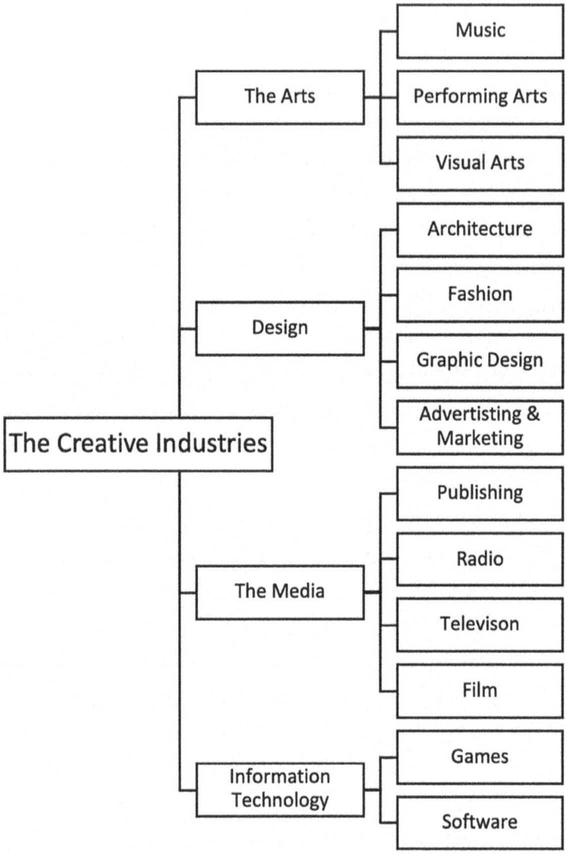

Fig. 2.3 Creative industries lists represented as a hierarchical structure

functions such as public relations, strategic communication and others. Radio would include all forms of broadcast and narrowcast radio, including, free-to-air, digital radio, podcasting and streaming services. This is true of each of the 11 sub-sectors of design, the media, IT and the arts. And of course, this map could be scaled upward as well so that creative industries themselves sit alongside agriculture, mining, health, education, finance, manufacturing, biotechnology and all other designated industries that make up various parts of the economy. Representing the creative industries in this hierarchical tree pattern does not imply that one scale level in this system is any more or less important than any other scale level. There are no top down or bottom up hierarchies in systems.

In summary, we can say that we now have in place a detailed account of the literature which initially covers the development of the singular term "culture industry" to the pluralized term "cultural industries". This review then moved on to connect these terms with the term "creative industries", which was followed by an overview of the authoritative, rationally argued and empirically derived research into creativity. After this, we made a comparison of the way creativity, as a concept, has been conceived of in the research literature on creative industries. The problematic issue of defining the creative industries was raised before we set out an operational definition for this book and the reason why it is apposite. In conclusion we supplied a scaled understanding of the subsectors of the creative industries. Next, we turn our attention to what we see as the key reports on the creative industries which have attempted to quantify the creative industries globally, nationally and regionally and look at their assumptions about creativity.

References

Alexander, V. (2003). *Sociology of the arts: Exploring fine and popular forms.* Blackwell.

Amabile, T. (1983). *The social psychology of creativity.* Springer.

Amabile, T. (1996). *Creativity in context.* Westview Press.

Bailin, S. (1988). *Achieving extraordinary ends: An essay on creativity.* Kluwer Academic Publisher.

Becker, H. (1982). *Art worlds.* University of California Press.

Bergquist, C. (1999). A comparative view of creativity theories: Psychoanalytic, behaviouristic and humanistic. *Vantage Quest.* Retrieved June 7, 2006, from http://www.vantagequest.org/trees/comparative.htm

Boden, M. (1994). *Dimensions of creativity.* MIT Press.

Boden, M. (2004). *The creative mind: Myths and mechanisms* (2nd ed.). Routledge.

Bourdieu, P. (1977). *Outline of a theory of practice.* Cambridge University Press.

Bourdieu, P. (1993). In R. Johnson (Ed.), *Field of cultural production.* Columbia University Press.

Bourdieu, P. (1996). *The rules of art: Genesis and structure of the literary field.* Polity Press.
Capra, F., & Luisi, P. (2014). *The systems view of life: A unifying vision.* Cambridge University Press.
Caves, R. (2000). *Creative industries: Contracts between art and commerce.* Harvard University Press.
Csikszentmihalyi, M. (1988). Society, culture and person: A systems view of creativity. In R. Sternberg (Ed.), *The nature of creativity: Contemporary psychological perspectives* (pp. 325–329). Cambridge University Press.
Csikszentmihalyi, M. (1997). *Creativity: Flow and the psychology of discovery and invention.* Harper Collins.
Csikszentmihalyi, M. (1999). Implications of a systems perspective for the study of creativity. In R. Sternberg (Ed.), *Handbook of creativity* (pp. 313–335). Cambridge University Press.
Csikszentmihalyi, M. (2014). *The systems model of creativity.* Springer.
Cunningham, S. (2011). *The CCI narrative: Research for a creative Australia.* Retrieved September 27, 2012, from http://www.cci.edu.au/sites/default/files/alawrence/CCI_narrative_2011_public_FINAL.pdf
Cunningham, S. (2012). From cultural to creative industries: Theory, industry and policy implications. In B. Moeran & A. Alacovska (Eds.), *Creative industries: Critical readings, Vol 1—Concepts* (pp. 206–218). Berg.
Dacey, J., & Lennon, K. (1998). *Understanding creativity: The interplay of biological, psychological, and social factors.* Jossey-Bass.
Davies, R., & Sigthorsson, G. (2013). *Introducing the creative industries: From theory to practice.* Sage.
Davis, H., & Scase, R. (2000). *Managing creativity: The dynamics of work and organization.* Open University Press.
Dawson, A., & Holmes, S. (2012). *Working in the global film and television industries: Creativity, systems, space, patronage.* Bloomsbury Academic.
DCMS. (2001). *Creative industries mapping document.* HM Dept for Digital Culture Media and Sport.
Dodgson, M., & Gann, D. (2010). *Innovation: A very short introduction.* Oxford University Press.
Drucker, P. (1991). The discipline of innovation. In J. Henry & D. Walker (Eds.), *Managing innovation* (pp. 9–17). Sage.
Eisenberger, R., & Shannock, L. (2003). Reward, intrinsic motivation and creativity: A case study of conceptual and methodological isolation. *Creativity Research Journal, 15*(2–3), 121–130. https://doi.org/10.1080/10400419.2003.9651404

Feldman, D., Csikszentmihalyi, M., & Gardner, H. (1994). *Changing the world: A framework for the study of creativity*. Praeger.
Flew, T. (2012). *The creative industries: Culture and policy*. Sage.
Florida, R. (2002). *The rise of the creative class*. Basic Books.
Freud, S. (1976). Excerpts from the relation of the poet to daydreaming. In A. Rothenberg & C. Hausman (Eds.), *The creativity question* (pp. 48–54). Duke University Press.
Gardner, H. (1993). *Creating minds: An anatomy of creativity seen through the lives of Freud, Einstein, Picasso, Stravinsky, Eliot, Graham and Gandhi*. Basic Books.
Glaveanu, V. (2014). *Distributed creativity: Thinking outside the box of the creative individual*. Springer.
Godin, B. (2015). *Innovation contested: The idea of innovation over the centuries*. Routledge.
Greenfield, S. (2008, June 25–27). Creating creative brains. In *Creating Value: Between Commerce and Commons Conference, Queensland University of Technology, Brisbane, Queensland, Australia*. Retrieved July 29, 2009, from http://cultural-science.org/creatingvaluesusan1.html
Gross, J. (2020). *The birth of the creative industries revisited: An oral history of the 1998 DCMS mapping document*. King's College London.
Gruber, H. (1988). The evolving system approach to creative work. *Creativity Research Journal, 1*(1), 27–51. https://doi.org/10.1080/10400418809534285
Hartley, J. (2005). *Creative industries*. Blackwell.
Hartley, J. (2012). *Digital futures for cultural and media studies*. Wiley-Blackwell.
Hartley, J., Potts, J., Cunningham, S., Flew, T., Keane, M., & Bandk, J. (2013). *Key concepts in creative industries*. Sage.
Hennessey, B. (2017). Taking a systems view of creativity: On the right path toward understanding. *The Journal of Creative Behavior, 51*(4), 341–344. https://doi.org/10.1002/jocb.196
Hennessey, B., & Amabile, T. (2010). Creativity. *Annual Review of Psychology, 61*, 569–598. https://doi.org/10.1146/annurev.psych.093008.100416
Hesmondhalgh, D. (2007). *The cultural industries* (2nd ed.). Sage.
Hesmondhalgh, D. (2011). *The cultural industries* (2nd ed.) [reprint]. Sage.
Hesmondhalgh, D. (2019). *The cultural industries* (4th ed.). Sage.
Hofer, R., & Polt, W. (1998). Evolutionary innovation theory and innovation policy: An overview. In K. Bryant & A. Wells (Eds.), *A new economic paradigm: Innovation based economic systems* (pp. 5–16). Dept of Industry Science and Resources: Science and Technology Policy Branch.

Holt, J., & Perren, A. (2009). *Media industries: History, theory, and method.* Wiley-Blackwell.
Howe, M. (1999). *Genius explained.* Cambridge University Press.
Howkins, J. (2001). *The creative economy: How people make money from ideas.* Penguin.
Hume, D. (1952). *An enquiry concerning human understanding.* Routledge and Kegan Paul.
Inglis, D., & Hughson, J. (2003). *Confronting culture: Sociological vistas.* Polity Press.
Kaufman, J., & Sternberg, R. (Eds.). (2019). *The Cambridge handbook of creativity* (2nd ed.). Cambridge University Press.
Kerrigan, S. (2013). Accommodating creative documentary practice within a revised systems model of creativity. *Journal of Media Practice, 14*(2), 111–127. https://doi.org/10.1386/jmpr.14.2.111_1
Laszlo, E. (1972). *The systems view of the world: The natural philosophy of the new developments in the sciences.* George Braziller.
Lebuda, I., & Glaveanu, V. (2019). *The Palgrave handbook of social creativity research.* Palgrave Macmillan.
Luhmann, N. (1990). *The science of society.* Suhrkamp.
McIntyre, P. (2008, November). The systems model of creativity: Analyzing the distribution of power in the studio. *Journal of the Art of Record Production, Issue 4: Supplement to ARP08, The Peer Reviewed Proceedings of the 2008 Art of Record Production Conference.* University of Massachusetts, Lowell. Retrieved June 24, 2010, from http://www.artofrecordproduction.com/content/view/214/126/
McIntyre, P. (2009, July 8–10). Rethinking communication, creativity and cultural production: Outlining issues for media practice. In T. Flew (Ed.), *Communication, Creativity and Global Citizenship: Refereed Proceedings of the Australian and New Zealand Communications Association Annual Conference, Brisbane, Australia.* ISBN 987-1-74107-275-4.
McIntyre, P. (2011, July 6–8). Bringing novelty into being: Exploring the relationship between "creativity" and "innovation". In *ANZCA 2011—Communication on the Edge: Shifting Boundaries and Identities.* The University of Waikato, Hamilton, New Zealand. Retrieved April 26, 2015, from http://www.anzca.net/conferences/anzca11-proceedings.html.
McIntyre, P. (2012). *Creativity and cultural production: Issues for media practice.* Palgrave Macmillan.
McIntyre, P. (2013). Creativity as a system in action. In J. Chan & K. Thomas (Eds.), *Handbook of creativity research* (pp. 84–97). Edward Elgar.

McIntyre, P. (2022). Songwriting practice and production: The past, present and future. *Songwriting Studies Journal, 1*, 5–26.

McIntyre, P., Fulton, J., & Paton, E. (Eds.). (2016). *The creative system in action: Understanding cultural production and practice*. Palgrave Macmillan.

McQuail, D., & Deuze, M. (2020). *McQuail's mass communication theory* (7th ed.). Sage.

McWilliam, E. (2009). Teaching for creativity: From sage to guide to meddler. *Asia Pacific Journal of Education, 29*(3), 281–293. https://doi.org/10.1080/02188790903092787

Mockros, C., & Csikszentmihalyi, M. (1999). The social construction of creative lives. In A. Montuori & R. Purser (Eds.), *Social creativity* (Vol. 1, pp. 202–234). Hampton Press.

Moeran, B., & Alacovska, A. (Eds.). (2012). *Creative industries: Critical readings—Vol 1: Concepts*. Berg.

Montuori, A., & Purser, R. (1995). Deconstructing the lone genius myth: Toward a contextual view of creativity. *Journal of Humanistic Psychology, 35*(3), 69–112. https://doi.org/10.1177/00221678950353004

Negus, K., & Pickering, M. (2004). *Creativity, communication and cultural value*. Sage.

Niu, W., & Sternberg, R. (2006). The philosophical roots of Western and Eastern conceptions of creativity. *Journal of Theoretical and Philosophical Psychology, 26*(1–2), 18–38. https://doi.org/10.1037/h0091265

NSW SRD. (2009). *NSW creative industry: Economic fundamentals*. NSW Department of State and Regional Development. Retrieved February 24, 2018, from https://www.industry.nsw.gov.au/__data/assets/pdf_file/0007/55384/NSW_creative_industry_economic_fundamentals_090204.pdf

O'Connor, J. (2012). Surrender to the void: Life after creative industries. *Cultural Studies Review, 18*(3), 387–410.

O'Connor, J., & Gu, X. (2012). Developing a creative cluster in a post-industrial city: CIDS and Manchester. In T. Flew (Ed.), *Creative industries and urban development: Creative cities in the 21st century* (pp. 156–203). Routledge.

OED. (n.d.-a). Create. *Oxford English Dictionary*. Retrieved February 9, 2011, from http://0-dictionary.oed.com.library.newcastle.edu.au/cgi/entry/50053519?query_type=word&queryword=create&first=1&max_to_show=10&sort_type=alpha&result_place=2&search_id=NNeg-EfiJcU-1356&hilite=50053519

OED. (n.d.-b). Innovation. *Oxford English Dictionary*. Retrieved February 9, 2011, from http://0-dictionary.oed.com.library.newcastle.edu.au/cgi/entry/50117397?single=1&query_type=word&queryword=innovation&first=1&max_to_show=10

Olsen, F. (1954). The nature of creative thinking. *The Phi Delta Kappan, 35*(5), 198–200. http://www.jstor.org/stable/20332414

Paul, E., & Kaufman, S. (2014). *The philosophy of creativity: New essays*. Oxford University Press.

Peterson, R. (1985). Six constraints on the production of literary works. *Poetics, 14*(1–2), 45–67.

Petrie, D. (1991). *Creativity and constraint in the British film industry*. Macmillan.

Pope, R. (2005). *Creativity: Theory, history, practice*. Routledge.

Praz, M., Davidson, A., & Kermode, F. (1970). *The romantic agony*. Oxford University Press.

PWC. (2020). *The economic contribution of Australia's copyright industries 2006–2018*. Australia Copyright Council. Retrieved April 12, 2023, from https://www.copyright.org.au/static/ACC_pdf/The_economic_contribution_of_Australia%E2%80%99s_copyright.pdf

Rogers, E. (2003). *Diffusion of innovation* (5th ed.). The Free Press.

Rothenberg, A., & Hausman, C. (Eds.). (1976). *The creativity question*. Duke University Press.

Runco, M., & Pritzker, S. (1999). *Encyclopedia of creativity*. Academic Press.

Ryan, B. (1992). *Making capital from culture*. Sage.

Sawyer, K. (2006). *Explaining creativity: The science of human innovation* (1st ed.). Oxford University Press.

Sawyer, K. (2012). *Explaining creativity: The science of human innovation* (2nd ed.). Oxford University Press.

Sawyer, K. (2019). Individual and group creativity. In J. Kaufman & R. Sternberg (Eds.), *The Cambridge handbook of creativity* (2nd ed., pp. 567–586). Cambridge University Press.

Sawyer, K., & DeZutter, S. (2009). Distributed creativity: How collective creations emerge from collaboration. *Psychology of Aesthetics, Creativity, and the Arts, 3*(2), 81–92.

Schiffer, L. (Ed.). (1998). Definitions. *Creative basics*. Retrieved July 28, 1998, from http://www.ozemail.com.au/~caveman/Creative/Basics/definitions.htm

Schumpeter, J. (1939). *Business cycles: A theoretical, historical, and statistical analysis of the capitalist process*. McGraw-Hill.

Simonton, K. (2003). Creative cultures, nations and civilisations: Strategies and results. In P. Paulus & B. Nijstad (Eds.), *Group creativity: Innovation through collaboration* (pp. 304–325). Oxford University Press.

Simonton, K. (2004). *Creativity in science: Chance, logic, genius and zeitgeist*. Cambridge University Press.

Stein, M. (1953). Creativity and culture. *The Journal of Psychology, 36*(2), 311–322. https://doi.org/10.1080/00223980.1953.9712897
Sternberg, R. (Ed.). (1999). *Handbook of creativity*. Cambridge University Press.
Sternberg, R., & Lubart, T. (1991). An investment theory of creativity and its development. *Human Development, 34*(1), 1–32. https://doi.org/10.1159/000277029
Thomas, W. (1967). *The unadjusted girl: With cases and standpoint for behavioral analysis*. Harper & Row.
Thomas, W., & Thomas, D. (1928). *The child in America: Behavior problems and programs*. Knopf.
Tidd, J., Bessant, J., & Pavitt, K. (1997). *Managing innovation: Integrating technological, market and organizational change*. Wiley.
Tschmuck, P. (2006). *Creativity and innovation in the music industry*. Springer.
Varbanova, L. (2001). *The creative industries mapping document 2001: Department for Culture, Media and Sport*. National Archive. Retrieved October 19, 2012, from http://webarchive.nationalarchives.gov.uk/+/http://www.culture.gov.uk/global/publications/archive_2001/ci_mapping_doc_2001.htm
Watson, P. (2005). *Ideas: A history from fire to Freud*. Weidenfeld & Nicolson.
Weisberg, R. (1988). Problem solving and creativity. In R. Sternberg (Ed.), *The Nature of creativity: Contemporary psychological perspectives* (pp. 148–176). Cambridge University Press.
Weisberg, R. (1993). *Creativity: Beyond the myth of genius*. W.H. Freeman and Co.
Weisberg, R. (2006). *Creativity: Understanding innovation in problem solving, science, invention, and the arts*. Wiley.
Williams, R. (1958). *Culture and society, 1780–1950*. Penguin.
Williams, R. (1981). *Culture*. Fontana.
Wolff, J. (1993). *The social production of art*. Macmillan Press Ltd..
Zolberg, V. (1990). *Constructing a sociology of the arts*. Cambridge University Press.

3

Creative Industries: Global and Local Perspectives

Creative Industries Reports

There have been a number of reports that have attempted to describe and, importantly, quantify the creative industries internationally, nationally and regionally (e.g., CIIC, 2013; Cox, 2005; Lhermitte et al., 2015, NESTA, 2006; Work Foundation, 2007). A broad review of these reports suggests that there is general agreement that: the creative industries deliver economic value and provide the foundation for other significant sectors; the creative industries play a key role in innovation and solving problems and challenges and they contribute to strategies to respond to community objectives for sustainability, livability, social cohesion and urban densification; and cultural and arts sub-sectors of the creative industries are important in the personal and social lives of people, the development of ideas and future-shaping. Despite ongoing attempts to report on these industries there are problems as 'the economic weight of cultural and creative industries (CCI) in mature and emerging economies is partially described, misunderstood and undervalued' (Lhermitte et al., 2015, p. 11). While differing models and definitions of the creative

P. McIntyre et al., *Creativity and Creative Industries in Regional Australia*, Palgrave Studies in Creativity and Culture, https://doi.org/10.1007/978-3-031-45972-6_3

economy, industries and workforce certainly illuminate the sector, the lack of a workable operational definition, an agreed nomenclature and a common taxonomy of sectors, makes comparability between reports difficult. As a result, while an understanding of the broader concepts and measures of activity help to ascribe value, those developing policy and considering action for economic development tend to lack data that is highly differentiated, localized and insightful.

There are a range of creative industries' definitions and descriptors used across both the international scene and national and local policy areas. As mentioned in Chap. 2, there is a substantial crossover discernible between the idea of creative, cultural and copyright industries (Hartley, 2005, pp. 30–31); there are also differences in terminology between countries (Flew, 2012, p. 4). Additionally, there is a persistent use of variable "clustering" systems for data gathering. For example, architecture is sometimes clustered with design and visual arts and sometimes with the built environment and yet it can be argued on one level that these business and professional profiles and industry organizations are distinctly different. In some papers, software is seen as the major economic contributor, but in one (NSW CIT, 2013, p. 9) it is not included in the analysis at all, other than in a fleeting referral to the increasing influence of digital technologies across all sectors. This situation makes comparisons and trend-watching from publicly available data difficult. The difficulty is further compounded when figures are broken down into creative goods and services or attributed to the various work contexts of practitioners. While such variability across reports can drive new insights, it can also lead to confusion in measurement and particularly in policy direction.

Globally Focused Reports

To elaborate, the United Nations Conference on Trade and Development (UNCTAD) stated in 2008 that the creative industries 'are among the most dynamic sectors in world trade' (2008, p. 4) and reported in 2015 that international trade in creative industries had shown sustained growth in the previous decade with traded *creative goods and services* (combined) at a record $547 billion in 2012, as compared with $302 billion in 2003.

A later UNCTAD report noted the:

> Cultural and creative industries significantly contribute to the world economy. The cultural sector accounts for 3.1 percent of global gross domestic product (GDP), while UNCTAD estimates that in 2020, creative goods and services represented 3 and 21 per cent of total merchandise and services exports, respectively. In addition, cultural and creative industries provide 6.2 per cent of all employment, generating nearly 50 million jobs worldwide, and employ more young people (15–29-year-olds) than other sectors. (2022, p. 2)

They noted that while the creative economy advances social inclusion, cultural diversity and human development, 'the COVID-19 pandemic had a devastating impact on certain creative industries and deepened their pre-existing vulnerabilities' (UNCTAD, 2022, p. 2). UNCTAD Secretary-General Rebeca Grynspan said:

> The report is published at a time when the global community faces some of the most significant challenges in decades: the COVID-19 pandemic, looming climate change and environmental crisis, geopolitical tensions and a major cost-of-living crisis. Despite these challenges, the creative economy remains a critical sector for sustainable development. (Fairley, 2022)

The resultant contraction has been alarming. We will return to it later in the book, but what concerns us immediately here is the basic assumptions of the earlier report. It asserted that the concept of creativity had to be enlarged 'from activities having a strong artistic component to 'any economic activity producing symbolic products with a heavy reliance on intellectual property and for as wide a market as possible' (Fairley, 2022). In this case, they came much closer to what the research into creativity is telling us (see Chap. 2), in contrast to many other reports at the time such as the Cox Review (2005) or the Work Foundation (2007) report that uncritically used historically specific sets of cultural assumptions.

Contrasted to the UNCTAD position, the figures provided by Marc Lhermitte, Solenne Blanc and Bruno Perrin, the consultants from Ernst & Young Ltd. who compiled the *Cultural times: The first global map of cultural and creative industries* report for the Confederation of Authors and Composers Societies, are slightly different. They quote Irina Bokova, the Director-General of UNESCO, who states that 'capitalizing US$2,250 billion and nearly 30 million jobs worldwide, the creative and cultural industries are major drivers of the economies of the developed as well as the developing countries indicating that they are among the most rapidly growing sectors worldwide' (Lhermitte et al., 2015, p. 5).

While these two reports show trends moving in the same direction, the underlying assumptions about trade, capitalization and jobs vary widely. It should be noted here that while there were acknowledged methodological issues which were reflected in that data, the 2015 UNCTAD Report also suggested that increasing demographics [sic], better access to ICTs and dynamic shifts to new lifestyles associated with both creative products and services, means that the creative services sectors continue to grow as the knowledge-based economy expands. In this regard, Guillermo Valles, the Director of the Division on International Trade in Goods and Services, and Commodities, at UNCTAD asserted that:

> [The] creative economy leverages creativity, technology, culture and innovation in fostering inclusive and sustained economic growth and development ... generate(s) income through trade (exports) and intellectual property rights and create(s) new jobs in higher occupational skills, particularly for small and medium sized enterprises. With advancement in technology, especially the digital revolution, education and innovation, creative and knowledge-based industries have emerged as among the dynamic sectors of the global economy. (UNCTAD, 2015, p. ii)

The estimates produced for the Ernst & Young report, in the absence of reliable aggregated statistical data, were based for each region on 'national statistics, market research analysis, existing CCI studies (such as WIPOs), industry reports and technical interviews' (Lhermitte et al., 2015, p. 117). Where they could not obtain regional data, they made estimates of employment and revenues using their own tailor-made assumptions. In doing this they:

> Scaled up available data from the main markets in each region with a representative sample (for instance, Brazil, Mexico, Argentina and Colombia for Latin America). [They] used world data and applied a market share scaling-down factor. When absolutely no data was available for any country in a region, [they] used a ratio based on data collected in other regions, adjusted by indicators to take into account the structural specificities of each region (productivity ratios, literacy rates, GDP per capita, etc.). (Lhermitte et al., 2015, p. 117)

They also 'conducted 150 interviews during the study to construct [their] key hypothesis and market assumptions' (Lhermitte et al., 2015, p. 117). Lhermitte et al. noted that 'the 11 CCI sectors are an integral, massive and universal cornerstone of the global economy. In 2013, they generated US$2,250b of revenues (3% of world GDP) and 29.5 million jobs' (2015, p. 117) and that 'creative industries and cultural tourism have become strategic assets for local economies' (2015, p. 117). They also recognized that not only was there a significant formal contribution to regional economies but also most importantly much of the output of the creative industries escaped detection in the official estimates of most countries' GDP. This primarily informal exchange of goods and services was at times central to certain regional cultures as it is how they have operated culturally for some time. However, its existence also includes physical piracy as well as unauthorized internet distribution of protected works. They do, however, go on to caution that the informal economy in toto must not simply be 'considered as criminal activities: it represents cultural activities and content traded by creators using informal distribution channels' (Lhermitte et al., 2015, p. 28).

These ideas also serve as a timely reminder that, as UNESCO's *Creative economy report, 2013, special edition: Widening local development pathways* contends, the 'creative economy is not a single superhighway, but a multitude of different local trajectories found in cities and regions' (UNESCO, 2013, p. 12) around the world. Apart from activity going on in the developing world, for the BRICS countries – Brazil, Russia, India, China and

South Africa, which are seen as the countries with greatest economic potential as a result of their demographics—there is a growing contribution from the creative industries to their economies. Nonetheless, there is much more to be done before they can fully leverage that potential. *The creative industries and the BRICS* (CISAC, 2014) report reviews the state of the creative economy in each of these countries and was carried out for the Confédération Internationale des Sociétés d'Auteurs et de Compositeurs [International Confederation of Societies of Authors and Composers] (CISAC). The report states that 'the modern global economy today relies on creativity like never before and the creative economy makes up a growing proportion of national economic output and job creation in many countries around the world' (CISAC, 2014, p. 10). The report noted BRICS countries are also 'lagging behind their ability to generate income from the use of their intellectual property (including from creative goods and services)' (CISAC, 2014, p. 10). In 2011, Korea alone generated US$4.5 billion from its intellectual property assets, while the average for the BRICS markets was less than US$0.5 billion (CISAC, 2014, p. 10). In summary, this report does two things at once: it maps the state of the creative economy in the BRICS countries and, like most reports on the creative industries, recommends policy initiatives to help each BRICS nation develop its creative economy.

In the bloc of countries that now constitute Europe, the European Commission has been active in recognizing, understanding and promoting their highly valuable creative sector. For example, in the *Innovative instruments to facilitate access to finance for the cultural and creative sectors (CCS): Good practice* (2016) report, the European Commission recognized that:

> Cultural and creative industries (CCIs) are, at the dawn of the 21st century, undergoing considerable change as a result of increased digital technologies, the economic crisis of the past several years, and considerable changes in the regulatory framework. Support to CCIs has, likewise, evolved rapidly, witnessing core changes in intellectual property law, increased support through state aid, and a greater recognition of their potential contribution to the economy. Despite the considerable potential of CCIs, estimated to be responsible for over 3% of the EU's gross domes-

tic product and jobs, they remain undervalued and unrecognized, especially in terms of their ability to access start-up capital and financing. The challenges facing CCIs are compounded by a lack of clear evidence and information in the sector, which further limits the ability of financial backers to recognize their potential, as well as other legislative hurdles, such as intellectual property rights, varying tax regimes, and mobility issues. (EC, 2017, online)

In June of 2021, using the Trident Methodology (Higgs & Lennon, 2014) as its basis, Deloitte produced *The future of the creative economy* report. It focused on six large economies in Europe and three large economies in the Asia Pacific (APAC): Japan, South Korea and Australia. It was commissioned by streaming service Netflix. The report noted that the 'creative economy is an ecosystem that comprises a wide range of occupations' (Deloitte, 2021, online). What distinguished this sector was the idea, drawn from the DCMS definition of the creative industries, of 'the generation of wealth and jobs through individual creativity driving the generation and use of intellectual property' (Deloitte, 2021, online). The report found that the 'creative economy employed nearly 20 million people across those nine economies in 2018' (Deloitte, 2021, online), representing approximately 7% of total employment. Despite the COVID pandemic, the report concluded that 'it is reasonable to expect that the sector will return to its long-term trend of growing faster than the wider economy' (Deloitte, 2021, online).

Nationally Focused Reports

The role played by the creative industries has not only been recognized at the international level. At a national level there have been a number of reports produced. For example, the formative UK Mapping Document in 2001, which gave both a national and regional perspective, concluded that the creative industries in the UK generated:

revenues of around £112.5 billion and employ some 1.3 million people. Exports contribute around £10.3 billion to the balance of trade, and the

> industries account for over 5% of GDP. In 1997–98, output grew by 16% compared to under 6% for the economy as a whole. (Varbanova, 2001, p. 10)

The influential *Cox review of creativity in business: Building on the UK's strengths* came out in 2005. One of its major flaws was that it privileged from within one disciplinary area what are now seen, in research terms, as highly contestable concepts and used these as its basic and uncritically examined assumptions. For example, it noted that creativity was 'the generation of new ideas' with innovation being 'the successful exploitation of new ideas' (Cox, 2005, p. 2). As was mentioned above and dealt with more fully in McIntyre (2011), these ideas can be seen as largely conventional truisms rather than evidence-based and rational understandings of both concepts.

The National Endowment for Science, Technology and the Arts (NESTA) in the UK also produced a report in 2006 entitled *Creating growth: How the UK can develop world class creative businesses*. This report echoed the idea that the creative industries made up a very significant part of the UK economy. It stated that these industries 'constitute a larger part of the economy and employ more people than the financial services sector' (NESTA, 2006, p. 3) and recommended that 'policymakers from across national governments, and not just the traditional advocates for these sectors, need to concentrate on the opportunities and challenges facing these industries from an economic point of view' (NESTA, 2006, p. 3). The NESTA report, however, also criticized the DCMS approach, which had become increasingly popular with policymakers. One problem for them was the inclusion of sectors that NESTA did not conceive of as "creative" (see, for example, NESTA, 2006, p. 53) but they appeared unaware that they were also uncritically using the common-sense understanding that being creative was somehow equivalent to being artistic or cultural. This, of course, ignores the recent empirically and rationally validated research into this phenomenon (see Chap. 2).

Another UK report, *Staying ahead: The economic performance of the UK's creative industries* (2007), was commissioned by the Department for Culture, Media and Sport (DCMS). It provided an analysis of the creative industries, what factors shaped their success in the UK and what the challenges were that this sector faced (Work Foundation, 2007, p. 9). This report by Work Foundation gave an overview of the creative industries as well as detailing their economic performance. It set out what the knowledge economy is before defining the creative industries and identifying the drivers of those industries. However, one major problem is that it perpetuated the Cox Report's problematic conception of creativity and innovation and they defined creativity as being:

> about the origination of new ideas—either new ways of looking at existing problems, or of seeing new opportunities, while innovation is about the successful exploitation of new ideas. It is the process that carries them through to new products and services or even new ways of doing business. (Work Foundation, 2007, p. 16)

In making these assumptions, they pay little attention to the research into creativity and, instead, they echo familiar cultural assumptions. They state, that 'the creative industries are not underpinned by a large scientific or technical base with formal logical structures. The process of learning and creating tends to be intuitive, iterative and trial and error rather than analytical and explicit' (Work Foundation, 2007, p. 102). With these simplistic and problematic conceptions underpinning their ideas, they offer a stylized typology of the creative industries. This assumption is based on an analysis set out in *The economy of culture* report from the KEA European Affairs for the European Commission and:

> deploy the notion of expressive value to map the creative industries in a series of concentric circles radiating out from the "bull's-eye" of core expressive value creation. The "bull's-eye" represents where pure creative content is generated. This is the domain of the author, painter, film-maker, dancer, composer, performer and software writer. (Work Foundation, 2007, p. 102)

Work Foundation do suggest that the "bull's-eye" does not only represent traditional art forms but also 'the writing of computer software, the establishment of a 2.0 website or the evolution of a new character in a video game all belong here' (2007, p. 104). Drawing uncritically on the "pure art" versus commerce dichotomy, underpinned as it is by romantic thinking, they suggest the next ring represents those industries that focus 'primarily or solely on the commercialisation of pure expressive value—the cultural industries—such as music, television, commercial-radio, publishing, computer games and film in the industrial classification' (Work Foundation, 2007, p. 104).

> The next concentric circle represents the focus of the creative industries. These are analytically first cousins to the cultural industries; distinct while belonging to the same family of activity. Architecture, design, fashion, computer software services and advertising are all creative industries whose market offerings pass both an expressive and workability test. They deliver both expressive and functional value. They tend to respond to the close demands of clients for creative offerings that work to their specifications; they constitute intermediate input in sectors in the wider economy. (Work Foundation, 2007, p. 105)

In 2017, Peter Bazalgette produced his *Independent review of the creative industries* report. This report was commissioned by the UK Business and Culture Secretaries and drew heavily on industry knowledge in the UK, in particular the Creative Industries Council and the Creative Industries Federation. In his report, Bazalgette noted that the UK creative industries 'exported £19.8bn of services in 2014 (9% of the UK total) and is a net exporter of creative services overall' (2017, p. 56). He went on to claim that 'it is human creativity that drives the success of this sector' (2017, p. 5). With the UK being one of a limited number of net exporters of music, Bazalgette also claims that, along with other creative occupations, these industries 'are highly resistant to automation with 87% of creative workers in the UK at low or no risk' (2017, p. 5). However, as Tim Cross points out, AI and machine learning are set to allow software to write songs for mass consumption by 2025 (2017, p. 144). Nonetheless, Bazalgette suggests that:

> The digital era, often referred to as the Fourth Industrial Revolution, represents an enormously exciting opportunity for a further wave of growth and innovation. But we will need to work hard to harness the value of the IP in these sectors and invest in R&D to secure our reputation as the most innovative place to make creative content. We need to exploit technologies

such as Virtual and Augmented Reality, 5G, 3D printing and other new techniques to keep innovation strong. We need to reimagine this as a "creative-tech" sector. The value that they bring is not only to the Creative Industries themselves but also as enablers to the wider economy. (2017, p. 5)

This report acknowledges that the creative industries in the UK are extremely innovative, but it also recognizes that they are constituted predominantly, as elsewhere in the world, 'by an abundance of SMEs, micro-businesses and individuals spread across the arts, design, cultural, digital, entertainment and media sectors' (Bazalgette, 2017, p. 28). As a result, there is limited 'capacity for strategic, cross-sectoral R&D which, if properly recognized and supported, could propel growth' (Bazalgette, 2017, p. 28). In this case, Bazalgette argues that leveraging government financial support is essential.

While the UK has produced a number of national-level reports like this, boosting the very real potential of the creative industries, in the USA an understanding of the creative industries has tended to be limited to two basic groups. Attempts to quantify it have been, as Terry Flew (2012) has indicated, bifurcated between a poorly funded arts sector and the commercially oriented global powerhouses of the entertainment and software industries. Each, the arts sector and the commercial giants, collects data on their own spheres. However, it is at the regional and local levels that the creative industries as a concept has gained some traction in the USA, particularly with the success of Richard Florida's (2002) work on creative cities.

China, on the other hand, has produced a number of reports primarily on what is known as the cultural/creative industries. Many of the reports coming specifically from China have been done in tandem with European scholars such as Justin O'Connor (e.g., O'Connor & Gu, 2012) or observed offshore, as it were, by scholars such as Michael Keane. His document *China's creative industries: Challenges matched by opportunities* indicates that:

Cultural projects (*xiangmu*) are the subject of numerous government-funded reports. The proposition that greater investment in cultural and creative industries will transfer the unattractive "world factory" label else-

> where while resolving environmental problems is appealing; it is a good news story. The cultural and creative industries range from esoteric kunqu opera to animated videos, artworks, toys and fashion accessories. Artifacts are displayed for sale in theme parks, galleries and online sites. Content is generated in software farms, media clusters, incubators, factories and art zones. (2014, p. 11)

Many Asian countries, as revealed by the UNCTAD (2008) study, are benefiting from a dynamic creative industries sector 'and are putting in place tailored cross-cutting policies to enhance their creative industries. China, which is leading this process, became the world's leading producer and exporter of value-added creative products' (UNCTAD, 2008, p. 5). Keane argues that there are now visible signs of the Chinese government's 'intention to fast-track the cultural economy. All first-tier cities and most second-tier cities have poured funds into constructing cluster projects' (2014, p. 11). He goes on to note that 'the digital landscape is evolving at a frightening pace' (2014, p. 12) while 'intellectual property remains a key hurdle' (2014, p. 12).

Further south, Boni Pudjianto, the Director of International Marketing for the Indonesian Agency for Creative Economy (Badan Ekonomi Kreatif—BEKRAF), which 'deals with policy making, coordination between Government bodies, guiding and supporting the creative sectors' (2016, p. 21), reported at the Asia-Pacific Digital Societies Policy Forum in 2016 that there are 16 'creative subsectors under the Indonesian Creative Economy. These include Apps & Games, Architecture, Interior Design, Visual Communication Design, Product Design, Fashion, Film, Animation & Video, Photography, Craft, Culinary, Music Publishing, Advertising, Performing Art, Fine Art, Television & Radio' (2016, p. 21). Understanding the significance of these creative subsectors, BEKRAF:

> aims to expand Indonesia's creative economy with a target to reach a 12 percent contribution to GDP by 2019, almost twice the 7.1 percent in 2014. It also aims for a 13 million-member workforce by 2019, 1 million more than in 2014 and a rise from 5.8 percent contribution to exports in 2014 to 10 percent in 2019. (Yosephine, 2015, online)

The 2003 *Economic contributions of Singapore's creative industries* document (Heng et al., 2003) charts the scope of the creative industries in Singapore. It sees these as 'comprising both "upstream" arts and "downstream" applications' (Heng et al., 2003, p. 51). Heng, Choo and Ho contend that:

> One can think of the creative industries as comprising basic and applied arts industries. Basic or "upstream" arts refer to traditional arts such as the performing, literary and visual arts, whereas "downstream" arts refer to the applied arts such as advertising, design, publishing and media-related activities. While "upstream" art activities may have commercial value in themselves, "downstream" art activities derive their commercial value principally from their applications in other economic activities [and] suggests the existence of a mutual relationship between upstream and downstream arts, so that each is an essential component of the arts "ecosystem". (2003, p. 52)

This composite view allowed the researchers to ascertain the economic impact of the creative sectors in Singapore and 'benchmarks Singapore's creative industries against those of leading countries, to give an idea of Singapore's current position and scope for advancement' (2003, p. 52). The paper recognizes that the creative industries are fueled by the 'intersection of the arts, business and technology. It leverages on the multi-dimensional creativity of individuals—artistic creativity, entrepreneurship and technological innovation—to create new economic value' (2003, p. 52) for Singapore.

In Australia, there have been a number of reports on the creative industries at the national, state, regional and city level. These include Higgs et al. (2007), Grace (2009), Price Waterhouse Cooper (PWC, 2020), Northern River Arts (NR Arts, 2012), Creative Industries Innovation Centre (CIIC, 2013), NSW Trade and Investment (NSW T&I, 2013), Essential (2013) and Lea et al. (2009) to name just a few. Of these, Higgs et al. (2007) found in their *Australia's creative economy: Basic evidence on size, growth, income and employment* report, that in 2001, 437,000 people comprised what they called the creative workforce. They found that this workforce:

was equivalent to 5.4% of the total Australian workforce. Almost 300,000 people were employed in firms specializing in the production of creative goods and services while an additional 137,000 people worked in Creative Occupations (CO) embedded in other industries. (2007, p. 4)

Not surprisingly, they found there were more people undertaking creative occupations by working inside other businesses than those working in businesses designated specifically as creative industries. They also noted that 'during 2001, the value of salaries and wages of people in the creative workforce was almost $21 billion, representing 7% of the earnings from all Australian employment' (2007, p. 4). Interestingly, they also found that:

Approximately 155,000 creative enterprises were registered for the Goods and Services Tax (GST) on the Australian Business Register (ABR), which was 6.6% of the total number of GST-registered enterprises in operation at the end of April 2006; [and] There were some 253,000 creative enterprises without GST registration, mostly sole traders, representing 10.8% of the total number of non-GST-registered enterprises in operation at the end of April 2006. (2007, p. 4)

Moving forward to 2013, the then Australian Federal Minister for Industry, now chief executive of the Queensland Resources Council, Mr. Ian MacFarlane, stated in the *Valuing Australia's creative industries final report* from the Creative Industries Innovation Centre (CIIC) at UTS, that 'Australia depends not only on its traditional industries, but on its creativity and innovation—qualities on which our vibrant creative industries are built' (2013, p. 5). MacFarlane also stated that:

These industries contribute more than $90 billion to our economy annually in turnover, add more than $45 billion to GDP and generate annual exports of $3.2 billion. And quite separate is the intangible but undeniable worth of knowing our nation creates great software, films, TV, radio, music, theater, dance, design, media, writing, marketing and architecture ... These agile, sophisticated and digitally savvy businesses and the creative professionals they support are more significant in number than you might expect. In 2011 there were more than 600,000 people working in the cre-

> ative industries in Australia and over 120,000 creative businesses. (CIIC, 2013, p. 5)

Drawing in part on the Creative Trident Methodology developed at the Centre for Creative Industries and Innovation at QUT (discussed more fully in Chap. 4), the CIIC report presented information on a number of creative industries' sectors. However, they warned that:

> Due to their dynamic nature, the creative industries are not simply defined and consist of a wide variety of businesses and individuals. They include cultural sectors like the visual and performing arts, as well as those sectors that are often dubbed digital media or multimedia including film and television, broadcasting, computer animation, web design and music. They also include a range of other sectors like architecture and urban design, industrial design, designer fashion, writing and publishing. Understanding the extent of the creative economy is even more problematic due to the way that creative and non-creative workers and businesses intersect. (2013, p. 7)

The CIIC report goes on to say that 'within the creative industries, the creative segments are shown to have varying structure and varying levels of performance' (2013, p. 12).

In 2020, using the same basic methodology, the ANA think tank produced *Australia's cultural and creative economy: A 21st century guide.* This report saw the creative economy, that is the creative industries plus those embedded in so-called non-creative sectors of the economy:

> contributing $111.7 billion to the Australian economy (6.4% of GDP) in 2016-17, and employing more than 800,000 people (8.1% of the total workforce), this is an industry area that is internationally recognized as resistant to automation and as a jobs-rich area of the economy. The cultural and creative economy has significant growth potential to 2030 and beyond. (Trembath & Fielding, 2020, p. 8)

This report used a scaled approach seeing creative and performing arts (0.3% of total workforce) as a subset of the creative art' (1.8% of total workforce), which is a component part of the creative industries (6.0% of total workforce), which was a component part of the creative economy

(8.1% of total workforce), which was itself a part of the whole economy (100% of total workforce). As the report indicated, 'several Australian states and territories are currently employing cultural and creative industries approaches, with the goal to diversify their economic base and social and cultural opportunities (Trembath & Fielding, 2020, p. 10).

State-Based Reports

Working our way down to that state level, in 2013 the NSW Creative Industries Taskforce (CIT), appointed by then NSW Deputy Premier Mr. Andrew Stoner, who was also Minister for Trade and Investment, and Minister for Regional Infrastructure and Services, estimated that, as per the 2011 Census, the NSW creative industries directly employed approximately 147,600 people. This number accounted for a 39.6% share for NSW of national employment in the creative industries. This is also equivalent to 4.7% of total NSW employment. In summary, the Taskforce found that NSW creative industries directly employ almost as many people as the financial and insurance services industries in NSW and more people than mining, agriculture, rental and real estate services, and the wholesale trade (NSW CIT, 2013, p. 11). In the State of Victoria during 2020–21:

> The creative industries added a gross value of $34.4 billion to the Victorian economy. This figure has grown an average of 5.6 percent annually over the last five years. Since 2018, the Australian Bureau of Statistics has published data on Victorian businesses by sector. The latest data shows there were 44,960 creative businesses operating in Victoria by the end of 2021. The creative sector employs 9 per cent of the total workforce in Victoria. (Creative Victoria, 2023)

There were 316,000 people employed in the creative industries as their principal job and there was a '2.9% Increase in creative industry employment from August 2021 to August 2022 [against] 2.5% total increase in Victorian employment over the same period' (Creative Victoria, 2023) with the bulk of those figures being located in the Melbourne and major regional centers like Ballart and Bendigo.

In terms of specific Australian cities that are *not* one of the major east coast metropolitan centers, the creative industries that feature in Darwin, for example, were mapped in the report *Creative tropical city: Mapping Darwin's creative industries* (Lea et al., 2009). This report indicated the creative industries generated a diverse set of jobs and, in 2006, 'these industries employed 1,918 people in Darwin across 44 industrial sectors and over 130 types of jobs' (2009, p. 14). This comprised 3.5% of the total workforce in Darwin making the sector comparable to other more visible industries. Startlingly, it employed more people than mining, finance and insurance, agriculture, forestry and fishing combined. While not as numerically significant 'as government administration, defence and communities services (all of which employ substantially more people)' (Lea et al., 2009, p. 14), the comparison would be more favorable if 'part-time, intermittent and "pro-am" creative workers were to be included (these types of workers are not successfully captured in the census)' (Lea et al., 2009, p. 14). Significantly, the creative industries share a direct link with the tourism industry 'through activities such as festivals and cultural tours' (Lea et al., 2009, p. 14) making the creative industries statistically equivalent with the tourist industry 'in terms of its contribution to Darwin's workforce' (Lea et al., 2009, p. 14). The report indicated more generally that:

> CI [creative industries] is relatively invisible, tending to be associated with fringe activities or the visual and performing arts, and not viewed as a core industry sector in its own right. It gets less policy attention in terms of framing the future of Darwin than its close cousin, tourism. Yet, as this report reveals, CI is not just culturally but also commercially important to the city of Darwin and its future. While traditional resource industries and tourism remain vulnerable to sudden changes in global conditions, the creative industries are the means by which communities have the diversity, talent and resourcefulness to respond to rapid global, technological and political shifts. CI is the link. (Lea et al., 2009, pp. 4–5)

Regionally Focused Reports

Bringing the examination down to a regional level, the Regional Australia Institute (RAI) conducted a study into four industries that might contribute to regional growth. They concluded in the report, *Regional Growth Prospects: Strategic Investment in Food Processing, Tourism, Advanced Manufacturing and Creative Industries* (Achurch, 2019), that:

> Employment in creative industries is growing in regional Australia but there are very few regions which are specialized in the industry. There is often a positive relationship between population size and creative employment and these places also have a higher number of creative services, or business-to-business, jobs such as graphic designers, web developers and other. Places with a high proportion of jobs in creative industries are largely places where people want to live. Creative industries play a role in local innovation and liveability, which may include attracting and/or retaining population in regional areas. This industry has an important presence in some smaller and more remote Indigenous communities where there is an opportunity to build on growing international and domestic demand for Indigenous art. (Achurch, 2019, p. 5)

Focusing in North Queensland, Townsville City Council, in a project led by James Cook University, also recognized the importance of the creative industries to northern Australia. The report, entitled *Growing the creative industries in Townsville* focused specifically on architecture, design, advertising and marketing, software and digital content, and film and investigated both supply and demand side issues for these subsectors of the creative industries. The report noted that:

> The supply of creative industries services is quite strong. While there are some instances where specialist skills are lacking in the city or not easily identifiable, in general the majority of services needed for effective industry activity can be found within the city. (Daniel et al., 2015, p. 6)

Raising the need for these sole traders and SMEs to brand and profile themselves more readily, the report also noted that 'there is a significant loss of creative work to capital cities, online or other providers, with many major projects lost to local practitioners' (Daniel et al., 2015, p. 6). This presents both challenges and opportunities for creative industries practitioners who need 'to look at collaborating, clustering and developing a stronger brand presence in order to win some of the lucrative contracts and projects that will continue to be available' (Daniel et al., 2015, p. 6). The report also recognized that all creative industries' sectors are changing very quickly mainly due to rapid advances in technology and digitization and globalization more generally. While competition is coming from global and capital city providers, the operatives on Townsville are also being 'challenged by the rise of the self-taught practitioner in such areas as photography, film and design, with entry costs to the market declining and with no regulation of entry or operation' (Daniel et al., 2015, p. 10). The creative industries' professionals in Townsville have thus had to work hard to 'maintain currency and to keep up to date with the latest industry developments' (Daniel et al., 2015, p. 10). They do this through a number of strategies which include: online learning in both paid work time and through self-education; networking and holding local industry events; selective travel to events beyond Townsville; and sharing of equipment and resources (Daniel et al., 2015, p. 10).

The City of Wollongong in NSW has also had researchers focus their attention on it as a small creative economy. As Gordon Waitt and Chris Gibson wrote:

> The City of Wollongong was one of the first Australian municipal authorities to embrace culture, establishing a creative cities agenda and the aspiration to become the City of Innovation prior to the "Richard Florida phenomenon". That this was the case is in itself a challenge to presumptions about large cities driving the creativity agenda. Yet, despite early aspirations to creative transformation, Wollongong has struggled to achieve sustained successes in repositioning the city's economy and image. (2009, p. 1224)

Wollongong has clung to its manufacturing industry, which affords it a unique set of circumstances that differentiates this city from others. It cannot claim to be completely post-industrial with the city still 'clustered around the port and steel mills' (Waitt & Gibson, 2009, p. 1228). In their study, Waitt and Gibson cite two reports. The first *Point of take off: Cultural policy framework and cultural plan 1998–2003* and the second is *The Wollongong cultural industries audit* in which 'culture, creativity, the arts and cultural industries appeared as an integral part of Wollongong's social and economic future' (Waitt & Gibson, 2009, p. 1229). Both of these reports suggest that 'for too long Wollongong Council had ignored the economic potential of culture' (Waitt & Gibson, 2009, p. 1229) with the first of them outlining 'the metropolitan economy of Wollongong in the context of globalization' (Waitt & Gibson, 2009, p. 1229). Waitt and Gibson conclude by suggesting that:

> Where it did occur, the story of creative regeneration in Wollongong had little to do with official planning schemes, global trends, desires on the part of creative producers to cluster together or the rise of the sorts of entrepreneurial creative cultures documented in larger cities elsewhere. Instead, organically developed creative "hamlets" emerged along a scattered string of beachside villages. This was more to do with changing narratives of proximity to Sydney, the circulation of discourses in Australia of beach-side living as idyllic quality of life … and the vernacular pursuits of grass-roots artists, musicians, writers and documentary makers who could work from home studios and would prefer scenic locations in which to live and be inspired … but who could only afford relatively inexpensive property prices. (2009, p. 1243)

As far as specific regionally focused reports are concerned, Essential Economic P/L delivered its *Creative industry in rural Victoria: Economic analysis* in 2013 to Rural Councils Victoria. It found that approximately 5500 creative businesses were located in rural Victoria, representing approximately 7% of all businesses. However, 'many workers in the sector commute to other locations for employment (especially those who live close to major regional and metropolitan centers)' (Essential, 2013, p. 72). Compared with the metropolitan center of Melbourne, rural areas also have a much lower share of 'jobs associated with IT, computer, telecommunications, engineering design and advertising' (Essential, 2013, p. 72), but the share of jobs in the more traditional creative industries 'such as newspaper publishing, printing, libraries, archives, arts education, photographic services, and employment for creative artists, musicians, writers and performers' (Essential, 2013, p. 72) is much higher. In NSW, as of 2012, 34% of people over the age of 15 from outer regional and remote areas did not use the internet, compared with 23% in capital cities (NSW DI, 2012, p. 22) but PriceWaterhouseCoopers reported in 2017 that, with 27% of the NSW population living in regional and rural areas, it has been estimated that a 10% increase in regional Australia's internet connectivity would result in a 0.53% increase in regional output, compared with a 0.38% increase in metro areas.

On the Mid North Coast of NSW, a predominantly rural region with a few centers of urban agglomeration, the *Mid North Coast creative industries research project* reported that the creative industries directly employ 1765 people from within this region. The report estimated that the value of the creative industries to the region sits at $80.6m (Grace, 2009, p. 6). In terms of employment, most of this was concentrated in the more urbanized and demographically larger centers of Coffs Harbour and Port Macquarie. The report noted that it did not set out 'to provide comprehensive economic analysis from the outset, rather an overview of the current situation' (Grace, 2009, p. 8). It did indicate that 'outside of clusters in screen industries within the Coffs Harbour and Bellingen [centers] (identified and supported by ScreenLinks) there were no identifiable industry clusters in the region' (Grace, 2009, p. 6).

The *Northern Rivers arts and creative industries strategy 2009–2012 mapping report*, which was prepared by Positive Solutions for Arts Northern Rivers, set out to 'provide a blueprint for managed, strategic, longer-term engagement in the development of the creative industries in the region by industry stakeholders, the three levels of government, and the business sector' (NR Arts, 2012, p. 5). This report found that the number of people employed in the creative industries in each of the local government areas (LGAs) that comprised the Northern Rivers Region sat at 1866 people in 2001 and, following a growth rate of 3.9%, sat at 2254 people in 2006. This growth rate was above the growth rate for all other industries in the region (NR Arts, 2012, p. 22). The report also found that 'mean incomes in the region are highest in the software/digital content sector and the advertising and marketing sector and lowest in music and the performing arts' (NR Arts, 2012, p. 26). Significantly, for our purposes, the NR report also 'compared the development of creative industries employment in Northern Rivers with that in several other Australian regions' (NR Arts, 2012, p. 27) which they believed could be used to eventually compare progress. One of these was the Hunter Region (Tables 3.1 and 3.2).

The earnings for creative occupations across the five regions compared in the report, looking at three Census periods, had the Hunter Region with the highest earnings figure (NR Arts, 2012, p. 28). The report also stated that 'in common with other regions, the software and digital content sector displayed the highest levels of earnings in the Northern Rivers' (NR Arts, 2012, p. 28) (Table 3.3).

Table 3.1 Comparison of creative occupation employment numbers by region (original in NR Arts, 2012, p. 27)

Region	1996	2001	2006	% inc 96-06
Hunter CI	3132	4019	4566	46%
Hunter all industries	177,904	148,779	163,219	
Illawarra CI	2719	3548	3646	34%
Illawarra all industries	133,261	136,768	123,149	
Northern Rivers CI	1230	1625	2055	67%
NR all industries	30,911	18,623	63,457	
Western District CI	588	465	442	-25%
Western all industries	8905	6391	15,239	
South West CI	789	1065	1174	49%
SW all industries	20,258	3276	27,199	

Table 3.2 Total creative occupation earnings for the five regions (original in NR Arts, 2012, p. 28)

Region	1996	2001	2006
Hunter	$95,021,212	$149,181,136	$217,269,104
Illawarra	$83,724,628	$145,550,132	$186,515,058
Northern Rivers	$27,946,048	$44,239,988	$71,986,356
Western District	$15,166,684	$13,278,200	$16,277,404
South West	$20,681,752	$30,198,220	$47,847,956

Table 3.3 Regional comparisons of mean income for all creative occupations (original in NR Arts, 2012, p. 28)

Region	1996	2001	2006	CAGR* 1996–2001	CAGR* 2001–2006
Hunter	$30,339	$37,119	$47,584	4.12%	5.09%
Illawarra	$30,792	$41,023	$51,156	5.91%	4.51%
Northern Rivers	$22,720	$27,225	$35,030	3.68%	5.17%
Western District	$25,794	$28,555	$36,827	2.06%	5.22%
South West	$26,213	$28,355	$40,756	1.58%	7.53%

Creative Industries in the Hunter

In the Hunter Region, specifically in the regional capital Newcastle, there has been a concerted effort to create an innovation ecosystem that has belatedly recognized the importance of the creative industries to the region and their use of digital technologies. It has been estimated, for example, that small businesses in the Greater Newcastle area could unlock an additional economic output of nearly $100,000 each, over ten years, through better use of internet and mobile technologies (PWC, 2017, online).

Dr. Sarah Pearson, employed as the University of Newcastle's Pro Vice Chancellor Industry Engagement and Innovation, also produced a report entitled *Connecting innovation to opportunity* (2017). It was primarily supported by the Hunter Founders Forum and was completed to review and identify the region's support pathways for business growth and innovation through mentoring, capability building and connecting to opportunity. Its significance lies in the fact that the resulting region-wide strategy draws together the major support, education and training organizations in a collaborative approach to supporting those industries related to creativity, invention and innovation. While it was not specifically focused on the creative industries, they were briefly recognized as an integral element and their contribution to other endeavors became evident in this process. The broad findings are therefore impactful to the creative industries and provide an added insight into the sector.

Using an innovation ecosystem framework developed by herself, 'based on her experience building an innovation ecosystem in Canberra (CBR

Innovation Network, CBRIN), her visits to international innovation ecosystems, and literature searches' (Pearson, 2017, p. 11), Pearson's report covered innovation activity as it relates to existing companies, large and small, as well as government input and diverse start-ups. Pearson reported that:

> The Hunter has a well-educated community; a world class research driven university that is increasing its engagement with, and commitment to industry and entrepreneurship; a TAFE dedicated to advanced manufacturing and future industries; national labs represented by CSIRO. (2017, p. 13)

Pearson noted that the Hunter Region has a number of accelerator and incubator programs which included CSIRO ON, the Regional Incubator, Slingshot and the partnership between Slingshot and UON through the ICON Accelerator and also reported that:

> Several training programs are available (such as Lean Startup and Business Model Canvas workshops) [and] the Integrated Innovation Network (I2N) is also setting out to connect and leverage investment in growth support across several innovation hubs in the region for start-ups and SMEs. (2017, p. 13)

Pearson's *iF Report* also sketched a regional construct of the creative industries that sees them as an integral, and integrated, part of the regional industry ecosystem. She recommended that an 'engagement with UON's [University of Newcastle] School of Creative Industries (SOCI) would also be highly valuable' (2017, p. 6). This school had been set up in response to the recommendations of the Allen Consulting Group (ACG) report delivered to UON in 2013 but the programs it delivered have, since 2021, been housed in the School of Humanities, Creative Industries and Social Sciences. This ACG report, entitled *Scoping a research and innovation cluster in the creative industries in Newcastle and the Hunter Region*, used the Trident Methodology (Cunningham & Higgs, 2008; Higgs et al., 2007; Higgs & Lennon, 2014), outlined more fully in Chap. 4, and ventured a best estimate of numbers employed in the creative

Table 3.4 Creative employment trident in Newcastle and Hunter Region 2011 (original in ACG, 2013, p. 34)

Source: ABS 2011a		Creative	Industry—other	Total
Occupation	Creative	2431	6862	9293
	Other	2273	251,386	253,659
	Total	4704	258,248	262,952

industries in the region. At the same time, they cautioned that 'the data is only available at the 4-digit ANZSCO occupation level, while creative occupations are defined by Cunningham at the more specific 6-digit level' (ACG, 2013, p. 33). ACG suggested that this process likely 'overestimates the size of the sector' (2013, p. 33). With that caveat in mind, they asserted that, for the Hunter Region, '11,500 people were employed in the creative industries in 2011' (2013, p. 31) (Table 3.4).

ACG then asserted that for 'Newcastle and the Hunter Valley, the creative industries represent 4.4 per cent of employment compared with 6.6 per cent in NSW and 7.2 per cent in Australia' (2013, p. 34) (Table 3.5).

The ACG Report broadly asserted that:

> While the region's reliance on mining is forecast to grow, the manufacturing industry is forecast to decline, indicating further diversification of the economy will be needed in the future. The creative industries have an important role in this diversification: as a source of employment growth; more broadly, by helping to retain talented young people in the region; and helping to attract and retain people and families with high levels of educational attainment, incomes and aspirations. These contributions will help to build labor force participation levels, help to ensure that important services are available in the region and add to the human capital base in the region—a key element in investment attraction for high value-adding industries. (2013, p. 31)

Creative Work

While the numbers for the creative industries appear, at first glance, to be heartening, the assumption that creative work is inherently free and easy 'have proved somewhat less than convincing' (Banks & Hesmondhalgh,

Table 3.5 Number of people employed in creative occupations in Newcastle and Hunter (original in ACG, 2013, p. 37)

4-digit occupation	Newcastle and Lake Macquarie	Hunter Valley excluding Newcastle	Total	Total growth *2006–2011*
Actors, dancers and other entertainers	85	23	108	7%
Advertising and marketing professional	415	156	571	33%
Advertising, public relations and sales managers	1027	425	1452	15%
Architects and landscape architects	234	30	264	10%
Architectural, building and surveying technicians	836	481	1317	40%
Archivists, curators and record managers	53	20	73	13%
Artistic directors, and media producers and presenters	94	18	112	-12%
Authors, and book and script writers	45	20	65	36%
Fashion, industrial and jewelry designers	68	17	85	49%
Film, television, radio and stage directors	73	23	96	7%
Graphic and web designers, and illustrators	380	142	522	36%
ICT support technicians	419	168	587	28%
Interior designers	55	21	76	7%
Jewelers	29	12	41	-25%
Journalists and other writers	232	84	316	15%
Multimedia specialists and web developers	91	17	108	108%
Music professionals	159	42	201	-1%
Other engineering professionals	162	58	220	29%

(*continued*)

Table 3.5 (continued)

4-digit occupation	Newcastle and Lake Macquarie	Hunter Valley excluding Newcastle	Total	Total growth *2006–2011*
Other miscellaneous clerical and administrative workers	230	110	340	1%
Other miscellaneous technicians and trade workers	218	186	404	41%
Other specialist managers	584	345	929	33%
Performing arts technicians	122	44	166	5%
Photographers	125	64	190	29%
Software and applications programmers	567	158	725	15%
Urban and regional planners	166	80	246	30%
Visual arts and crafts professionals	34	45	79	-18%
Total	**6504**	**2789**	**9293**	**23%**

Source: ABS, 2011 Census of Population and Housing

2009, p. 419). For example, workers within the creative industries in Europe and elsewhere face a range of difficulties that can 'reflect the often exploitative and precarious nature of the work process' (Banks & Hesmondhalgh, 2009, p. 419). As of 2009, Banks and Hesmondhalgh found that creative work is often project-based and irregular, contracts tend to be short term, and there is little job protection. There is a predominance of self-employed or freelance workers; career prospects are uncertain and often foreshortened; earnings are usually slim and unequally distributed, and insurance, health protection and pension benefits are limited. Creatives, they report, 'tend to be younger than other workers, and to hold second or multiple jobs. Women and ethnic and other minorities are underrepresented and disadvantaged in creative employment' (Banks & Hesmondhalgh, 2009, p. 420). Little has changed in the decade since. In 2019, Hesmondhalgh noted that creative workers typically have more than one job, are self-employed, have irregular and uncertain work with very few, if any, protections and an unequal pay distribution (2019, p. 351). Hesmondhalgh also noted that these features are 'recurring, persistent and seemingly worsening' (2019, p. 351).

Internationally, according to Lhermitte et al. (2015), cultural and creative workers also display certain qualities. This study found that these industries were characterized by youth, high productivity, independence and entrepreneurship and a high level of education. However, cultural and creative industries work in some countries also provides some economic opportunities for women in some sectors compared with more traditional industries (Lhermitte et al., 2015, p. 18) although that report does not indicate whether they remain under-represented. In the UK, as Banks and Hesmondhalgh (2009) suggest, because of an oversupply of creative labor, there is a correspondingly large contribution made through the "gift" economy or for low wages. These characteristics tend to confirm the pattern of differences in income between embedded workers and those working directly in creative workplaces. For the 44,000 practicing professional artists working in Australia many predominantly have portfolio careers, with just 17% working full-time on their creative practice (Australia Council, 2015, p. 4), attesting to the idea that people who work in certain sectors of the creative industries often have several occupations, working across a number of creative sectors, or work where their creative occupation is not their main employing occupation. For example, a person who teaches drama at TAFE but performs in their spare time would be assessed as belonging to the Education and Training industry rather than the creative industries (ACG, 2013, p. 33).

Creative labor, outside larger or specialist workplaces or where workers are embedded in other industries, tends to be individualized and reliant on individual talent, personalized according to certain modes of work, thus reducing opportunities for collective approaches to negotiations. This situation encompasses a different view taken of the "creative" or "knowledge" economy than in other areas. Self-employment and freelancing are becoming dominant modes of work and high-success role models do not reflect the reality of many others. In their UK study, Banks and Hesmondhalgh (2009) concluded that creative industries policy was increasingly linked to educational and employment policy in the interests of asserting national identity and consolidating economic interests. They suggest that 'there must be serious concerns about the extent to which this business-driven, economic agenda is compatible with the quality of working life and of human well-being in the creative industries' (Banks & Hesmondhalgh, 2009, p. 428). In comparison, Susan Luckman's case studies on rural, regional and remote creative work, demonstrate 'the ways in which cultural industries are gaining strength in rural and regional areas and the degree to which this is linked to a focus on lifestyle, in particular to life beyond, or as intertwined with, paid work' (2012, kindle). As Mark Deuze reports, 'people in all sectors of the economy have to come to terms with the challenges and opportunities of contingent employment, precarious labor, and an overall sense of real or perceived job insecurity' (2007, p. 2). If the reports from Deloitte (2021) and the Oxford Martin Working Paper *The future of employment: How susceptible are jobs to computerisation?* (Frey & Osborne, 2013) are both correct, many workers will find it necessary to create income from wherever they can, rather than gain full time employment, as digitally driven automation takes hold. For some it will be business as usual. Taylor and Luckman also point out, employing Berlant's notion of "cruel optimism", the hope that goes with the possibility of success 'promotes the intensification of labor and, too often, the acceptance of limited rewards for large effort' (2018, kindle).

For Hesmondhalgh and Baker 'the great army of freelancers sustaining the cultural industries have little access to the financial and psychological benefits accruing from strong union representation' (2011, p. 137). This view is leavened, and perhaps supported, by the idea that numerous creative freelancers reported that:

> pleasure in autonomy and freedom, that their work was complex, challenging, interesting and varied. It may be demanding, but it offers considerable opportunity for a sense of completion, and of having done a job well. There was widespread appreciation of the fact that this is work socially recognized as interesting, even glamourous. (2011, p. 138)

Dawson and Holmes (2012) also report that while the rewards are primarily non-material and the creative industries continue to attract freelancers willing to undercut each other for these non-material rewards, this increasing casualization, sub-contract and freelance work may actually be detrimental to creativity and innovation as these workers move toward risk averse behavior in order to maintain network contacts and regular contracts in an effort to please their clients. These clients are, of course, those who have increasingly outsourced their content production, design capability and IT support. There is little doubt these businesses will continue to pursue these activities so long as they see a financial advantage in them. For Davies and Sigthorsson:

> In a media ecology in which a few large multinational companies tend to control the distribution of products (along with PR, marketing and other business activities), the majority of freelancers and small companies, who are supplying products and services to the larger ones, find themselves in a buyer's market and in fierce competition with each other. (2013, p. 52)

All of this goes to support the notion of a 'whales and plankton' ecology (Evans in Davies & Sigthorsson, 2013, p. 49) where the contemporary creative industries can be depicted, on the whole, by 'a high number of freelancers and microbusinesses, which are largely involved in content creation and the dominant presence of extremely large, often multinational, corporations' (Davies & Sigthorsson, 2013, p. 49). This situation, dependent as it is on the triple drivers of neoliberalism, digitization and globalization, means that many of the skills and services at the heart of business competitiveness are being outsourced to regions with low costs and large pools of technical expertise. Further, as the ACG report suggested:

> The economic and social importance of creative industries is emphasized by their contribution to GDP, employment, income, as well as innovation, social cohesion and creativity. While the economic contribution of the creative industries can be quantified to an extent—using measures such as employment numbers and industry value added—quantitative measures do not fully capture the contribution of creative industries. (ACG, 2013, p. 6)

In summarizing these ideas we have examined what we see as the key reports on the creative industries. The review we presented of these reports encompasses the way they have described and, significantly, quantified the creative industries globally, nationally and regionally. This chapter then necessarily delved into the assumptions made in these reports about creativity in particular. Finally, we took a look at the nature of creative work in the creative industries especially in the light of neoliberal ideology as it took hold of the policies that govern the creative industries. It is to the statistical side of understanding the creative industries in one of the most important regions in Australia that we will now turn.

References

ACG. (2013). *Scoping a research and innovation cluster in the creative industries in Newcastle and the Hunter Region: Report to the University of Newcastle*. Allen Consulting Group.

Achurch, H. (2019). *Regional growth prospects: Strategic investment in food processing, tourism, advanced manufacturing and creative industries*. The Regional Australia Institute.

Australia Council. (2015). *Arts nation: An overview of Australian arts*. Australia Council for the Arts.

Banks, M., & Hesmondhalgh, D. (2009). Looking for work in creative industries policy. *International Journal of Cultural Policy, 15*(4), 415–430. https://doi.org/10.1080/10286630902923323

Bazalgette, P. (2017). *Independent review of the creative industries: Report to the UK Business and Culture Secretaries*. Boston Consulting Group.

CIIC. (2013). Valuing Australia's creative industries: Final report.. Prepared by SGS Economics and Planning for the Creative Industries Innovation Centre.

CISAC. (2014). *The creative industries and the BRICS: A review of the state of the creative economy in Brazil, Russia, India, China and South Africa*. Communications Department of CISAC.

Cox, G. (2005). *Cox review of creativity in business: Building on the UK's strengths*. HM Treasury.

Creative Victoria. (2023.). *Victoria's creative economy—Data*. Creative Victoria. Retrieved March 26, 2023, from https://creative.vic.gov.au/resources/2021-22-victorian-creative-industry-employment

Cross, T. (2017). Human obsolescence. *The World in 2018: The Economist*. The Economist Newspaper. Retrieved March 23, 2023, from https://theworldin.economist.com/edition/2018/article/14586/human-obsolescence

Cunningham, S., & Higgs, P. (2008). Creative industries mapping: Where have we come from and where are we going? *Creative Industries Journal, 1*(1), 7–30.

Daniel, R., Fleischmann, K., & Welters, R. (2015). *Growing the creative industries in Townsville*. Townsville City Council and James Cook University.

Davies, R., & Sigthorsson, G. (2013). *Introducing the creative industries: From theory to practice*. Sage.

Dawson, A., & Holmes, S. (2012). *Working in the global film and television industries: Creativity, systems, space, patronage*. Bloomsbury Academic.

Deloitte. (2021). *The future of the creative economy: A report by Deloitte*. Deloitte Access Economics. Retrieved March 15, 2023, from https://www2.deloitte.com/content/dam/Deloitte/uk/Documents/technology-media-telecommunications/deloitte-uk-future-creative-economy-report-final.pdf

Deuze, M. (2007). *Media work*. Polity Press.

EC. (2017). *Supporting cultural and creative industries*. European Commission. Retrieved July 21, 2017, from https://ec.europa.eu/culture/policy/cultural-creative-industries_en

Essential. (2013). *Creative industry in rural Victoria: Economic analysis*. [Essential Economics P/L for Rural Councils Victoria]. Municipal Association of Victoria.

Fairley, G. (2022, October 14). *Global report takes pulse on creative industries*. Arts hub. Retrieved March 30, 2023, from https://www.artshub.com.au/news/features/global-report-takes-pulse-on-creative-industries-2586294/

Flew, T. (2012). *The creative industries: Culture and policy*. Sage.

Florida, R. (2002). *The rise of the creative class*. Basic Books.

Frey, C., & Osborne, M. (2013). *The future of employment: How susceptible are jobs to computerisation?* Oxford Martin Working Papers. Retrieved March 1, 2017, from http://www.oxfordmartin.ox.ac.uk/downloads/academic/The_Future_of_Employment.pdf

Grace K. (2009). *Mid North Coast creative industries research project*. Evolve Network Australia. Arts Mid North Coast.

Hartley, J. (2005). *Creative industries*. Blackwell.

Heng, T., Choo, A., & Ho, T. (2003). *Economic contributions of Singapore's creative industries*. Singaporean Ministry of Trade and Industry.

Hesmondhalgh, D. (2019). *The cultural industries* (4th ed.). Sage.

Hesmondhalgh, D., & Baker, S. (2011). *Creative labor: Media work in three cultural industries*. Routledge.

Higgs, P., Cunningham, S., & Pagan, J. (2007). *Australia's creative economy: Basic evidence on size, growth, income and employment*. CCI Technical Report. QUT Faculty Research Office, CCI. Retrieved June 25, 2010, from http://eprints.qut.edu.au

Higgs, P., & Lennon, S. (2014). *Applying the NESTA dynamic mapping definition methodology to Australian classification*. Queensland University of Technology. Retrieved March 27, 2023, from https://eprints.qut.edu.au/92726/

Keane, M. (2014). China's creative industries: Challenges matched by opportunities. *Ticker: Business Journal of German Chamber of Commerce in China, 4*, 11–13.

Lea, T., Luckman, S., Fitzpatrick, D., Brennan-Horley, C., Willoughby-Smith, J., & Hughes, K. (2009). *Creative tropical city: Mapping Darwin's creative industries*. Northern Territory Government.

Lhermitte, M., Blanc, S., & Perrin, B. (2015). *Cultural times: The first global map of cultural and creative industries*. Ernst & Young Report for the Confederation of Authors and Composers Societies. EYGM Ltd..

Luckman, S. (2012). *Locating cultural work: The politics and poetics of rural, regional and remote creativity*. Palgrave Macmillan. Retrieved from https://www.amazon.com.au/Locating-Cultural-Work-Politics-Creativity-ebook/dp/B00A208S52/ref=tmm_kin_swatch_0?_encoding=UTF8&qid=&sr=

McIntyre, P. (2011, July 6–8). Bringing novelty into being: Exploring the relationship between "creativity" and "innovation". In *ANZCA 2011—Communication on the edge: Shifting boundaries and identities. The University of Waikato, Hamilton, New Zealand*. Retrieved April 26, 2015, from http://www.anzca.net/conferences/anzca11-proceedings.html

NESTA. (2006). *Creating growth: How the UK can develop world class creative businesses: NESTA research report*. NESTA.

NR Arts. (2012). *Northern Rivers arts and creative industries strategy 2009–2012—Mapping report*. Arts Northern Rivers.

NSW CIT. (2013). *Industry action plan: NSW creative industries*. NSW Dept of Trade and Industry. Retrieved April 12, 2014, from https://wecreate.org.nz/wp-content/uploads/2018/02/iap_nsw_creative_industries.pdf

NSW DI. (2012). *Industry action plan: NSW digital economy*. Digital Economy Industry Task Force, NSW Department of Industry. Retrieved June 27, 2017, from https://www.industry.nsw.gov.au/buy-fromnsw/industry-capabilities/information-and-communication-technology/industry-actionplan-Digital-economy

NSW T&I. (2013). *Visual arts, design and new media sectors snapshot*. Trade and Investment ART NSW. Retrieved February 24, 2018, from https://www.create.nsw.gov.au/wp-content/uploads/2013/04/2013-Visual-Arts-Design-and-New-Media-Sector-Snapshot_Website-Final2.pdf

O'Connor, J., & Gu, X. (2012). Developing a creative cluster in a post-industrial city: CIDS and Manchester. In T. Flew (Ed.), *Creative industries and urban development: Creative cities in the 21st century* (pp. 156–203). Routledge.

Pearson, L. (2017). *Connecting innovation to opportunity*. Hunter Founders Forum.

Pudjianto, B. (2016, 27–28 April). *Empowering nations through creative economic sector*. Asia-Pacific Digital Societies Policy Forum 2016. Indonesian Agency for Creative Economy [Badan Ekonomi Kreatif—BEKRAF]. Retrieved June 27, 2017, from https://www.itu.int/en/ITU-D/Regional-Presence/AsiaPacific/Documents/Events/2016/Apr-Digital2016/S7_Present_Boni_Pudjianto.pdf

PWC. (2017). *The potential for internet and mobile technologies to transform small business*. PriceWaterhouseCoopers. Retrieved July 13, 2017, from www.digitalinnovation.pwc.com.au/smallbusiness-digital-growth

PWC. (2020). *The economic contribution of Australia's copyright industries 2006–2018*. Australia Copyright Council. Retrieved March 27, 2023, from https://www.copyright.org.au/static/ACC_pdf/The_economic_contribution_of_Australia's_copyright.pdf

Taylor, S., & Luckman, S. (Eds.). (2018). *The new normal of working lives: Critical studies in contemporary work and employment*. Palgrave Macmillan. Retrieved from https://www.amazon.com.au/New-Normal-Working-Lives-Contemporary-ebook/dp/B0785V412R

Trembath, J., & Fielding, K. (2020). *Australia's cultural and creative economy: A 21st century guide*. New Approach and Australian Academy of the Humanities.

UNCTAD. (2008). *Creative economy report 2008*. United Nations Conference on Trade and Development. Retrieved June 27, 2017, from http://unctad.org/creative-economy

UNCTAD. (2015). *Creative economy outlook and country profiles: Trends in international trade in creative industries*. United Nations Conference on Trade and Development (UNCTAD). Retrieved June 27, 2017, from https://unctad.org/system/files/official-document/webditcted2016d5_en.pdf

UNCTAD. (2022). *Creative economy outlook 2022 (Overview)*. United Nations Conference on Trade and Development (UNCTAD). Retrieved March 26, 2023, from https://unctad.org/publication/creative-economy-outlook-2022

UNESCO. (2013). *Creative economy report, 2013, special edition: Widening local development pathways*. UNESCO. Retrieved March 30, 2023, from https://apo.org.au/sites/default/files/resource-files/2013-03/apo-nid183651.pdf

Varbanova, L. (2001). *The creative industries mapping document 2001: Department for Culture, Media and Sport*. National Archive. Retrieved October 19, 2012, from http://webarchive.nationalarchives.gov.uk/+/http://www.culture.gov.uk/global/publications/archive_2001/ci_mapping_doc_2001.htm

Waitt, G. F., & Gibson, C. (2009). Creative small cities: Rethinking the creative economy in place. *Urban Studies, 45*(5&6), 1223–1246.

Work Foundation. (2007). *Staying ahead: The economic performance of the UK's creative industries*. DCMS/The Work Foundation.

Yosephine, L. (2015, November 4). Indonesia to optimize intellectual property rights to boost creative economy. *The Jakarta Post*. Retrieved July 21, 2017, from http://www.thejakartapost.com/news/2015/11/04/indonesia-optimize-intellectual-property-rights-boost-creative-economy.html

4

Statistical Analysis

Introduction

As you will see immediately below, this research project revealed a wealth of both quantitative and qualitative data. The first action taken in this research process was a literature review (see Chaps. 2 and 3) and the next, a statistical analysis of the creative industries in the Hunter Region. We start here with Statistical Measure 1.

Statistical Measure 1: Using 2011 Census Place of Residence Data Across Selected 6-Digit ANZSCO '06 Occupations

The Hunter catchment is an area that is geographically, socially and industrially diverse and is comprised of 11 local government areas (LGAs), that is, Lake Macquarie, Newcastle, Maitland, Port Stephens, Cessnock, Great Lakes, Upper Hunter, Singleton, Dungog, Gloucester and Muswellbrook. The region is also: 'divided into the urban areas, based

P. McIntyre et al., *Creativity and Creative Industries in Regional Australia*, Palgrave Studies in Creativity and Culture, https://doi.org/10.1007/978-3-031-45972-6_4

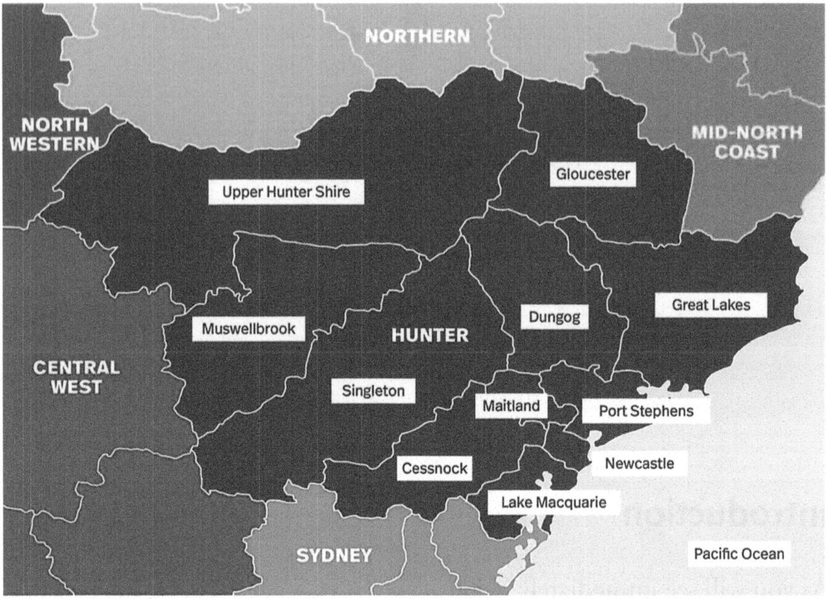

Fig. 4.1 Map of Hunter Region Local Government Areas (LGAs)

around Newcastle and Lake Macquarie, and the remaining semi-rural and rural areas' (Wilkinson, 2017, online) (Fig. 4.1).

The total population of the Hunter Region sat at 675,199 in 2017. Together, Newcastle and the Lake Macquarie LGAs had 54.17% of the region's total population with Lake Macquarie, as a major domiciliary location, holding the larger of the two urban populations (Wilkinson, 2017, online).

Estimated from Remplan data, which incorporated Australian Bureau of Statistics (ABS) June 2016 Gross State Product, 2013/2014 National Input Output Tables and 2011 Census Place of Work Employment data, the Gross Regional Product (GRP) for the Hunter Regions, that is, its net measure of generated wealth, was estimated to sit at $48.351 billion in 2017. As an example of scalability at work:

> Newcastle's Gross Regional Product is estimated at $16.985 billion. Newcastle represents 35.13% of Hunter Region's GRP of $48.351 billion, 2.95% of New South Wales' Gross State Product (GSP) of $576.716 bil-

lion and 0.97% of Australia's GRP of $1.755 trillion. (Remplan, 2017, online)

With the creative industries constituting approximately 2% of the employed population in the region, they were estimated in simple and approximate terms to contribute close to $1 billion, that is, $967 million or $0.967 billion, to the GRP of the Hunter Region. Lake Macquarie, Maitland and Newcastle LGAs, contributed 75.49% of the $41.124 billion value added in the Hunter Region (Remplan, 2017, online) with the region contributing '1.65% of the $501.134 billion value added in New South Wales and 0.54% of the $1.545 trillion value added in Australia' (Remplan, 2017, online). The creative industries' contribution to the regional gross value added (GVA) at this time was constituted, at least according to this measure, by the Information Media & Telecommunications and the Arts & Recreation Services industry categories. It was estimated to be $727,783 million. Of this figure, $534,072 million or 73.4% was contributed by the urban center of the region, which is commensurate with the total industry figure.

The occupations designated to exist within the creative industries are derived from the same 6-digit ANZSCO '06 Occupations codes as used in the *Valuing Australia's creative industries final report* (CIIC, 2013, pp. 30–31). These were then divided into a standard set of sectors and, with that in mind, a customized data report from the ABS using 2011 Census Place of Residence data across the selected 6-digit ANZSCO '06 Occupations, by Age and by Sex, within the 11 LGAs of the Hunter Region (2011 boundaries) was produced.

This ABS customized data showed that the Advertising and Design sector in the Hunter Region constituted 43.9% of all people engaged in the creative industries. This sector also contains Marketing and Public Relations. There were 18.1% engaged in the Electronic Games and Interactive Content sector, but we note here that this percentage is based on all digitally oriented occupations, including all those who work within other creative industries sectors. The next largest sector is Architecture at 13.4%. In total, these three sectors represent at least 75% of the total creative industries people living in the Hunter Region. The lowest level of occupation numbers is within the Film sector at 1% followed by Radio at 1.3%, Fashion at 1.5%, Television at 1.9% and Performing Arts at 2%.

In order to see how many creative industries occupations were represented in each LGA in the Hunter Region, a cross tabulation of two factors, i.e., occupation and LGA, revealed that the urban center of this region had, as expected, the greater number of people from the creative industries living in these areas. Of this urban center, Newcastle has the greater share with 2539 people and Lake Macquarie with 2074. Of the rural and semi-rural areas, Maitland houses 584 closely followed by Port Stephens with 481 people engaged in the creative industries. The Dungog LGA has the lowest number of creative industries' residents with the Upper Hunter contributing just 65 to the overall total of 6535.

The creative industries were also divided, following Flew (2012), into four major sectors. These are Design, the Media, Information Technology (IT) and the Arts. Using the NSW Creative Industries Taskforce sector categories (NSW T&I, 2013), and the NSW Department of State and Regional Development (NSW SRD, 2009, p. 7) as a basis, we amalgamated Architecture, Fashion and Advertising and Design (including marketing and public relations) into the Design subsector. The Media subsector was constituted by Publishing (including newspaper, magazines, books and new media), Film, Television (broadcast and digital) and Radio (broadcast and digital). The Information Technology subsector is constituted by Electronic Games (including popular and serious games) and Interactive Content (including software and app development). The Arts subsector included Visual Arts (including painting, sculpture and photography) and Performing Arts (including popular and serious music, in all its forms, as well as theater and dance). These subsectors were then broken down per LGA in Table 4.1.

We can see that there were 580 people (9%) working in the Media, 928 in the Arts (14%), 1180 in IT (18%) and 3847 working in Design (59%) in the Hunter Region.

Our analysis also revealed the gender and age spread in creative industries in the region is similar to but not precisely the same as other studies. For example, the Ernst & Young report outlined in Chap. 3 found that the creative industries were oriented toward youth and in some countries provided more economic opportunities for women in certain sectors

Table 4.1 Primary sectors in the creative industries by LGA in the Hunter Region

LGA	Design	The arts	Media	IT	Total
Cessnock (C)	165	85	28	45	323
Dungog (A)	30	0	0	21	51
Gloucester (A)	12	9	0	6	27
Great Lakes (A)	134	28	18	17	197
Lake Macquarie (C)	**1234**	**286**	**154**	**400**	**2074**
Maitland (C)	358	80	48	98	584
Muswellbrook (A)	33	18	15	6	72
Newcastle (C)	**1456**	**324**	**251**	**508**	**2539**
Port Stephens (A)	287	73	48	76	484
Singleton (A)	89	18	9	3	119
Upper Hunter Shire (A)	49	7	9	0	65
Total	**3847**	**928**	**580**	**1180**	**6535**

Source: Customized Data Report from the ABS using 2011 Census Place of Residence data across selected 6-digit ANZSCO '06 Occupations, by Age and by Sex within the 11 LGAs of the Hunter Region (2011 boundaries)

compared with more traditional industries (Lhermitte et al., 2015, p. 18). Banks and Hesmondhalgh's 2009 study also revealed that creatives 'tend to be younger than other workers, and to hold second or multiple jobs' (2009, p. 420) with an under-representation of women. In terms of age, most people employed in the creative industries in the Hunter Region are in the 25–34 year age band, followed closely by the 35–44 year age band, and this share is similar for both females and males. For the Hunter Region, the breakdown of age and gender is as follows (Graph 4.1):

This graph indicates that, overall, the peak age period for workers in the creative industries are between 25 and 44 years old. For males, the figures hold relatively steady across the 25 to 54 year age bracket while for females, there is a peak at 25 years of age with a slow decline until around 44 years old and then a sharp drop off from that point onward with fewer females maintaining longer-term positions in the creative industries. There are, of course, sector and LGA differences. When females are cross-tabulated with LGA we observed that there were, for example, 554 females occupied in Advertising and Design in the creative industries in Newcastle compared with 507 males. We deduced overall that at certain sectoral levels and in certain LGAs, the Ernst & Young assertions held true, while for some sectors and LGAs, the trend was reversed. For

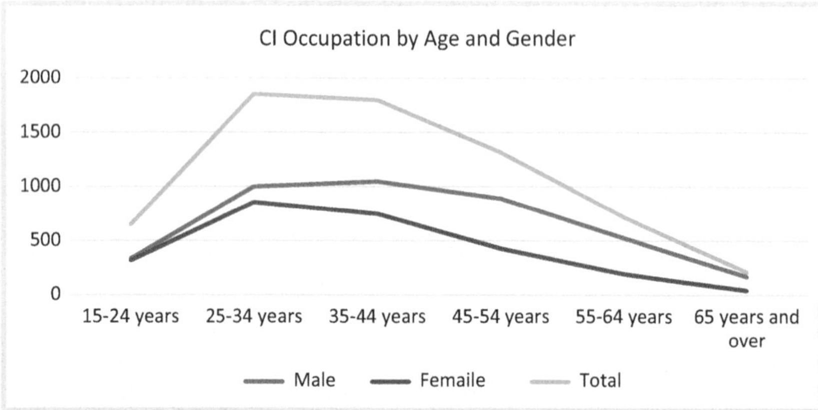

Graph 4.1 Creative industries occupations in the Hunter by age and gender. (Source: Customized Data Report from the ABS using 2011 Census Place of Residence data across selected 6-digit ANZSCO '06 Occupations, by Age and by Sex within the 11 LGAs of the Hunter Region (2011 boundaries))

example, in the Electronic sector, there were 64 females and 336 males engaged in IT in Lake Macquarie. These results differ somewhat from the findings of the studies mentioned above. Given the mix of results, and the various collection methods used to ascertain them, these figures need to be refined to gain a comprehensive and cohesive picture of what is actually going on. Similarly, certain sectors exhibit older populations than others. For example, in the Performing Arts and Fashion sectors the major age category is 35–44 years while for Architecture the major age category is 45–54 years. However, for Advertising and Design the major category is 35–44 years, followed closely by 25–34 years (816).

Of the 6535 people working in the creative industries in the region in 2011, males and females of all ages, 11.2% (719) were estimated to be self-employed, with most of these working in the region's urban center. The caveat here is that many of the positions in the creative industries in certain sectors such as Film or Visual Arts are predominantly freelance, contract or sessional. To label these as employees or employers may be misleading. However, The World Bank has measured the self-employed in Australia, as a percentage of total numbers employed. It sat at 16.3% in 2020 (Trading Economics, 2020). Self-employed workers were defined as:

> those workers who, working on their own account or with one or a few partners or in cooperative, hold the type of jobs defined as "self-employment jobs" i.e. jobs where the remuneration is directly dependent upon the profits derived from the goods and services produced. Self-employed workers include three subcategories: employers, own-account workers, and members of producers' cooperatives. (Trading Economics, 2020)

What can be reasonably asserted in general from the statistics presented above is that all of the sectors belonging to the creative industries are certainly represented in the Hunter Region. As indicated in the table below, out of the total working population of 330,837 in the Hunter Region, 6535 people work in the creative industries, a share that appears to be below the national average (CIIC, 2013) and most of the creative industries occupations are taken up by males (3957) in comparison with females (2578). As a whole, the creative industries contributed $0.967 billion to the GRP of the regional economy in the Hunter with a GVA of $0.820 billion (Table 4.2).

At this point, we want to emphasize that these early statistics from Measure 1 appear, prima facie, to be close to what could be expected for the creative industries in the region at this time. However, hidden

Table 4.2 Composite creative industries statistics for the Hunter region

	All industries	Creative industries
Population figures		
Total working	330,847	6535
Employed	293,793	5810
Self-employed	37,054	719
Females working	–	2578
Males working	–	3957
Economic contribution		
Contribution to GRP	$48.351 billion	$0.967 billion
Contribution to GVA	$41.124 billion	$0.820 billion

Sources: (1) Customized Data Report from the ABS using 2011 Census Place of Residence data across selected 6-digit ANZSCO '06 Occupations, by Age and by Sex within the 11 LGAs of the Hunter Region (2011 boundaries); (2) Remplan data, incorporating Australian Bureau of Statistics (ABS) June 2016 Gross State Product, 2013/2014 National Input Output Tables and 2011 Census Place of Work Employment data)

alongside and within many of these occupational categories are other unidentified positions such as, in music, songwriter, record producer and audio engineer, of which there are quite a number in the Hunter region, as detailed in our own prior research (e.g., McIntyre, 2015). These are not listed in the ABS Data set we worked with, with some occupations not accounted for at all in the 6-digit ANZSCO '06 Occupations list.

While this list looks intuitively accurate, there are a number of questions to be asked as to its veracity. For example, this 6-digit ANZSCO '06 Occupations by Creative Industries Sector list employed in Measure 1 only indicates two occupational roles for the radio sector, that is, Radio Presenter and Music Director. Yet occupations in radio generally include Station Manager, Program Director, Music Director, Traffic Scheduler, Creative Director, Audio Engineer, Technical Officer, Sales Manager, Accountant, Sales Representative, Audience Research Executive, Announcer/Presenter, Stringer, Broadcast Journalist and News Director/Producer. This over-simplification operates in a similar way for many of the other creative industries sectors. In this case, we advise that the statistics from Measure 1 must be read with this major caveat in mind, as they are based on the supplied 6-digit ANZSCO '06 Occupations list, rather than the number of occupations each sector is actually constituted by.

With this knowledge in mind, we then looked at the occupational problem we perceived in this data set from the other direction, as it were. We went to the industry and asked what occupations exist there. This further list was derived from an extensive web search of company, employment and organizational websites, as well as from our own knowledge of these sectors as practitioners. We did this for *all* the sectors identified as belonging to the creative industries. We will give just two examples here: Television and Film. The 6-digit ANZSCO '06 Occupations codes for the Film sector only list Video Producer, Film, Television, Radio and Stage Directors, Technical Director and Make Up Artist. We noted the following occupations for Film: Second AD, Producer's Assistant, Production Manager, Unit Manager, Public Relations Officer, Rigger, Company manager, House manager, Usher, Ticketing Agent, Art Director, Choreographer, Accountant, Construction Manager, Editor, Location Manager, Camera Operator, Sound Designer, Carpenter, Associate Producer, Stunt Performer, Assistant Producer, Casting

Director, Wardrobe Supervisor, Chargehand Painter, Concept Artist, Storyboard Artist, Costume Assistant, Set Decorator, Costume Designer, Costume Maker, Director, Actor, Unit Stills Photographer, Agent, Director of Photography, Editor, Stagehand, Executive Producer, First Assistant Camera, Painter, First Assistant Director, HoD Plasterer, Production Runner, Property Master, HoD Rigger, Line Producer, Make-up and Hair Artist, Hair Designer, Marketing Executive, Scenic Artist, Marketing Manager, Model Maker, Animator, CGI, Painter, Plasterer, Screenwriter, Producer, Unit Manager, Production Designer Script Supervisor and Production Coordinator.

Similarly for Television, the 6-digit ANZSCO '06 Occupations Television list included: Film, Television, Radio and Stage Directors, Director (Film, Television, Radio or Stage), Artistic Directors, Media Producers and Presenters, and Media Professionals. However, the occupation list we compiled, in the opposite direction, as it were, for Television included; Actor, Variety Artist, Walk-on and Supporting Artist, Agent, Camera Assistant (Studio and OB), TV Broadcast Journalist, News Director, Chief of Staff (TV News), Camera Operator (Portable Single Camera), Production Manager (TV), Costume Designer, Director (TV), Executive Producer, Gaffer (TV), Lighting Director, TV Presenter, Accountant, Location Manager, Make-up and Hair Artist/Designer, Transmission Engineer, Marketing Executive, Sound Supervisor, Stunt Performer, Marketing Manager, Network Operations Assistant, Public Relations Officer, Researcher, Script Supervisor, Sound Assistant (TV), Art Director, Boom Operator, Camera Operator (Studio and OB), Sound Recordist and Vision Mixer.

What is also important to note here is that many of these occupational types have not been comprehensively accounted for in any statistical analysis so far. To put this in the frame we are presenting here, we argue that the lists we compiled are closer to constituting a major part of the various "fields" of these creative industries sectors, excluding audiences as per Sawyer (2012), than the ANZSCO Six Digit ones available are. To give this some perspective, we suggest the processes used by the ABS to define occupational classifications are understandably reactive not proactive. The ABS as a data gathering entity is operating in an environment that is continually changing and must react to those changes rather than anticipating or predicting them. There is thus a disparity in the ABS lists due to the inability to reflect current practice as it is occurring. At a technical level, there may also be a "frame of reference" issue associated with occupational classifications, leaving some doubt about the adequacy of the questions used to collect occupational data to fully encapsulate working practices and the associated perceptions of what constitutes an occupation in the creative industries.

We also noted there is a wide variety of occupations within the creative industries that cross between sectors. For example, whether we are talking about networked, broadcast, cinematic or virtual screen industries, there are a number of film or television directors actually working within design and advertising or embedded in other industries (McIntyre & Kerrigan, 2014), yet they identify in some parts of their professional lives with the film sector.

Additionally, work, employment and job creation in the creative industries continue to be dependent on the contextual structures within which they occur. Manuel Castells pointed out that the occupational structures of many societies around the globe have been transformed by new technologies. He stated that 'the processes and forms of this transformation have been the result of the interaction between technological change, the institutional environment and the evolution of relationships between capital and labor in each specific context' (2010, p. xxiv). As noted in Chap. 1, with these larger forces increasingly at play, operating at varying scales within the system, interlinked with the increasing dominance in the economic sphere of neoliberal free market forces, there has been a concerted move away from full-time employment toward freelancing and casualization in creative industries' workforces. At the same time, there is an increasingly entrepreneurial bent amongst creative workers. This situation indicates that we need to look beyond traditional models of labor market employment, that is, look beyond an individual 'who works for a public or private employer, who receives remuneration in wages or salary, and is engaged under a contract of service/employment contract' (ABS, 2015).

Because of this dynamic environment, new creative industries' occupations are emerging and creative industries' professions are undergoing radical change. For example, Transmedia Storyteller is an occupation the

ABS has not even begun to consider, let alone classify or gather data on. As Davies and Sigthorsson pointed out in 2013:

> the creative industries regularly generate job descriptions that previously did not exist—terms like "app developer" or "community manager" crop up suddenly and become ubiquitous. [People] will apply to jobs that don't exist yet, in businesses yet to be established. (2013, p. 229)

This process has evolved and developed at a rapidly accelerating rate since then. To add to the complexity of these issues of the constitution of the creative industries, there is the matter of core, embedded and support services to be considered. It is at this point we turned to the Creative Trident Methodology (Cunningham & Higgs, 2008; Higgs et al., 2007; Higgs & Lennon, 2014), which we believed was designed to potentially circumvent the problems the methodological disadvantages of Measure 1 presented.

Statistical Measure 2: Using 2011 and 2016 Census Data with the Creative Trident Methodology

To give this study a second statistical measure, the Creative Trident Methodology was also employed. This time we drew from both the 2011 and 2016 Censuses. A second customized table from the ABS containing the number of persons employed, the total who stated income and mean income for 35 selected industries (4-digit IND06P) and all other industries by all occupations (6-digit ANZSCO), was then sought. The resultant data for this second measure was not drawn from LGAs, as for Measure 1 above, but was based instead on SA4 geographical areas. This geographic level is aggregated for ASGS 106 Hunter Valley (excluding Newcastle) and 111 Newcastle and Lake Macquarie. Unlike Measure 1, it excludes the Great Lakes and Gloucester. However, before proceeding to present the statistical results for Measure 2, there are a number of assumptions and definitions that underpin the Trident Methodology that need to be further explored.

For Peter Higgs and Sasha Lennon, the creative industries have been variously conceived. They assert that to 'define and measure creative industries according to a fixed set of industry sectors or codes is insufficient to measure the true extent of Australia's creative workforce' (2014, p. 1). They argue that the creative industries are not discrete sectors of the economy but are instead 'a pervasive input to many, if not all industries' (2014, p. 1). They further suggest that the Trident Methodology, which they use, not only quantifies employment in creative industries but 'also identifies the employment of creative workers (by occupation) "embedded" in other so-called "non-creative" industry sectors' (2014, p. 1). For Higgs and Lennon:

> The creative trident focuses on the activities that define creative production capacity in both occupations and industries. It includes three categories: (1) creative occupations within the core creative industries (what we term "specialists"); (2) creative occupations employed in other (non-creative) industries (termed "embedded" creatives); and (3) non-creative occupations ("support staff") employed in the creative industries. (2014, p. 1)

To put this another way, if we are to measure the creative industries' portion of the Australian workforce it is necessary 'to include "specialist" creative activity and "creatives" employed in other sectors of the economy' (Higgs & Lennon, 2014, p. 4). This inclusion helps to 'capture the full range of employment types' (Higgs & Lennon, 2014, p. 4). It is thus necessary to identify those specialists working within what are seen to be core creative industries, those support staff directly employed in those core creative industries, and those who are embedded in other supposed non-creative industries. It should be noted that these categories depend in many ways on a maintenance of above-the-line and below-the-line characterizations of occupational roles, one where the line is drawn by industry type, and one which Dawson and Holmes argue needs to be interrogated. As outlined in Chap. 2, Dawson and Holmes assert, somewhat similarly to Howard Becker (1982), that 'we need other ways to understand creativity in an industry with a complex social division of labor involving large numbers of people working cooperatively' (2012, p. 14).

The Trident Methodology is based on the NESTA approach of measuring and defining creative employment. For Higgs and Lennon, these forms of employment are centered on 'the activities that define core creative production capacity in both occupations and industries' (2014, p. 4). Using this approach gives the possibility of evaluating Australia's occupation classifications using five criteria to establish a form of what they call 'creative intensity' which is then used to designate an industry as creative or not. These five criteria are:

1. *non-uniformity*, where the output of the occupation is not the same but results from the interplay of a number of factors;
2. *creative output*, where that occupational output is perceived as novel and not mechanistic;
3. *not mere transformation*, where the occupational role does not just transfer someone else's creative work into another form;
4. *novel process*, where the occupation solves a problem or achieves a goal in novel ways; and
5. the occupation is *mechanization-resistant* as it is assumed that 'creative occupations are arguably less exposed to substitution through mechanization' (Higgs & Lennon, 2014, p. 4).

Of course, these factors are absolutely dependent on a particular set of assumptions being drawn from Higgs and Lennon's own understanding of what constitutes the phenomenon of creativity itself, which may or may not align with the authoritative, well-reasoned, empirically derived research into creativity outlined in preceding chapters. Nonetheless, from this perspective those occupations 'scoring 4 or 5 are considered "creative occupations"' (Higgs & Lennon, 2014, p. 4). A calculation is then made to derive the 'share of employment that creative occupations account for in each of the standard (ANZSIC) industry classifications to generate what is then termed "creative intensity"' (Higgs & Lennon, 2014, p. 4). A high score gives a high-intensity level and, of course, the reverse is applicable. This calculation of creative intensity is then used to decide whether an industry is creative or not.

The assertion is also made for this methodology that the sectors the creative industries are usually constituted by (using a list-based approach), 'fall into one of two sub-groups' (Higgs & Lennon, 2014, p. 5): creative services or cultural production.

Creative services enterprises and those who work within them, such as freelancers, self-employed subcontractors and so on, provide inputs deemed to be crucial to many other industries and the businesses that constitute them. These other industries range from 'manufacturing and construction to retailing and entertainment' (Higgs & Lennon, 2014, p. 5). The creative services sub-group then represents, for Higgs and Lennon, what is virtually a 'creative services economy' where 'creative enterprises and individuals add value to production through design, technical performance, packaging and branding' (Higgs & Lennon, 2014, p. 5). The sectors that are designated here as creative services include architecture and design, advertising and marketing, and software and digital content.

Cultural production, on the other hand, according to this methodology, includes those occupations which 'embody the role of arts and cultural assets as contributors to quality of life and community well-being and as important contributors to economic activity and economic development in their own right' (Higgs & Lennon, 2014, p. 5). The sectors that are designated as cultural production for this methodology include film, television and radio, music, visual and performing arts, and publishing.

There is also the issue of creative workers normally having a compendium of jobs in an attempt to make up a full-time wage, a situation endemic to most employment within the creative industries, as the qualitative material presented in later chapters reveals. In this regard, the primary limitations of using census data to measure creative employment lies in the fact that national datasets like those derived for the 2011 Census by the ABS use standardized classifications to acquire the data. As Higgs and Lennon point out, 'the census questions, the answers given, and the processes used to encode them, also shape the data' (2014, p. 6). For example, a person's employment may range across a number of sectors but their census information 'can only be encoded with one out of the approximately 600 standard industry codes that encompass all economic activity' (Higgs & Lennon, 2014, p. 6). Similarly, a person's occupation may be classified according to 'approximately 1,000 occupations of which some 90 are considered to be "creative"' (Higgs & Lennon, 2014, p. 6). Furthermore, as Higgs and Lennon discuss, various occupation codes are specifically described, such as "landscape architect", with other occupations seeming to be relatively vague and may include a mix that seem 'relatively unrelated—for example, the ANZSCO3 code 211499 Visual Arts and Crafts Professionals n.e.c. (not elsewhere classified) includes New Media Artist, as well as Leadlighter and Textile Artist' (Higgs & Lennon, 2014, p. 6). Furthermore, for this methodology:

> the term "employed" is used inclusively and synonymously with "work", as many in the creative economy are self-employed or employers, rather than employees. It also includes all those employed in their primary job whether on a full-time or part-time basis. (Higgs, 2017)

As a result, Peter Higgs reminds us, 'the analysis … ignores second jobs' (Higgs, 2017). This declaration is important as we will see from the qualitative aspect of this project and our conclusions from that outlined later in the book. As stated, the Census only gathers information on the "main job" performed across a certain timeframe and also does the same for the industry of employment. This is a regrettable limitation when dealing with the creative industries since employment, as revealed in the qualitative data, is often cross-sectoral and multi-occupational. For example, Higgs and Lennon themselves point out the Throsby data gathered for the Arts Council 'indicates that some 37% of artists have only a single job, 33% have an additional arts-related job and 23% have an additional non-arts job while 8% have three jobs' (2014, p. 6).

Unfortunately, there is generally little way of telling if the main job 'provides the bulk of the income for an individual and if the creative component of overall income is improving or reducing' (2014, p. 6). Despite these caveats, Higgs and Lennon believe the Census data is currently the best we have as 'a valuable and authoritative source of data for assessing the quantum and growth of creative employment in Australia and for making direct comparisons between states/territories, cities and regions' (2014, p. 6).

Another important factor about the statistics emerging from the application of the Trident Methodology to small population sizes at the regional level is particularly pertinent to the 2016 data. Around this time, the ABS had recently changed their strategy for ensuring that the identities of those who fill out the census remain confidential where there are counts of cells with fewer than three people. As Peter Higgs (2017) explained, where there are only one or two people in a cell it is easy to identify, for example, one radio presenter in a region. Randomization is thus necessary to maintain privacy. However, the change from software-based randomization to a simplified "find and replace" technique to suppress low cell counts means the aggregation totals will not be as accurate as hoped for. This situation has produced certain distortions in the results, especially for cities and regions with smaller workforces and lower populations than many of the capital cities. In short, the numbers become coarse approximations only, due to the necessary compromises and inconsistencies. The following statistics are therefore presented with the above set of assumptions and limitations in mind.

Proceeding under these assumptions, we drew on the ABS Census of Housing and Population 2011 and 2016. It is worth noting that the resultant statistics, set out in much more detail in our final report (McIntyre et al., 2019), are divided between those derived from either place of residence (POR) or place of work (POW) population data and the final numbers for each reflect that difference. The summary tables presented below are sorted into the four basic CI categories of design, the media, IT and the arts, and their subsectors of music, performing arts, visual arts, advertising and marketing, architecture, graphic design, fashion and other design, software (including games and app development), film, publishing, radio, TV and other media. They are also divided between what are called creative industries and creative occupations. Creative industries are measured by those specialists and support staff employed within what are designated as creative businesses. It is to be noted that this situation does not account for "embeddeds". Using the idea of creative occupations, on the other hand, enables us to slice the data slightly differently. The category of creative occupations are seen here as those who work as specialists in creative businesses or as embedded creatives in other industries. An alternative term could be "the creative workforce". It is worth noting, though, that this does not account for "support" staff.

Pressing on, we can say that, based on POR, the number of people employed in the creative industries is rising in the Hunter Region with nearly 9600 people employed in 2016. The share of the total workforce also increased between 2011 and 2016 with a compound annual growth rate (CAGR as opposed to AGR) of 2.0% compared with an annual growth in the general workforce of 0.6%. While the percentage share of employment of specialist and support workers has dropped marginally, there has been substantial growth in the employment of embedded creatives, that is, those operating within other industries (Tables 4.3, 4.4, and 4.5).

If we now base our analysis on POW data instead of POR data, the figures change slightly. The number of people employed in the creative industries, in this case, now sits at approximately 8800 for 2016. In comparing POR and POW data for employment, one can see that there is a slight drop in overall numbers employed in the region's creative industries workforce when POW data is used. This difference may be the result of personnel who live in the region working elsewhere. For example, a number of people work in Sydney and commute on a daily basis into the metropolitan center and other creative industries practitioners being resident in the Hunter but take on project work internationally, so their place of work is external to the Hunter Region.

For POW figures, the share of the total workforce also increased year on year between 2011 and 2016 with a compound annual growth rate (CAGR not AGR) of 2.8% compared with an annual growth in the general workforce of 2.0%. While the percentage share of employment of specialist and support workers has also dropped marginally, based this time on POW figures, there had been steady growth in the employment of embedded creatives, that is, those operating within sectors of other industries, as indicated by the following Table 4.6.

Portions of this POW data may be represented differently as set out in the tables below (Tables 4.7 and 4.8).

Examining the data using place of work (POW) figures gives, as was the case for employment above, a slightly diminished amount of earnings for creative industries, that is, those specialists and support staff employed

Table 4.3 Trident employment in the Greater Hunter Valley, 2011 & 2016, by place of residence

Trident employment (POR)	Employed 2011	Employed 2016	Share of workforce 2011	Share of workforce 2016	Share of creative employment 2011	Share of creative employment 2016	CAGR 2011 to 2016
Specialist	**2349**	**2431**	0.89%	0.89%	27.05%	25.33%	0.7%
Support	**2698**	**2803**	1.02%	1.03%	31.07%	29.21%	0.8%
Total creative industries	5050	5239	1.92%	1.93%	58.15%	54.60%	0.7%
Embedded	**3636**	**4360**	1.38%	1.60%	41.87%	45.44%	3.7%
Total trident	**8683**	**9594**	3.30%	3.53%	100%	100%	**2.0%**
Creative occupations	5986	6797	2.27%	2.50%	68.93%	70.84%	2.6%
Total workforce	**262,944**	**271,408**					**0.6%**

Source: Analysis of customized extract of ABS Census of Housing and Population

Table 4.4 Employment by creative and other sectors, place of residence, 2011 (persons)

8683 *2011* *Total creative*	Creative industries	Other industries	Total
Creative occupations	**2349** *Specialist*	**3636** *Embedded*	5986
Other occupations	**2698** *Support*	254,263 *Other*	256,962
Total	5050	257,893	262,944 *Workforce*

Source: Analysis of customized extract of ABS Census of Housing and Population

Table 4.5 Employment by creative and other sectors, place of residence, 2016 (persons)

9594 *2016* *Total creative*	Creative industries	Other industries	Total
Creative occupations	**2431** *Specialist*	**4360** *Embedded*	6797
Other occupations	**2803** *Support*	261,808 *Other*	264,614
Total	5239	266,170	271,408 *Workforce*

Source: Analysis of customized extract of ABS Census of Housing and Population

within what are designated as creative businesses. The total earnings for both creative industries and creative occupations located within each sector, that is design, the arts, the media and IT, as well as the subsectors that sit within each of these broader categories, and using a slightly different process of analysis, we can see that, once again, embedded workers have increased their share of workforce earnings. There is a marginal increase for creative occupations with an increase in creative earnings. Share of workforce earnings for specialists has remained static but dropped once we look at share of creative earnings. Support worker share of workforce earnings and share of creative earnings have remained fundamentally the same. The annual growth rate of the set of total Trident workers, that is all specialist support and embedded workers, rose from 2011 to 2016 a little more markedly than for the total workforce (Table 4.9).

In terms of mean weekly income, there had been an increase in income levels across the board. However, it is in the support sector where incomes

Table 4.6 Trident employment in the Greater Hunter Valley, 2011 & 2016, by place of work

Trident employment (POW)	Employed 2011	Employed 2016	Share of workforce 2011	Share of workforce 2016	Share of creative employment 2011	Share of creative employment 2016	CAGR 2011 to 2016
Specialist	**2056**	**2199**	0.88%	0.86%	28.70%	24.99%	1.4%
Support	**2388**	**2585**	1.03%	1.01%	31.22%	29.38%	1.6%
Total creative industries	4444	4787	1.92%	1.87%	58.11%	54.41%	1.5%
Embedded	**3203**	**4014**	1.38%	1.56%	41.88%	45.62%	4.6%
Total trident	**7647**	**8798**	3.30%	3.44%	100%	100%	**2.8%**
Creative occupations	5261	6214	2.27%	2.43%	68.79%	70.62%	3.4%
Total workforce	**231,430**	**255,694**					**2.0%**

Source: Analysis of customized extract of ABS Census of Housing and Population

Table 4.7 Trident employment by creative and other sectors, place of work, 2011 (persons)

7647 2011 *Total creative*	Creative industries	Other industries	Total
Creative occupations	**2056** *Specialist*	**3203** *Embedded*	5261
Other occupations	**2388** *Support*	223,788 *Other*	226,183
Total	4444	226,994	231,440 *Workforce*

Source: Analysis of customized extract of ABS Census of Housing and Population

Table 4.8 Trident employment by creative and other sectors, place of work, 2016 (persons)

8798 2016 *Total creative*	Creative industries	Other industries	Total
Creative occupations	**2199** *Specialist*	**4014** *Embedded*	6214
Other occupations	**2585** *Support*	246,895 *Other*	249,479
Total	4787	250,912	255,694 *Workforce*

Source: Analysis of customized extract of ABS Census of Housing and Population

rose most, followed closely by those working as embedded personnel. As a reminder, this form of "embedded" employment occurs in industries not normally designated as creative where typical creative industry workers may gain employment. Illustrative cases might include a video maker in the service of the Police Force, a web designer working in the mining industry or a PR person working in the corporate world. As the table below indicates, this group of embedded creatives tended to have the highest level of weekly income (Table 4.10).

Annual income overall increased within the broader creative industries, most often sitting just above the average annual increase for the total workforce generally.

We then compared the share of workforce and employment with capital cities in Australia in 2011, noting that the creative industries constitute approximately 2.8% of the total workforce in 2011 in the Hunter Region (as defined by SA4—the smallest geographical area that is

Table 4.9 Comparison of earnings in the specialist, support and embedded CI workforce 2011 to 2016

Trident earnings	2011	2016	Share of workforce earnings 2011	Share of workforce earnings 2016	Share of creative earnings 2011	Share of creative earnings 2016	CAGR 2011 to 2016
Specialist	**$92,813,812**	**$121,498,468**	0.8%	0.8%	27%	24%	5.5%
Support	**$136,277,492**	**$193,338,340**	1.2%	1.2%	39%	38%	7.2%
Total creative industries	$229,091,304	$314,836,808	1.9%	2.0%	66%	62%	6.6%
Embedded	**$120,162,744**	**$194,641,616**	1.0%	1.2%	34%	38%	10.1%
Total trident	**$349,254,048**	**$509,478,424**	3.0%	3.2%	100%	100%	**7.8%**
Creative occupations	$212,976,556	$316,140,084	1.8%	2.0%	61%	62%	8.2%
Total workforce	**$11,818,150,032**	**$16,074,953,024**					**6.3%**

Source: Analysis of customized extract of ABS Census of Housing and Population

Table 4.10 Comparison of mean weekly income in the specialist, support and embedded CI workforce 2011 to 2016

Trident mean weekly income	2011	2016
Specialist	$940.00	$1050.00
Support	$1030.00	$1250.00
Total creative industries	$990.00	$1170.00
Embedded	$1180.00	$1390.00
Total trident	**$1050.00**	**$1240.00**
Creative occupations	$1060.00	$1230.00
Workforce	$980.00	$1140.00

Source: Analysis of customized extract of ABS Census of Housing and Population

Table 4.11 Comparison of share of workforce for selected cities across Australia for 2011

Workforce 2011	Sydney	Perth	Melbourne	Brisbane	Adelaide	Newcastle
Specialist	2.5%	1.2%	2.1%	1.4%	1.2%	0.8%
Support	4.0%	1.9%	2.7%	2.3%	1.7%	1.1%
Total CI	6.4%	3.1%	4.8%	3.7%	2.9%	1.9%
Embedded	2.6%	1.4%	2.2%	1.7%	1.4%	0.8%
Total trident	**9.1%**	**4.5%**	**7.0%**	**5.4%**	**4.4%**	**2.8%**
Creative occupations	5.1%	2.6%	4.3%	3.1%	2.6%	1.7%
Total workforce	100.0%	100.0%	100.0%	100.0%	100.0%	100%

Source: Analysis of customized extract of ABS Census of Housing and Population

statistically valid). The question is whether this is a high percentage or a low percentage for a region. The figure may be low in comparison with 9% in Sydney (where there is a heavy concentration of creative industries, as would be expected), but may not be low compared with Perth at 4.5% or Adelaide at 4.4%, noting that Adelaide has approximately twice as many workers and Perth has approximately four times the total workforce. With these qualifications in mind, the following tables give an indicative set of comparisons (Table 4.11).

The following table allocates numbers to these percentages (Table 4.12).

It should be noted that when making comparisons like this across a diverse set of cities operating within a wide variety of contexts, what needs to be investigated is what is normal and what is exceptional in each of these cases. In this case density, that is, the number of workers calculated in that occupation in a given area, becomes important to

Table 4.12 Comparison of employment in the creative industries for selected cities across Australia for 2011

Trident employment for 2011	Sydney	Perth	Melbourne	Brisbane	Adelaide	Newcastle
Specialist	51,111	9927	40,753	13,658	6598	1893
Support	81,698	15,498	50,814	22,938	9545	2549
Total CI	132,809	25,425	91,567	36,596	16,143	4442
Embedded	54,457	11,379	41,769	16,438	7861	1964
Total trident	**187,266**	**36,804**	**133,336**	**53,034**	**24,004**	**6406**
Creative occupations	105,568	21,306	82,522	30,096	14,459	3857
Total workforce	2,063,246	824,401	1,904,800	984,952	547,913	231,438

Source: Analysis of customized extract of ABS Census of Housing and Population

understand. Once this number is calculated, the figure can then be mapped against the total workforce. The question raised is this: is a low number of fine artists in one region, for example, reflective of the norm? As a benchmark, manufacturing tends to be evenly distributed around the country, but creative industries workforces tend to be attracted to higher population areas, particularly capital cities, and are therefore clustered more densely in these areas. The further question, then, arises as to whether a concentration of the creative population in urban centers is a matter of economic necessity for these workers or if some other attractor is at work. All of these questions need further and more thorough investigation. However, by using the same methodology, region to region, we have a basis for comparing regions of similar size and asking whether, for example, the Hunter Region is under-performing or over-performing in relation to cities of a similar type and context, for example Wollongong. With these figures as a basis we can also begin to ask, analytically, whether something such as the BHP steel mill closure in Newcastle had an effect on the creative industries in the region. In this case, a national study, state by state, region by region, using this methodology was called for. We will return to that exact matter in our final chapter.

Further Considerations

Taking this approach one step further, but staying within the above specified limits and using the assumptions outlined above, we could argue that the Creative Trident Methodology is actually trying to measure in a somewhat limited way the *field*, a term used specifically by both Mihaly Csikszentmihalyi (1988) and Pierre Bourdieu (1993) to describe all those who form part of the social structure of creative activity in a certain domain of creative action. If we assume this is the case, what this situation then requires is one further step for analysis. There is a requirement to look at *all* those who constitute *the field* of each sector of the creative industries, rather than what occupations might or might not occur there, since it is the field that forms a crucial contribution to the emergence of creative processes, products and ideas within any entrepreneurial system. This additional perspective might reveal—in a slightly different way—who is involved and what they contribute to the emergence of creative activity in these industries. These fields—collections of agents who contribute to the emergence of objects, services and experiences typical of design, architecture, film, theater and so on—are not the same as an industry occupation list although they do share commonalities. What is being highlighted here by making this suggestion is the idea that there is an increasing difficulty in accounting for changes in not only business operation but also employment types that have arisen as a result of the massive digital revolution sweeping the post-industrial world. In other words, the creative industries are fast moving beyond the tangible structures of production that typify traditional economies: 'firms, labor, production network, industrial districts, and markets—that is the normal stock in trade of industrial investigation' (Hutton, 2009, p. 139). Instead, what we are tending to see are 'shifting boundaries of function, evolving technical divisions of labor, and emergent product sectors' (Hutton, 2009, p. 139). This shift in thinking is bound together with conceptions of creativity that have moved, in research terms at least, away from the commonly held cultural assumptions about it. Instead, what we see now are highly confluence-based approaches.

Given these changes, we deemed it necessary to conduct a more in-depth, qualitative investigation, including participant observation and interviews, with key operatives in each CI sector, as this promised to reveal far more of the detail of what is occurring qualitatively in the creative industries than a statistical analysis can to this point.

But before we do that we can summarize what we have so far by stating that this chapter has covered in detail the two statistical analyses used in the research. As we also indicated in the Introduction of this book, while the principal methodological framework employed for this project was that of ethnography, the project also depended on a quantitative element within this ongoing and detailed ethnographic work. As we set out above, the quantitative aspects of the project involved two statistical measures. Along with the analysis of the data, the various limitations of these two measures were detailed as well. Despite these limitations, the resultant quantitative data, outlined in some detail above, was used to complement, inform and support the extensive qualitative aspects of the study and contributed to the far more immersive aspects of the ethnography. As such, the overall conduct of this research followed the key methods and principles of ethnography. To that end, this study now reports on the ethnographies conducted into the creative industries in the Hunter Region which include, following an adaptation of the NSW Creative Industries Taskforce sector list, music, performing arts, visual arts, architecture, fashion, advertising, PR and design, publishing, radio, film and television, and electronic games and interactive content, as well as the supporting organizations that enable these creative industries to work effectively as per our creative (eco)systems in action model. We start with the music sector.

References

ABS. (2015). *6105.0—Australian labor market statistics*, July 2011. Australian Bureau of Statistics. Retrieved March 26, 2015, from http://www.abs.gov.au/ausstats/abs@.nsf/products/348E1C0EC48A648BCA257922000E2F51?OpenDocument

Banks, M., & Hesmondhalgh, D. (2009). Looking for work in creative industries policy. *International Journal of Cultural Policy, 15*(4), 415–430.
Becker, H. (1982). *Art worlds*. University of California Press.
Bourdieu, P. (1993). *Field of cultural production* (R. Johnson ed.). Columbia University Press.
Castells, M. (2010). *The rise of the network society* (2nd ed.). Wiley-Blackwell.
CIIC. (2013). Valuing Australia's creative industries: Final report.. Prepared by SGS Economics and Planning for the Creative Industries Innovation Centre.
Csikszentmihalyi, M. (1988). Society, culture and person: A systems view of creativity. In R. Sternberg (Ed.), *The nature of creativity: Contemporary psychological perspectives* (pp. 325–329). Cambridge University Press.
Cunningham, S., & Higgs, P. (2008). Creative industries mapping: Where have we come from and where are we going? *Creative Industries Journal, 1*(1), 7–30. https://doi.org/10.1386/cij.1.1.7_1
Davies, R., & Sigthorsson, G. (2013). *Introducing the creative industries: From theory to practice*. Sage.
Dawson, A., & Holmes, S. (2012). *Working in the global film and television industries: Creativity, systems, space, patronage*. Bloomsbury Academic.
Flew, T. (2012). *The creative industries: Culture and policy*. Sage.
Higgs, P. (2017). *Sheet 1 notes Greater Hunter Valley 2011 and 2016 updated report*. [Source: Analysis of customized extract of ABS Census of Housing and Population].
Higgs, P., Cunningham, S., & Pagan, J. (2007). *Australia's creative economy: Basic evidence on size, growth, income and employment*. CCI Technical Report. QUT Faculty Research Office, CCI. Retrieved June 25, 2010, from https://eprints.qut.edu.au/225659/1/8241.pdf
Higgs, P., & Lennon, S. (2014). *Applying the NESTA dynamic mapping definition methodology to Australian classification*. Queensland University of Technology. Retrieved March 27, 2023, from https://eprints.qut.edu.au/92726/
Hutton, T. (2009). Cultural production in the transnational city. In A. Pratt & P. Jeffcutt (Eds.), *Creativity, innovation and the cultural economy* (pp. 139–160). Routledge.
Lhermitte, M., Blanc, S., & Perrin, B. (2015). *Cultural times: The first global map of cultural and creative industries*. Ernst & Young Report for the Confederation of Authors and Composers Societies. EYGM Ltd.
McIntyre, P. (2015). Tradition and innovation in creative studio practice: The use of older gear, processes and ideas in conjunction with digital technolo-

gies. *Journal on the Art of Record Production, 9*, 1–26. Retrieved from https://www.arpjournal.com/asarpwp/tradition-and-innovation-in-creative-studio-practice-the-use-of-older-gear-processes-and-ideas-in-conjunction-with-digital-technologies/

McIntyre, P., Balnaves, M., Kerrigan, S., King, E., & Williams, C. (2019). *Creativity and cultural production in the Hunter: An applied ethnographic study of new entrepreneurial systems in the creative industries*. Retrieved March 30, 2023, from https://hciss.newcastle.edu.au/hci/final-report/

McIntyre, P., & Kerrigan, S. (2014). Pursuing extreme romance: Change and continuity in the creative screen industries in the Hunter Valley. *Studies in Australasian Cinema, 1*(1), 1–17. https://doi.org/10.1080/17503175.2014.960680

NSW SRD. (2009). *NSW creative industry economic fundamentals*. NSW Department of State and Regional Development. Retrieved March 31, 2023, from https://www.industry.nsw.gov.au/__data/assets/pdf_file/0007/55384/NSW_creative_industry_economic_fundamentals_090204.pdf

NSW T&I. (2013). *Visual arts, design and new media sectors snapshot*. Trade and Investment ART NSW. Retrieved February 24, 2018, from https://www.create.nsw.gov.au/wp-content/uploads/2013/04/2013-Visual-Arts-Design-and-New-Media-Sector-Snapshot_Website-Final2.pdf

Remplan. (2017). *City of Newcastle economy profile*. Retrieved February 16, 2018, from http://www.economyprofile.com.au/newcastle/industries/gross-regional-product

Sawyer, K. (2012). *Explaining creativity: The science of human innovation* (2nd ed.). Oxford University Press.

Trading Economics. (2020). *Self-employed—Total (% of total employed) in Australia*. Trading Economics. Retrieved April 15, 2023, from www.tradingeconomics.com/australia/self-employed-total-percent-of-total-employed-wb-data.html

Wilkinson, J. (2017). *The Hunter Region: An economic profile*. Parliament of NSW. Retrieved July 10, 2017, from https://www.parliament.nsw.gov.au/researchpapers/Documents/the-hunter-region-an-economic-profile/Newcastle%20and%20the%20Hunter%20GG%202.pdf

5

Music

History of the Popular Music Industry: Its Accumulated Heritage

The popular music industry is a global one (Miller & Shahriari, 2012). If you choose China's music industry as an example of a national music industry you can see that its commercial history runs for the past 900 years (Fangjun, 2014). However, histories of Western popular music tend to emphasize the American/British nexus, to the exclusion of most others (see for example Frith in Martin, 1983). This emphasis is understandable given the social, economic and political dominance of a major portion of the planet by both of these countries during the last century and a half (Macintyre, 1999).

If we concentrate on Australian popular music (see Beilby & Roberts, 1981; Cockington, 1992; Creswell, 1993; Creswell & Fabinyi, 1999; Freud, 1997; Hayward, 1992; Homan & Mitchell, 2008; Jenkins, 1994; Leiber, 1996; Mathieson, 1996; Mitchell, 1996; Rogers, 1975; Sly, 1993; St. John, 1994; Walker, 1996; Wilmoth, 1993; Zion, 1987, 1988) we do need to keep in mind how deeply connected Australian popular music

P. McIntyre et al., *Creativity and Creative Industries in Regional Australia*, Palgrave Studies in Creativity and Culture, https://doi.org/10.1007/978-3-031-45972-6_5

has been to those British and US traditions. Taking a much broader view we can also see that there is a continuum for Western popular music that has stretched beyond the development of jazz, rock and roll and electronic dance music (EDM) in the US back to Europe and Africa. In fact if one took a very broad view, Western popular music itself could be traced convincingly to the murky beginnings of recorded time (Menuhin & Davis, 1979). It is only relatively recently, for instance, that an appreciation of the long history of Australian indigenous music is beginning to be incorporated into mainstream tastes (Breen, 1989; Ellis, 1985; Mitchell, 1996). This broad view could also encompass the music hall tradition of Britain, the Celtic folk song tradition, Viennese operettas and the rhythmic pulses of West Africa. Country and western, or the more aptly titled hillbilly music, plus big band swing, the standards produced by Tin Pan Alley and the hits from major Broadway shows which have, at some stage during the twentieth century, all held a position as one of the most popular forms of music in Australia (Whiteoak & Scott-Maxwell, 2003). Rock, in its all-encompassing types and forms, held sway in Australia in the last half of the twentieth century (Masterson & Gillard, 1999) moving through phases of growth, consolidation and internationalization (McIntyre, 2004). This form has been superseded, complemented and reworked by a list of styles that includes R&B, rap, hip-hop, house, jungle, gabba, dub and many, many others, all existing under the broad umbrella term EDM, as well as world music and the continuing traditions mentioned prior.

Just as the introduction of the technologies of recording, tape, LPs, 45s and cassettes and the dominance of radio and Tin Pan Alley had significant impacts on the music industry after the peak of the industrial revolution and across the twentieth century (Fink, 1996), the ongoing digital revolution in the twenty-first century continues to reshape the industry, its songwriting, recording, performance and business models.

Structure of the Popular Music Industry: The Shape of the Interconnected Field

While the field of popular music is broader than the industry, the music industry is still an important constituent part of the field. There are a number of structural models of the music industry available (e.g., Wikstrom, 2009, pp. 47–84). While some argue that there is not one music industry per se but a set of music industries (Williamson & Cloonan, 2007), in general it can be claimed that there are three major sectors within the industry: publishing, recording and live performance. There are ancillary sectors as well such as manufacture, retail and media (McIntyre, 2011). These sectors and their relationships can be best illustrated in the following way (Fig. 5.1):

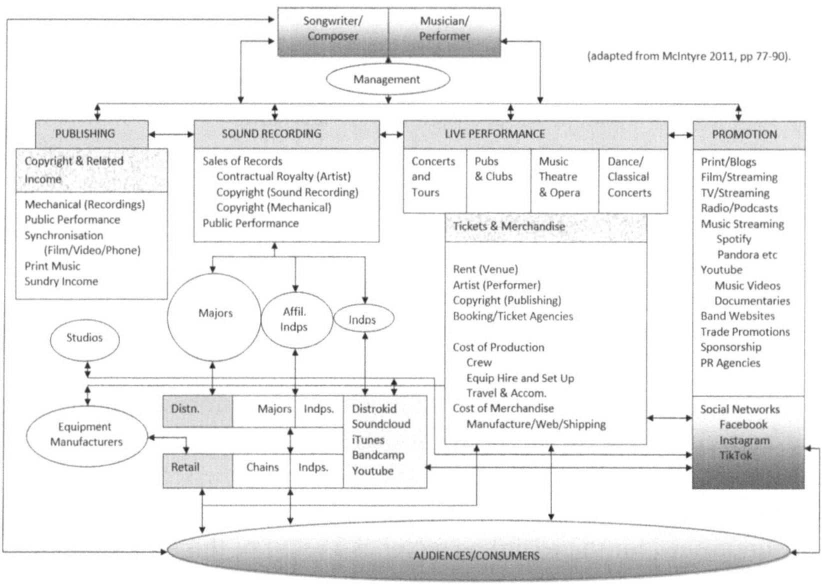

Fig. 5.1 The music industry—graphic. (Adapted from McIntyre (2011, p. 86))

Business Models as Necessary and Shared Domain Knowledge

Various business models continue to operate across the music industry and understanding these are necessary forms of domain knowledge for those existing in the field. As noted above, there are three sectors. The publishing sector is concerned with the copyright of songs. A songwriter sells or licenses a song to other parties usually through a publisher. In doing so, they agree to write songs in exchange for an advance (loan) from the publisher and the publisher agrees to promote and sell the songs, usually in exchange for 50% of the copyright royalty income on the song. Royalties are required to be paid by law on each public performance of the song wherever that might occur i.e. in concert, broadcast, as part of a film soundtrack, played as a ringtone or streamed, although streaming fees for copyrighted songs is minimal in comparison to streaming income from mechanical rights for the recording of the song.

The recording sector still derives some income from direct sale of product and incurs costs through recording, distribution and marketing. Musicians may be given an advance by a record label to make a recording and will repay this loan before receiving any income. Alternatively, they will incur the cost themselves and lease the recording to the record company for distribution and promotion or, increasingly, use an automated distribution service and promote their own recordings via multiple forms of legacy and social media. Royalties are also paid to the owners of the mechanical rights of these recordings, usually record companies, in addition to other rights. As a result of digital distribution, retail income has moved from stores to web-based outlets but as streaming has become ubiquitous, the income from direct sales has been superseded by income from mechanicals and associated streaming fees. However, overall income has diminished for the recording sector as a result of this supersession.

Income in the live performance sector is derived primarily from direct ticketing and merchandising sales and it is usual for the performers to take the risk of success. This risk is also spread across agents and promoters who generally operate on a percentage of the derived income from these performances. Income from concert performances has progressively diminished over the last 20 years for the bulk of touring musicians as costs have increased with fees generally stagnant, in real terms, for most working musicians.

Operational Methods of the Field

Musicians legally operate as sole traders, partnerships or in some cases as companies. Once a musician, sometimes called an artist, has developed a reputation as a "good live act", usually in small venues where they "play for the door", they will engage a talent or booking agent who has a list of venues, clubs or pubs that the agent exclusively books. The agent matches the performer to these venues for a percentage of the performance fee (usually 10%). The artist often incurs all promotional costs for these concerts including printing of posters and photo shoots for press releases. The artist will usually hire or buy a public address system for those venues that don't have them installed. The artist will need to consider public liability insurance and all necessary insurance and compensation packages for the operators and, eventually, a touring crew. A tour is a series of one-night engagements across a given geographical territory. Tours are usually organized through a touring company for a percentage of the concert appearance fee and the touring company will negotiate with local promoters for fees, security, promotional costs etc. The touring artist may also need to hire a support act at each local venue who may also be required to pay to be on the tour and provide additional luggers to aid the crew. At this point, the touring operation can be described as a major live production and, accordingly, the artist will need to engage a larger touring crew and hire all the necessary equipment for the duration of the tour. This equipment includes an adequate PA system and lights for all types of venues, a truck to transport it and a bus or plane to transport the band as well as accommodation for all of these personnel. Legal contracts are drawn up and the operation is tightly planned and executed using written schedules such as tour sheets, which detail times of performance, venue address and layout, conditions of performance and all necessary technical information to allow the concert to proceed.

A recording musician, who may or may not also be a touring performer, will incur the full costs of their own personal equipment such as instruments and amplifiers. They will generally buy their own recording gear or hire it. This gear is often housed in a home studio, that is, a controlled audio environment. The use of professional studios will necessitate the hiring of an audio engineer for a negotiated fee. The recording artist may also feel the need to hire a producer, who often works for a set fee or a percentage of the royalties or what is called points. Other costs may include rehearsal space, freight, session musician hire, equipment rentals, meals and accommodation and arranger's fees. These costs of recording may be offset by an advance or loan from a record company. The record company advances the monies to cover recording costs and acts in the manner of a venture capitalist, doing various deals dependent on the leverage an artist has. These may range from 360-degree deals, where the record company takes a percentage of all forms of a musician's income, through to a standard royalty deal, or a licensing deal, profit share deal, promotion and distribution deal or alternatively an artist may bear all the costs and risks and garner 100% of the profits. While manufacturing and distribution costs are becoming minimal with web-based delivery now the norm, promotion and marketing is still a time-consuming cost that may necessitate the hire of a dedicated music promotions company. At this point, the artist will need to interact with all broadcast, non-broadcast and narrowcast media in order to promote, and thus sell, the recording.

Songwriters write songs, the core artifact of the music industry. While in decades past, songwriting was a separate profession 'songwriters of today frequently wear more than one hat, doubling as singers, musicians, record producers or even managers' (Barrat in Martin, 1983, p. 59). This presents certain complexities but, for legal purposes, songwriters and performers are generally treated as separate entities. As Siegel (1990), Whitsett (1997), Wilson (1999), Passman (2002) and Simpson (2006) variously explain, once a song is written and exists in a material form it is copyrighted. At this stage, the songwriter owns 100% of the written song. Most often they engage a publisher, a separate business entity, to publish, promote and administer the song. The royalties earned from the song are split in two. There is a writer's share, usually 50%, and a publisher's share, also usually 50%. If there is more than one writer the writer's share is split between the writers according to a, usually written, writer's agreement. The publisher takes the publisher's share to administer and promote the song. The publisher usually has the rights in the song assigned to them, that is, the ownership of the song, for a certain period or term.

> This means the publisher can control the use of the song for this period and may be entitled to maintain ownership in the song for the life of the copyright. However, if a publisher does not do the best thing by the song and does not actively promote it, a reversion clause will allow the song's rights to be returned to the songwriter. With these conditions in place, the publisher is then able to issue licences for others to use the song. The publisher is, in essence, obligated to try to get other people to do cover versions, place the songs in movies, in TV shows and any other places where income can be derived. The publisher should thus actively sell the song for the songwriter. This is their job. They do not, and should not, just collect and administer royalty income (McIntyre, 2009, p. 7).

Increasingly, musicians are taking on many of these operational functions themselves. Twenty-first-century musicians must be able to write songs, maintain and update playing skills, sing, buy, use and maintain performance and recording equipment, produce recordings, mix and master those recordings, shoot videos, hire rehearsal space, pay for transport to move gear and fellow musicians to and from venues, load in and out, negotiate performance fees, pay for promotion and website costs, regularly upload material to the website, maintain a regular blog, be highly active on social media, cover insurance costs, file tax returns, file APRA returns, and pay agent and manager fees, as well as cover food, housing, bills and living expenses.

As well as operating in these legal and financial ways, musicians also operate within a gift economy. What this means, effectively, is that as well as being cooperative in performance, many musicians need to be collegial in the way they operate with each other, supporting each other's gigs, loaning equipment to fellow performers at no expense and generally helping each other out. There are exceptions to these generalities of course but these values tend to be generally accepted. At the core of most musicians' value judgments 'are the values on which successful performance depend: values concerning collaboration, the ability to play with other people; the values of trust, reliability, a certain sort of professionalism' (Frith, 1996, p. 53).

> Even the most anti-professional punk band needs its members to turn up at rehearsals or gigs, to be in a fit state to take to the stage. This is the context in which skill and technique become valued not as abstract qualities but by reference to what must be done in a particular musical genre, what fellow players can take for granted … as part of this collaborative work, musicians are expected to have a certain basic knowledge of their instrument and of technology—they need to be able to change a string, tune a drum, program a sampler. (Frith, 1996, p. 53)

As Simon Frith writes, within this process:

> musicians have to make a series of decisions—should I play this note, use this take, hire this musician, change the melody here, that order of the set there, shorten my solo, change the key; and these decisions rest on a constant process of evaluation—that's the wrong chord, the wrong tempo, the wrong sound, the wrong mix—and a constant process of encouragement: that's good, leave it! Such decisions are both individual, a reflection of one's own talent (musical talent describes, among other things, the ability to make the right decisions about what's good), and social. (1996, p. 52)

Just as other people in small businesses do, members of musical collectives must plan their activities and this usually involves a lot of mundane details.

> Once they're famous or rich, or preferably both, they'll have a manager, a host of roadies, a sound tech, a lights and rigging tech and the odd spotlight operator. Until then, it's the band members who have to see to getting bookings and hiring vans, people and a tonne of equipment. They have to sort out any technical problems, have to get everything to the gig in time to set up the hardware, run sufficient sound checks to satisfy everybody, make sure the light rig is up and going, reassure the management, make

> sure they'll get paid the agreed amount, do the gig brilliantly, bump all the equipment out quickly—especially if there's another band on straight afterwards—then return all hired gear promptly and in good order tomorrow morning at an indecently early hour. People who [are musicians] are not lazy. Their commitment to their music and performance skills is such that they often become their own entrepreneurs, working intensely hard in order to keep doing the job they have chosen to do. (Wilson, 1997, p. 57)

Important Personnel in the Interconnected Field

Musicians are the people who perform musical instruments, that is, any object that produces sound including the voice. Managers look after the business affairs of the musician usually for a commission of up to 25% of all the artist's income from all sources. Agents match venues to performers for approximately 10% of the concert fee. Promoters organize, stage and promote a touring concert performance once again for a percentage of the concert returns. A touring crew is necessary in order to stage a concert tour. The crew will consist of at least a tour manager, a front of house engineer and lighting operator, a stage manager and a monitor engineer. Venue operators operate venues at which performances take place. These can range from small hotels through to large stadiums. A&R operatives are record company talent spotters whereas record producers are like directors on a film set. They have overall creative responsibility for a recording. Audio engineers have the technical responsibility to capture and manipulate sound just as a cameraperson in the film industry captures light. A publisher administers and promotes the songs a songwriter writes. Publishers have clients they service not only in the live performance sector but also the film and advertising industries. Without an audience none of these personnel would continue to subsist in the music industry. Each of these members of the field have a unique but shared background each brings to the actions of the field and each is a case that illustrates all the above.

The Hunter Music Scene: An Interconnected Field, Shared Domain Knowledge and Set of Choice Making Agents

The music industry in the Hunter is diverse, vibrant and dynamic although it has had its challenges with broader structures such as the urbanization of key locations, lockout laws and, as is the case with the industry overall, changes in delivery platforms and other digital transformations. What can be seen, though, is how digital changes such as social media play a role in how music is distributed and promoted. Music in the Hunter ranges from jazz, country, folk, opera, electronic dance music (EDM) and rock with choirs, brass bands, orchestras, DJs, pipe bands and rock bands. The Hunter has produced national and international success stories. There is a recognizable creative (eco)system in the Hunter music scene in performance and recording with support from retailers, promoters, instrument manufacturers and repairers, local media and social media, and venue operators.

Live Performance in the Hunter Region: Gigs and Venues

Audiences are drawn to good performance venues. These venues are crucial to the live music sector. Not only are they important for audiences but they are a major employer, source of income and a training ground, as well as being a promotional tool, for many musicians (Groeneveld, 1998, p. 21). While the number of popular music performance sites in the Hunter Valley has decreased significantly since the Seventies and Eighties (Sheather, 2016, pp. 194–197), several still cater to the local industry. Andrew Goodwin wrote on his blog post:

> Until recently I was responsible for running an online gig guide for Newcastle ... Over four years … I published over 60,000 events … from Gosford in the South, to Taree in the North, and West to Merriwa in the Upper Hunter Valley. (2021, online)

Taking a Hunter snapshot across one week in March 2017, there were over 100 live venues operating with 81 quartets or trios, 15 duos, and 6 DJs (Goodwin, 2017, online) in work. These figures for one week do not include festivals such as Groovin' the Moo, one-off international touring concerts or the numerous weddings taking place in the Valley. Many venues in the hinterland have intermittent functions where live bands perform. In the next major city in the valley, Maitland, the Grand Junction Hotel, known as The Junkyard, maintains a strong band roster and is a venue of choice for many local musicians. In Newcastle, while most venues only employ cover bands, some venues highlight musicians who perform largely self-written music or are slightly out of the mainstream. These included, until recently, The Great Northern, which attracted independent musicians from the capital cities, as does Lizotte's in suburban Lambton. Along with a platform for nationally recognized musicians from the Oz/pub rock period, Lizotte's hosts many touring groups and roots music performers from the USA while supporting local musicians as they release recorded material. Other venues include the Cambridge, a nationally iconic venue closing in mid-2023 as developers encroach on its precinct. It hosts young local acts and national touring groups.

Other venues encourage an eclectic and rich range of music from the Lass O'Gowrie's support for local independent artists, to The Black Malabar's world and roots music. Offerings such as American blues master Kirk Fletcher, the Bandaluzia Flamenco troupe and Miriam Lieberman and her kora (21 string African harp) appear there. Some venues cater to a more traditionally oriented roots, blues and rock scene or support cover bands with advice from venue consultants like the Eastern Acoustic Organisation (EAO), while others depend on duos and solitary performers and some outdoor locations feature young buskers. In Islington, the Small Ballroom hosts "under-age" events, like Vibes for Tribes, featuring all young regional bands such as Stranger Than Friends, Smacked Youth, Cherry Stain, Fungus, Looseleaf IV and Sienna Lace in 2017. Catering to an older crowd, the Central Bar plays regular house music, hosts hip-hop dance nights, and features performers such as Alex Lloyd or the Temptresses of Tease Burlesque Revue. Touring bands, EDM and DJs with cutting edge sound and lights add to the options.

However, many venues that serviced live performances in the recent past have closed with buildings being demolished or re-purposed. Many of these sites have become exemplars of change as Newcastle has morphed from its steel-making past to a more cosmopolitan scene or have been impacted by early lock-out regulations responding to late-night violence. Tomsen et al. suggest that despite the closures, 'serious conflict and violence at licensed venues is not yet uncommon in the local region' (2003, p. 2). These circumstances resulted in a national news story in *The Australian* reporting that:

> Researchers from the University of Newcastle and the NSW Bureau of Crime Statistics and Research [asserted] a 1 am lock-out combined with a 3 am closing time at 14 licensed premises from March 2008 reduced the number of assaults in the area by almost 200 in the following 18 months … The Newcastle restrictions … were bitterly opposed by hoteliers, who now say the measures have caused insolvencies and harmed Newcastle's night life. (Dusevic, 2010, online)

The researchers claimed that the curfew approach was 'unique internationally' and provided the possibility for policy implementation around the world: 'The trend internationally has been to longer trading hours. This study presents a bold challenge to that trend' (Dusevic, 2010, online). These Lock Out Laws, replicated in Sydney in 2014 in an attempt to reduce alcohol-fueled violence, also had a detrimental effect on the night time economy. These are not the only restrictions venues face. Newcastle-based music entrepreneur, Steven Pickett, stated that:

> The lock-out laws did nothing but decimate the Newcastle social scene … It's being strangled ... There needs to be two things: number one, entertainment precincts that are protected from that type of thing, and secondly, a first occupancy rule … where if you've moved next door to a pub that has live music you know that you can't do anything about that. (Pickett, i/v Oct 2015).

While nighttime venues struggle with these issues, intermittent daytime festivals have become increasingly popular. As one example, the Fat as Butter Festival 'has attracted international and Australian acts to Newcastle each spring since it began in 2008' (Tarala, 2013, p. 3).

For the established music industry these one-off events contribute little long-term income to the industry itself since local acts, if they are added to the bill, are paid little compared to the out-of-town headline acts and production is often sourced from Sydney. What they do contribute are opportunities to study how professionals in other areas conduct their business (McIntyre & Sheather, 2013). In addition, one of the city's other long-term promoters, Peter Anderson of Rock City Event Marketing (REM), diversified his promotions and moved into becoming an event organizer now rarely dealing with local music. He laments the loss of a business driver of policy frameworks like the Australian radio quota system. During 30 years of existence, REM brought artists such as The Beach Boys, Bob Dylan, Cold Chisel, Crowded House, The Cure, Faith No More, Garth Brooks, INXS, Oasis, Reba McIntyre, The Seekers, Soundgarden, Split Enz, Sting, The Supremes, Paul Kelly and Pink (REM, 2013, online) to city venues and went on to compete with concerts staged in the wine region. For example, having completed their 'purpose built 19,000 capacity outdoor amphitheater at our Hunter Valley Winery' (Hope Estate, 2013, online), this winery bought Fleetwood Mac and has staged other concerts by artists such as Carole King and Leonard Cohen and Bruce Springsteen to perform there. Needless to say, these shows draw large crowds, along with their discretionary entertainment income, from across the valley and out of its major city, Newcastle.

Recording: Record Producers and Studios in the Hunter

Recording, on the other hand, does not have an overly strong presence in the Hunter. Those studios that are operating are generally owned and operated by local record producers and audio engineers with extensive careers in the industry. Robbie Long, for example, is an experienced session player, multi-instrumentalist, Australian Flat Pick Guitar Champion and record producer who owns and operates Sound Ideas. Rob Taylor is an award-winning engineer and producer who has worked nationally and internationally (UON, 2018, online). With radio and studio experience, he produced the highest selling independent album in Australian history, The Whitlams' *Eternal Nightcap*, had his recorded work named four times as Triple J Album of the Week, produced ARIA award winning albums, worked with INXS and re-mixed Madonna's *Like a Prayer* (Ian Sandercoe, 2014, online). With Tony Heads from The Velvet Underground, Mark Tinson established Maitland's Cordial Factory, then built and managed Studio 21 for Peter Andersen's Rock City organization, before moving to Sydney. After returning to Newcastle he set up Overhead Studios, now the digitally focused Steelville Studios in Kotara. Musician/composer/producer Gareth Hudson has his studio downstairs in his house and continues to tour internationally and record with his quartet, Hudson Arc. He has produced albums across genres and 'recorded and written arrangements for artists including The Hilltop Hoods, The Last Kinection, Briggs and The Beards' (Hudson Arc, 2014, online). His last major project is writing and staging a musical called *Between Worlds* (Hudson Arc, 2014, online).

Being in a regional center, the local industry is typified by the need to engage in a diversity of operations. For example, Tommirock, run by producer Joel Black and his team, offers music production, studio recording, mixing and mastering as well as video production, professional photography, website design and artwork, CD and DVD manufacturing, song writing, voice overs and social network marketing. Similarly, the former 90 Degree Studio, then run by Allon Silove and Andy Lindsay, offered single, EP and album packages for bands and artists and also provided voice-over material for radio, TV, web and telephone-hold services as well as post-production facilities for film and television work. Sawtooth Studios has a recording studio and rehearsal space as well as media production studio, and green screen and animation capabilities.

Other Hunter recording studios can be found in the Kurri Kurri/Maitland area, inner and western suburbs of Newcastle and in Lake Macquarie. Newcastle based record producer, Terry Latham, is a classical guitarist who teaches guitar, music technology and sound production (Latham, i/v Oct 2014). His Impromptu Studio in Tighes Hill provides 'a wide range of current and vintage equipment' (Impromtu,

2013, online). Latham, along with Grant Walmsley from the Screaming Jets, also formed One Henry Records. One Henry Records was one of a few local record labels. Peter Anderson's own label was another, as was Bloody Fist Records run by Mark Newlands. Bloody Fist sold material for hardcore techno groups like Syndicate, Xylocaine and Memetic but is best known for the Nasenbluten recordings which did well in Germany. Steven Pickett's case is also illustrative.

Early in Pickett's career as a music entrepreneur he owned and operated a recording studio before moving into agency, events and design work. Pickett was motivated at one period to operate like a regional record label:

> We even started our own distribution network. We invested in a number of original music acts over a ten-year period, and … lost well over a million dollars … that we'd invested in local musicians only to have them [change direction] … So, virtually from the end of one year to the start of the next, EAO turned from being recording studio, managing original artists, and supporting [them] financially, to becoming a cover agency. Financially it was the best thing we ever did. For the soul I'm not sure. (Pickett, i/v Oct 2015)

While the recording scene is comparatively minimal, Instrument manufacture, repair and retail are fundamental to the industry. For example, Hunter Valley Violins is an instrument repair business. David Robertson, the luthier who owns this business, has years of experience building and repairing violins, violas and cellos. He is a master craftsman who sells his own instruments. He also has some remarkable antique instruments available for inspection (HVV, 2017, online). His counterpart in the popular music world is Len Biglin who, as well as fixing and making guitars and amps, plays guitar and blues harp with Big Daddy's Cajun Blues Party. He also played with the Mutineers, Voodoo Daddy, the Polecats, Serious Business and The Witchdoctors (Biglin, 2017, online). One Hunter musical institution is Musos Corner, a retail outlet with an extensive online presence. Run by Sandra Lindsay, this company has supplied equipment to amateur and professional alike since 1967. It employs a large roster of music professionals as sales advisors as well as a digital sales team catering to its national and international customer base. Their in-house studio, training facility and hi-tech showroom are industry standard (Musos Corner, 2017, online). They also run the Drum Shop, Foley's Pianos and 90 Degree Studio. Their nearest competitor was Music Headquarters in New Lambton, which also presented musical instrument sales, teaching, recording and rehearsal studio space. Other rehearsal rooms can be found at venues such as Sawtooth Studios, which doubles as a studio for recording, photography and videos (Sawtooth, 2017, online).

The demise in the physical sale of CDs impacted on the Valley's smaller and family-owned retailers of recorded music. These included Sound World and Beaumont St Beat. The Sanity chain store also had a presence but the JB HiFi chain located in suburban malls is now the only outlet for hardcopy recordings. Second-hand vinyl and CDs can be purchased at Snafu Records and Rice's Bookstore. The situation for record retail reflects the globalized and digitized music world. Most music consumers in the Valley are now familiar with downloads from websites such as iTunes and streaming services such as Spotify but are also cognizant of downloading material, for example, by accessing YouTube clips and converting these to MP3 files via converters such as Video2MP3. As a discussion paper for the Australian Law Reform Commission noted, 'worthy individuals and citizens ... are knowingly, ignorantly or indifferently finding themselves in breach of international and national copyright law. And they intend to keep on doing exactly as before' (ALRC, 2013, p. 46) necessitating a rethink of all related business models.

Structural Support for the Music Industry

Servicing the live sector, Centauri Audio provides 'support services to musicians and the industry' and 'repairs and modifications to professional music production equipment … PA and lighting systems' (Centauri Audio, 2017, online) while Scion Audio operates as a music industry hire company and, since the mid-1970s, has been supplying 'public address systems and lighting rigs of all sizes and types, the crews to run them [with] theme lighting, draping, event equipment and staging (Scion, 2017, online).

An important structural feature of the field of popular music is the media. The ABC Radio has been generally supportive to local musical activity as has the University-run community radio, 2NURFM, but apart from occasional stories on NBN television, local commercial radio plays few local recordings although other outlets, such as *The Herald*, provide promotional space. The national broadcaster's Triple J Unearthed project has been important for younger musicians like Rum Jungle. Social media, particularly Facebook and Instagram, has been embraced by local working musicians to augment and now supplant traditional promotional devices such as poster runs, radio interviews and press stories. Online sites such as Newcastle Live (NL), started by Steven Pickett, claims to be 'the Hunter's premier online music, entertainment and lifestyle guide' (NL, 2017, online). Pickett suggests that it has been:

> hard to get support from the local paper and radio stations, and virtually impossible from TV. But … as the 21st century dawned, the digital world came into being, and it occurred to me that I might be able to … *become* the media. (Pickett, i/v Oct 2015)

Media support for local musicians is now predominantly coming from online sources. Ison Live Radio (ILR), which runs regular popular music charts often featuring Hunter musicians, has been one of the unheralded success stories in this area. Its programs, syndicated online, 'are heard by over three million free to air radio listeners each week covering most major western markets' (ILR, 2016, online). Its support has been crucial for some musicians.

Brass and Concert Bands, Choirs and Orchestras: Communal Creative Practice

The history of the regions and its tensions have also influenced what people value in music. While Indigenous song lines have not earned the respect they deserve, the convict, mining, manufacturing and maritime experiences of European workers and their need for community has marked the Valley's music. A deep tradition of brass and concert bands grew from its working-class roots. A love of jazz, folk music and choirs has been integral to that history. Dr. Helen English from the University of Newcastle has documented many of the Hunter's forgotten musicians involved in these styles of music. For example, mining communities 'were remarkably active, supporting brass bands and choral unions—and organizing concerts and eisteddfods' (UON, 2017, online). Many of these are still alive and effective.

There are many choirs in the valley including Newcastle Gay and Lesbian Choir, Novatones and a men's harmony choir. There is also the Australian Celtic Singers and the Waratah Girls' Choir which has 'performed well in many prestigious international singing competitions' (NMD, 2021, online). The Newcastle University Choir itself has a proud 40-year history and is regarded highly. Philip Matthias is a specialist in Australian church music and leads the University's Chamber Choir—Echology. His compositions are primarily for choir, psalms for churches, or anthems for individual performers or film soundtracks. When reflecting on the range of gigs he undertakes, he acknowledges his motivations:

> If I wrote a piece of music that I want to write, for me, I'll do my best to be creative and put my all into it ... If it's not for myself [but] for others like a film ... I put myself into it but it's a job, like doing anything else. (Matthias, i/v July 2016)

Over the last few years, Philip has developed works with Torres Strait Islanders and Indigenous singers including David Leha. As a result, there was a report of an Indigenous record label starting (Gregory, 2018), based on Leha's extensive contacts which include Dr. Karl Neuenfeldt, a former UON anthropology lecturer and record producer who has been collecting, preserving and producing records of Indigenous culture. The valley's orchestras include Orchestra Nova (ON, 2017, online), a 50-piece symphony orchestra that collaborates with Opera Hunter staging operas such as *Les Miserables* and *Carmen* and performing with choirs including the Newcastle University, Newcastle City and Waratah Girls' choirs. Broadcasts of their concerts regularly feature on community radio, featuring classical and non-traditional composers. The City of Newcastle RSL Pipe Band, the city's oldest, was founded in 1924 (CNRPB, 2017, online) and has performed for 93 continuous years. In its early days, the band maintained itself through public subscriptions and membership fees. It played every night except Sunday at a 'fun fair' in the city 'for two pounds two shillings per night and in Hamilton where shops donated between one shilling to four shillings per week' (CNRPB, 2017, online). It remains popular with paid engagements, subsidizing free events and band equipment. The Hunter Wind Ensemble has performed at Christchurch Cathedral (HWE, 2017, online) while other large community ensembles are represented in centers as widely spread as Cardiff/North Lakes, Maitland, Lake Macquarie, Muswellbrook, Scone, Singleton, Port Stephens, Toronto, Wangi Wangi and Waratah, as are the United Mine Workers, the world-famous Marching Koalas, and the Newcastle Ukulele Orchestra. Many of these bands belong to the Hunter Regional Band Association (HRBA) participating in annual competitions and community entertainment (HRBA, 2017, online) and many of these players take their cornets, trumpets, clarinets and saxophones into the jazz scene.

The Jazz Scene

One of the jazz sector's premier events is the annual Newcastle Jazz Festival hosted by The Newcastle and Hunter Jazz Club (NHJC) for 30 years and 'regarded as one of the best Jazz Festivals in Australia' (NHJC, 2017, online). One regular performer is Peter Gray who played with the New York Music Collective, performing professionally with over 250 gigs per year. Other players mix work with pleasure. For example, GP Dr. Ben Ewald performs with Le Minibus, a band specializing in European Gypsy music, French tracks and tangos, Greek, klezmer and American jug band music. Ewald also plays soprano sax, alto sax and flute in the jazz trio It's Time. Then there are various trad and Dixieland bands like Eric Gibbon's New Orleans Jazz Band. Andy Firth's Big Band keeps the swing tradition alive. Firth has been playing from a very young age and has performed at Carnegie Hall. He is an accomplished composer and arranger and has received an MO Award for best live jazz performance and an Australia Day Honors award and has worked with national and international artists. With 25 albums to his name, he teaches privately. The jazz scene he belongs to has recently been given further impetus through the Newcastle Improvised Music Association (NIMA).

NIMA began its life through the work of Capree Gaul. Gaul grew up in Maitland beginning her performance career at 16, continuing in rock bands and country tours performing keyboards; a career highlight being an appearance on national television on *Hey Hey It's Saturday* and ABCTV's *Countdown*. Gaul's current band is Trancemission and they play alternate 80 s and David Bowie sets in local pubs. Gaul believes her live performance experiences contributed to her career as a social entrepreneur. She insists that she 'wouldn't be doing what I'm doing … if I hadn't done all those things beforehand' (Gaul, i/v Sept 2015). Gaul creates opportunities for other musicians to showcase their talents in live venues and understands how to harness social networking. She connects individuals through their common interests in new and improvised music, in particular, live jazz where NIMA has become important to the Newcastle scene. They draw four or five international acts throughout the year from countries such as the Netherlands, Austria, Germany and France (Gaul, i/v Sept 2015).

Folk Music: A Popular Tradition

Dr. Peter Allsop, an anesthetist, has reinvigorated the folk music scene in Newcastle with his Trade Winds (TW) concerts. Allsop, who worked professionally as a folk singer in the USA, and his wife Dr. Nicola Ross, bring 'folk, world, acoustic, blues and community music from professional and semi-professional artists' (TW, 2017, online) to perform locally. These touring bands and others are often supported by Ross and Allsop as well as locals such as Carole Garland, Michael Fine, Rob, Sarah and David Smith and Hannah Duque. Trade Winds cooperates with the Newcastle Hunter Valley Folk Club, which started in 1964 with a coffee house environment (NHVFC, 2017, online). Interesting groups attracted to appearing for these two organizations have included String Theories, a Blue Mountains based trio 'exploring the world of "New Acoustic" music (TW, 2017) and The Mothers of Intention, a Celtic-inspired four-piece band featuring 3-part vocal harmonies, rhythm guitar, fiddle, mandolin, Irish whistles, recorders and Bodhran (Irish frame drum)' (NHVFC, 2017, online).

Electronic Dance Music (EDM): The New Mainstream

At the other end of the spectrum, EDM is generally disparaged within the regional rock community. It is, nonetheless, a form of music making that, like all other forms, manipulates logically organized sound. On this basis, DJs, turntablists and sampling producers are as much musicians as those traditionally classified as such. Noting that, Leiber and Stoller claimed that, 'we didn't write songs; we wrote records' (Palmer, 1996, p. 35). It is also asserted that the 'action and interaction of technology with popular music has changed its expression, form, reproduction, promotion and even its creation' (Durant, 1990, p. 176). The 'techniques of collage, involving recycling, parodies and pastiches' (Walker, 1983, p. 2) points to the fact that the 'process of musical performance has become so complex through its links with technology that it can no longer be mastered simply by a musician, let alone be set down in musical notation by a composer as it used to be' (Wicke, 1990, pp. 15–16). These ideas can be applied to the work of regional EDM producers like DJ Sasch who 'remixes and creates electronic and dance music and plays them live at gigs' (Triple, 2017, online). Jacob Grant, who works under the name Just A Gent, was a winner of Triple J's Listen Out competition in 2017 and is also an accomplished electronic producer and DJ.

Musicians: Choice Making Agents Within the Creative (Eco)System

Skilled musicians like Jacob Grant hold a special place in all cultures, but not necessarily one that is well rewarded financially. For instance, the University of Newcastle's Conservatorium provides a critical adjunct to the industry and Professor Frank Millward, previously Head of the School of Creative and Performing Arts, suggests that:

> No one really makes a living out of being a creative artist. There's like a pyramid with a pinpoint at the top, and on the pinpoint are the number of people who make about $150,000 a year or more. There are a lot of people who live on thirty, fifty, sixty, seventy thousand … A lot of success in the creative arts is about personality, luck, and … skill. It's about being virtuosic, being different, having something to say. (Millward, i/v June 2016)

The International Federation of Phonographic Industries (IFPI), 'an investor in human creativity' (IFPI, 2003, online), confirms that 'only a tiny minority … will ever prove commercially successful' (IFPI, 2003, online). Local music entrepreneur, Steven Pickett suggests that in terms of comparative incomes, between the 1980s and now, a four-piece band would:

> be lucky to see a 10/20 per cent difference. Soloists get a bit more ... We still get hotels wanting "a six-piece band, $600, supply your own PA". It's in no way kept up with everybody else's wage increases. (Pickett, i/v Oct 2015)

This experience appears to be region-wide with live performance income, adjusted for inflation, dropping steadily over the decades. Mark Tinson, a producer of seven film soundtracks, six theater cast recordings, 25 radio jingles, 64 albums and who has 154 songs registered with APRA, noted that many musicians have low financial status but a high cultural importance:

> If you're in a popular band … you're considered to be an exciting person and you probably get to experience more exciting things than other people. The trade-off for that is, generally, you don't have as much money as everybody else has … but we've contributed to the culture. That's important. (Tinson quoted in Sheather, 2016, p. 80)

The Hunter rock band whose early recordings were produced by Tinson, Supersonic, found that for them, that was not enough. Supersonic achieved its initial distinction through national band competitions and became 'one of our biggest selling local acts' (Supersonic, 2003, p. 25). Supersonic maintained its activities primarily through live performance. Production and management costs were contributed by their management *gratis* in expectation of eventual success and they sourced finance from small local investors to record their last album, produce a video, hire Australian Music Biz to promote an east-coast tour and release a CD through MGM Distribution. After the tour and CD release, Supersonic disbanded having realized that, without financial input from the major record companies (Haynes, 2011), expansion would be difficult.

Supersonic's songwriters then diversified. Matt Plummer moved into graphic design and Xanders performed solo in the UK. He then took up professional photography in Melbourne and moved back to Newcastle. Mark Wells is now well established in country music. After winning the Telstra Songwriter's Prize at the Tamworth Country Music Festival in 2008, he went to the USA:

> to work with some of Nashville's best songwriters and US music industry heavyweights ... The lead single from his debut alt. country EP, the bluegrass infused *You're Still on My Mind* … reached the top 20 of the CMC Music Chart. His song *Big Skies* co-written with Morgan Evans, reached the ARIA Australian Top 50 … He has [performed] center stage at the Sydney Entertainment Centre, and appeared on bills with … Lee Kernaghan, Troy Cassar-Daley and Kasey Chambers. He was named Best Male Vocalist at the 1233 ABC Music Awards. (Wells, 2013, online)

Wells' song-writing collaborator, Morgan Evans, has pushed his successes even further. Evans began his career working live in Newcastle before venturing into the country music realm working as a presenter on country music television programs and being named New Oz Artist of the Year at the CMC Music Awards. He eventually relocated to Nashville, signed to Warner Bros and now records and tours internationally (see McIntyre et al., 2023, pp. 140–141). The skills he developed playing and writing in Newcastle, were critical to his success in the USA and around the globe.

> I think the biggest skill you take, apart from being able to play a guitar and sing, is the ability to deal with the unknown … The biggest thing from those bar gigs is a culture [of live performance], as well as collaboration in song writing. I've got a bunch of mates here and, they're like, "Hey come, jump up and sing a song with us." And I'm totally comfortable in situations like that because I've done it a million times at Wells's gigs and Wells's done it a million times with me … it's like what's the worst that can happen, it's already happened. (Evans, i/v April 2016)

Mark Wells' band still consists of friends, all of whom are full-time professional musicians and continue as journeymen musicians with him. For example, Justin Ngariki has been described by his peers as '[t]ruly one of our most remarkable hidden treasures. He is currently signed to ABC records and is in great demand as a guitarist, vocalist, drummer and songwriter' (Tinson, 2012, online).

In Kurri Kurri, Kirsty Lee Akers has also successfully taken up country music. She is an ARIA Top 10 Artist and an ARIA #1 Australian Country Artist. In 2007, she won the Toyota Star Maker talent search, a win she shares with Keith Urban and Lee Kernaghan. In 2008, she won the Golden Guitar Award for Best New Talent. While she is 'proud of her Indigenous heritage, she has embraced a global musical culture and now spends her time between Australia and the USA' (Akers, 2018, online):

> A lot of women might doubt themselves and normally it's more of a man's world in the recording studio, but I have been doing this my whole life … I released my first album 11 years ago, so I think I know what I'm doing by now. I'm just glad I had the courage to step into the producer's seat … I'm lucky I'm surrounded by amazing people. (Leeson, 2018, online)

Amy Vee is an award winning fully independent artist and completed her last album via a successful crowdfunding campaign with her fans effectively acting as her record label. Her awards include, among others, the 2018 Studios 301 All Access Winner, 2009 Winner of the APRA/ABC Publishing Songwriter of the Year and 2005 MUSICOZ Artist of the Year. She has released a number of singles and the *Same Skin* LP in 2019, *Fits and Starts* LP in 2013 and her first recording *Sleeping Dogs Lie* in 2010. Her digital only single *Ten Years*, released in 2016, gained Top 20 chart positions on iTunes and Triple J Unearthed. Her digital singles are available:

> on all the streaming platforms. I have a distributor who takes care of all that for me. They're kind of available anywhere you find music. My last single was recorded at Hazy Cosmic Jive Studio which is owned by Gareth Hudson in Newcastle. There was also one that I self-produced last year that actually just went out on YouTube and Facebook. I've been self-producing my songs because I was in lockdown. I just did an EP on [software] Garage Band which is surprisingly quite functional. The beauty of it is, it's copyright free. (Vee, i/v 2021)

She sees herself as a singer and a songwriter, but:

> I also work as kind of a hired gun for a few other bands as well, so being a multi-instrumentalist, I get to work in a variety of different settings, different genres, so that keeps me working, keeps me busy, and keeps me match-fit. What else? I work as a session artist in a recording studio sometimes. I go and do vocal sessions for people. I've done a little bit of teaching in music as well. I have also dabbled in other performing arts, so I do a little bit of theater and music theater. (Vee, i/v 2021)

Until recently Les Hall from the Ted Mulry Gang, Mark Tinson from The Heroes and Grant Walmsley from the Screaming Jets, all important musical personnel in the field of popular music, contributed their extensive industry expertise to the teaching of music industry programs at TAFE. This expertise was often acquired via a deep commitment to their profession. For example, Les Hall from Maitland, guitarist and songwriter for the nationally successful touring and recording group the Ted Mulry Gang, now finds time, after his teaching functions at TAFE ceased, to write songs for, and produce, young dance artists for the European market. Grant Walmsley was a founding member of the Screaming Jets. The Screaming Jets, initially played at such venues as Tubemakers in Mayfield before making a national name for themselves while signed to Rooart records. They had come to national attention by winning the first Triple J National Band Competition. They eventually toured Europe and the United States a number of times, where they were released on Atlantic Records, and acquired enough national chart hits to enable the compilation of a "best of" recording *Hits and Pieces*. They are still based in Newcastle and continued to tour nationally at least until 2012. Since then they have reformed a number of times.

Newcastle's most famous alumni include Daniel Johns, Ben Gillies and Chris Joannu from Silverchair. In their early days, they attended the TAFE's Ausmusic Basic Music Industries Skill course as part of the combined JSST TAFE program to enable them to complete their secondary education while recording and performing. After signing to Murmur Records, a subsidiary of Sony, they released the internationally successful album *Frogstomp* and each of their successive studio albums all placed at Number 1 with three singles reaching the top of the charts. Across their career, they toured internationally, broke records previously established internationally by bands like INXS, and went on to win 21 ARIA music awards and six APRA awards.

A bright new crop of the Hunter Valley's popular musicians exist in bands like Rum Jungle who are signed to an independent record label, Sureshaker, based in Sydney and home of Sticky Fingers, a band who have toured Australia, Mexico, the United States, the United Kingdom, Germany, the Netherlands, New Zealand and Indonesia. Rum Jungle are managed by Ripple Effect and their website, www.rumjungleband.com, houses the band's branded merchandise as well as advertising for tour dates. Their booking agent from Cult Artists, a firm who are affiliated with Live Nation, had them headlining a nationwide tour after they had broken into the national festival circuit with a successful showing at the Byron Bay Falls Festival and elsewhere. One of their tunes, *Keep*, has over 2 million hits on Spotify and their new single, one of a number of them, was premiered on national broadcaster Triple J. Their distribution occurs through an automated system operating out of the United States, Distrokid, which places their songs on iTunes, Spotify, Pandora and a host of other streaming services. Promotion takes place primarily on Facebook, Instagram and TikTok and their analytics indicate a large and diverse international following. Benny, their singer and one of their songwriters, also works, courtesy of the online environment, full time from home as Roland Australia's social media marketing manager.

Summary

The performers named above, and many others listed in the Newcastle Music Directory (NMD, 2021, online), have contributed significantly to the recording and live performance sectors of the Hunter's music industry. It is still the case that the most significant choice making agents or decision making entities in the field of popular music include songwriters, musicians, managers, touring crews, venue operators, agents, promoters, producers, engineers, publishers, and, of course, the audience. Many of them find an immersion in both the shared knowledge of the domain and interconnected networks of the field of music through the community-based music clubs, brass bands and orchestras that provide opportunities for on-the-job training in ensemble skills which enrich areas like the jazz scene. Many popular music virtuosos find work as session players in local recording studios but a number have diversified to provide other industry-related services. While opportunities in the live realm, particularly for popular musicians, are extensive, incomes are diminished with gig fees having stayed static, in terms of real income, across decades. Many musicians struggle to earn income commensurate with the rest of the population. Nonetheless, driven by factors other than the financial, such as social, cultural and symbolic capital, there are still many musicians continuing to write, perform and record.

Changes wrought by digital technologies have also had an effect at the local and global level. The structure of social media, streaming services and automated distribution, in particular, have changed the way musicians and music businesses promote and distribute their work. Not that this is as profitable as it used to be, for both songwriters and performers. Diminishing income for international recording artists, due to the digital turn and the deals made with streaming services to specifically compensate record companies, has meant these acts are increasingly chasing a return from live sector markets traditionally serviced locally. At the same time, the loss of city performance venues through urban redevelopment, tightened security and nighttime curfews, coupled with the rise of the festival touring circuit, has meant shrinking opportunities for residencies for regional performers. However, people in this field of interconnected networks still collaborate, compete, mentor and support each other through both a gift and financial economy trading at various scaled levels—locally, nationally and globally. This basic framework has not changed. Overall, it can be concluded that the Hunter's music industry is not a collection of isolated parts but a dynamic interlocking set of interconnected networks that produce and circulate musical goods, ideas and shared knowledge across a variety of genres and styles. The choice making agents who work within these structures are part of a much larger creative (eco)system at work.

References

Akers, K. (2018). *Bio & media*. Kirsty Lee Akers. Retrieved August 24, 2018, from http://www.kirstyleeakers.com/bio-media/

ALRC. (2013). *Copyright and the digital economy: Final report*. The Australian Law Reform Commission. Retrieved July 15, 2017, from https://www.alrc.gov.au/wp-content/uploads/2019/08/final_report_alrc_122_2nd_december_2013_.pdf

Beilby, P., & Roberts, M. (Eds.). (1981). *Australian music directory*. AMD P/L.

Biglin, L. (2017). *Len Biglin*. Facebook. Retrieved June 10, 2017, from https://www.facebook.com/len.biglin

Breen, M. (Ed.). (1989). *Our place, our music*. Aboriginal Studies Press.

Centauri Audio. (2017). *Home*. Centauri Audio. Retrieved August 27, 2017, from http://www.centauriaudio.com.au/

CNRPB. (2017). *History*. City of Newcastle RSL Pipe Band. Retrieved June 8, 2017, from http://www.newcastlerslpipeband.com.au/history2.htm

Cockington, J. (1992). *Mondo weirdo: Australia in the sixties*. Mandarin.

Creswell, T. (1993). *Too much ain't enough*. Random House.

Creswell, T., & Fabinyi, M. (1999). *The real thing: Adventures in Australian rock & roll*. Random House.

Durant, A. (1990). A new day for music? Digital technologies in contemporary music-making. In P. Hayward (Ed.), *Culture, technology & creativity in the late twentieth century* (pp. 175–196). John Libbey and Co and Arts Council of Great Britain.

Dusevic, T. (2010, September 16). *Curbs on drinking results in fall in assault rate in Newcastle*. The Australian. Retrieved June 12, 2013, from https://www.

theaustralian.com.au/nation/nation/curbs-on-drinking-results-in-fall-in-assault-rate-in-newcastle-/news-story/f5fb04d4ba50d3d5a75f4eee0335ecaa

Ellis, C. (1985). *Aboriginal music: Education for living*. University of Queensland Press.

Fangjun, L. (2014). *China's music industries: Evolution, development and convergence*. Unpublished PhD Thesis. Department of Media, Music, Communication and Cultural Studies, Macquarie University, Sydney.

Fink, M. (1996). *Inside the music industry: Creativity, process and business*. Schirmer Books.

Freud, S. (1997). *Thank you, good night: A backstage pass to Australian rock 'n' roll*. Random House.

Frith, S. (1996). *Performing rites: Evaluating popular music*. Oxford University Press.

Goodwin, A. (2017). *Visualising Newcastle's live music scene. On a tangent*. Retrieved June 11, 2017, from http://www.goodwin.id.au/2011/04/26/visualising-newcastles-live-music-scene/

Gregory, H. (2018, March 8). University of Newcastle launches record label, Baraya Records, to help emerging musicians. *The Newcastle Herald*. Retrieved April 12, 2023, from https://www.newcastleherald.com.au/story/5270075/university-of-newcastle-launches-baraya-records-to-help-emerging-musicians/

Groeneveld, J. (1998). *Growing the Hunter contemporary/popular music industry feasibility study*. HAC & DEWRSB.

Haynes, B. (2011, June 22). What are the odds of succeeding without a record deal? *Music think tank: Where the music industry thinks out loud*. Retrieved May 25, 2013, from http://www.musicthinktank.com/blog/what-are-the-odds-of-succeeding-without-a-record-deal.html

Hayward, P. (Ed.). (1992). *From pop to punk to postmodernism: Popular music and Australian culture from the 1960s to the 1990s*. Allen & Unwin.

Homan, S., & Mitchell, T. (2008). *Sounds of then, sounds of now: Popular music in Australia*. ACYS.

Hope Estate. (2013). *Home*. Hope Estate. Retrieved April 12, 2013, from https://www.hopeestate.com.au

HRBA. (2017). *Hunter Regional Band Association*. Retrieved June 6, 2017, from http://hrba.org.au/

Hudson Arc. (2014). *Home*. Hudson Arc. Retrieved June 11, 2014, from https://www.hudsonarc.com

HVV. (2017). *Hunter Valley Violins*. Retrieved June 10, 2017, from http://www.huntervalleyviolins.com.au/newcastleviolinsalesrepairs.html

HWE. (2017). *Hunter Wind Ensemble*. Facebook. Retrieved August 5, 2017, from https://www.facebook.com/hunterwindensemble/

Ian Sandercoe. (2014). *Rob Taylor*. lanSandercoe.com. Retrieved October 14, 2014, from http://robtaylor.iansandercoe.com/

IFPI. (2003). *Music: One of the great global industries*. International Federation of Phonographic Industries. Retrieved May, 29, 2013, from http://www.ifpi.org/

ILR. (2016). *Home*. Ison Live Radio. Retrieved July 19, 2016, from http://www.isonliveradio.com/index.html

Impromtu. (2013). *Home*. Impromptu Studios. Retrieved October 14, 2013, from http://www.impromptumusic.com.au

Jenkins, J. (1994). *Ego is not a dirty word: The skyhooks story*. Kelly & Withers.

Leeson, J. (2018, August 4). Akers making ground. *The Newcastle Herald*.

Leiber, S. (1996). *History and styles of rock music in Australia*. Ausmusic.

Macintyre, S. (1999). *A concise history of Australia*. Cambridge University Press.

Martin, G. (1983). *Making music: The essential guide to writing, performing and recording*. Pan.

Masterson, A., & Gillard, S. (1999). *Rocking in the real world: An introduction to the music industry in Australia*. Ausmusic.

Mathieson, C. (1996). *Hi-Fi days: The future of Australian rock*. Allen & Unwin.

McIntyre, P. (2004). *Creativity and cultural production: An ethnographic study of contemporary Western popular music songwriting*. Unpublished PhD Thesis. Macquarie University, Sydney.

McIntyre, P. (2009). Songwriting, creativity and the music industry. In R. Sickels (Ed.), *The business of entertainment: Vol. 2. Popular music* (pp. 1–20). Praeger.

McIntyre, P. (2011). Rethinking the creative process: The systems model of creativity applied to popular music songwriting. *Journal of Music Technology and Education, 4*(1), 77–90. https://doi.org/10.1386/jmte.4.1.77_1

McIntyre, P., Fulton, J. M., Kerrigan, S. M., & Meany, M. M. (2023). *Entrepreneurship in the creative industries: How innovative agents, skills and networks interact*. Palgrave Macmillan.

McIntyre, P., & Sheather, G. (2013). The Newcastle music industry: An ethnographic study of a regional creative system in action. *International Journal of Music Business Research (special issue on the Australian Music Economy), 2*(2), 36–60.

Menuhin, Y., & Davis, C. (1979). *The music of man*. Methuen.

Miller, T., & Shahriari, A. (2012). *World music: A global journey* (3rd ed.). Routledge.

Mitchell, T. (1996). *Popular music and identity: Rock pop and rap in Europe and Oceania*. Leicester University Press.

Musos Corner. (2017). *About us*. Musos Corner. Retrieved June 10, 2017, from https://www.musoscorner.com.au/about-us/

NHJC. (2017). *Newcastle and Hunter Jazz Club*. Retrieved June 6, 2017, from http://www.newcastlejazz.com.au/

NHVFC. (2017). *History of the Folk Club*. Newcastle Hunter Valley Folk Club. Retrieved June 6, 2017, from https://www.newcastlehuntervalleyfolkclub.org.au/history-of-the-folk-club/

NL. (2017). *About*. Newcastle Live. Retrieved June 6, 2017, from http://newcastlelive.com.au/about/

NMD. (2021). *Newcastle Music Directory.* Retrieved February 10, 2023, from https://newcastlemusic.com/

Palmer, R. (1996). *Dancing in the street: A rock and roll history*. SBC Books.

Passman, D. (2002). *All you need to know about the music business*. Penguin.

REM. (2013). *About us*. Rock City Event Marketing. Retrieved June 16, 2013, from http://www.rockcity.com.au/page12067/About-Us.aspx

Rogers, B. (1975). *Rock 'n' roll Australia: The Australian pop scene 1954–1964*. Cassell.

Sawtooth. (2017). *Home*. Sawtooth Studios, Retrieved June 10, 2017, from http://www.sawtoothstudios.com.au/home

Scion. (2017). *Scion Audio*. Retrieved June 10, 2017, from https://scionaudio.com.au/

Sheather, G. (2016). *Rock this city: Live music in Newcastle, 1970s–1980s*. Hunter Press.

Siegel, A. (1990). *Breaking into the music business*. Simon & Schuster.

Simpson, S. (2006). *Music business: A musician's guide to the Australian music industry*. Omnibus Press.

Sly, L. (1993). *The power and the passion: A guide to the Australian music industry*. Warner/Chappell.

St. John, E. (1994, September). *Species deceases*. Rolling Stone.

Supersonic. (2003). Unpublished Business Plan (Newcastle: Supersonic).

Tarala, K. (2013, June 8). *Rock, unroll a swag*. Newcastle Herald.

Tinson, M. (2012). Liner notes. *Mark Tinson's Steelville cats II*. CD available at https://marktinsonmusic.com/shop/

Tomsen, S., Homan, S., & Russo, D. (2003). *Masculinity and public drinking violence in Newcastle and the Hunter ('Boozers and Bouncers')*. Interim Report for the School of Social Sciences. University of Newcastle.

Triple J. (2017). *DJ Sasch*. Triple J Unearthed. Retrieved June 6, 2017, from https://www.triplejunearthed.com/artist/dj-sasch

TW. (2017). *Events*. Trade Wind Folk Events. Retrieved June 6, 2017, from http://tradewindsfolk.com/

UON. (2017). *Music making in the colonial city*. University of Newcastle. Retrieved June 6, 2017, from http://www.newcastle.edu.au/research-and-innovation/publications/music-making-in-the-colonial-city

UON. (2018). *Music producer mixes postgraduate research with career change*. University of Newcastle. Retrieved April 25, 2023, from https://www.newcastle.edu.au/newsroom/featured/music-producer-mixes-postgraduate-research-with-career-change

Walker, C. (1996). *Stranded: The secret history of Australian independent music 1977–1991*. Macmillan.

Walker, J. (1983). *Art in the age of mass media*. Pluto Press.

Wells, M. (2013). *Biography*. Mark Wells. Retrieved June 15, 2013, from http://www.markwells.com.au/bio.html

Whiteoak, J., & Scott-Maxwell, A. (2003). *Currency companion to music and dance in Australia*. Currency House.

Whitsett, T. (1997). *Music publishing: The real road to music business success*. MixBooks.

Wicke, P. (1990). *Rock music: Culture, aesthetics and sociology*. Cambridge University Press.

Wikstrom, P. (2009). *The music industry: Music in the cloud*. Polity Press.

Williamson, J., & Cloonan, M. (2007). Rethinking the music industry. *Popular Music, 26*(2), 305–322. https://doi.org/10.1017/S0261143007001262

Wilmoth, P. (1993). *Glad all over: The countdown years*. McPhee Gribble.

Wilson, L. (1999). *Making it in the music business: The business and legal guide for songwriters and performers*. Allworth Press.

Wilson, P. (1997). *The singing voice: An owner's manual*. Currency Press.

Zion, L. (1987). The impact of the Beatles on pop music in Australia 1963–66. *Popular Music, 6*(3), 291–311. https://doi.org/10.1017/S0261143000002336

Zion, L. (1988). The sound of Australian music. In V. Burgman & J. Lee (Eds.), *Constructing a culture: A people's history of Australia since 1788* (pp. 209–222). McPhee Gribble.

6

Performing Arts

The Accumulated Heritage of Performing Arts in Australia: A Brief History

While not identified as such, performing arts have a long history in Australia which predates white settlement with First Nations performances occurring over 60,000 years as an intrinsic part of Indigenous culture. Indigenous practices, values and beliefs were shared within and across language groups, using song and dance as 'stories and ceremony moved back and forth across the landscape' (Dunn, 2020, p. 15).

Western art forms were imported with the British colonists and included English-style musical theater, comedies and pantomimes. The first Western play to be performed in the colony, *The Recruiting Officer*, was staged largely by convicts in 1789 (AG, 2018, online) though it was written by Irish playwright, George Farquar in 1706. The first musical ensembles were the regimental bands of the British military (Whiteoak & Scott-Maxwell, 2003, p. 482), with the first concert performed in 1803. Employment in the performing arts began as theaters emerged and offered work for actors and musicians (AG, 2018, online) with Australia's

P. McIntyre et al., *Creativity and Creative Industries in Regional Australia*, Palgrave Studies in Creativity and Culture, https://doi.org/10.1007/978-3-031-45972-6_6

oldest continuously operating theater being Hobart's Theatre Royal, which opened in 1837. The first ballet was performed in Sydney at the Theatre Royal in 1835 (Whiteoak & Scott-Maxwell, 2003, p. 79).

Entrepreneurs realized that there were opportunities to be exploited in Australia, particularly as the population grew with the 1850s Gold Rush. International companies, like the New York Serenaders (1851) and the Backus Minstrels (1855) (AG, 2018, online), toured Australia and opera became a significant element of the performing arts in Australia with Irish entrepreneur William Lyster, bringing The Royal English and Italian Opera Company to tour in 1861. Lyster's brother Fred, a baritone and also an entrepreneur, built up a musical touring company, employing singers and musicians as it toured Australia (Whiteoak & Scott-Maxwell, 2003, p. 470). In 1908, the National Opera Company was established and imported stars were eclipsed by home-grown and internationally successful performers such as Dame Nellie Melba.

Under the guidance of Harry Rickards in the late nineteenth century, the Tivoli in Sydney became the preeminent popular theater in Australia. It drew on both American minstrel shows and the British music hall tradition, giving them a peculiarly Australian character. At the same time jugglers, lion-tamers, bearded ladies and freak shows continued to tour the country in traveling circuses, although 'Australia's tradition of circuses stretches back to the early 19th century' (Landragin, 2011, online).

Australian show business started to emerge at the end of the nineteenth century (Van Straten, 2003, p. 2) with more opulent playhouses in the provincial centers employing locals and staging international productions, while traveling shows performed in humble halls and under canvas and '[e]ntrepreneurs such as J.C. Williamson and George Musgrove presented carbon copies of the latest overseas successes' (Van Straten, 2003, p. 2).

The Great Depression forced many live venues to shut their doors at a similar time as the Golden Age of Radio began. In 1920, opera singer Dame Nellie Melba broadcast from Essex, England to listeners in many parts of the world via Marconi's innovative invention—the radio transmitter. (Holloway, 1975, p. 9). Following this, radio began to broadcast plays, musical comedy, dance music, grand opera, band concerts, orchestral concerts, vaudeville, symphony concerts, community singing and revues, effectively promoting these art forms and keeping many professional performers in work. People tuned in nightly to hear their favorite serial and the most enduring drama program in Australia was *Blue Hills* (1949), written by Gwen Meredith that ran continuously until 1976 (Lane, 1992, p. 234). ABC Radio in particular became the home of a number of symphony orchestras and opera was often broadcast.

After WWII, in 1948, the National Theatre company was set up and this period saw the beginnings of a national dramatic identity with the first Festival of Perth held in 1953 as well as the establishment of The Australian Elizabethan Theatre Trust in 1954. Australian playwright Ray Lawler's *Summer of the Seventeenth Doll* was first staged in 1955, and the National Institute for the Dramatic Arts (NIDA) was founded in 1958 to train professionals for the theater. In 1968, The Australian Council for the Arts, soon to become The Australia Council, was set up to provide funding sources for major state theater companies (AG, 2018, online). Australian live performance was reimagined and re-invented through the circus performances in the late 1970s, which seeded 'the establishment of long-lived companies that have endured to today, such as *Circus Oz* and the *Flying Fruit Fly Circus*' (Arrighi, 2013, p. 2). Performing arts festivals proliferated and included the Perth International Arts Festival, established in 1953, The Adelaide Festival and the Adelaide Fringe, established in 1973, the Darwin Festival and Melbourne's International Comedy Festival.

The 1970s saw a further flourishing of theatrical expression boosted by the second wave of the Australian film industry. Playwrights such as David Williamson came to the fore and the Australian Performing Group and Nimrod Theatre (now Belvoir) were established. As one later reviewer commented:

> Some of the plays may be rough around the edges, indulgent or consigned to the bin of noble failures, but they were rarely half-hearted and reveled in the might and mastery of words. McNeil, Buzo, Hibberd, Romeril, Williamson, Hewett and company were far too passionate about the stage, and its promise, for them to have been anything less. (SMH, 2002, online)

The 1990s saw a diversity in performance styles, companies and venues with *Bran Nue Dae* by Jimmy Chi and the band Kuckles premiering at the Festival of Perth. The Bell Shakespeare Company was established in Sydney and there was an Australian musical theater revival with '*Bran Nue Dae*, *Hot Shoe Shuffle* (1993) and *The Boy from Oz* (1998–99)' (AG, 2018, online).

These diverse forms of performing arts have continued well into the twenty-first century. Some of the shows that have had international success include musicals like *Priscilla Queen of the Desert, The Boy From Oz, Tap Dogs* and Sydney Theatre Company's *Hedda Gabler* on Broadway. Australian talent continues to impress on the world stage and these include, among many others, opera director Barrie Kosky, theater director Simon Stone and Bangarra Dance Theatre, 'an Aboriginal and Torres Strait Islander organization and one of Australia's leading performing arts companies, widely acclaimed nationally and around the world' (BDT, 2023, online). Bangarra have been in existence for three decades and tour their work regionally and internationally. They engage in workshops and education programs and inspire the next generation of First Nations performers and storytellers.

Structural Elements: The Shape of the Interconnected Field

The performing arts industry is a global ecosystem that supports activities in theater, dance, opera, orchestral performances and concerts (Fig. 6.1).

It is made up of global and locally independent theater companies that invest in staging original and traditional shows which intend to turn a profit when taken on national or international tours. The sector is also supported by national funding bodies and dominated by large professional organizations and companies that hire venues, stage festivals and engage with training institutions. Most capital cities and some regional centers host arts festivals which have proven to be a boon to tourism and economic development (Fig. 6.2).

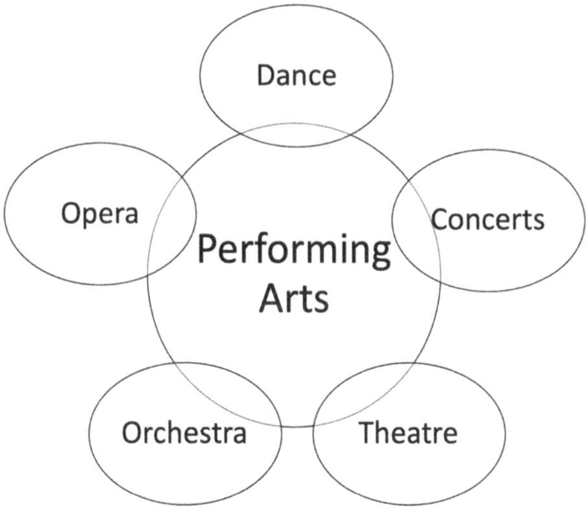

Fig. 6.1 Performing arts industry sectors (or clusters or disciplines). (Original from Annukka Jyrama School of Business, Aalto University)

Added to the structure of the industry are organizations such as The Media, Entertainment and Arts Alliance (MEAA) which is the union and industry advocate for performing artists in Australia while the Australian Major Performing Arts Group (AMPAG) is the umbrella group for Australia's 28 major performing arts companies and gives members 'a national voice and presence' (AMPAG, 2017, online).

Business Models: Shared and Crucial Domain Knowledge

There are several ways that this industry makes money. Ticket sales and subscriptions remain the primary income stream in the performing arts where practitioners create a product and sell attendance to realize a profit. Profits are only made when attendances exceed the cost of staging the performances. Payments of residuals may also accrue for re-use of produced or recorded work. Agents market and sell a performance, usually collecting a percentage-based fee. Agents also represent some performers,

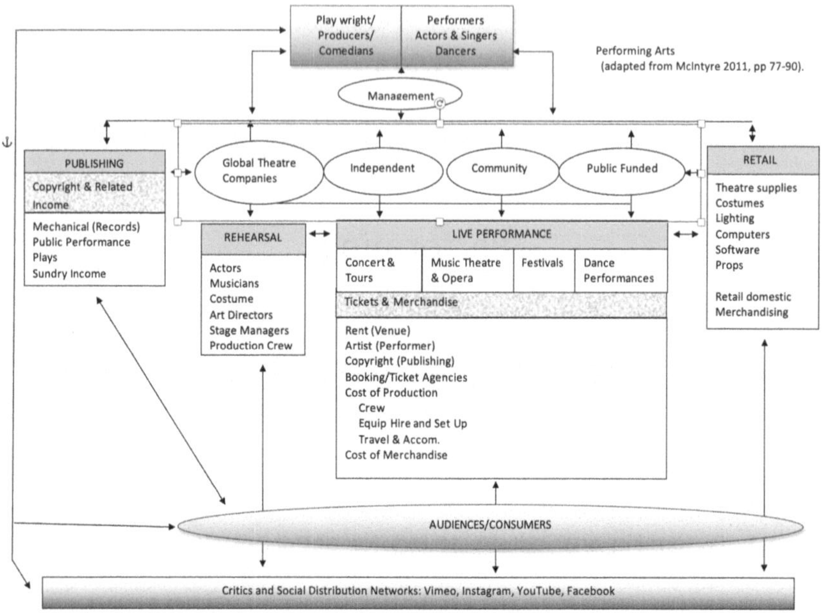

Fig. 6.2 Performing arts industry—generalized structure

although others self-manage their careers. Performers usually provide services on a freelance/contract basis, operate with a profit sharing arrangement, or give their time without payment as part of the gift economy. For profit sharing these may be split with prominent performers, depending on the popularity of the performance. Continuing work—on a long-running musical theater production or tour—is rare although some ongoing paid employment is available in, for example, teaching the performing arts, managing venues and as employees of local government operating cultural programs.

Limited funding is available from federal government organizations such as The Australia Council for the Arts or state-based organizations including Create NSW, Arts Queensland, Create Victoria and Arts South Australia. Local governments provide support via venue hire subsidies or other "in kind" support. Private funding is rare. Arts philanthropy in Australia is not strong although investors will sometimes take a chance on a high-risk investment and fund producers with a track record. It should also be noted that the gift economy is strong in this sector, and is generally a key part in the business model, with performers often working for free for the exposure and experience. On a similar note, those providing peripheral services in the performing arts often volunteer.

Operational Methods of the Field

In the theatrical world, a show will be developed by playwrights or choreographers to the point where it can be staged, while dramaturgs ensure the viability of theatrical scripts prior to a production going ahead. As well as hiring venues for a season, a performer or company may also tour, which requires outlays for venue hire, accommodation, insurances, travel costs, vehicle hire, crew payments and production costs. Income comes mainly from ticket sales or merchandising like t-shirts, posters and program booklets. The difference between outlays and income determines whether the next production can be staged.

Following a successful tour, a season may be booked at a major venue requiring similar financial balancing. Rental for theater spaces, payments for performers, stage manager, and lighting and sound designers still apply although the venue supplies house management and box-office services. A promotions company may also be needed but, more recently, social media in the form of Facebook and Twitter are playing a key role in promoting a new performance with smaller companies and individuals increasingly using these low-cost promotional methods. Digitization is now incorporated into the core part of marketing, box office functions and production as well as being the basis of providing a forum for interactive participation (Towse, 2013). Websites and social media are now ubiquitous with ticketing and financial controls also undertaken digitally. In terms of production, digitally controlled scenery changes and lighting have reduced the need for certain backstage staff while streamed live performances are becoming more common (Towse, 2013).

Important Personnel in the Field: Choice Making Agents

Actors, dancers, singers, comedians, jugglers, gymnasts and so on are the core onstage presence in the performing arts. These creatives may develop their skills through formal study but many are self-taught or learn on the job. Performers seek work through auditions and casting calls, through agents or a manager paid on commission, or by creating their own work as entrepreneurs. They generally self-manage a "portfolio" career. Festivals are often useful for performers, mostly in terms of promotion as many are lucky to cover costs. They are like trade shows and allow the performer to show off their wares and establish a presence in the marketplace.

Other roles in this (eco)system include musicians, playwrights, producers, directors, art directors, stage managers and backstage crew. Further affiliated with the performing arts in peripheral but crucial roles are agents, those who sell tickets and merchandise, and theater critics. The core performance work may be supported by creative, technical and administrative staff, such as those noted above, or, as is the case for micro-theatre, a core band of company members may take on multiple roles themselves. In other words, different sectors of the performing arts have different needs when it comes to important personnel (Fig. 6.3).

As an example, musical theater, a subsector of performing arts, exists in a deeply intertwined system and depends on a number of crucial roles. These include those who compose the book, score and lyrics, a set of texts which become the blueprint for the performance. While musical directors are responsible for the musical elements, directors control the artistic elements and producers ensure that all other tasks such as financing, legal and administration are taken care of. Producers must ensure production costs are covered. Agents find the cast or hire musicians to fit the theatrical event and venue managers will ensure the performance is right for the venue and may supply limited in-house lighting and sound facilities, staging requirements and marketing. For large-scale productions, entertainment lawyers and accountants are crucial and then there is, of course, the audience. Critics act as knowledgeable intermediaries between the audience and the performances.

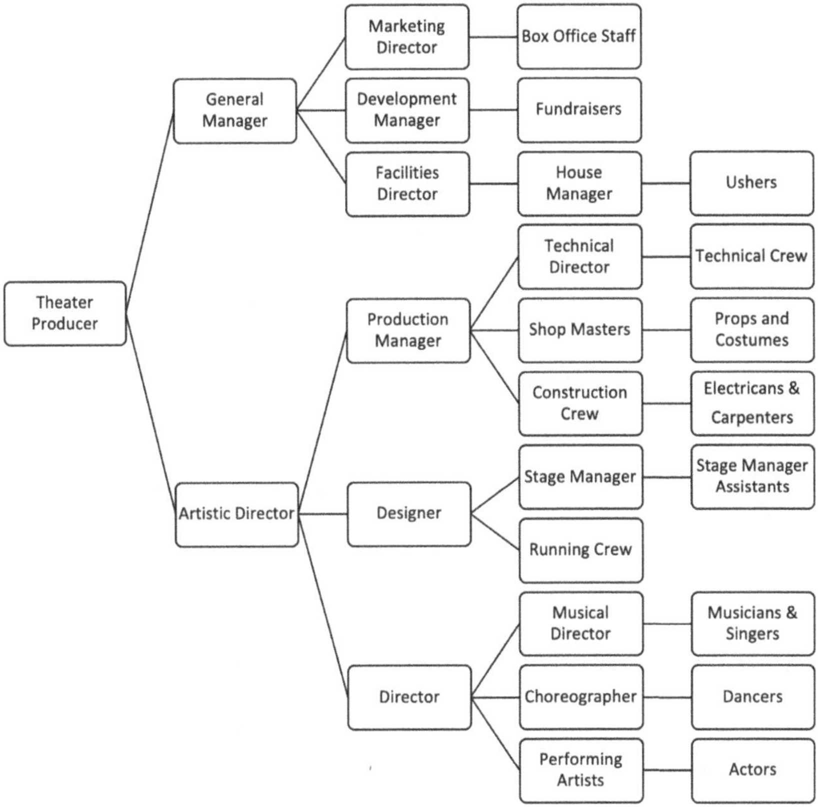

Fig. 6.3 Performing arts industry personnel

Hunter Region Performing Arts: An Interconnected (Eco)System

In the Hunter, the performing arts are primarily found in drama and musical theater, dance, opera, music, circus, mime and comedy. Many performers have achieved significant careers nationally and internationally with many of these creative workers operating between the pro-am and amateur spaces. A significant amount of activity occurs within the gift economy with an extraordinary number of volunteers and amateurs ensuring the viability of the creative (eco)system. Given its prominence in the region we will initially focus our attention on theater.

The Newcastle theater industry is supported through the professional body, the City of Newcastle Drama Association (CONDA), which was established in 1979. And, while a 2018 study into the Newcastle theater sector found that it was vibrant and active with $3.1 million generated in ticket sales, there were only 17 full-time equivalent theater jobs in this sector in the region (Bransdon, 2021, p. 253). What was comparatively astounding was there were 11,000 people also participating in volunteer gigs in theater in Newcastle. A survey of all local productions found 'that a range of between 5 and 380 volunteers were utilized for each production staged by typical companies' (Bransdon, 2021, p. 125). This level of activity was generated by 48 local companies, who mount 118 local productions a year across 45 venues, providing creative opportunities for 1000 local actors, musicians and artists (Bransdon, 2021 p. 254). The ABS statistics from 2016 similarly indicate a low level of professional activity with only 2% employment for the sector across the Hunter Region but these did not account for the numerous amateurs and volunteers who ensure this sector keeps running successfully.

Looking back we can see that the 1980s was a vibrant period in the Hunter with two professional theater companies (Hunter Valley Theatre Company and Freewheels) as well as Opera Hunter, The Workers Cultural Action Committee of Trades Hall and various groups including Zeal Theatre and The Castanet Club, all supporting a set of full time professionals. Since then, there have been venue closures and a significant defunding of companies. Now there are no fully professional theater companies existing in this region. However, there are companies that aspire to and achieve professional standards and commit to paying performers on a profit-share basis. These include Two Tall, Knock and Run, Stray Dogs and Stooged Theatre Company. Others, such as musical theater company Metropolitan Players, represent a surprising hybrid of professionalism and amateurism in that the quality of work, the budgets and the operational methods are of the highest industry standards while relying on a veritable cast of volunteers. Newcastle's Young People's Theatre is also run by volunteers and has 'provided training and performance opportunities for young people between the ages of 8 and 18 for over 75 years' (YPT, 2023, online).

The argument can be made, then, that even though there is not a significant amount of employment income, there are many avenues for experience, with the region consequently acting as a significant "rookery" for performers, many of whom go on to work elsewhere and then return, bringing expertise and connections for next generation aspirants. Notable exports are actor and writer Jonathan Biggins, comedians Rhys Nicholson and John Doyle ("Rampaging" Roy Slaven), music theater performers Jye Frasca and David Harris, and actors Abbie Cornish, Sarah Wynter, Susie Porter, Stephen Peacocke, John Bell and Ben Mingay. The Hunter was also home to playwright Nick Enright and musical director John Foreman. The Tap Dogs dance troupe has toured internationally while local dancers often appear with international dance companies including the Moulin Rouge.

While local employment options are limited (Bransdon, 2021, p. 253), there are examples of successful, full-time professional companies working in the region. Paper Cut is one example. They create their own work. Similarly, Chris and Debbie Kelly have for many years run Ship O'Fools which provides entertainment for children. However, interviews with members of the performing arts scene reveal that it is intrinsic rewards that drive the gift economy in this sector. The co-founders of Paper Cut: Contemporary Performance Collective, Sarah Coffee, Tamara Gazzard and Lucy Shepherd, create, produce and stage original theater and movement work and contribute to the discussion of unpaid performance work. Shepherd points to this issue:

> A lot of people do it for free, they do it as a passion and they do it for the high they get from it but when does that line cross over to professionalism? … When do you start getting paid? (Shepherd, i/v May 2016).

Sarah Coffee argues that working for free is 'not sustainable' and more thought needs to be put into creating professional opportunities 'instead of just talking about the lack of them' (Coffee, i/v May 2016). Coffee feels that in the Hunter there is an 'expectation associated with the creative industries that you should be doing it for free' (Coffee, i/v May 2016), while Gazzard says:

> One thing that characterizes working in the creative industries is unpredictability. The work doesn't happen nine to five, five days a week, and you don't get paid a regular wage ... There are periods of amazing energetic creation, and then there's nothing for a while. So, you have to ride those waves. (Gazzard, i/v May 2016)

And, as another anonymous interviewee stated, not being paid for creative work challenges the notion of an industry: 'We talk about the industry a lot but in actual fact it's not an industry, because people who work in industry get paid' (Anon 2, i/v 2016).

Performers' financial security is also challenged by the travel required and selection processes which require auditions and call-backs. Some actors live in the region and work elsewhere, including Stephanie Priest, Angie Diaz, Katy Carruthers, Anne Rzechowicz, Barry Shepherd and Todd Lasance. This is also the case for opera performer Guilhereme Noronha. Others have relocated to major cities but remain involved in Newcastle. These include Singleton-born director and actor Chloe Perrett who works at Sydney Theatre Company in customer service, Medowie-born Daniel Cottier (recently assistant director of a professional production in Sydney) and Mat Lee. They all remain involved with Stooged Theatre where the core team work for free unless engaged on a profitable production (Lee, i/v April 2017).

Dance in the Hunter: Domain Acquisition Through Institutional Training

In terms of dance in the Hunter, it is clear that there are 'a lot of highly respected training institutions and dance schools but there's not a place for professional artists to work' (Anon, i/v 2016). The unpaid performances of dancers in Newcastle affect the status of dancers in the city as they struggle for their work to be seen as a professional activity rather than a hobby. Dancers, while they have strong skills, must leave the region to work professionally. Nonetheless, private dance academies are well established and many students move on to the national and international stage. Timothy Gordon, who teaches at the National College of Dance, says Newcastle punches above its weight in terms of dancers succeeding at the highest level and quips that 'there's nothing else to do here, except go to the beach!' (Gordon, i/v Aug 2016). More seriously, he speaks of the difference in culture, especially youth culture, in Newcastle:

> these kids come from the country, way out in NSW, Coffs Harbour, Mudgee, Orange, the outback, all of that western country area. They would rather come to us than go to Sydney ... One feels safe. The kids can wander around and do all sorts of things outdoors ... They look after each other. They have an amazing camaraderie. (Gordon, i/v Aug 2016)

Gordon agrees with a comment made to him by Dame Peggy van Praagh, the founder of the Australian Ballet. She said that 'the future of dance in Australia would not be in the main centers; the future of dance in Australia would be in the regions' (Gordon, i/v Aug 2016).

Choice Making Agents in the (Eco)System: Individual Performers, Writers, Choreographers, Composers, etc.

Individuals have varied options in performing art in the Hunter with some freelancing locally, nationally and internationally. For example, David Fitzgerald is a CONDA award winning musical director and head of audio, he works in Australia and overseas recruiting musicians for shows he directs and supplying technical specifications of their audio parameters (Fitzgerald, i/v April 2017). He completed an MBA and now operates under his own trading name of Full Fat Jazz (Fitzgerald, i/v April 2017). Fitzgerald's break in musical theater came when he moved to Melbourne to study at the Victorian College of the Arts. He was awarded the Millfield Fellowship, and relocated to the UK for 12 months where he was mentored by Cameron McIntosh, the director of *Phantom of the Opera.* Even though he trained as a classical pianist, he moved into synthesizers and the related digital technology. Fitzgerald, who lived in Sydney before relocating to Newcastle, has found the move to be beneficial for his lifestyle and work life balance. He acknowledges that there are a few jobs he has said no to because of a lack of proximity but he feels he has continued to be creative, 'because I can say no to jobs. It's allowed me a lot of great experiences' (Fitzgerald, i/v April 2017).

Interviews like that with Fitzgerald revealed several issues confronting the performing arts. For example, an anonymous local performing arts creative noted from their perspective that artists in the region 'often lack entrepreneurial skills and spirit' (Anon 2, i/v 2016). Other issues revealed include: the need for even the most successful performers to adapt, diversify and be mobile; the way sub-sectors work together; the different expectations held for Australian and overseas practitioners; and significant legalities involved in copyright, understanding finance and touring.

Of those who took on touring, the alumni of the now defunct Hunter Valley Theatre Company (HVTC) are still involved in the performing arts locally, nationally and internationally. Among the young actors who inhabited the local stage at HVTC before setting out were Celia Ireland, David Wenham and Susie Porter. Others sitting in the audience 'saw their future' (Bevan, 2017, online). For example, Vanessa Hutchins, the former Civic Theatre Manager in Newcastle, got her start working as a stage manager and lighting operator with HVTC (Bevan, 2017, online). She has gone on to a significant national career as a music and arts touring and event manager. Jonathan Biggins was also an early convert to theater, dropping out of university to perform professionally with the HVTC before becoming a nationally recognized comedic personality working on stage, in television and at corporate events. Barry Shepherd, still working as a professional actor, is another example. He was working as a schoolteacher in a regional town in the 1980s and traveled to Newcastle to perform in amateur productions where he was spotted by a Sydney talent agent. Shepherd's expertise is still in strong demand, often traveling interstate to act in commercials. He is also an assistant director for film productions and has edited a television series and acted in movies such as *McLean's Money* and in the *Rake* television series (IMDB, 2018, online).

Perhaps one of the best-known performers from the HVTC is John Doyle. A former schoolteacher, Doyle studied drama at the University of Newcastle. The playwright John O'Donoghue recognized that Doyle had the gravitas needed for a part in O'Donoghue's play *Essington Lewis, I am Work*. After this success, Doyle worked steadily for a number of years at HVTC, eventually leaving his teaching position. While his credits include the films *Bliss* and *Babe*, he has inhabited the now iconic comedic character of "Rampaging" Roy Slaven as well as many more:

> Roy and his co-host HG Nelson have appeared continuously on radio since 1986 as well as creating television programs including *Club Buggery, The Channel Nine Show, Win Roy and HG's Money, The Dream, The Monday Dump, The Ice Dream, The Cream* and *The Memphis Trousers Half Hour* for ABC TV. Doyle himself hosted the weekly mid-afternoon shift on 702 ABC Sydney in the late 1980s and early 90s … Over the last decade Doyle has developed a very successful parallel career as a writer of serious television drama … Doyle's contribution to Australia's cultural scene has been recognized through a multitude of awards. He has also published a number of books and was presented with an OAM in 2010. (Celebrity Speakers, 2018, online)

Daniel Stoddart is a typically multi-dimensional performer. He is an award-winning actor, singer and director and is the artistic director of Hunter Drama, an independent academy for young actors. Stoddart has had a portfolio career; as a drama graduate from the University of Newcastle, he worked for two years at L!vesites, a place activation initiative, and he developed the concept for *The Ultra-Swing Lounge*, a 1950s-style jazz music show. He is of the view, however, that there is a lack of commitment to professionalism within the sector (Stoddart, i/v Oct 2015). He also refers to a lack of professionalism, 'a lot of back-patting, a mentality that effort equals quality' (Stoddart, i/v Oct 2015). Stoddart also underscores the expense and risk involved in staging productions, not least because of royalty payments of 16.5 percent on a show's gross. In 2014, his company, Hunter Drama, staged Disney's *The Little Mermaid Jr* at the Civic Theatre and it failed to cover costs.

Agencies, Support Workers, Venues and Festivals: Completing the Interconnected Networks of the Field

In addition to performers, the Hunter also boasts agents. While many local performers sign with Sydney agents, local agencies for performing artists include longstanding agents Models and Actors, CHAAYS Model and Talent Management, and Gina Stoj Management. When Gina began representing Newcastle actors, others from Sydney and beyond joined the agency (GSM, 2018, online). While she operates her Australian agency from Newcastle, she is a global player. Her USA management company has offices on Hollywood Boulevard in Los Angeles and Lexington Avenue in New York. She has placed actors in numerous television series, films and commercials (GSM, 2018, online).

As a creative (eco)system, the sector involves technical, organizational and administrative workers including venue and festival crews, training institutions, companies and enablers such as investors and funding bodies. Shane Bransdon (2021) points out the flow-on significance of funding for the sector. Our interviews revealed a shared sense that performing arts in the Hunter is not receiving its fair allocation of government funding. Some of this funding is available from Create NSW and The Australia Council for the Arts, and local government support is generally "in kind". Tantrum Youth Theatre's Tina Hardingham sums it up: 'Finances are tight. We really just survive. You know, we work so hard on these tiny grants, and there's never any respite' (Hardingham, i/v Nov 2015). All of this signifies a mismatch between industry education and policy settings that fail to generate outcomes commensurate with the social and cultural value the performing arts have.

Venues, many with long-term social and cultural value in the regions, play a key role in the performing arts and the region's major venues are in the city of Newcastle with the Entertainment Centre, the historic Civic Theatre and two clubs with large auditoriums that regularly hold performances. It is noted, though, that there is a lack of mid-size venues (seating 400 to 600) in the urban center. University of Newcastle's Griffith Duncan Theater holds just over 800 but increased fees have made it unusable for most theater companies. Across the region, community halls are used for theatrical and music performances, and Tantrum is known for its site-specific works at Newcastle Ocean Baths, Fort Scratchley and the shores of Lake Macquarie. Festivals use non-traditional venues for innovative work, notably the annual TINA (This is not Art) Festival, which stages experimental performance artists from all over Australia in shopfronts, streets, and unused buildings.

Successful creative entrepreneur Daniel Stoddart is frustrated by the lack of suitable venues. He is Australia's only recipient of the Freddy Gershon Fellowship (presented by Music Theatre International, New York) for his work with young people: 'It's the age-old problem—the need for a medium size theater … [it] is needed as a stepping stone to get to the next level business' (Stoddart, i/v Oct 2015). Stoddart noted Newcastle's Civic Playhouse, a 200-capacity venue associated with the Civic Theatre, as an intimate space to hold plays, but there is a great leap between the Playhouse and the 1400-capacity Civic Theater. And while Stoddart praised the Playhouse as a venue, since a hire increase and associated take of 11% of net box office sales, the venue remains largely unoccupied.

Performing arts festivals staged in the Hunter primarily focus on new and experimental work and alternative venues. Crack Theatre Festival grew from the National Young Writers' Festival (Crack, 2017, online) and is now part of the annual TINA (This is not Art) Festival, which bills itself as a place 'where experimental performance artists come from all over Australia to unleash their wildest ideas' (Crack, 2017, online). In 2017, the Newcastle Fringe Festival offered 'over 100 unique shows and performers' across a range of city venues 'within walking distance of the Newcastle CBD' (NFF, 2018, online). The Hunter Valley Arts Centre was instrumental in producing Theatrefest Hunter, a festival of one-act plays performed by the region's theater groups and held in the Cessnock Performing Arts Centre (Stage Whispers, 2018, online).

Performing Arts Companies Operating in the Hunter: Staging Traditional and Innovative Work

Among the successful performing arts companies operating in the region are Circus Avalon, an active community circus company that is 'one of Australia's largest non-government-funded community circus organizations' (Circus Avalon, 2018, online). Opera Hunter has also successfully mounted large productions such as *The Magic Flute, The Marriage of Figaro, Sweeney Todd, West Side Story, Oliver, Les Miserables* and *Cats* (Sticky Tickets, 2018, online). This company often works with the Lake Macquarie Philharmonic Orchestra and The Hunter Orchestra but is dedicated equally to opera and musical theater, using 'popular musicals to support financially the mounting of opera productions' (Opera Hunter, 2018, online).

Perhaps the most ambitious company in the region is Metropolitan Players, a musical theater company that has been operating for 40 years. Julie Black is Artistic Director of the company while Graeme Black is often Set Designer and Stage Manager for productions as well as being President of the Player's committee. *Les Miserables*, in August 2017, was the ninth show they have staged at Civic Theatre in Newcastle. The company has been the recipient of numerous CONDAs (City of Newcastle Drama Awards) over the years.

> The Company was first formed in 1977 and has been producing quality musicals ever since. We produce one major musical each year, although in the past there were sometimes 2 each year … For many years we have used the 924-seat Griffith Duncan Theatre at Newcastle University. Our most recent productions have been at Newcastle's premier theater, the 1400-seat Civic Theatre. The Company is run by a Committee that is elected each year at the Annual General Meeting in February. We used to rehearse at Broadmeadow Uniting Church Hall in Broadmeadow, but after 33 years have now moved to Glendale High School. Set construction is at our warehouse in Cardiff. Over the years our productions have received many City of Newcastle Drama Awards (the CONDAs). The most successful was *The Producers* in 2008 which won 6 Awards. However, this has now been beaten

> by our 2014 production of *The Phantom of the Opera* which won 7 Awards. After *Wicked* in 2016 the Company has now won the CONDA Best Musical production 5 years in a row. We make all our own costumes for each show and many of these are for hire. (MP, 2018, online)

Metropolitan Players currently receive neither government nor corporate support. They have had some in-kind support from Newcastle City Council in the past but were unsuccessful in 2016 in their application for event funding which offered up to $20,000. With budgets of approximately $400,000 per show, Graeme Black suggests:

> It's a huge financial risk. It could be the last show every time ... Last year's production took nearly $500,000 at the box office but the costs are significant. Performing rights cost 16–18% of gross which was $80,000 last year, theater hire was $140,000, $80,000 was spent on sound and lighting hire, and $8,000 on billboards. (G. Black i/v May 2017)

Metropolitan Players represents a surprising hybrid of professionalism and amateurism in that the quality of work, the budgets and the operational methods are of the highest industry standards, yet everybody involved works on a voluntary basis. Graeme Black explains that this allows them to work to a scale and level that would otherwise be impossible. As Julie says, they all do it for the love of it. Those who compete for roles with Metropolitan Players shows appear to be happy to work for nothing, attracted by the opportunity to be part of a successful, high quality show where they can develop their experience, skills and profile in a positive atmosphere. Daniel Stoddart, who has performed in several Metropolitan Players shows, says that to ask for pay would be 'pricing yourself out of the market' (Stoddart, i/v Oct 2015). He bluntly asks, 'Why would Metropolitan Players pay you if there are ten other people lined up who are happy to do it for nothing?' (Stoddart, i/v Oct 2015). Indeed, roles with Metropolitan Players shows are hotly contested: in 2016, 207 people auditioned for 50 roles, only nine of which were leads.

Importantly, experience with Metropolitan Players can assist performers develop the skills and knowledge they need for professional careers. Graeme Black says the company tries to give performers 'as close to a professional experience as possible and a rare opportunity to work in a theater such as the Civic Theatre' (G. Black, i/v May 2017). Several performers who have worked with Metropolitan Players have gone on to significant professional careers. Jye Frasca came to the company as a young tap dancer and is now working in shows in the West End of London, David Harris has had professional leads in Australian musicals and now lives and works in Los Angeles, Costa Nicholas worked as a singer/dancer and now runs a casting agency in the USA, Nigel Turner Carroll directs shows nationally, and Tyran Parke and Seth Drury are both currently appearing in the musical *Big Fish* at the Hayes Theatre in Sydney.

While Metropolitan Players' shows do not pay performers, the economic value they generate is significant. Daniel Stoddart estimates that the 2015 production of *Mary Poppins*, in which he was a lead, had possibly one hundred people working on the show. (In actual fact that production of *Mary Poppins* included a production crew alone of 100 plus a full cast of 56 actors, accompanied by a 17-piece orchestra):

> Each of those people was going into town for up to two weeks. They were all putting money in the parking meters, they were all going into the little shop next door buying iceblocks. How much money did they spend on petrol to get their car into town? How much money was spent on buying stockings for that production from Lowes up the road, and costumes, fabric, wood from Bunnings to make sets and things? If there was some way of quantifying that in a really tangible, practical way and saying the arts contribute X amount of revenue to the local economy … comparing that to a packed-out Newcastle Knights stadium, I think we would probably give them a red hot run for their money. (Stoddart, i/v Oct 2015).

Other theater companies in the region include Stooged Theater, Stray Dogs Theatre Company and Tantrum Youth Arts. Tantrum is a prominent, well-established company that started in Newcastle in 1976 as 2 Til 5 Youth Theatre Co-op. It presents a range of art forms including 'performance, filmmaking, writing, physical theater' (Tantrum, 2018, online) for young people aged 3 to 26. The Tantrum name was first used in 1996, and it does receive government arts funding, albeit a small amount.

Stooged Theatre began in 2003 under Carl Young's leadership as a not-for-profit company operating on a profit-share basis. Artistic Director Mat Lee explains that their 'product is bringing contemporary … plays to Newcastle that other companies have not yet staged, or classical/modern work that has a social message' (Lee, i/v April 2017). For more than a decade, it has staged three or four shows a year and has received numerous CONDAs (City of Newcastle Drama Awards). Stray Dogs Theatre Company is a co-op headed by playwright, director, actor and educator Carl Caulfield and his partner, director Felicity Biggins. The company stages new plays written by Caulfield, whose main income comes from teaching drama and creative writing at the University of Newcastle and NIDA. Noting that a playwright's work is constrained by theater budgets, he comments that:

> Theater companies won't look at your work if you're writing for more than seven actors … it's great to have the chamber pieces, but we also want to see the large-scale work that deals with big social issues or the movements of history. (Caulfield, i/v May 2015)

Training Organizations: Necessary Domain Immersion in Action

The limited nature of theater training available in the region has been identified as an issue, however. Mat Lee from Stooged Theatre talks of the strong talent base and high degree of theater-related activity in the city but he points to the loss of institutional training opportunities on offer:

> Newcastle is both thriving and at a loss. We currently have more companies producing contemporary work and theater in general, than I think we ever had before (especially in the case of dramatic theater), we have a great assortment of up-and-coming talent graduating high school and producing or performing in excellent work—In terms of dramatic actors, there isn't really another viable avenue to study theater in Newcastle (this is not including musical theater with many options available). The University doesn't really offer real acting training like it once did, and young actors—

> if they wish to pursue a career in this field—have to study in Sydney. (Lee, i/v April 2017)

Drama schools offer programs mostly for children and young people and they include Tantrum Youth Arts, Hunter Drama, Young People's Theatre and Pantseat Performing Arts as well as the Hunter Valley Actors Centre (HVAC). Young People's Theatre (YPT) is of particular note as they are one of the few companies to return substantial profits according to the audit reports available publicly from acnc.gov.au:

> It has provided training and performance opportunities for young people between the ages of 8 and 18 for over 70 years … 400 students attend weekly classes at YPT. As well as staging 6 productions a year, YPT provides technical training and mentors youth directors. (YPT, 2018, online)

HVAC, located in the Polish Hall in Maitland, has provided acting and theater courses since 2010. Tantrum Youth Arts also offers a range of programs for young people aged 3 to 26 and Pantseat Productions was formed in 2007 to assist young people develop their performance skills with a specific music theater focus. UpStage Youth Theatre in Maitland holds a number of classes where 'students are given the opportunity to learn about the dramatic arts through a practical, hands-on approach to performance' (Upstage, 2018, online). Their classes cover a wide variety of skills pertinent to the performing arts including 'improvisation, audition preparation, playbuilding, physical theater, mask, voice work and speech, mime, technical productions, circus skills, performance, script work, stage craft, social development, individual tuition, musical theater and acting for the camera' (Upstage, 2018, online).

Drama Karma has been operating in Morisset since 2008 and offers courses in acting, public speaking, mime, script writing, performance and theater sports (AA, 2018, online). The Australian Dance and Talent Centre in Cardiff, The Pasvolsky Actors Studio in Cooks Hill and Barnes Music in Broadmeadow are family-run training businesses. In the Upper Hunter, the Platinum Dance Centre is located in the main street of Muswellbrook and The Hunter Dance Academy also operates out of Singleton while the Newcastle Premier Dance Co at Caves Beach provides dance tuition (AA, 2018, online). At the coastal end of the valley, Newcastle is renowned for its talent in dance with many local dancers finding placements in leading companies internationally, from ballet companies to the Moulin Rouge. Dance schools include Newcastle Ballet Theatre, Tap Pups and the National College of Dance as well as Catapult which is a not-for-profit contemporary dance organization for professional artists, emerging artists and young people (McCarthy, 2018, online). The studio has received funding from Create NSW, the City of Newcastle, the NSW Department of Education & Training, and Ausdance NSW (McCarthy, 2018, online). The National College of Dance (NCD) in Lambton, Newcastle was formerly the renowned Marie Walton Mahon dance school. Her Academy was bought in 2012 by Brett Morgan, formerly of the Australian Ballet Company and Associate Director of Sydney Dance Company. NCD teaches classical and contemporary dance and jazz from Certificate to Diploma (semi-professional) level.

Shane Bransdon runs OzTheatrics with Daniel Stoddart and their aim is to 'grow Australia's musical theater industry by providing young people with quality musical theater programs' (OzTheatrics, 2018, online). Bransdon is a long-time performer in acting, singing and dancing roles and has built a highly successful performing arts education business in Newcastle called OzTheatrics. Bransdon describes himself as 'an actor/director and educational specialist' who has appeared in *Les Miserable* (2017), *Wicked* (2016), and *Mary Poppins* (2015)' (OzTheatrics, 2018, online). Bransdon, discussing the performing arts in Newcastle, pinpoints dance as the most popular and visible but also agrees with Stoddart about working in the gift economy:

> When we are talking about the performing arts as a subsector of the creative industries in Newcastle, I think dance will be the biggest chunk of the pie. If we can somehow capture the economy created just by parents taking their kids to dance class every week, creating costumes and performances! ... In fact, on any list of the employed there are dancers. And musicians, they just don't work for free ... If an actor was to say 'I won't work unless you pay me' there would be ten lined up behind them willing to do it for free. (Bransdon, i/v Oct 2014)

As a glimmer of hope in the employment stakes, performers are in demand for training videos, promotional films and television commercials such as those produced by award-winning production company Good Eyedeer, or local television stations and advertising agencies which produce commercials. And, in a demonstration of how the creative industries are embedded in the non-creative industries, performers were employed with The Arts Health Institute (AHI). More than 80 performers in music, dance, theater and comedy were trained to work in aged care facilities and hospitals, implementing various programs that both entertain and engage people while also bringing therapeutic benefits (Connell, 2016, online) until the program ceased in 2017.

Summary

The performing arts sector in the Hunter exhibits an intricate intertwining of choice making agents and support services that enable a vibrant industry offering professional-level works. However, that industry is highly dependent on volunteers and those who engage for the love of the craft. By surveying theater companies in the urban areas of the city, Shane Bransdon was able to capture the passion and deeply engaged level of activity of these choice making agents that allow many theatrical traditions, in particular, to continue, even if these theater productions are economically nonviable. His research captured the extent of the gift economy operating in the Hunter. We can, however, see what a remarkable incubator the Hunter has been for developing talent across all the broad spectrum of the performing arts with those trained here making their mark nationally and globally. Learning their craft from the shared domain knowledge they have had access to and building interconnected networks within the field not only give them access to the system but also demonstrates the enduring nature of this creative (eco)system in action. We can also see how even a sector that could be considered traditional has embraced the innovations of digitization in the form of social media, websites and interactive performances to enhance the experience for the performers and the audience. The performers discussed in this book chapter, all considered to be choice making agents, have engaged with education structures such as dance academies, drama schools, circus training and youth theater companies. They battle with the structures of government and each other for funding and access to venues. They use ticket sales and subscriptions and sponsors to earn a living and to ensure the creative system stays afloat so they can stage their next performance, allowing their audiences to continue to enjoy the theater, musical theater, dance, music, opera, comedy, circus, mime and many other forms of performing arts.

In conclusion, we can see that the Performing Arts sector of the creative industries operates as a complex (eco)system of creative activity. It is a mature creative industries sector. It covers all aspects of artistic expression that involve people using their bodies and/or voices, or extensions of those, to communicate with an audience. The shared knowledge of the domain of performing arts also includes the business structures and operational methods that make the performing arts sector commercially viable. Creative performers working in the sector are field members who employ these operational business methods to stage performances, original and traditional, through theatrical production companies for audiences. As we do in other chapters, we discussed the history and structure of the sector, and the business models and operational methods of performing arts before discussing the important personnel or choice making agents operating within the system. We then told the stories of these creatives, and in that process demonstrated how each one of these decision making entities has internalized the opinions of the interconnected networks that comprise the field and immersed themselves in the shared knowledge of the domain, allowing them to creatively contribute to the Hunter's Performing Arts creative (eco)system. We will now follow a similar pattern in examining the creative industries' sub-sector of Architecture.

References

AA. (2018). *Drama classes & lessons for kids in the Hunter Valley*. Active Activities. Retrieved January 24, 2018, from https://www.activeactivities.com.au/directory/category/performing-arts/drama/drama-classes-lessons/location/nsw/hunter-valley/

AG. (2018). *Highlights in Australian theater history*. Australian Government. Retrieved January 18, 2018, from https://www.australia.gov.au/about-australia/australian-story/highlights-in-austntheatre-history

AMPAG. (2017). *AMPAG welcomes ministerial changes to arts funding framework*. Australian Major Performing Arts Groups. Retrieved June 5, 2017, from http://www.ampag.com.au/article/ampagwelcomes-ministerial-changes-to-arts-funding-framework

Arrighi, G. (2013). *Re-routing traditional circus performance: Towards a cultural history of community circus in Australia*. Paper for circulation within the Popular Entertainments Working Group, IFTR, 1–14. Retrieved January 1, 2018, from http://acapta.org.au/wp-content/uploads/2014/08/Re-routing-traditional-circus-performance-towards-a-cultural-history-of-community-circus-in-Australia-G-Arrighi-2013.pdf

BDT. (2023). *About*. Bangarra Dance Theatre Knowledge Ground. Retrieved April 16, 2023, from https://bangarra-knowledgeground.com.au/about

Bevan, S. (2017, July 21). The people and stories of Hunter Valley Theatre Company. *The Newcastle Herald*. Retrieved January 25, 2018, from http://www.theherald.com.au/story/4801875/memories-of-a-golden-age/

Bransdon, S. (2021). *Valuing Newcastle's theatrical performing arts industries: A systemic approach to unpacking the economic, structural and social challenges faced by the Newcastle theater industry*. Unpublished PhD Thesis, University of Newcastle.

Celebrity Speakers. (2018). *Inspiring people—John Doyle*. Celebrity Speakers. Retrieved January 25, 2018, from http://www.celebrityspeakers.com.au/john-doyle/

Circus Avalon. (2018). *Home*. Circus Avalon. Retrieved January 21, 2018, from http://www.circusavalon.com.au/

Connell, T. (2016, March 6). Healthcare pioneer named Newcastle woman of the year. *The Newcastle Herald*. Retrieved May 4, 2017, from https://www.newcastleherald.com.au/story/3773408/dr-maggie-haertsch-named-newcastle-woman-of-the-year/

Crack. (2017). *About the festival*. Crack. Retrieved January 10, 2017, from http://cracktheatrefest.com/aboutcrack/

Dunn, M. (2020). *The convict valley: The bloody struggle on Australia's early frontier*. Allen & Unwin.

GSM. (2018). *About*. Gina Stoj Management. Retrieved January 22, 2018, from http://www.ginastoj.com/AUS/about-aus.php

Holloway, J. (1975). *Radio in Australia*. Reed Education Publications.
IMDB. (2018). *Barry Shepherd*. IMDB. Retrieved February 24, 2018, from http://www.imdb.com/name/nm1788098/?ref_=nv_sr_2
Landragin, A. (2011). *The history of the circus in Australia*. The Wheeler Centre. Retrieved January 19, 2018, from https://www.wheelercentre.com/notes/4b7d9f9ba9e3
Lane, R. (1992). *The golden age of Australian radio drama: 1923–1960*. Melbourne University Press.
McCarthy, C. (2018). *Director Cadi McCarthy*. Catapult Dance. Retrieved February 25, 2018, from http://www.catapultdance.com.au/director-cadi-mccarthy/
MP. (2018). *About*. Metropolitan Players. Retrieved December 29, 2017, from https://metropolitanplayers.com.au/about/
NFF. (2018). *About us*. Newcastle Fringe Festival. Retrieved January 22, 2018, from http://www.newcastlefringe.com.au/
Opera Hunter. (2018). *About: History*. Opera Hunter. Retrieved January 25, 2018, from https://www.operahunter.org.au/about/history/
OzTheatrics. (2018). *About us: What we do*. OzTheatrics. Retrieved August 14, 2018, from https://www.oztheatrics.com/aboutus
SMH. (2002, April 8). A stretch of the imagination, downstairs Belvoir. *Sydney Morning Herald*. Retrieved August 14, 2018, from https://www.smh.com.au/entertainment/art-and-design/a-stretch-of-the-imaginationdownstairs-belvoir-20020408-gdf6h1.html
Stage Whispers. (2018). *Theatrefest Hunter*. Stage Whispers. Retrieved January 22, 2018, from http://www.stagewhispers.com.au/community-theatre/theatrefest-hunter
Sticky Tickets. (2018). *About Opera Hunter*. Sticky Tickets. Retrieved January 25, 2018, from https://www.stickytickets.com.au/operahunter
Tantrum. (2018). *About*. Tantrum Theatre. Retrieved January 22, 2018, from http://www.tantrum.org.au
Towse, R. (2013). Performing arts. In R. Towse & C. Handke (Eds.), *Handbook on the digital creative economy* (pp. 311–321). Edward Elgar.
Upstage. (2018). *Upstage youth theatre*. Culture Hunter. Retrieved January 24, 2018, from http://culturehunter.org/upstage-youth-theatre/
van Straten, F. (2003). *Tivoli*. Thomas C. Lothian P/L.
Whiteoak, J., & Scott-Maxwell, A. (2003). *Currency companion to music and dance in Australia*. Currency House.

YPT. (2018). *Over 70 years of theater making*. Young People's Theatre. Retrieved June 20, 2018, from https://ypt.org.au/about/

YPT. (2023). *About*. Young People's Theatre. Retrieved April 14, 2023, from https://ypt.org.au/about/

7

Architecture

Introduction

Architecture is an example of a creative services sector of the creative industries. It sits 'at the center of Australia's built environment industry, a $100 billion sector employing over a million people' (AACA, 2023). As such, architecture, like visual arts, music, dance, publishing, television and radio, is a mature example of the creative industries. It could be claimed, perhaps, that more than with many of the other sectors of the creative industries, it had an "industry" link early in that it, or its ancestral forebears, has fulfilled an instrumental service function across history.

Architects have an image of being creative and innovative. However, they are much more than designers of function and beauty. Their designs have to be functional and sustainable and that takes deliberate and conscious application of intellectual processes and significant skills. It has been argued that there are two types of architecture: firstly, there are buildings that result from professional designs, known as the high style; and, secondly, a category called vernacular architect which is built from within the building industry (Cox, 2011 [1984], online). In Australia in

P. McIntyre et al., *Creativity and Creative Industries in Regional Australia*, Palgrave Studies in Creativity and Culture, https://doi.org/10.1007/978-3-031-45972-6_7

2014, there were approximately 12,000 registered and practicing architects, working in businesses with a total income of $6.4 billion, generating a profit of $603 million. Only 11% are based outside capital cities.

Some Hunter architects find satisfaction in problem-solving, some feel the need to have a 'pencil in my hand' and others confess to seeing buildings as 'beautiful art'. All of these architects rely on the affordances that technologies provide to help them prepare their designs and are equally constrained by government building regulations. It is a creative service that has a deep history.

A Brief History of Architecture in Australia: An Accumulated Heritage

There were villages and towns in Australia long before the Europeans arrived. Indigenous communities lived in sturdy dwellings designed to accommodate the climate and the geography of the regions they existed in. As Bruce Pascoe asserts, 'design features had been developed to make harsh environments habitable' (2014, p. 78) and these buildings were strong, aesthetically pleasing and comfortable (2014, p. 78). According to Pascoe, '[b]uilding types varied according to the material available' (2014, p. 88) with open cane-roofed dwellings in the north and thatched-roof permanent dwellings further south, as well as strong houses in the alps where stone was often used as a basic building material. Gardens and wells were also part of these establishments which were situated alongside cultivated grassland. In fact, 'large populations of Aboriginal people were manipulating the Australian environment and husbanding plants to produce surplus food of such great quantities that populations could lead more or less sedentary lives in the vicinity of their crops' (Pascoe, 2014, p. 78). Much of this was documented by explorers and surveyors and, later, "protectors" but, as Pascoe (2014) argues, this evidence has not been given the cultural weight it deserves. The Europeans, largely ignorant of the conditions they were sailing into, bought their own architectural designs with them.

Prefabricated buildings were brought out with the First Fleet, made of timber and canvas and unsuitable: 'As Governor Phillip complained … the roof of his "home" leaked, vermin had free reign and it was excruciatingly hot in summer and freezing in winter' (van Teeseling, 2018, online). The first European buildings in Australia were related to the immediate needs of the colonies—prisons, hospitals, public buildings, lighthouses, forts, barracks and churches. Over time the buildings came to exemplify what became known as the colonial style, drawing on Georgian architecture, with single story dwellings with verandahs that were used to cool the house in the summer heat. Where available, sandstone was used even though it 'had to be quarried and then moved to site, which made it expensive' (van Teeseling, 2018, online). As with other sectors, Australian colonial architecture followed changing trends in Britain and in the mid- to late nineteenth century, Victorian architecture began to dominate urban areas rather than the buildings that had been so popular: 'The simplicity of the Georgian buildings was replaced by the over-the-top style of the Gothic Revival' (van Teeseling, 2018, online). In the 1870s, NSW architects began to form themselves into Institutes or Associations and from that time on, housing styles drew primarily on the international scene except perhaps for what is now known as the Queenslander which, as Peter Newell argues, represents 'the strongest regional identity in creation of a native Indigenous style' (1979, p. 1).

In a good example of the sociocultural relationship the creative work of architecture had, the history and scope of Australian identity can be seen through its "vernacular" architecture, from the shearers' shacks to the mini-mansions of Point Piper, Toorak and the Balmoral Slopes, to the Queenslander, the wool shed, the beach house and the twenty-first-century McMansion. As Sophie Hill indicates:

> architecture shapes our cities. It creates iconic skylines, signals great civilizations and builds must-see landmarks which define entire countries. Architecture has the power to capture imaginations hundreds, even thousands, of years after it was built. Less obviously, it guides and controls our way of living, the way we use space, navigate our cities and create communities. (2018, online)

The Hunter Region was no different. Its built environment reflects its historic foundation on agriculture, coal mining, manufacturing and heavy industry (Reedman, 2008). In the mid-1800s, towns in the Hunter Region had many buildings designed by local architects (Maitland & Stafford, 1997) suggesting an already established and effective local profession. For example, the architecture of High Street in Maitland, still the main street in the city of Maitland, features government, commercial and residential buildings from colonial days (Charlton, 1961), designed by Colonial and District Architects. There were also, of course, building designs imported from England, both of which emphasize the early localized and global nature of architecture in the valley.

Many other Australian cities showcase award winning architecture. These include the Academy of Science in Canberra and, in Sydney, the Frank Gehry-designed Dr. Chau Chak Wing Building (also known as the Paper Bag building). And, of course, the iconic and internationally recognized Sydney Opera House, now a UNESCO World Heritage site. These are all examples of what Philip Cox described as "high" style where architecture is 'a conscious, deliberate and intellectual process' (1984, online). It lives on in the many buildings designed by local creative architects, like Brian Suter, in the Hunter.

Structure of the Architectural Field

Structures are an important part of the creative system providing both constraints and enablers for practice. They are the source of the possibility of action. In Australia, architects have to be registered to practice. This creative services sector has been regulated since 1921 through an Act of Parliament. To accommodate this formal requirement, Australia has a number of professional associations. These include: the Institute of Architects, (representing some 12,000 members and, similar to an employee group, providing services and professional development to members); the Australian Architecture Association which promotes architecture to the public; Professional Architects Australia; the Association of Consulting Architects (representing employers); the Architects Accreditation Council of Australia; State and Territory

Architects' Boards; and other specialist groups such as the Association of Architecture Schools of Australasia and Government Architects Network of Australia. This mature sector also sits alongside a number of related fields in construction, design, building design and landscaping—all groups from the diverse sectors recognized by the ABS. There is also a well-established system of industry awards and prizes that acknowledge achievement in the field giving highly valued symbolic capital to the creative professionals in this sector (Fig. 7.1).

Architectural organizations appear more fragmented than other professional service areas like accounting or law, with a greater representation of smaller and, at times, boutique practices—perhaps reflecting its creative individualism. That said, there are also large global companies at work, often invested in major international and national projects with successful smaller firms being bought out by larger, often international, architectural firms. The work of architects also impacts on aspects of public safety, environmental concerns and building integrity, demanding different approaches to accountability, regulation and compliance. Most architectural firms are located in Sydney and Melbourne and many

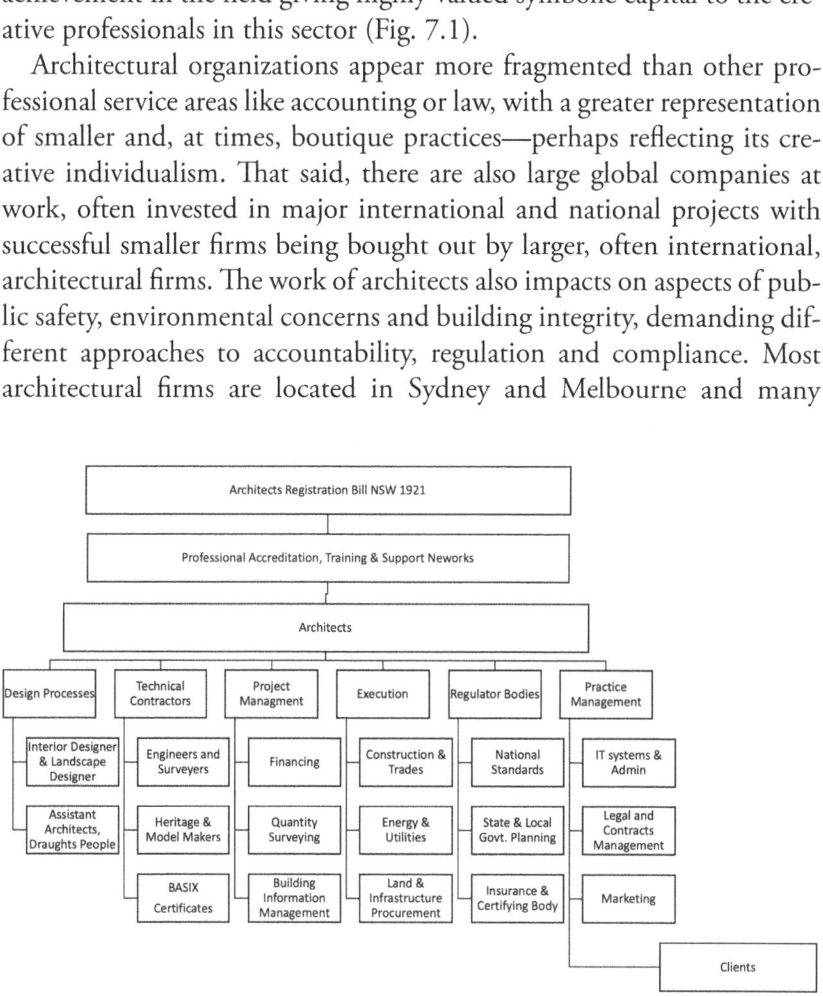

Fig. 7.1 Structure of the architecture industry

employees work full time with females accounting for almost a third (31%) of the workforce (AACA, 2018). Many architectural firms are seeking to broaden their revenue base and this can be achieved through strategic partnerships between firms as well as outsourcing labor-intensive tasks to offshore agents (Hays, 2017, p. 1).

Importantly, the issue of copyright applies to architecture, as it does to many other creative industries. However, in terms of attributing the creative element supposedly remunerated through copyright, there is the principal question of moral rights to be considered. Moral rights are designed to protect the creative reputation of the "author" of the work. These principles are embedded in an architectural Code of Conduct that sets out how to deal with other architects who take over a job from the original designer and indicates how to acknowledge the work of the previous architect. This code is necessary as changes of architect occur frequently with the refurbishment of big buildings, particularly if it has been a building that has received awards for its creative contributions.

Business Models that Support the System

Architecture is a fee-based, service industry, closely linked to cycles in the building industry. Normally an architect may take approximately 1% to 2% of a building's budget but this is always negotiable. Some architects may also lower their fee in order to take a stake in some building projects or initiate the projects themselves, meaning they engage in property development and real estate investment in addition to their architectural work. This is more typical for partners in firms rather than for architects as employees. The client base for fee-based work is split between designing for residential buildings, commercial/industrial buildings, public works and other non-building work. Typically, design and documentation work constitute around two thirds of work undertaken by architectural practices (IBIS World, 2016). The larger architectural practices are growing at the expense of mid-tier firms, where the focus is on delivering whole projects at the lowest cost possible (AACA, 2018, p. 8) often achieved through efficient pre-design approaches.

Operational Methods and Important Personnel: Choice Making Agents in the Field

Australian architects are registered by an Architects' Registration Board after a minimum two years of professional practice, completion of set logbook hours and further professional examinations. However, there are few professional services reserved for architects in Australia, meaning building designers who are not registered can also offer similar services. Not all who study architecture go on to register, with about half following related roles such as generalist management or other fields of design such as landscape architecture, interior design or urban planning. Many in this group are women. There is a fast track registration process for experienced overseas-trained architects and reciprocal rights allow Australian architects to work overseas. The daily tasks of an architect include: pre-design, scoping and feasibility work; building design and documentation; procurement of building services, contract administration, oversight of works and post-occupancy evaluation; design services and consultancy; education; and service to the profession (AACA, 2018). Typically architects own and manage their businesses, which suggests smaller enterprises, and they work long hours compared with other professionals. Architects work closely with draughtspersons, designers, planners, surveyors, and technicians and they work alongside many other occupations like building contractors, engineers, lawyers, accountants and tradespeople. Generally the profession is represented by an older male demographic with women being under-represented. While many women study architecture they tend not to pursue professional registration and, by the age of 30, women start to leave the profession or move to part-time work (Connolly, 2013, p. 22). Good architects are known for their design work and their ability to deliver on a client's wishes and preferences while still meeting the demands of planners and environmental regulations alongside national building codes, budgets and other constraints.

Hunter Region Architecture

Most architects in the Hunter work as sole traders or for large firms that are increasingly moving toward multinational agglomeration, using cost-saving processes such as offshoring and casualization of what were once in-house positions. It is an industry that suffered a downturn from the 2008 Global Financial Crisis and it is also an industry that depends heavily on technology. There are challenges with technology, globalization and global, national and local regulations. But it is also an industry that has strong roots in the region. Both Maitland and Newcastle have substantial architecturally designed buildings and, in Greater Newcastle, of the 127 being built between 1840 and 1940, half were designed by local architects suggesting that an effective local architectural profession was in operation in the region by then (Maitland & Stafford, 1997). In 2016, architecture was the third-largest creative industries sector in the Hunter (13.4%) with 876 employed in the urban center. This is higher than the number of accredited architects, because the ABS statistical employment category for architecture also covers draughtspersons, designers, planners, surveyors and technicians. Nonetheless, the relatively large number of architects in the region is credited to the strong, collaborative, professional networks created by the University of Newcastle's approach to training which builds connections between students and the profession, resulting in young architects wanting to stay in the city to work. A further incentive is the attraction of working in a regional center. Local architect Edward Duc sees the value in doing business in a regional area: 'Newcastle architects are often more affordable than Sydney architects. And, in fact, Newcastle architects are influencing other places—designing buildings in Sydney. And Melbourne. And internationally' (Duc, i/v March 2014).

Global and Local Businesses in the Hunter Region

As noted in earlier chapters, the whales and plankton ecology of the creative industries is exemplified in architecture in the Hunter where there are a variety of small, boutique-style firms along with large national and international firms based mainly in the urban center of Newcastle. One major company, Suters Architects, which started in Newcastle, has grown to employ 170 staff operating across five offices nationally. In 2017, it was taken over by international company Bangkok-based DWP after four years of collaboration (Bleby, 2017, online). This merger reflects the industry downturn since the GFC in 2008. For Suters, this merger resulted in a reduction of local staff by about 75%, and the dispersal of local staff to other locations (McKendry Hunt, i/v May 2015). It also points to the issue of having people working overseas where, apart from the concerns around the off-shoring of local jobs, quality can become problematic for something done thousands of kilometers away in a different country with language barriers and different construction codes.

Another example of a Newcastle-based company is GHD, which offers comprehensive services across multiple disciplines that are integrated in-house. GHD, founded in 1928, now has 200 offices across five continents (GHD, 2023, online). It is a professional services company operating in the global market sectors of water, energy and resources, environment, property and buildings, and transportation. They explain that the company 'engages in a vast array of projects at all scales, linking multiple disciplines to provide design solutions to private, commercial, community and government groups' (GHD, 2017, p. 1). They employ a 'design management approach that analyzes and synthesizes constraints and opportunities to realize new possibility [through] a global network … [and a focus on] creative thinking; research, modeling, pursuit of broad alternatives and the testing of innovative solutions' (GHD, 2017, p. 1). This is a local reflection of the trend for big engineering and project companies to integrate architectural services and employ operational methods that are global in their implications. The comprehensive service also contrasts with the capabilities of smaller companies, which rely on their specializations to capture niche areas of the market.

An innovation in the Hunter for architects is the availability of co-working spaces that offer newly registered architects, such as Cassie Stronach, low overhead costs on office space and networking opportunities with other young professionals in related fields. When interviewed, Stronach was a sole trader working in architecture, building design, interior design and art. At the opposite end of the architecture scale to companies such as Suters and GHD, Stronach notes that as a start-out professional she does everything. She acts as her own business manager, marketer and cleaner but she outsources her accounting and IT support. She also finds social media, such as Facebook and Instagram, has been helpful.

Participants in the study lamented the difficulties of working within the highly structured and very strict bureaucratic framework that typifies architecture in this country. Debra McKendry Hunt, who deals primarily with residential and other small projects such as child care facilities, has been practicing in Newcastle since she graduated from the University of Newcastle in 1990. She initially worked with larger firms like Suters and EJE learning how to design large commercial properties and collaborating with other independent professionals to comply with certification requirements. In 2002, she established her own firm, McKendry Hunt Architects, a small but productive practice. She has relied on reputation building through the acquisition of significant symbolic capital, winning more than 20 architectural design awards. Her practice has also won a Master Builders Association Award for Excellence and a Women in Building Recognition Award. McKendry Hunt is very active in the profession and is chairperson of the Australian Institute of Architects Newcastle Division and an Examiner with the AACA Architectural Practice Examinations NSW. She, like others, argues that complex planning legislation is 'becoming unworkable and unreasonable' (McKendry Hunt, i/v May 2015) but is also concerned about the process of architecture once a project passes the legislative phase:

> There are a lot of guides for architects—development control plans for every Council and State … the Building Code of Australia … and the

> Australian Standards for safe design. While architects collaborate to achieve all that, you [might] get it through the approval process and then the client brings in a project manager to oversee construction and you lose control. (McKendry Hunt, i/v May 2015)

Soaring costs of practicing are also part of those tight constraints. McKendry Hunt notes that 'being paid what you are worth' (McKendry Hunt, i/v May 2015) is an ongoing challenge while ongoing liabilities are problematic:

> Professional liability is expensive and liability never ceases as architects are responsible if people are hurt during the life of the building, that is, while it is being built, while it is being used, and when it is being demolished. (McKendry Hunt, i/v May 2015)

Edward Duc, a highly experienced architect, declares: 'God knows why we keep doing what we are doing!' (Duc, i/v March 2014). After graduation, Duc spent five years in England where he was exposed to the philosophy of designing low energy buildings and repurposing buildings:

> You need to be able to re-use the building for other purposes. Or if you need to pull the building apart you need to be able to keep the resources that you put into it. And … during its operation it needs to use as little energy as possible. (Duc, i/v March 2014)

Architects located in the Hunter must inevitably engage with local councils so Duc undertook postgraduate studies in Urban Design 'because when I had an argument with Councils, I wanted to have some knowledge, some qualifications that I could argue over' (Duc, i/v March 2014). He, like McKendry Hunt, has concerns about current approaches to casualized work and contracting.

> My role would be to find the work, to find the client. Sometimes you would see a project that had legs and put a bit of work into that and take it to an entrepreneur … So, I employed people, instructed them, trained them, produced designs and documentation, watched them being built. (Duc, i/v March 2014)

This contrasts to short-term contracting for specific jobs: 'I tended not to do that. I tended to employ people on a permanent basis. That way you have loyalty. I got reliable people and people who understood what I was about' (Duc, i/v March 2014). While he is now focused on factory-made sustainable housing, Duc also undertakes small residential developments, an increasingly common practice for many architects.

Debra McKendry Hunt commented on how technology has enabled the proliferation of architectural practices, particularly the scope of work smaller firms can handle:

> 10 or 12 years ago the big practices would tell you they did the big projects because they had the resources. But now, if you have a decent website and you've got the software and hardware and skills to run it, big projects can come out of small practices. (McKendry Hunt, i/v May 2015)

Technological affordances which present possibilities of creative action have changed architectural practice. Technological solutions such as ArchiCAD for design, REVIT Design Software and Building Information Management (BIM) have now become *de rigueur* for all architects. BIM is a powerful tool that has revolutionized and streamlined processes to allow complex collaborative work to be done quickly and easily. At the same time, the internet's global advertising potential has opened opportunities to secure contracts and source work overseas. There are practices in Newcastle with less than ten employees who have done buildings in Abu Dhabi and Mauritius, because they have been able to exploit the technological possibilities and also market themselves to the world.

In line with the idea of affordances, Reedman's analysis provides a succinct account of early architectural processes and in so doing shows how the potential for "novelty" and problem solving are shaped by the tools brought to the task:

> In early days architects drew everything by hand and produced what were often admirably precise and beautiful images ... Today architects employ 3-D CAD and rarely draw anything! This is not neutral ... the means we use to visualize architecture affects how we see and evaluate ideas and hence impacts on the character of the architecture that is the result. Since many

> computer operators know little about actual construction their digital drawings are truly "virtual" without much "reality". The architect in the 19th century was influenced by what he could draw and … his drawing instruments placed definite limits on his imagination ... The new unconstrained freedom in architecture in the 21st Century is mostly illusionary; in the 19th Century, T-squares, French curves, brass compasses, Indian ink, pens and ebony scale rules were handled with great delicacy to render the plans and elevations of the new architecture ... What could be imagined was, to an extent, limited by the means used to express the forms: hand drawn for an architecture based on hand made craft details and manual work. These days architecture has an impersonal quality untouched by hands. (2008, p. x)

There are other constraints that architects have identified when using technology. Edward Duc noted significant challenges in the construction industry worldwide that are intractable, where costs are indeterminate and government creates barriers with "nonsensical" rules. The use of the assessment tool BASIX (which is to do with water use, greenhouse gas emissions and thermal comfort) is one example. Duc argues that designing to satisfy a specific software tool puts constraints into the mix where other solutions may in fact offer better outcomes (Duc, i/v March 2017). There are further challenges which technology also present, for example, when architects work with other professions such as engineers where differing technology platforms are standard.

Creativity and Problem Solving in Regional Architecture

Erica McWilliam points out that 'recent scholarship has sought to unhook creativity from "artiness", individual genius and idiosyncrasy' (2009, p. 282). While most laypeople in the West still adhere to this commonsense view of creativity as artistic practice, this standard view is largely unexamined (Bourdieu, 1977, p. 80). However, as Hennessy and Amabile point out, most researchers now 'agree that creativity involves the development of a novel product, idea, or problem solution that is of value to the individual and/or the larger social group' (2010, p. 572). We found Hunter Region architects to be well aware of their role in creativity and problem-solving and this is evident in their marketing of creative practice. For example, Mark Lawler proposes architectural design is 'a process of creative problem solving. This requires analytical skills to firstly define the problems to be solved. Then, we use our design skills to propose creative solutions to address the identified problems' (2017, online). As another example, Edward Duc's practice is focused on functional designs and sustainability and he emphasizes the problem-solving aspect. His philosophy of design is pragmatic and he likes working with structure, services and new materials and techniques. He suggests that 'every project is different, so every solution is different' (Duc, i/v Mar 2014). Duc insists that architects have to find out what the 'real question is; and seek an answer to that real question' (Duc, i/v Mar 2014). For Debra McKendry Hunt, the old architectural adage that form follows function is true because 'there is a strong form of reasoning that comes from looking at the functional diagrammatic relationship and then looking at the built form of it' (McKendry Hunt, i/v May 2015). She also professes to 'getting a bit antsy, a bit irritated if I haven't got a design project going ... Something about the hand-to-eye thing where you can just sit and sketch and work something out' (McKendry Hunt, i/v May 2015). Newly qualified architect Cassie Stronach has a passion for the "art" end of the spectrum, believing that 'architects are on the cusp of science and art' (Stronach, i/v May 2015). For her, 'creativity is one of the biggest pressures in our industry, because creativity is not on tap' (Stronach, i/v May 2015). She feels it is necessary to showcase her art works as it 'shows that we are in the art of architecture—quite artful, beautiful spaces' (Stronach, i/v May 2015).

Specializations and Service Variety: Distinction in the Marketplace

Most full-service architectural firms that employ between 20 and 50 staff are concentrated in the lower Hunter where the population of the urban agglomeration is greater than in the hinterland. Many firms, however, tend to specialize. For example, EJE Architecture specializes in heritage architecture, interior design and urban planning (EJE, 2017, online). While other larger firms can offer a broad range of services, smaller practices work with other specialists to achieve the same range of multi-disciplinary services such as geo-tech, construction or civil engineering, quantity surveying or landscape architecture. Debra McKendry Hunt noted that architects frequently find themselves in competition with building designers who have less training (McKendry Hunt, i/v May 2015). That concern was confirmed in reviewing the smaller regional towns, where services meet local needs and are targeted to compliance and small building design, major projects being less in demand. Nevertheless, specialization is still evident. As examples we noted that SHAC Architects specialize in education and performing arts, health, regional airports, marinas and industrial buildings where efficiency and functionality are the primary need (SHAC, 2023, online). CoAssociates offer general architectural work, but have also found a niche in supplying staff to assist other architects with CAD and general drafting, building and site models, contract drafting and building surveys, providing solutions for those who need to outsource technical tasks or scale up for busy periods (2023, online). Small firm, Lewis and Zwart, highlight their integrity, quality and creativity addressing social and environmental responsibility and economic value (2017, online) and Towndrow (2023, online) emphasize their contemporary design. Seaside Homes Design, however, are strictly building designers (2019, online). All have had to provide some level of distinction in the marketplace.

In the smaller centers such as Port Stephens, Maitland, Cessnock and Forster, the services offered tended to be even narrower. In the case of Sorensen Design and Planning of Port Stephens, services tend to be defined in terms such as 'professional building design, delivering drafting, designing and town planning services' (2017, online). Often, they were limited to practical support such as Statements of Environmental Effects and BASIX reports (building sustainability) including reports on bushfires, complying development, rezoning, site feasibility and visual impact, shadow diagrams and master-planning. GPN architects extend this to focus on quality control, tender evaluation, contract management and assistance in marketing developments after completion.

This pattern undoubtedly reflects the nature of a localized market and the interdependence of the work of architects with Councils, local builders and tradespeople. As a regional pattern, it underlines the challenges faced as practices move into the international sphere.

University Education as a Source of Shared and Dynamic Domain Knowledge

The University of Newcastle, the only university located in this region, is one of 18 Australian universities offering qualifications in architecture and is proud of being rated within the top 45 according to the QS World University Rankings by Subject. It is recognized for being a pioneer in problem-based learning and offers programs in architecture, building and industrial design, construction management, disaster risk reduction, preparedness and reconstruction, project management and property.

Locally, however, the changing role of architecture and the competition from allied professionals has led to a diminished call for architects and these circumstances have been reflected at the University. As of 2017, the *Newcastle Herald* reported the University's Architecture staffing was restructured as 'architecture is in decline [and] twice as many construction students means change is needed' (Connell, 2017, online). Connell quotes Professor Brett Niness as stating that 'technological advances have changed the role of architects' (2017, online) creating a need to keep the degree 'relevant and future-orientated' (2017, online). In a further interview for the website *Architectureau*, Niness is quoted as suggesting that aspects of the way the program had been run were not benefiting students since 'we've had a focus on certain research that has taken away from teaching' (Harris, 2017, online). Debra McKendry Hunt raised concerns about some aspects of current professional training:

> I think we should be bringing out graduates who are proficient in the task of producing buildings—that's what we do. These days it's a two-degree process. The first degree is a science-based architecture degree. That's when you focus on the materials science and the building structure. Then the second degree is more about looking at large scale projects and design as a process and writing a thesis. If we are going to combine those two things together—the technical and the more esoteric and creative stuff—it's important that graduates be taught both. If you don't have that particular understanding of engineering structures and things like that, it makes me wonder how you can collaborate with others in the industry for the process. If you don't know the fundamental language about the structure and what makes a building stand up, how does that translate to the industry? It is incredibly important in building design to get the structure and services like the air conditioning, the plumbing, the electricals—whatever—to actually integrate seamlessly and there are certain tools that we can use within our BIM modeling to make that happen but if the people we are working with are not using that same software or we are using something that is incompatible, then it is almost useless. (McKendry Hunt, i/v May 2015)

Summary

The vibrant and contemporary nature of architecture in the Hunter is as a mature and sustainable creative industries sector that is subject to the dynamism of the creative (eco)system it resides within. It is a sector with a wide range of business modes from sole traders within boutique enterprises through to large international firms who are globally focused. It interacts with many of the other industries in the Hunter as well as by necessity and regulation having close relationships to local government. However, several issues emerged from this investigation and the first revolves around competition for traditional architectural services which is increasingly coming from building designers, building contractors, engineering concerns and industrial/ interior design firms. These practitioners are not as broadly qualified as architects, they do not share the same domain knowledge, and are not regulated by the field in the same way architects are, yet they undertake similar functions as choice making agents. There is no clear evidence as to the impact on quality outcomes, particularly in design, materials specifications and supervision of works but there is a well-publicized and emerging issue with recent building failures in Sydney as well as fire-linked tragedies overseas. This situation has affected the educational sphere where changes in role and demand for architects are now mirrored through lower demand and changing approaches to curriculum. Our interviews with Hunter architects also evidenced the number of support workers who facilitate the work of architects, including in management, administration, marketing, financials, client relations and IT, and the interdependence of the work of architects with Councils, builders and tradespeople. In other words they rely on interconnected networks. In terms of regional representation, there are low numbers of architects in rural areas, reflecting a general difficulty experienced by all rural parts of the region in attracting suitable professionals and providing sufficient work for them, making it difficult to prepare for registration or to link to other professionals. The profile of architects in the region exhibits low gender and ethnic representation. Female participation drops off sharply after graduation and continues to drop, apparently due to long hours, impact on families, relatively low pay and limited mentoring options offered by the field. There are also structural changes underway as architects face a progressive emptying out of the middle tier of business as is happening globally. Most architects in the region now work as sole traders or for large firms increasingly moving toward global multinational agglomeration, using cost saving processes such as offshoring and casualization of what were once in-house positions. The process of digitization, globalization and political-economic realities has driven a local reaction to these global imperatives this creative (eco)system operates under.

References

AACA. (2018). *Industry profile: The profession of architecture in Australia.* Architects Accreditation Council of Australia. Retrieved April 3, 2023, from https://www.aaca.org.au/wp-content/uploads/Industry-Profile.pdf

AACA. (2023). *Architecture in Australia.* Architects Accreditation Council of Australia. Retrieved April 1, 2023, from http://comparison.aaca.org.au/industry-profile

Bleby, M. (2017, April 3). *Architecture firm Suters throws lot in with Bangkok-based DWP to focus on Asia.* AFR.com. Retrieved September 25, 2017, from https://www.afr.com/property/architecture-firm-suters-throws-lot-in-with-bangkokbased-dwp-to-focus-on-asia-20170403-gvcsye

Bourdieu, P. (1977). *Outline of a theory of practice.* Cambridge University Press.

Charlton, K.D. (1961). *The architecture of High St, Maitland.* Unpublished PhD Thesis, University of NSW.

CoAssociates. (2023). *Home.* CoAssociates. Retrieved March 22, 2023, from http://www.coassociates.com.au

Connell, T. (2017, August 24). University of Newcastle proposes staff restructure as architecture in decline. *Newcastle Herald.* Retrieved August 24, 2017, from https://www.newcastleherald.com.au/story/4875775/uni-plans-as-architecture-in-decline/

Connolly, J. (2013). *Appendix C: Architects in Australia: A snapshot from the 2011 Census (Equity and diversity in the Australian architecture profession: women, work and leadership).* Presented to the project Steering Committee and the National Council of the Australian Institute of Architects, September 2013. Retrieved September 25, 2017, from https://parlour.org.au/wp-content/uploads/2014/08/Appendix_C_Census_Report_sml.pdf

Cox, P. (2011, November 29 [1984]). Australia's architectural identity. *ArchitectureAU.* Retrieved April 26, 2018, from https://architectureau.com/articles/philip-coxs-as-hook-address-from-1984/

EJE. (2017). *Home.* EJE Architecture. Retrieved July 25, 2017, from http://www.eje.com.au/

GHD. (2017). *Global services.* GHD. Retrieved August 11, 2017, from http://www.ghd.com/global/services/architecture/

GHD. (2023). *About us.* GHD. Retrieved April 3, 2023, from https://www.ghd.com/en/about-us/about-us.aspx

Harris, J. (2017, August 25). University of Newcastle trades architecture, industrial design for construction management. *ArchitectureAU.* Retrieved August

25, 2017, from https://architectureau.com/articles/university-of-newcastle-trades-architecture-industrial-design-for-construction-management/

Hays. (2017). *The role of an architect, today & tomorrow*. Hays. Retrieved July 2, 2017 from https://www.hays.com.au/architect/index.htm

Hennessy, B., & Amabile, T. (2010). Creativity. *Annual Review of Psychology, 61*, 569–598. https://doi.org/10.1146/annurev.psych.093008.100416

Hill, S. (2018). *Australia's top 10 iconic architectural sites*. University of Melbourne. Retrieved April 26, 2014, from https://pursuit.unimelb.edu.au/articles/australia-s-top-10-iconic-architectural-sites

IBIS World. (2016). *Australian architecture industry 2014-2015*. Architects Accreditation Council of Australia. Retrieved August, 23, 2017, from http://www.aaca.org.au/wp-content/uploads/Industry-Profile.pdf

Lawler, M. (2017). *About*. Mark Lawler Architects. Retrieved September 17, 2017, from http://marklawlerarchitects.com.au/

Lewis, A., & Zwart, T. (2017). *Home*. Lewis and Zwart Architecture. Retrieved September 24, 2017, from http://lewiszwart.com.au/

Maitland, B., & Stafford, D. (1997). *Architecture Newcastle: A guide*. RAIA—Newcastle Division. Retrieved September 24, 2017, from https://trove.nla.gov.au/work/23212577?selectedversion=NBD13254175

McWilliam, E. (2009). Teaching for creativity: From sage to guide to meddler. *Asia Pacific Journal of Education, 29*(3), 281–293. https://doi.org/10.1080/02188790903092787

Newell, P. (1979). The origins and development of the Queensland house. *espace*. Retrieved April 26, 2018, from https://espace.library.uq.edu.au/view/uq:205086/s00855804_1978_79_10_4_18.pdf

Pascoe, B. (2014). *Dark emu black seeds: Agriculture or accident?* Magabala Books.

Reedman, L. (2008). *Early architects of the Hunter Region—A hundred years to 1940*. Self-published.

Seaside Homes. (2019). *Home*. Seaside Homes. Retrieved April 3, 2023, from https://www.seasidehomesdesign.com.au/

SHAC. (2023). *Home*. SHAC. Retrieved April 3, 2023, from https://www.shac.com.au/

Sorenson Design. (2017). *Home*. Sorensen Design and Planning. Retrieved August 14, 2017, from http://www.sorensendesign.com.au/

Towndrow. (2023). *Home*. Towndrow. Retrieved April 3, 2023, from https://www.towndrow.com.au/index.html

van Teeseling, I. (2018). *History: Australian architecture*. Australia Explained. Retrieved April 25, 2014, from http://australia-explained.com.au/history/australian-architecture

8

Visual Arts

Introduction

Visual arts is made up of many creative fields, including painting, sculpting, illustration, photography, pottery and ceramics. There are points of intersection and shared practices operating between these artistic fields, so much so that the visual arts sector functions as a mature ecosystem extending from artistic practices to business structures and operational methods. For those who seek to make a living from their art, the interviews we conducted with those who practice in this space identify both the potential and the challenges they face, revealing that art is not the province of individuals alone but also made by community members who share their work in local exhibitions or markets, or as gifts for friends and family. This multitude of creative actors constitute the great underbelly of the arts community. Their novel creative contributions are valued socioculturally and, as Bourdieu (1996) indicated, for some sections of cultural production many artists' personal creative satisfaction often ranks higher than financial rewards while others value the benefits the marketplace brings. Some artists who work in this sector often run micro

P. McIntyre et al., *Creativity and Creative Industries in Regional Australia*, Palgrave Studies in Creativity and Culture, https://doi.org/10.1007/978-3-031-45972-6_8

businesses, exhibiting in galleries and selling their paintings, sculptures, jewelry, etc. at markets or online. The more successful artists will sell all their works through their exhibitions. The fortunes of the arts sector rise and fall with economic cycles so artists have long learned to secure their income in other ways. Teaching has been one such option. To be a successful artist, an active choice making creative agent, one sooner or later comes to realize the codes and conventions of the domain must be internalized and learn, as best they can, the complex methods of operation, as well as the variety of opinions and points of judgment the field holds as the (eco)system they work within continues to operate in a dynamic and robust way.

A Brief History of Visual Arts in Australia: An Accumulated Heritage Located in Deep Time

The visual arts in Australia have a very long history. In *Rattling Spears: A History of Indigenous Australian Art* (2016), Ian McLean indicates that Indigenous communities across the country produced symbolic work in visual form that carried meaning for its users for a possible 60,000 years. This is certainly well before colonization saw the paintbrushes of Europeans represent and reflect images of themselves in their new settlements imposed on the landscape by their very recent arrival.

Beginning with Joseph Banks' illustrations of flora and fauna during James Cook's voyage to Australia, European images of the continent emerged as new settler artists, some of them convicts, depicted their new home and its ancient people. Joseph Lycett, for example, painted *Corroboree at Newcastle* in 1818 while John Glover's *Corroboree at Mills Plains* in 1832 represented life in Van Diemen's Land as the European arrivals saw it. The landscape also intrigued colonial artists, although their work is very much seen through a European lens. In the production of such art works, and the uses to which they were put, we can see that visual artists in the colony had become part of the small but burgeoning local economy.

A number of works outline the history of European Art in Australia (see, for example Anderson, 2011; Grishin, 2013; Hughes, 1970; Sayers, 2001; Smith, 1979). Christopher Allen in *Art in Australia: From Colonization to Postmodernism* (1997) sets out the stages he believes Australian Art has progressed through, from the early colonial to high colonial, the Heidelberg School, Federation, Modernism, Abstraction and Social Realism, as seen in the work of the Angry Penguins, Postmodern pluralism and, more recently, contemporary art from the 1990s onward. We can see in that trajectory over the last two and a half centuries that the development of the visual arts in Australia, like architecture, was influenced by international innovations and practices. This occurred alongside the opening of cultural institutions from large to small. For example, the first art gallery opened in Hobart, Tasmania in 1831 and in Sydney in 1842, while photographer George Goodman also opened a daguerreotype portrait studio around this time.

As Australia's visual culture emerged, so did commercial activities, seen with a local overprint—the masculinity of a harsh existence and daily life, which became increasingly nuanced as women artists depicted other aspects. The Heidelberg School of painting emerged later in the eighteenth century and the next generation saw the bush in symbolist modes and mythologies while photographic showcases emerged. Photography advanced alongside camera technology and, in 1917, Frank Hurley became the country's first official war photographer (AGNSW, 2018, online). The work of photojournalist Damien Parer rose to prominence during WWII with his combat photographs of the Kokoda trail in Papua New Guinea. The interwar years also saw post-impressionism and modernist influences emerge in painting while the 1930s marked the beginning of the modern Aboriginal art movement with Albert Namatjira's watercolors of his Central Australian/Arrernte country. In the 1960s, Mervyn Bishop joined the *Sydney Morning Herald*, later becoming Australia's first Indigenous press photographer, and Indigenous artists at Papunya began 'dot painting' with acrylic paints—the Western Desert painting movement (AGNSW, 2018, online). In 1982, the National Gallery of Australia opened in Canberra and one of its collection highlights is 'The Aboriginal Memorial' (1986–88), an installation of 200 hollow log coffins by artists from Arnhem Land representing 200 years of colonization (and survival). From the late 1990s onward, digital technology and the internet have since globalized contemporary art across the world, Australia included.

The Structure of the Field of Visual Arts

Art schools and galleries provide two of the main structures for the visual arts world where artists are firstly educated and then connected to the commercial structures where their artifacts may be sold. Traditional support systems also include residencies, commissions and grants from funding bodies such as arts councils, government, foundations or sponsors. Residencies offer opportunities for artists to gain funding, build or increase their profile, and the space and time to work. Some seek private, public or corporate commissions. These are competitive and criteria based ways to increase an income and are not always easy to secure. Galleries, schools, residencies, and the administration of grants and commissions, make up the structures that form the basis of networks in the contemporary art world. These socioeconomic structures offer the artists an opportunity 'to enact and perpetuate the art world, while at the same time negotiating kinds and levels of cooperation in a mutually understood careerist and competitive context' (Irvine, 2009, online). This interdependent network operates on commercial structures that are centuries old. It shapes artistic choices, often contentiously or unknowingly throughout the stages of production—creation, production, distribution, sale and conservation of artworks. These stages of cultural production support the business organizations whose mission and purpose is to disseminate and distribute art. Individual artists initially produce artworks to be exhibited by small to medium organizations. Typically, these run contemporary art exhibition spaces and offer opportunities to artists through prizes, grants and residencies to build their symbolic capital while also offering limited economic capital to support their work. This patronage may also be covered with in-kind arrangements. When artists become more successful and their works of art are sought after, the major organizations operating at the state and national levels provide the necessary structures to support an artist's career (Fig. 8.1).

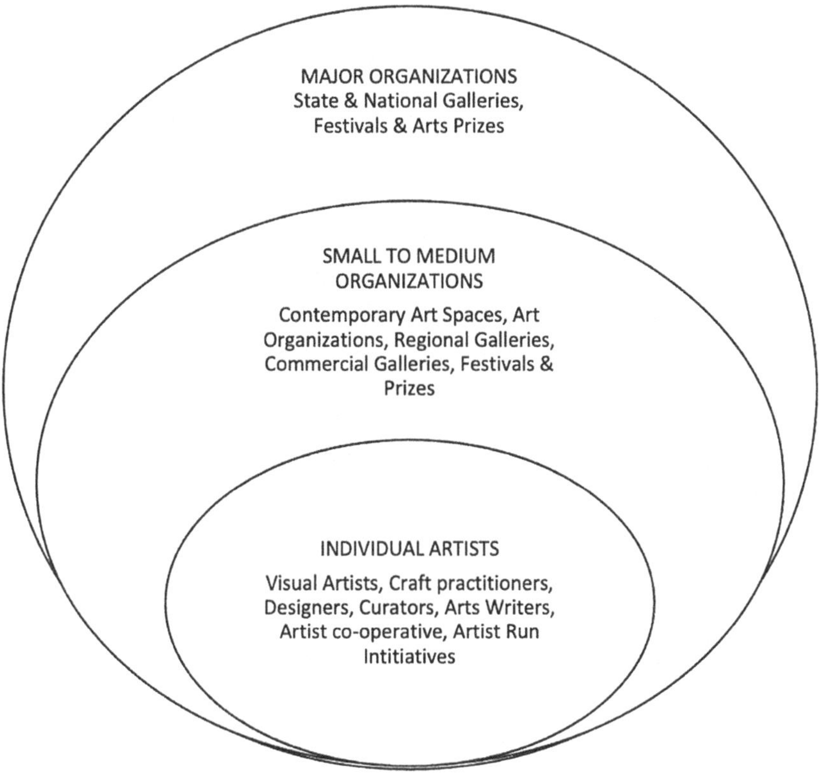

Fig. 8.1 Visual art industry operational structure

These stages of cultural production, briefly set out above, appear to be merging, even collapsing, which means that earning a workable income from art is as challenging as it has ever been. As a result visual artists often build their working life around a "day job" of some sort and many have embraced digital methods to help boost their income streams. As Arora and Vermeylen argue, 'the emergence of countless new interactive sites has added a new layer of infrastructure to the art market' (2013, p. 327).

Business Models: Part of Shared Domain Knowledge for the Visual Arts

Before digital methods existed, artists sought representation through a gallery to exhibit work with a commission paid on sales of 40–50%. Gallerists help manage artists' careers, supporting them through their patronage but also exerting control, usually restricting their freedom to show elsewhere and sharing in any prize money gained. Contemporary artists will often reduce those costs by selling direct to the public through "open studio" events and show in artist-run spaces where costs are proportionally less. Recently rising commission costs have accompanied a declining market with prices of artwork falling as much as 40% since the 1990s. Gaining incomes post-GFC has become very challenging. The structural opportunities where an artist can create sufficient income from their artistic practice continue to be challenging, so a paid income from a "day job" has almost become a necessity for many practicing artists. Typically, this day job is teaching, carried out as private lessons or through high schools or universities.

Traditional business models, patronage and commissions of artworks, have been recently modified by government support and corporate employment. As Raymond Williams (1981) explained in his discussion on patronage, when an artist produced a work for a patron, the work became the possession of the patron, not the artist, who was compensated with a set of living conditions that enabled them to keep working. This situation, however, has become less common. Related to this is a situation where an artist, as an individual professional worker, is placed on a retainer or works on commission. There are also market-based situations such as art fairs and markets, where an artist is remunerated directly by a paying public. Sometimes wealthy individuals subsidize the work and these individual's reputation helps ensure, to a degree, the support and attendance of that paying public. Many arts bodies are funded this way, for example, through Gallery Foundations populated by wealthy individuals or corporates seeking reputational enhancement. A fourth way of gaining revenue is from corporate or private sponsorship. Arts festivals such as the Sydney Biennale depend heavily on corporate sponsorship, while individual artists may be supported informally by patrons who are often art collectors. The fifth is public patronage where revenues are raised from taxation to encourage 'the deliberate maintenance and extension of the arts as a matter of general public policy' (Williams, 1981, p. 43). For Williams, 'certain arts which are not profitable or even viable in market terms are sustained by specific institutions such as foundations, by organizations of subscribers, and still by some private patronage' (1981, p. 55). These artist business models have been affected by digitization, 'causing a shift in the art market from an object based and supply side-oriented market to a more consumer driven market' (Arora & Vermeylen, 2013, p. 328). Digitization, though, has allowed artists to generate more income.

Different artists favor different approaches to their business models. Some maintain control by offering their work for direct sale and become 'dependent on the immediate market' (Arora & Vermeylen, 2013, p.44). Most, however, sell through intermediaries such as a gallery that takes a commission. These intermediaries may become, in effect, an employer. Related to this agent-based model is the artist who sells directly to an intermediary who invests in the work to make a profit. There are also market professionals who depend on the frameworks of copyright in the form of royalty payments and/or to engage in contracted work. In Australia in 2010, a resale royalty scheme started under which artists receive 5% of the sale price when eligible art works are resold commercially for $1000 or more. Payments are distributed by the Copyright Agency but there are issues with the registration of works to keep track of the number of times resale occurs so the royalty payment can be administered (Bradley, i/v Sep 2015). As Arora and Vermeylen argue, while the visual arts sector has been generally slow to adopt digital methods in marketing and production, use of websites and social media has been critical (2013, pp. 322–329). Strikingly, art museums, as they transition in their role from being custodians of cultural heritage to educators, have led the way as technological innovators (Arora & Vermeylen, 2013, pp. 323–324). In general, this gives art consumers more access to basic information relative to artist biographies, the provenance of the works they interact with, data on exhibitions and so on (Arora & Vermeylen, 2013, p. 327).

Operational Methods: Actions of the Interconnected Field

Artists produce their works in their own studios within their homes or in studio spaces hired in collaboratively run warehouses. These options help minimize studio costs, facilitate time to work and also socialize. When artworks are produced with minimal cost, then exhibition in a gallery, with its 40% commission fee, becomes a feasible financial proposition.

Once a work is produced, artists sell their work in art markets, and these are subject to intense competition for discretionary expenditure from the buyers. The operational attributes of a market changes with social and aesthetic trends and technologies. Artisan markets allow artists to set up stalls to sell their work directly to customers but there are also online markets. These are gaining favor with artists establishing websites and online catalogs while social media such as Instagram has become popular to promote works, advertise exhibitions and make sales.

Merchandising also provides artists with an alternative income stream. For example, Hunter artists John Bradley and Natalie Jane Parker sell their artworks and cups, placemats, calendars and jigsaws through a local Art Gallery. This merchandising income stream significantly supplements an artist's income so they can continue to produce original works of art. Galleries and art schools are significant too as, 'the emergence of countless new interactive sites has added a new layer of infrastructure to the art market' (Arora & Vermeylen, 2013, p. 327). There are also digital works of art that are curated and sold in online forums. Non-fungible tokens (NFTs) used as crypto assets have aided the online art market since you can use NFTs to represent ownership in any tangible or intangible asset. As the ATO points out, 'a non-fungible token is not interchangeable in the same way as crypto coins or tokens. NFTs typically record ownership of digital pictures or artworks' (2023, online).

Important Personnel: Choice Making Members of the Field of Visual Arts

The operational methods, business models and structures of the art world situate the artist as a central actor within the art world but the artist can only survive when placed within a distributed creative system that includes institutions, networks and nodes that house other actors such as gallery curators and art collectors. Martin Irvine, in his elucidation of the art market, indicates that this network is comprised of:

> Artists, dealers and galleries, collectors, buyers … auction houses, art consultants and advisors, art investment services and funds … museums and museum professionals, art media … art fairs, biennials … art market services … gallerists, curators, critics, patrons, funding bodies, teachers, auction houses. (2009, online)

Artists are typically seen to produce the work. Art dealers buy and sell works. Gallery owners typically take a portion of income for providing space for artists to exhibit while also prompting those exhibitions. Collectors are principal consumers in the art market. Those who work in auction houses facilitate the buying and selling of artworks to the highest bidder. Art consultants and advisors and art investment services work to ensure that investment funds in particular buy work that will appreciate in value over time. Museums and museum professionals have a vested interest in curating what they believe to be the very best work on offer while art media critics advise audiences of what is valuable in a cultural sense. Funding bodies are populated by arts administrators whose job it is to ensure the sociocultural viability of particular forms of visual art and art teachers, often artists themselves, ensure the domain knowledge, held in the accumulated heritage of the works themselves, is passed on to the next generation. Retailers, too, are important for the art world as these are, like galleries, places where original artworks or reproductions can be purchased.

Hunter Region Visual Arts: Field, Domain and Agency at Work

The Hunter has a long and strong reputation in visual arts. Our interviews reveal that Hunter artists feel valued by their community; they are well qualified, much traveled and innovative in their approach to art as a business. Notable artists long associated with the region include William Dobell and Margaret Olley while contemporary professionals include Archibald Prize and Moran Prize winner Nigel Milsom and Kilgour Prize winner Peter Gardiner. The 593 people who identified as visual artists in the 2011 Census were drawn from occupations such as photographer, illustrator, painter, sculptor, signwriter, potter, ceramic artist, body artist and gallery or museum curator. Leading local artists who are full-time professionals also include Dino Consalvo, Brett McMahon, Pablo Tapia, Aaron Kinnane, Dallas Bray, Rachel Milne, Nicola Hensell, John Turier, Lezlie Tilley, Vera Zulumovski and Jane Landers. Amongst the younger generation are Lottie Consalvo, Jen Denzin, Kelly Barlin and Shan Turner-Carroll. However, and as our interviews also reveal, art is also made by unsung community members who share their work in local exhibitions and markets or as gifts for friends and family. This latter group does not appear in ABS statistics as visual artists, but their participation is vital to the art world in the region as they actively support art classes and purchase equipment and supplies from art supply retailers such as Eckerlsys in Hamilton. They form the great underbelly of the arts community. As one example among many, Wonnarua woman Denise Hedges says: 'I'll be doing art until the day I die … It's not about selling, it's about telling the story' (Emberson, 2015, online).

Early Indigenous art in the Hunter can still be admired at Biami Cave and Mount Yengo with colonial artist Joseph Lycett painting early Newcastle life including the Awabakal and Worimi people. Art has been formally taught here from 1896 and, even during the era of heavy industry and steelmaking, progressive voices saw and argued for a role for culture. Newcastle Art Gallery's collection began in 1945. Artists such as William Dobell, a three-time Archibald Prize winner, emerged from this region (NAG, 2023, online) while Margaret Olley said of the regional capital:

> Newcastle produced a lot of painters. Besides Dobell, John Olsen came from there, Billy Rose, and Jon Molvig. It's a very painterly city. The sea breeze blows all the smoke out west. I just loved it. (Stewart, 2005, p. 381)

Other prominent Australian artists who were born or lived and worked in the region include Matthew Perceval, Mary Beeston, Shay Docking and Michael Bell. Margel Hinder's Captain James Cook Memorial Fountain located in Civic Park in Newcastle is seen as an outstanding example of modernist sculpture. Regional artists also enter hotly contested local, state and national art prizes. Australia's richest and most prestigious portrait prizes—the Archibald and Moran—have both been won by Newcastle artist Nigel Milsom. Two nationally significant prizes are run in the Hunter—the annual Kilgour Prize for figurative and portrait painting and the Muswellbrook Art Prize for works on paper and ceramics. The nationally focused Brett Whiteley Travelling Art Scholarship, won recently by Hunter artist James Drinkwater, provides cash and a three-month Paris residency, while regional artists are helped to travel via the Brenda Clouten Memorial Travelling Scholarship and the Jennie Thomas Travelling Art Scholarships. Hunter artists have also undertaken residencies overseas; Michael Bell undertook an Australia Council–funded residency at the *Cite Internationale des Artes* in Paris in 2011. A local residency scheme is operated by The Lock-Up Cultural Centre. Interviews with Hunter artists illustrate how these forms of patronage are vital to the regional creative (eco)system. Many are prizewinners, understanding the preferences of the field, and all have immersed themselves in the acquisition of domain knowledge, enabling them to pursue their part as active decision making agents in this creative (eco)system.

Hunter Artists: Active Choice Making Agents in the Creative (Eco)System

As a sculptor, painter and furniture designer, Jo O'Toole believes her job is to put art into public spaces, to exhibit in galleries and sell work. Jo has post-graduate qualifications and her studio is located in an industrial workshop that she runs as a business with her furniture maker husband Warwick O'Toole. The workshop houses a number of woodmakers and is fully equipped with woodworking tools and machinery for metalwork. The materials needed for sculpture can be costly and Jo chooses to use mostly timber and recycled materials for her 3-D sculptures. Her income comes from a portfolio career which includes sales of her work, teaching and art prizes. Jo says that winning prizes 'helps immensely … it means you can put that money into buying more expensive materials to do the next sculpture' (O'Toole, i/v Oct 2015). For her, art is unlike other professions in that:

> It's not a conventional business. You don't know your market. You don't know who the people are until they arrive on your doorstep, or you have that conversation or they walk into a gallery and like your work. (O'Toole, i/v Oct 2015)

Textile artist Meredith Woolnough 'draws with a sewing machine' (Woolnough, i/v, Sept 2015) and she approaches her form of cultural production differently to others. She stitches intricate designs often based on natural forms, such as coral or leaves, then washes the fabric away, leaving behind a colorful embroidered three-dimensional piece that is mounted and framed behind glass. Woolnough developed her embroidery technique during her Fine Arts Honors year at university. She draws inspiration from nature and finds scuba diving a great way to discover new designs. While she knows she has been fortunate, she does encounter a certain attitude known to artists everywhere:

> A lot of people undervalue the work of artists ... A lot of creative people don't take themselves seriously or have a hard time doing that, maybe

> because they enjoy it, so taking that step from hobby to professional is a hard thing to do. (Woolnough, i/v, Sept 2015).

While O'Toole and Woolnough work in three dimensions, Rachel Milne is a successful, full-time artist who paints in oils. She describes her style as impressionistic, figurative and painterly. She is inspired by the world she encounters:

> That reality is so beautiful when you really look at it, light on surfaces and the way edges disappear and colors and tones. You get a feel for a scene and desperately want to capture it. (Milne, i/v Sept 2015)

Milne attended the Royal West of England Academy where there was a strong emphasis on the intellectual side of art. Figurative painting was considered highly unfashionable if not irrelevant and Milne eventually became disillusioned. She wanted to paint figuratively, not to intellectualize about her work. After graduating, she went into set painting with a small company called Cod Steaks who subcontracted to Aardman, the animation company that produced *Wallace and Gromit*:

> Set painting is the making of a beautiful thing, and a lot of the sets don't get seen or are destroyed … That type of work was great training for my artistic practice because you don't get time to be precious, you can't be weird about it, you just have to crack on. (Milne, i/v Sept 2015)

When there wasn't much animation work, Cod Steaks created another company The Undetectables, where Milne worked as well, honing her artistic skills:

> The Undetectables disguised mobile phone antenna with fake hollow fiberglass chimney pots. They employed female artists … and we traveled around the country working on building sites, at the top of buildings, at heights, in all weathers painting these chimney pots to look like the original buildings. That was amazing training, it was physically hard and having to color match quickly—that was brilliant. (Milne, i/v Sept 2015)

Milne worked for 15 years in part-time jobs to support her practice. She has been a cleaner, delivered toilets, worked at the Crown Court and run an art gallery. She says 'everything was about facilitating the painting, painting, painting' (Milne, i/v Sept 2015). Milne has exhibited internationally and been successful in portrait prize awards. She describes her approach to the business of art-making: 'I want to paint all the time therefore I have to make money out of it … I have to think like a business' (Milne, i/v Sept 2015).

Peter Lankas is also a painter who brings a business-like approach to his work: 'I have very clear working times in the studio. I clock on and clock off. I am really strict about my work ethic … This is my job even though it is very creative and rewarding' (Lankas, i/v Dec 2014). Lankas grew up in a family of artists and completed undergraduate studies and a Master's degree. After graduation he traveled overseas and, on his return, taught himself the techniques and color theories of the Old Masters. He took ten years off from painting and lived in a Buddhist meditation center before returning to Newcastle. He mounts several solo and group shows a year and teaches painting and drawing. As an established artist, Lankas has seen the art market decline since the 1990s. While his larger works used to sell for $4500, they now sell for $2500. Sales used to provide 50% of his income and teaching 50%. Teaching now provides three quarters of his income. Lankas, however, is positive about Newcastle: 'I have always wondered why working towns, whether it be Glasgow, Newcastle, Wollongong, have this highly concentrated creative drive and people explode with this creative energy and ideas' (Lankas, i/v Dec 2014).

Kerrie Coles agrees. A landscape and portrait painter, Coles moved from Sydney in 1980 and observes that, 'in Sydney the opportunities seem greater and more diverse but I wonder if I would have had the same connections there as I have enjoyed here. Perhaps there are actually more opportunities here' (Coles, i/v Sept 2016). Coles, too, has formal qualifications and has worked as a secondary school teacher and curator and director of the John Paynter Gallery, serving on numerous art committees and boards. Coles has had many works selected for exhibitions and private collections, in Australia and overseas, and has completed commissions for private clients and corporates. Coles believes that, 'artists in

Newcastle are very lucky. The city reveres its artists and there have been some very significant artists working here' (Coles, i/v Sept 2016).

Not all artists who move to the region come to the urban center. John Bradley's 'studio looks out over the rolling hills of the Paterson Allyn Valley near the picturesque village of Vacy' (Bradley, 2023, online). His original paintings can fetch $20,000, he has over 400 images in print, is regularly seen in prestige calendars, has published two books and developed a range of jigsaw puzzles. He is known internationally for his Australian landscapes but also paints railways, seascapes, cityscapes and maritime and military craft. Bradley trained as an aircraft engineer and worked in marketing before becoming an artist full time. He runs two other businesses, one in photographing and printing artwork and another in framing. Bradley has observed a decline in the market, notably the loss of purchasers in the middle band:

> We used to have the bulk of our sales [in the] $2,000 to $5,000 bracket. We're finding now that they're down into the $1,000 to $1,500 and then they jump to the investors. We still sell $10,000 and $20,000 pieces but not a lot. The middle ground is gone ... It's very volatile. (Bradley, i/v Sept 2015)

In response, he diversified his practice with a licensing arrangement with a North American company which operates globally to provide images for merchandise.

Other artists from the Hunter Region who live and work outside the urban center include Tia Gabriellah, Hank Den-Ouden and Charlotte Drake-Brockman. They are among the 57 visual artists listed on the Arts Upper Hunter website (AUH, 2023, online). Also included is David Mahony, a painter who started an art gallery cum café in Sandy Hollow and has work represented across Eurasia. Didier Colstoun from Gresford creates two- and three-dimensional work in a variety of media including wood, metal, bronze, painting and photography. Janice Hanicar from the Upper Hunter is a ceramicist with an interest in painting, printmaking and sculpture. Irene Esteves of Muswellbrook won the Local Ceramic Prize, with her entry featuring 'her distinctive torsos and some particularly beautiful finishes' (Scully, 2008, online). Stuart Dawson was a protégé of the renowned Fred Roberts and Dawson's landscapes reflect this influence. Emily Esteves, who works in earthenware and porcelain, has 'exhibited widely, won many awards, and runs workshops and community art projects' (AUH, 2023, online). Andrew Davis, in Muswellbrook, has an abiding interest in long-term community mural projects. Georgina Mason has completed commissioned work, sold her pieces in galleries and mounted numerous exhibitions. Rene Braeger works in watercolor and has lived at Paterson since 1990. She studied Ceramics at the National Art School, East Sydney and completed a Master of Science (MSc) degree by research into the suitability for use in ceramic glazes of various rock types found in the Hunter Valley (AUH, 2023, online).

Painter Denise Hedges is a Wanaruah woman. Hedges, known as Aunty Denise in her community, has 'sold a lot of art to people from all over the world' (Emberson, 2015, online). Hedges has been associated with the highly successful Wupa Art Prize, which is organized by the Ungooroo Aboriginal Corporation in Singleton:

> The artworks go to seven or eight venues around the Hunter Valley, people can follow the trail around and see different artworks … We like to get some of the young ones so we can mentor and help them. Last year Ungooroo donated canvases and paint to the artists to help them along. (Emberson, 2015, online)

Graham Wilson, another visual artist with diverse skills and income sources, taught art vocationally for 20 years so he could continue his practice. His business, The Carved Greenman, offers stone carving and graphic design, and for some years he had a retail outlet where he sold T-shirts, mugs, prints, posters, cards and small sculptures. Wilson is also an award-winning actor and filmmaker. He has participated in stone carving festivals in Europe and the UK, winning at Trondheim in Norway, where he worked in the workshop at Nidaros Cathedral where there was stone masonry, carpentry, a blacksmith's forge, a stained-glass section and mold-making. Wilson explains that the residency allowed him to continue 'carrying on a noble medieval tradition … The cathedral is 900 years old' (Wilson, i/v June 2015). After leaving teaching, his wife's full-time income became very important. As Wilson asserts 'she makes a living and I augment it' (Wilson, i/v June 2015). As also noted by other artists, making money from visual arts can be difficult: 'The income can be low. But just when I'm thinking "This is hopeless, why am I here, I'm not making money"—I'll have a good week … I keep my head above water' (Wilson, i/v June 2015).

Jono Everett is a furniture designer and fabricator, mainly using timber but also steel, acrylic and other materials. He works on commission, his focus on 'galleries or small museums' (Everett, i/v Sept 2014), but he is concerned about a lack of leadership and vision in the Region:

> I can't get my head around how it's not being seized on by Council and powers that be … there is a real movement of crafted objects, food, fashion, design happening under their feet … we could put Newcastle on the map. (Everett, i/v Sept 2014)

Photographers as Creative Choice Making Agents

Many photographers work successfully in the region with an international following for their work. One is Roger Skinner, an award-winning photographer from Scone. Before taking up photography full-time, Skinner worked for Rio Tinto Coal. He now works on commission, doing weddings and portraits, and believes in photography as art. He has been awarded a number of prizes and has published photographic collections and historical reviews. Photography is Skinner's passion. He asserts that:

> Light is the basis of all life. Photography is described as light writing. Hence it becomes the written language of light. The light-etched image of itself, the new hieroglyphics, the storyteller of now for the future, the history of life. It is good to be an interpreter in that history. (ABC Open, 2017b, online)

Another well-known photographer, Allan Chawner, has exhibited extensively and collaborated with musicians and digital artists to create multi-dimensional presentations. His Kalkadunga Man multimedia work toured nationally and he visited Houston USA to take photographs in the Rothko chapel and produced a projection work for the opening of the Melbourne Recital Centre. He has also provided projection images of ANZAC Cove in Turkey to accompany The Consort of Melbourne and collaborated with composer Andrew Chubb on the *Meditation on Bar Beach*—a digital projection installation at the Newcastle Art Gallery and St Mary's University Gallery, Halifax, Nova Scotia.

Chawner's collaborative vision and interest in the environment is reflected in a project he began in 2008 with environmental ethicist Glenn Albrecht. Together Chawner and Albrecht photographed Hunter Valley mines from a helicopter. As they flew over the Valley, Chawner photographed the landscape, looking at the visual impact of the mines on surrounding farms and built up areas:

> His understanding of, and passion for the land and his intimate and long-established love of the Hunter Valley is apparent. [His] photographs reveal the devastation facing the people of the Hunter. They give visual form to Albrecht's project of solastalgia, aptly describing the sense of loss that might be felt by people affected by the mining industry directly or by its visual impact … the contrast between natural forested areas, cultivated farming land and the sprawling mines could not be greater. The places may still be there, but they have been irreparably changed. They are no longer "home" to the people who have lived on, and cared for, the land that has sustained them for generations. (Chawner, 2017, online)

With a different take on the rural areas of the valley, Katrina Partridge 'specializes in equine, real estate and rural photography' (Partridge, 2017, online) while Robert Watson photographs the city, creating overlays using historic images combined with modern photographs taken from the same spot the older ones were shot, drawn or painted from (ABC Open, 2017a, online).

In 2016, Newcastle photographer Catherine Croll was contacted by a documentary crew from Chinese state television network CCTV 'about her role in the re-creation of China's nationally significant Long March' (Virtue, 2016, online) in 2012 and she 'was allocated the Guizhou province to photograph' (Virtue, 2016, online).

> I was able to explore that area, I was able to take a driver and a translator, and … retrace a part of that Long March … We walked through stone villages with cobbled streets that were 600 years old [and] hadn't changed at all … The Chinese were very keen to document this new Long March that China is undertaking all over the country—marching towards prosperity. (Virtue, 2016, online)

This documentation led to a hardcover book, *China: The New Long March.* Croll was acknowledged for her contribution to the Australia-China relationship through her selection as a finalist in the inaugural Australia-China Achievement Awards (Croll, 2017, online).

Alexander McIntyre is a former musician turned photographer, having seen success as a songwriter, singer and bass player with the award-winning band Supersonic, before spending time as a soloist in Britain. He attended RMIT in Melbourne on his return to Australia and relocated back to Newcastle to run a photography business. McIntyre's business is an example of how the domain of photography has changed from hard copy to primarily digital with social media a key source of income:

> My income comes from small contract work ... My work comes from a referral basis … I do a lot of agency work because it's more of a funnel … These days advertising agencies mainly deal with online content for socials. Probably [only] ten percent of my work is print these days. (McIntyre, i/v Sept 2017)

Balanced against those income modes is his expenditure, which includes the hire of a photographic assistant and expensive equipment. As well as these items specific to his profession, there are the general costs associated with running a business.

> There's [also] a lot of online software and … cloud storage, hard drives. A big part of working in the digital sphere is having traceable backups and having that duplicated, if not in triple ... I'm using about five terabytes per

year just in storage and then every four years those need to be replaced. (McIntyre, i/v Sept 2017)

McIntyre was recently contracted to take stop motion footage of a building site. He installed cameras on light poles overlooking the site and these were controlled remotely through his own server in Melbourne. When he was in South America shooting, he was able to remotely command the cameras in Newcastle and download and Photoshop these images in situ on the Amazon, combining his aesthetic practice with his familiarity with digital technology.

Justin Gilligan is a freelance photojournalist who works to a very high standard. He has an Honors degree in Marine Science and has worked with the Commonwealth and State Fisheries Agencies 'in addition to being contracted to carry out independent research on some of Australia's most remote coral reef locations, such as Lord Howe, Christmas and the Cocos (Keeling) lslands' (Gilligan 2017, online). He specializes in nature and underwater photography. Gilligan has been awarded Australian Geographic Nature Photographer of the Year multiple times, the ANZANG Nature and Landscape Photographer of the Year, Ocean Geographic Picture of the Year, and many more. His images and feature articles have appeared widely in international publications in Asia, Russia, the UK, USA, South Africa and Europe.

Art Galleries: Support Organizations in the Interconnected Field

The regional Councils of the Hunter own and operate major art galleries in Newcastle, Lake Macquarie, Maitland and Muswellbrook. The Newcastle Art Gallery was started in 1945 and has a nationally important collection valued at over $80 million and presents 'a comprehensive overview of Australian art from colonial times to the present day' (NAG, 2017, online). The gallery moved to a purpose-built location in 1977 and is now fronted by Brett Whiteley's sculpture—Black Totem II.

The Maitland Regional Art Gallery was opened in 2009, it is a cultural hub for the city of Maitland and features Australian Art from the 1850s to the present day with a diverse collection that includes historical archives and contemporary sculpture and art. Located further south, Lake Macquarie Gallery mounts fresh, contemporary exhibitions and has an active program of classes and events. To the west, Muswellbrook Gallery has a strong collection based in part on the nationally significant Muswellbrook Art Prize which is acquisitive. Smaller galleries like Watt Space Gallery in Newcastle's CBD, a student gallery, operate in refurbished rooms. The University of Newcastle Gallery is located on the University's Callaghan campus. Its director Gillean Shaw feels that a gallery does more than simply show an artist's work. She argues being a successful artist is not just about creating work; artists must be connected, have a profile and be part of a community and the Gallery is the place where these networks are sustained.

Artists elsewhere in the region are supported by organizations such as Arts Upper Hunter (AUH), which actively supports programs such as the Art Trail Weekend with some 40 sites and exhibitions across the region (AUH, 2023, online). The AUH recently reported a 'strong culture of painting, exhibition and prizes throughout the region; textile art … [and] artists making ceramics, sculpture, jewelry, photography and furniture; [with] art societies/groups in each LGA' (RANSW, 2023, online).

Many Hunter artists work in other spheres to support their passion, such as retail or art galleries, and others reduce business costs by sharing studios, equipment or expertise. Teaching provides an important supplementary income for many, although, particularly in the University and TAFE sector, employment has been casualized and job opportunities are diminishing. Some artists, especially those with a craft or design focus, sell their work at markets. Merchandising is also an option. Michael Bell, for example, has designed for Mambo clothing and Trevor Dickinson for Fred Bare and Disney while James Drinkwater's prints are for sale through the Fairfax online marketplace. Graham Wilson's artwork features on T-shirts, mugs, posters, cards and prints and Liz Anelli and Trevor Dickinson sell work in various locations including the National Library while poet Richard Tipping's text-based artwork sells nationally. His visual art can be found in The Museum of Modern Art in New York with over 20,000 sales to date.

Collaborative Workspaces

Newcastle Community Art Centre (NCAC) has been operating for over 30 years to support artists, primarily by providing affordable studio spaces. NCAC artists include The Strutt Sisters, Rachel Milne, Peter Lankas and Meredith Woolnough. Woolnough says of the NCAC:

> It's basically a huge building full of artists and it's a heavily subsidized rent so that artists can afford to have a professional space that we can work in. And I got a studio space here about two years ago, beginning of last year, and it was a really big step for me and a really positive step for my business and my practice to have that professional space. The Community Art Centre has many other functions; it's got a gallery attached to it and it's got rooms that people can hire out to teach workshops and run events, there's a theater downstairs, so it's got all sorts of things going on in the broader art community, but it's also a community of artists within itself. (Woolnough, i/v Sept 2015)

Renew Newcastle offered similar workspaces for artists in unused city buildings for very low rent from 2009 till 2019. Renew tenants, typically artists, were operating under a 30-day license, renewable if the building owner agreed. This grass roots organization was a driver of cultural participation and urban renewal in Newcastle, activating abandoned shop fronts and streetscapes by providing artists, photographers and makers with studios, exhibition spaces and retail outlets.

The Creative Incubator is run by sculptor Braddon Snape. It was established in early 2017 and is located in a busy warehouse facility in Hamilton North, Newcastle. The space has been configured to accommodate a number of individual artists (including Graham Wilson) as well as a gallery for exhibitions.

Summary

The visual arts sector in the Hunter is extremely well populated with professionals and amateurs existing side by side. Those who work in this creative industry encompass two and three dimensional and digital artists along with those who service the industry, write about it, teach it or manage it. Photographers in the region range from freelance commercial operators who do advertising and design work to those who see themselves as artists.

The 593 people who identified as visual artists in the 2011 Census were primarily drawn from occupations such as photographer, illustrator, painter, sculptor, sign writer, potter or ceramic artist, body artist and gallery or museum curator. Some professional artists exhibit internationally as well as nationally and some find success in highly contested regional and national art prizes. They also secure scholarships. In other words, they have learnt the requirements of the field.

These regional artists tend to be well qualified, much traveled and innovative in their approach to art as a business. Many earned an income in all five income areas noted by Williams (1981), though it was typical that many of these artists had to diversify to earn an income from their creations. This diversification predominantly included teaching. Many of them understand the benefits of and work with digitization, including using it for distribution and marketing via websites and social media to reach their audiences.

While this creative (eco)system has changed in the last 30 years—less income, a drop in prices, and a change in the distribution model—those in the field have had to adapt their practices. In the Hunter, teaching provides an important supplementary income for many artists but employment, particularly in the University and TAFE sectors, has been casualized and opportunities for employment are diminishing. Capital city galleries have provided access to a larger, more lucrative market for the fortunate few from the region who exhibit there. A few artists have developed portfolios through designing for clothing companies and some have seen their prints sell well through retail outlets and online marketplaces. Others have developed merchandise. Still others depend on day jobs or partners to support their work. Regardless, the visual arts sector in the Hunter remains strong in practice for both professionals and amateurs.

In total we can say that this chapter has set out the deep history of visual arts on the Australian continent linking the Indigenous use of visually symbolic forms to the later arrival of the European tradition. It sets out the structure of the field of visual arts, its interconnected networks and the way artists, choice making agents within the system, and the rest of the field, including the multitude of amateurs and semi-professional, gain incomes, as well as who these members of the field are and how they go about doing what they do. Then it homes in on the Hunter Region looking at specific creative choice making agents, concentrating on artists and photographers as they interact within the interconnected networks of the field and immerse themselves into the shared knowledge of the domain of this complex creative (eco)system. Notably, the chapter delineated the role of support organizations in the field of visual arts in this region before looking at the collaborative workspaces that have sprung up as artists of all kinds try to curb costs while diversifying their activities to earn an income from their creative works as they negotiate their way through this creative (eco)system.

References

ABC Open. (2017a). *Images of Newcastle now and then.* 1233 ABC. Retrieved March 5, 2023, from http://www.abc.net.au/local/stories/2012/07/09/3541929.htm

ABC Open. (2017b). *Roger Skinner.* ABC Open. Retrieved September 19, 2017, from https://open.abc.net.au/people/14002

AGNSW. (2018). *Art sets. The photograph and Australia: Timeline.* Art Gallery of New South Wales. Retrieved March 5, 2023, from https://www.artgallery.nsw.gov.au/artsets/51b88k

Allen, C. (1997). *Art in Australia: From colonization to postmodernism.* Thames and Hudson.

Anderson, J. (Ed.). (2011). *The Cambridge companion to Australian art.* Cambridge University Press.

Arora, P., & Vermeylen, F. (2013). Art markets. In R. Towse & C. Handke (Eds.), *Handbook on the digital creative economy* (pp. 322–329). Edward Elgar.

ATO. (2023). *Non-fungible tokens.* Australian Taxation Office. Retrieved March 16, 2023, from https://www.ato.gov.au/individuals/investments-and-assets/crypto-asset-investments/transactions%2D%2D-acquiring-and-disposing-of-crypto-assets/non-fungible-tokens/

AUH. (2023). *Arts Upper Hunter.* Retrieved March 5, 2023, from https://artsupperhunter.com

Bourdieu, P. (1996). *The rules of art: Genesis and structure of the literary field.* Polity Press.

Bradley, J. (2023). *About.* John Bradley Fine Art. Retrieved March 16, 2023, from https://johnbradleyart.com/about-john-bradley/

Chawner, A. (2017). *Allan Chawner.* Retrieved September 9, 2017, from http://www.chawner.com.au/Allan_Chawner/Introduction.html

Croll, C. (2017). *Music photography.* Catherine Croll. Retrieved March 5, 2023, from https://catherinecroll.com/music-photography/

Emberson, J. (2015). *Meet the mob: Aunty Denise Hedges.* 1233 ABC. Retrieved March 5, 2023, from http://www.abc.net.au/local/audio/2015/02/16/4180843.htm

Gilligan, J. (2017). *Justin Gillian nature and conservation photography.* Retrieved March 5, 2023, from https://justingilligan.wordpress.com/about/

Grishin, S. (2013). *Australian art: A history.* Miegunyah Press.

Hughes, R. (1970). *The art of Australia.* Penguin.

Irvine, M. (2009). *The art market: The structure of the industry and economic network.* Georgetown University. Retrieved March 5, 2023, from http://faculty.georgetown.edu/irvinem/visualarts/ArtMarket/ArtMarketStructure.html

McLean, I. (2016). *Rattling spears: A history of indigenous Australian art.* Reaktion Books.

NAG. (2017). *Introduction.* Newcastle Art Gallery. Retrieved March 5, 2023, from http://nag.org.au/Collection/Introduction

Partridge, K. (2017). *About.* Katrine Partridge Photography. Retrieved March 5, 2023, from https://www.katrinapartridgephotography.com/about

RANSW. (2023). *Arts Upper Hunter.* Regional Arts NSW. Retrieved March 5, 2023, from http://regionalartsnsw.com.au/networks/arts-upper-hunter/

Sayers, A. (2001). *Australian art.* Oxford University Press.

Scully, A. (2008). *Photography prize winner confounds and challenges Muswellbrook art lovers.* ABC Upper Hunter. Retrieved March 5, 2023, from http://www.abc.net.au/local/stories/2008/10/13/2389317.htm

Smith, B. (1979). *Place, taste and tradition: A study of Australian art since 1788* (2nd ed.). Oxford University Press.

Stewart, M. (2005). *Margaret Olley: Far from a still life*. Random House.
Virtue, R. (2016). *Newcastle photographer to feature in Chinese documentary*. 1233 ABC. Retrieved March 5, 2023, from http://www.abc.net.au/news/2016-05-25/newcastle-photographer-to-feature-in-chinesedocumentary/7444672.
Williams, R. (1981). *Culture*. Fontana.

9

Fashion

Introduction

The fashion industry is associated with textiles, clothing and footwear (TCF). Alongside music and perhaps film, the fashion sector is a participant in global trends feeding massive related industry outputs in media and entertainment. Its connection to both "essential" expenditure (clothing) and discretionary choices (as in "type" of clothing and a desire for novelty) ensures repeat and ongoing consumption of its outputs. At the same time, while generating activity, this profile engenders volatility and global competition that impacts on all stages of the creation, manufacture, distribution and marketing of fashion items. For regional practitioners, these sometimes-competing characteristics of the industry call for skilled, responsive business practices. Fashion, as a way of embellishing life, has a long history in this country.

P. McIntyre et al., *Creativity and Creative Industries in Regional Australia*, Palgrave Studies in Creativity and Culture, https://doi.org/10.1007/978-3-031-45972-6_9

A Brief History of Fashion in Australia: A Tradition of Innovation

While the Indigenous possum-skin cloaks were a prevalent mode of adornment for thousands of years in certain regions of the Australian continent, fashion itself was a European concept that arrived when European colonizers took over the country. However, the mode of attire for convicts and colonial soldiers alike was not of their choosing. A little later, early Australian dressmakers and tailors adapted European fashions to the class system and climate and it is documented that lightweight silk coats were being worn in summer along with a trend for sunhats (Penberthy, 2012, online).

The Industrial age in England and the mass production of clothes that resulted made these items of clothing affordable and, together with the Australian Gold Rush, allowed the average laborer to purchase the latest garments (MacDowall, 2016, online). During this period 'as reproducible photos became more common, ladies would retire to their living room to flick through [their] 19th century photo albums and see Queen Victoria' (Riley quoted in Penberthy, 2012, online) who was a source of certain modes of dressing. Styling and fashion trends were beginning to be communicated through images and many sought new fashions at Australian department stores (NGV, 2015, online). One of Australia's largest department stores, Myer's, was established in 1900 and began 'catering to stylish men and women who wanted to not only reflect the spirit of their age, but also its human element with fashion seen as a by-product of our independence and impertinence' (MacDowall, 2016, online). The 1950s saw a golden age of department store shopping and the "Paris end" of Collins Street in Melbourne, established in the late 1800s, boasted high-end boutiques such as La Petite, Hall Ludlow, Beril Jents and La Louvre, which is still in business today in South Yarra (MacDowall, 2016, online).

The color and experimentation of the 1960s became a significant part of the fashion scene and mini-dresses designed by Prue Acton helped her become the first female Australian designer to show in New York (NGV, 2015, online). In the 1970s, Jenny Kee's Flamingo Park boutique was established to sell the designer's 'landmark range of Australiana-inspired garments' (NGV, 2015, online) and, in 1983, the Fashion Design Council (FDC) was established 'to nurture independent Australian fashion design' (NGV, 2015, online). As Riley wrote in *From the Bush to the street: A change in direction for Australian fashion* (1997, pp. 43–45), the lead up to Australia's 1988 Bicentennial produced 'a cacophony of Australian themes being explored by local designers in an attempt to translate our culture and lifestyle into a distinctive look' (Riley, 1997, p. 44). Up to this point, Australian designers had little to draw on when it came to fabric choice. They had to make do and 'some experimented with the production of their own materials as a reaction against their isolation from the huge overseas textile markets' (Riley, 1997, p. 44).

At this time, Australian fashion lagged behind the global fashion centers of Paris, London and New York and this played into what became known as "the cultural cringe" as many Australians 'seemed to prefer international labels to local designs' (Riley, 1997, p. 44). This perception began to change during the 1990s with many Australian designers perceived to be at 'the cutting edge of international fashion design' (Riley, 1997, p. 44). In 1995, Collette Dinnigan was the first Australian designer invited to present a groundbreaking runway show at Paris Fashion Week (NGV, 2015 online).

Surfwear and swimsuit designers such as Speedo swimsuits, Mambo, Hot Tuna and Rip Curl rose to become prominent international global brands. The media started promoting local brands to Australians and, at the same time, 'Australian fashion was ready to launch itself, wholesale, into the world arena' (Riley, 1997, pp. 44–45). In May 1996, Mercedes-Benz Australian Fashion Week was launched, and 'officially put Sydney on the international fashion map as a developing fashion center' (1997, p. 45). But this exuberance and the claims attached to it, may have been premature.

The introduction of trade liberalization measures in the early 1990s affected Australian fashion brands and wholesale manufacturers like Pacific Brands, who made the iconic Bonds, Berlei and Stubbies garments, could no longer afford to manufacture in Australia. They had employed thousands at various sites around Australia but, in 2009, relocated most of the manufacturing to Asia to take advantage of lower labor costs. China, Vietnam and Bangladesh began to dominate the mass clothing market and products were sold in huge quantities through retail outlets such as Target, KMart, and department stores Myer and David Jones.

Despite the shrinking size of the local industry, Australian fashion designers are still acclaimed. Ellery, Toni Maticevski, Romance Was Born, Scanlan and Theodore, Zimmerman and Dion Lee, for example, have achieved international success, often after making appearances at Australian Fashion Week. However, the small size of the local market means that local fashion labels are unable to take advantage of profitable economies of scale. Local fashion designers encounter difficulties with distribution and transport across both domestic and international markets, not least because of the seasonal mismatch of the southern with the northern hemisphere. The ethical clothing movement also began to emerge, based on concerns about poor worker safety and unfavorable labor conditions in some countries that were mass-producing garments for the Australian market. There has been an associated move towards more sustainable manufacturing, with smaller, bespoke companies gaining more market share.

Despite or possibly because of these circumstances, the first major survey of Australian fashion opened at the National Gallery of Victoria in March 2016 (NGV, 2015, online). This exhibition presented over '120 works from over 90 designers and celebrated Australia's unique voice in the fashion industry' (NGV, 2015, online). In 2021, Australia's Fashion Council reported that the Fashion and Textile industry is a vibrant part of Australia's creative economy which is diverse and globally connected. They determined that Australia's fashion industry contributes $27.2 billion to the economy and has more than 489,000 workers, 77% of which are women (Australian Fashion Council, 2021, p.4).

Structure of the Fashion Industry: The Organization of the Interconnected Field

Global fashion industries are made up of a complex ecosystem of interlinked industries. As a loosely coupled system of production these include design, manufacturing, retailing and educational activities. It's important to note that the fashion ecosystem is much broader than designer labels. The Australian fashion industry 'is heavily interlinked with the broader economy, including with wool and cotton production, tourism and creative professional services' (Australian Fashion Council, 2021, p. 5). As well as being a contributor to the creative industries, fashion is also part of the diverse textiles, clothing and footwear (TCF) industry which includes raw materials processing through to the production, sale and promotion of final goods (Fig. 9.1).

Manufacturing, distribution, wholesale and fashion retail companies are important parts of the fashion industries' value chain. Retail outlets include large department stores, specialty stores and specialty retailers of private label apparel who may also be manufacturers. Digital distribution and online retailing is an increasingly important arm of this sector with social media used as a promotion model. Factory outlets, both online and at physical locations, give manufacturers and stockists the opportunity to sell directly to the public. Periphery industries such as modeling agencies and event companies are also important as is the fashion media, press and blogs. And to take this process further, finance, marketing and PR, including events such as Australian Fashion Week, are crucial elements in the structure of the industry with educational and training institutions acting as complementary auxiliaries.

The structure of the industry is deeply rooted in what has been called a 'linear, cradle-to-grave, or take/make/waste manufacturing system' that 'encourages a throwaway culture' (Piller, 2023, p. 289). Calls for a sustainable circular model are increasing and one such model is consumers buying and selling pre-loved clothes. In an increasingly sustainability-aware environment, on-selling used clothes has become another key element of the structure of the fashion industry with apps, websites, markets and special events facilitating the increasing sale of pre-loved clothes.

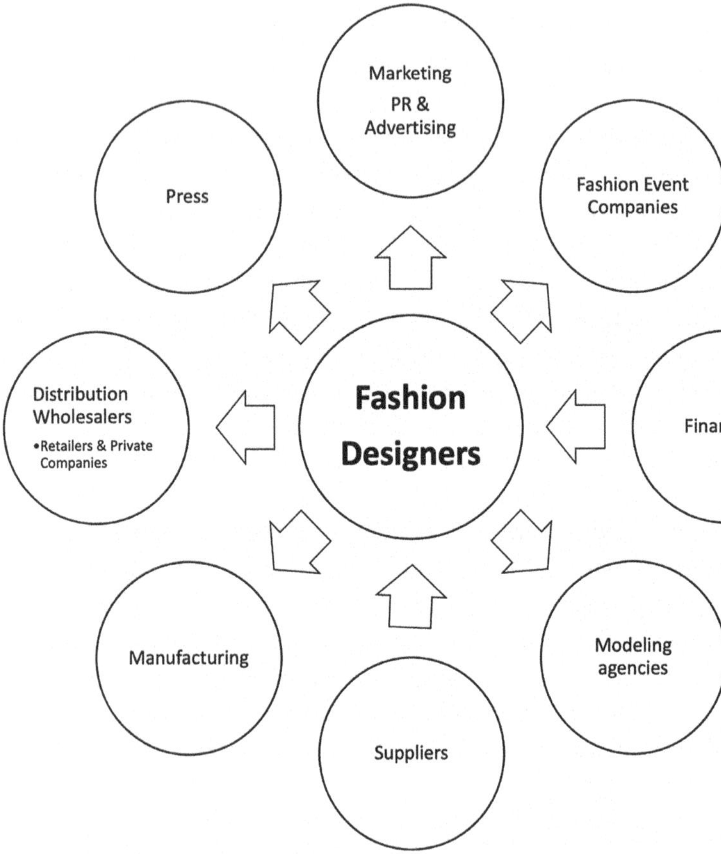

Fig. 9.1 Structure of the fashion industry

On the periphery of the core business of fashion is publishing, a crucial part of the field of fashion, which includes magazines such as *Vogue, Marie Claire* and *Elle*, all part of a large, international publishing empire, and general women's magazines, which typically include a fashion section, aimed at their particular audience. "Home-grown" publications such as *Frankie* and *Façon* are rare but survive through advertising or subscription revenue. Major newspapers also feature Australian fashion, especially in the weekend color magazines, to attract readers that can then be on-sold to advertisers in the form of aggregated readerships.

Business Models: Important Domain Knowledge of How the Field Gains Revenue

Most revenue in the fashion industry is derived from the sale of products or from the services associated with it.

Designers make money from engaging with members of the field by leveraging their reputation, their symbolic capital, to deliver a service to their clients. Costs for designers may include the expense of putting together collections to show. They will employ seamstresses, select and buy fabric, and organize photoshoots where they will need to hire models from agencies, photographers, stylists, makeup artists, hairstylists and so forth. They will also need to "wine and dine" buyers from the retail arm of the industry, all of which must be included as part of any business plan. They may also have infrastructure costs associated with the premises they work out of. Returns come in the form of commissions and contracts for collections and from direct sales if they also maintain a retail outlet.

Product sales form the basis of most revenue for manufacturing and retail within the industry. Suppliers sell the basic material and these, as well as production expenses, are baseline costs for manufacturers. They on-sell to wholesalers. Wholesalers will mark up the price of goods from the manufacturers and then on-sell the goods to retailers for a mark-up usually of 50%. Some companies import clothing from overseas for distribution and sales nationally.

Retailers will take the price from the wholesaler and nominally mark it up at a 50% rate (i.e. 33.3% of retail price) but often at three times the wholesale cost. The sale of accessories, perfumes and cosmetics is possibly the most lucrative source of revenue for the industry as often these are relatively cheap to make or purchase but, if branded well, the markup can be very profitable.

Selling products online is increasing in importance with Australian "bricks and mortar" stores moving into the online space. Some businesses, including outlets such as Vine Apparel and ASOS, are fully online. International retailer ETSY provides a global online marketplace for artisan and craft-based designers and makers (ETSY, 2017, online).

Operational Methods of the Field

Fashion designers generally work as part of a fashion business that also manufactures clothing. Most fashion manufacturing businesses are small but it is rare for fashion businesses not to have the backing of an investor or family support. Manufacturers produce clothing in local factories, in home-based businesses, through out-sourcing (sometimes to home-based operatives working on contract or on hourly rates), and increasingly off-shore, to take advantage of lower labor costs. Sourcing materials, pattern-making, grading for sizing, cutting, assembly, sewing and finishing are the key steps in the manufacturing process. Some fashion designers are freelance, selling designs to companies for manufacturing on a commission or contrast basis. Most designers are also manufacturers who have their own factories but many choose to outsource manufacturing for cost reasons.

The services sector of the fashion industry includes styling, consultancy and design. Designers deliver their service to clients or as employees of larger fashion houses. Another service is styling, a growing area serving television, fashion magazines, advertising and promotions. Big retailers and shopping center owners such as Westfield are increasingly engaging stylists to promote their fashion ranges, sometimes by providing a personal styling service for customers (Fig. 9.2).

Marketing and distribution vary according to the size of the business and its place in the market. While mass-produced clothing is distributed by wholesalers to major retail stores, couture may be displayed at fashion shows such as Australian Fashion Week and in fashion magazines as well as individually to retail buyers. Sales are conducted by retail assistants working in various retail outlets ranging from national department stores, to small designer stores to markets, with online retail increasing its market share.

Some who work in the fashion industry have trained at private or public fashion colleges, while some are self-taught or have learned on the job. These forms of domain acquisition may also accompany internships which are an increasingly common way of developing knowledge and skills as well as networks in the field. In terms of formal training, TAFE

Fig. 9.2 Fashion supply chain

colleges in the larger centers offer fee-based courses in fashion design, fashion business and clothing manufacture. A limited number of colleges and individual designers offer training in fashion design, fashion business and/or clothing manufacture.

Important Personnel in the Field: Choice Making Agents

While personnel in the fashion industry do not constitute the whole field of fashion they are, nonetheless, considerably important. They include designers, manufacturers, wholesalers, buyers, retailers, stylists, models and consultants. Other field members are fashion bloggers, magazine and newspaper publishers and journalists, teachers in fashion colleges, and the operators of design and craft markets. In Australia, 77% of the fashion and textiles roles are held by women, and this is consistent 'across the value chain, especially in sectors like retail, media and design' (Australian Fashion Council, 2021, p. 15). According to *Fashion Journal,* a range of expanding roles has made its way into fashion including trend forecaster, customer relationship manager, fabric researcher, sustainability officer, authenticity expert (for the pre-loved market) and fashion psychologist. Interestingly, and to demonstrate how a creative industry sector such as IT can affect all other sectors, data analysts are in high demand: 'A data analyst stays on top of trends and consumer behavior. This is done by collecting and analyzing all visitor data from the brand's channels (Instagram, Facebook, websites, and so on)' (Bammant, 2023, online).

The Fashion Sector of the Creative Industries in the Hunter Region: The Field at Work

The textile, clothing and footwear industry in the Hunter Region has been dynamic and diverse, ranging from design to the manufacture of clothing and sports, leisure and workwear. Despite many changes, the Valley still has a significant retail sector and a small but thriving design and styling sector. Locally, the industry began to decline in the 1970s, accelerated by the adoption of neoliberal policy by the federal government, including a move toward trade liberalization measures in the 1990s. These changes in policy resulted in significant job losses from import competition. Coupling these with technological change and shifting household expenditure, Hunter fashion manufacturing largely ceased in 2010 with the departure of Pacific Brands. However, smaller-scale design and production for the consumer market remains and is driven by quality design, innovative practices and solid work standards. Surfwear designed and made by Fashion Fish Design is a good example of this move. Currently, the industry operates in an increasingly digital and global marketplace which has led to a diversification of services and, in some cases, a plethora of income streams. While education and training in fashion has diminished at an institutional level, it is notable that there are designers in the area who hold master classes to teach the domain of fashion. As also noted in the publishing chapter, there are successful specialist fashion magazines operating in the Hunter.

Design and Manufacturing in the Hunter

Apparel manufacturers have operated in the Hunter Region for some time and have a long history. From 1893 the Mutual Help Society was founded in Newcastle to clothe destitute women and children (Harrison, 2006) and that eventually became Rundles Tailoring, founded in 1908. Rundles is now a manufacturing, retailing and hiring business specializing in men's clothing. Rundle's name is so well known locally they can market by reputation alone. They are located in Newcastle West and are the region's premier tailors and one of the few remaining large-scale mainstream clothing firms. Despite a downturn in the sector, there are still examples of other manufacturing businesses willing to find a niche and carry on. For instance, Wax Converters Textiles manufactures weatherproof textiles for the architecture, leisure and defense sectors. Other products reflecting the region's agricultural base are made by Airds of Lochinvar and Mortels Sheepskin Factory. There are also, though, designers that manufacture in the high-end women's market including Jean Bas and High Tea with Mrs Woo.

High Tea with Mrs Woo is a fashion label known for its originality and quality. Owned and operated by sisters Rowena, Angela and Juliana Foong, whose family migrated from Malaysia in 1988, the label has stopped manufacturing overseas because of quality, sustainability and lifestyle concerns. Their garments are designed and manufactured from a suburban studio factory in Islington, an inner-city area of Newcastle. They all collaborate on the designs and share the retail side too, but each brings specific strengths to the business. Juliana is the retail manager and does the pattern-making, Angela manages the legals and finances and Rowena does the marketing, websites and graphics for their corporate identity (Rowena & Angela Foong, i/v March 2016).

The Foong sisters business model is focused on sustainable small scale manufacturing, which is both ethical and a lifestyle choice. The choice to operate fully within Australia and sell their fashions online, with some international sales, was shaped through experience. Their business was globally successful; at its peak, High Tea with Mrs Woo had a retail outlet in Treviso, Italy and two shops in Sydney, employing ten staff with a turnover of $700,000 pa and supplying garments to 35 retailers. Their success began at the 2005 Sydney Fashion Week and ended with the GFC, which crippled them financially, with the high rents forcing them to close their doors (Rowena & Angela Foong, i/v March 2016). Their turnover in 2016 was less than half what it was at their peak. Now their aim is to pay themselves, their staff and put aside a bit of money (Rowena & Angela Foong, i/v March 2016). The GFC experience led them to be committed to a sustainable operation:

> Most of our colleagues have gone offshore to produce their work and we are one of a few to insist on staying here. That means to us a lifestyle choice and it's also a sustainability choice because we don't want to go and spend three quarters of the year or whatever managing production overseas … We are not interested in spending half our life in China chasing issues ... when you produce overseas, the minimum quantities are high. That means you are producing more than you actually need and all of that excess ends up going on sale … and anything that doesn't get sold gets dumped. We don't want to be part of that process. (Rowena & Angela Foong i/v March 2016)

They source high quality cotton, linen and merino wool on-shore and when large orders come in they turn to Sydney-based manufacturers (Green, 2013, online).

Another boutique operator, Jean Bas, has been a high-end fashion house in Darby Street, Newcastle for over 40 years. The company designed and manufactured corporate uniforms until intellectual property rights became an issue for them with their design being used without recompense. While there is protection for sketches, "utilitarian" three-dimensional products are not protected (Coffey, i/v Jan 2015). At that time the company, owned by Jean Bas and Kevin Coffey, was on the verge of relocating to Sydney. However, they took a risk and set up a shopfront in busy, fashionable Darby Street in Newcastle. This allowed the business to change focus and switch to "couture" bespoke fashion designs. Kevin Coffey suggests that a regional city like Newcastle refreshes the creative drive and he also recognizes the appeal of regional areas for creative people where it is possible to be globally connected as well as allowing them to congregate together in a local and mutually beneficial community

(Coffey, i/v Jan 2015). The retail outlet he and Jean Bas built also accommodated the designing and manufacturing arms of the business and, in 2018, the shop opened by appointment only. The made-to-measure garments they produce have top-end prices unmatched in the city and are necessary because of the high costs of their business, including the rates they pay to the highly experienced seamstress who works on-site (Coffey, i/v Jan 2015).

Another example of a small, local designer/manufacturer with a flexible, innovative business model is Gina Ermer whose business is Fringe Dweller. Ermer hand-dyes silk and linen fabrics for small-run clothing ranges and makes the patterns, but outsources the cutting and sewing. For a time she rented space within Jean Bas' shop in Darby Street, where a collaborative "style collective" operated, but in 2017 opened her own shop in Wolfe Street, Newcastle. Like many successful local fashion businesses, Fringe Dweller demonstrates a high level of both vertical and horizontal business integration and this, Ermer asserts, ensures she has complete creative control of her business (Ermer, i/v May 2017).

Jewelry and accessories manufacturing bridges the gap between visual art and fashion and is strong in the Hunter Region. A highly successful example of this is Studio Melt, a jewelry design studio owned and managed by Ange Hailey and her business partner Suzy Manning. Both are jewelry designers. Studio Melt emerged from the Renew Newcastle project, and sells studio-made work, mostly local, and conducts jewelry-making classes, and their focus is always on "the makers".

There were also a number of small fashion design/manufacturing start-ups including accessories and millinery businesses that operated from The Emporium in Newcastle, a Renew Newcastle initiative that closed in 2017 to make way for commercial redevelopments.

The Retail Arm of the Fashion Industry: How the Field Funds Itself

In 2016, there were at least 207 clothing retail outlets and approximately 118 fashion accessory outlets in Newcastle and Lake Macquarie Local Government Areas (Local Search, 2017/18, pp. 116 & 181–183). There are many more outlets in each of the major towns and centers across the Hunter Region. Fashion retailing in the region is dominated by the national chains Myer and David Jones who do not stock local designers, (although the Jean Bas label was sold in David Jones' Sydney store for some time). Malls such as Charlestown Square, Westfield at Kotara, High Street Mall in Maitland and Stockland at Green Hills are the principal centers of fashion retailing in the valley. They house outlets for national brands such as Sussan, Jeans West, Cotton On and Sportsgirl while international brands Zara and H&M established themselves around five years ago. There are smaller boutique fashion outlets in Maitland, Morpeth, Port Stephens, Shoal Bay, Muswellbrook and Scone. There are also some smaller companies in the region that provide repairs and alterations.

Several fashion retailers have found their place in a market which increasingly values the small, bespoke and personal. As previously mentioned, Darby Street in Newcastle is where Jean Bas is located and so was High Tea with Mrs Woo, although after COVID-19, High Tea with Mrs Woo joined their retail business with Studio Melt on Newcastle's Hunter Street. High Tea with Mrs Woo does retail online to both domestic and international customers in Europe and the USA, representing approximately 5% of their business. This is a growing part of their business even though they are very committed to customers coming into the shop to feel the fabrics and wear the clothes (Rowena & Angela Foong, i/v March 2016). Hunter fashion and jewelry is also sold at local weekend markets such as Olive Tree and Hunt and Gather, interstate art and design markets, and online. There are many other boutique operations dotted throughout all the major centers and suburbs in the region.

The purposeful use of social media, active websites and blogs typify the specialty retail enterprises that use it to build loyalty and a personal brand story. Jean Bas Studio, High Tea with Mrs Woo and Guanabana are examples of businesses that actively engage online and loyalty building and personal connections are enabled through the use of websites and blogs, Facebook, Pinterest, Tumblr and Instagram. The growing interest in narrow-band fashion is also driven by social media with companies such as MisKonduct Clothing and House of Androgyny communicating this way. These techniques have enabled growth in the small design and manufacturing start-ups emerging through collaborative spaces and those who retail through weekend markets or online.

Fashion Styling: Creating a "Look"

Fashion styling's main proponent in the region is Lara Lupish, an entrepreneur who has worked internationally, dressing many noteworthy people. She suggests it's a tough and competitive business and has worked in many areas in fashion: covering fashion editing in-house for magazines, freelance magazine work, red carpet events, TV, and costume design for film and music videos.

Soon after graduating from the University of Newcastle, Lupish moved overseas to Vancouver where she says she 'got thrown into the creative industries there' (Lupish, i/v Oct 2016). Lupish moved on to successfully forge 'an international career as a celebrity stylist, dressing some of the most beautiful and noteworthy people in the world' (Façon, 2017, online). She worked on music videos and as a wardrobe stylist for the film industry and eventually became a costume designer and worked with stars like Naomi Watts, Sir Ian McKellen, Laura Dern and Mark Ruffalo (Lupish, 2011, online). In 2009, Lupish returned to Australia and began to do more fashion styling with celebrities. She has worked with Danni Minogue, Delta Goodrem, Megan Gale, Jennifer Hawkins, Heath Ledger, Mel B and many others (Façon, 2017, online). In 2013, she returned to Newcastle and set up her agency Façon Creative.

In 2015, Lupish founded the glossy fashion magazine *Façon* which eventually switched to digital editions and in 2022 became freely available online (Façon, 2023, online). The Façon business is described as a collaboration of creative people producing world-class advertising imagery and a high-end fashion publication in Newcastle. Lupish recognizes that while Sydney has the status, Newcastle is more livable:

> I think still big cities dominate. Absolutely. I'm saying it loud and proud because there are a lot of Sydneysiders I work with who are struggling with the cost of Sydney and what it is to live there. I like to boast now that I have a nice home in Newcastle and we go to the beach after school and it's affordable, all that kind of stuff. Now I'm proud of it. But I have to admit that there are a lot of times I am doing business in Newcastle that I'm reminded of why I left and it happens every week. (Lupish, i/v Oct 2016)

Acquiring Domain Knowledge: Fashion Training in the Region

Hunter TAFE College offers a range of national accredited courses in fashion design, fashion business and clothing manufacture from Certificate to Advanced Diploma level. Students gain a solid grounding and employment outcomes are strong with a number of graduates establishing their own businesses, gaining positions with fashion companies in the capital cities, or finding work in related roles such as Head of Wardrobe for television programs.

In the private sector, short courses are offered by some designers including Jean Bas who conducts Master Classes in design and tailoring in her workroom. Gina Ermer now teaches from her home studio, although she previously operated from her studio at Newcastle Community Arts Centre.

Summary

By way of concluding, we stress that fashion designers and manufacturers have operated in the Hunter Region for a long time, although only 38 people remained employed full time in the sector in 2011. While large-scale manufacturing of textiles and garments has ceased, niche businesses serve high-fashion, bridal, sports and leisure, dance and workwear, footwear and jewelry. The services sector includes design, styling, tailoring, alterations and consultancy. There is a small international market for Hunter-manufactured goods, and fabrics and trim are often imported. Increasingly, aspects of manufacture (for example, cutting and sewing) are outsourced either locally or offshore. Most revenue in this sector is derived from the product sales or associated services and, while selling online is increasingly important, it enables overseas-based competition. Returns for designers come from commissions, contracts for collections and from direct sales and hiring. Fashion retail has maintained a strong presence in all of the major centers of the region, especially in the large malls, but as well as the larger national and international franchises, there are a number of boutique stores targeting particular market segments. Furthermore, craft and design markets have opened up new opportunities. It's worth pointing out that some designers and fashion stylists had established reputations in the fashion industry either in the capital cities or overseas before returning to the Hunter, bringing that experience back. This industry has been impacted by global shifts in manufacturing and trade and individual creative people have responded well to these larger structural forces adapting their boutique businesses to them. Customer service, the use of social media and engagement with positive networks, all field related activities, alongside domain elements such as training and experience in national and global markets, seems to underpin the personal creative stories of many of these talented fashion creatives.

In summary, we can say that in the Hunter Region of NSW, fashion is intensely personal. Its success in the creative industries is linked to the stories of talented individuals, choice making agents whose work is underpinned by training, broad experience, and a focus on customer service and promotion through social media, active websites and blogs. Many Hunter-based fashion designers are highly entrepreneurial, most operating as sole traders who also manufacture. That said, there is a very significant retail sector and a small design and styling sector. The 2011 Census revealed that most people who said they work in the Hunter's fashion industry lived in the coastal areas of the region and our interviews confirmed that fashion creatives like to congregate. There are several clusters where similar businesses operate and, while the sector has experienced rapid change through digitization and globalization, niche businesses in high fashion, bridal, sports and leisure, dance, babywear, workwear and footwear continue to survive. This snapshot of fashion in the Hunter demonstrates how this industry has been impacted by global shifts in manufacturing and trade and how individual creative people have responded to forge boutique businesses. Ultimately it demonstrates an interplay of the elements of the system of creativity: active choice making agents, domain immersion in shared knowledge as the basis for creative work, and a reliance on a deeply interconnected network called a field to allow creative works to emerge from this fashion-centered creative (eco)system in action.

References

Australian Fashion Council. (2021). *From high fashion to high vis: The economic contribution of Australia's fashion and textile industry*. Australian Fashion Council. Retrieved March 12, 2023, from https://ausfashioncouncil.com/wp-content/uploads/2021/05/From-high-fashion-to-high-vis-EY-final-report-31-May-2021.pdf

Bammant, H. (2023, January 20). A list of fashion industry jobs you didn't know existed and how to get them. *Fashion Journal*. Retrieved from https://fashionjournal.com.au/fashion/job-titles-fashion-industry/

ETSY. (2017). *About*. ETSY Retrieved August 31, 2017, from https://www.etsy.com/au/about?ref=ftr

Façon. (2017). *5 minutes with Lara Lupish*. Facon Australia Retrieved August 12, 2017, from https://www.faconaustralia.com/5minuteswith-lara-lupish/

Façon. (2023). *Homepage*. Facon Australia, Retrieved April 18, 2023, from https://www.faconaustralia.com/magazine/

Green, P. (2013, February 20). Smaller is better for Woo. *The Herald*. Retrieved August 31, 2017, from http://www.theherald.com.au/story/1315950/smaller-is-better-for-woo/

Harrison, P. (2006). *Captain Henry Newton—From assistant pilot to superintendent of navigation in the port of Newcastle 1873–1906*. Self-published.

Local Search. (2017/18). *Local Search 2017–2018 phone directory—Newcastle and Lake Macquarie*. Robin Qld.

Lupish, L. (2011, January 1). *Bio*. Lara Lupish. Retrieved December 21, 2021, from http://laralupish.com/bio.html

MacDowall, C. (2016). *200 years of Australian fashion: Colonialism to modernity*. The Culture Concept Circle: Art, Design, Music, Fashion and Style, Past, Present and Future. Retrieved September 12, 2017, from https://www.theculture concept.com/200-years-of-australian-fashioncolonialism-to-modernity

NGV. (2015). *200 years of Australian fashion* (Media Release, December 3, 2015). Retrieved August 30, 2017, from http://www.ngv.vic.gov.au/media_release/200-years-of-australian-fashion/

Piller, L. W. (2023). Designing for circularity: Sustainable pathways for Australian fashion small to medium enterprises. *Journal of Fashion Marketing and Management, 27*(2), 287–310. https://doi.org/10.1108/JFMM-09-2021-0220

Penberthy, N. (2012, September 7). Australia's fashion history. *Australian Geographic*. Retrieved August 30, 2017, from https://www.australiangeographic.com.au/topics/history-culture/2012/09/australias-fashion-history/

Riley, M. (1997). From the bush to the street: A change in direction for Australian fashion. *Art, 17*(1), 43–45.

10

Advertising, PR and Design

Introduction

Advertising, public relations (PR) and design is a composite, dynamic and competitive sector. This sector, with its numerous subsectors, is of high value because of the activity it generates not only for other industries but also within the related creative fields of visual and performing arts, publishing, interactive software, fashion, film, TV and music. As it capitalizes on changes in technology and communication trends, the sector, which appears to devour others as it grows, influences opportunities for growth in the creative industries as well as the economy overall.

Advertising, PR, and design are sectors that have grown significantly as part of the global creative industries landscape. The work they carry out is part of creative services where the production, management, circulation and selling of, as Raymond Williams (1981) puts it, signifying practices is the primary activity. The creative services offered through advertising, marketing, PR, and design businesses, known as agencies, allow for strategic campaigns to be created to deliver symbolic cultural messages, typically underpinned by a client's commercial desires or by

P. McIntyre et al., *Creativity and Creative Industries in Regional Australia*, Palgrave Studies in Creativity and Culture, https://doi.org/10.1007/978-3-031-45972-6_10

social or ethical movements, for example, those surrounding climate change. Advertising, PR or marketing campaigns are developed to be carriers of symbolic meaning (Davies & Sigthorsson, 2013, p. 1) and are most often engaged in a process of persuasion (Grunig & Hunt, 1984; Mattelart & Mattelart, 1998; Tungate, 2007). They engage broad and niche audiences, who are typically described as consumers. The recent convergence of many of these areas was to be expected as these businesses developed and capitalized on changes in technology, communication trends and new media forms (McLuhan in Gordon, 2003, p. 237). These, in turn, shaped and influenced opportunities for growth in the creative services sectors. This is an example of creative innovation and disruption at work and can be seen through the cultural melding of other creative arts sectors drawn into advertising, marketing and PR, and graphic design.

Intertwining Histories of Advertising, Marketing, PR and Design: An Accumulated Heritage

Advertising and marketing are historically viewed as 'the force that sustains all commercial media' (Sinclair, 2014, p. 209). Previously, new products were advertised in newspapers and to attract the right buyers commercial artists, now graphic designers, were engaged and their work became important (Young, 2015) as manufacturers used advertising alongside other marketing strategies (Young, 2015, pp. 211–212) to promote their products. While advertising in newspapers had been going on for some time, particularly for iconic Australian brands such as Rosella, Arnotts and Fosters, it was in the golden age of radio in the 1930s that advertising companies such as George Patterson Pty Ltd. began to influence programming through their purchase of air time for shows such as *Dad and Dave*, the *Lux Radio Hour*, *Australia's Amateur Hour*, *The Quiz Kids* and *Pick-A-Box* with performers promoting the sponsor's products (Baird, 1992, p. 8). The production of such programs in conjunction with revenue from traditional advertising strengthened the advertising industry and reinforced the media's dependence on it (Crawford, 2008, online). The arrival of television as the prime mass medium after the Second World War consolidated this trend. As Sinclair asserts:

> The international manufacturing-marketing-media complex we know today did not really emerge until after World War II, as US corporations seized opportunities to invest overseas in industrial development ... Among these corporations were the new US television networks and the advertising agencies of Madison Avenue. (2014, p. 212)

While Australian agencies took on the gendered characteristics of Madison Avenue, women were not entirely locked out of the advertising world. Dickenson suggests that as 'increasing numbers of educated, middle class Australian women sought paid work [and] advertising provided an acceptable route ... to enter the workforce' (2016, p. 11). Advertising and marketing became 'established as an integral part of the new age of corporate capitalism' (Dickenson, 2016, p. 11), while other specialties such as public relations also emerged.

Public relations, commonly called PR, has a complex history in Australia (Sheehan, 2014; Zawawi, 2009). Strategic planning, which is a key element of PR 'developed out of the advertising industry [when] ... advertising [had] been operating at a sophisticated level for more than a century' (Knights, 2001, p. 5). This relationship is important to understand since: 'Although it was much younger, and had smaller budgets ... and was perhaps a little harder to define, it was growing at a fast rate and ... [modeled] itself on its older advertising sister' (Knights, 2001, p. 5).

With PR becoming important, the advertising world also incorporated design into its orbit. Graphic design and advertising are intertwined in a symbiotic relationship (Young, 2015) with Australian design traceable to the 1880s (Bogle, 1998). The realm of graphic design has been expansionary, engaging a broad array of professions (Fry, 1988) and is now integral to product development with aesthetics affecting salability and functionality (Naiman, 2017, online), flagging an increasing recognition of the role of design in branding. The Design Council suggested in 2013 that:

> a brand is a set of associations that a person (or group of people) makes with a company, product, service, individual or organization … Design is what translates the ideas into communication. And many designers will work through both the strategy and the implementation to ensure that the results are consistent, adaptable and in-keeping with your original brand attributes. (2013, online)

The Design Institute of Australia (DIA) drew its members from 'disciplines in both established and emerging fields of design. They include (but are not limited to) spatial designers, communications designers, industrial designers, design educators, systems designers and design managers' (DIA, 2017, online). There are also those working in digital media, exhibition and display, systems and service design, industrial design, jewelry design, fashion design, textile design, furniture design, interior design, architectural and set design, UX design and many other forms recognized by the DIA. Some of these forms of design have been instrumental in the more recent popularity of "bespoke", hand crafted products where many consumers have tired of the uniformity and short life span of many mass-produced goods. However, it is graphic design that has most often been associated with advertising, most recognizably in the development of logos or brand marks and the associated consistency of visual presentation across media, packaging and products. The Australian Graphic Design Association was founded in 1988 and is now 'a lead member of the International Council of Graphic Design Organisations, forming a global network of 187 member associations in 56 countries and consultative status with UNESCO, UNIDO, ISO and WIPO' (AGDA, 2017, online).

Structure of the Fashion Industry: The Shape of the Interconnected Field

Three shaping forces—the commercial sale of products, consumer behaviors and innovations in new media technologies—allowed for new consumer products to be sold as novel advertising and marketing strategies converged (McIntyre et al., 2023). The structural forces at work included 'consumer preferences, various regulations, and economic and cultural factors' (Vujnovic & Kruckeberg, 2020, pp. 338–339). Faced with these pressures, the way creative agencies are structured evolved 'as rapid media developments, changing consumer behavior, and shifting industry goals have impacted its shape and form' (Rosengren, 2019, p. 39). With this sector re-defined as 'brand-initiated communications intent on impacting people' (Dahlen & Rosengren, 2016, p. 334), the signifying practices of the creative services who deploy symbolic messages for persuasion through the creation, production and management of media artifacts become meaningful for audiences and consumers. As a part of these broader structural forces at play, innovation, which may be 'new to the firm, to the market or to the world' (Mazzarol & Reboud, 2020, p. 21) appears to emerge naturally in a process of creative destruction (Schumpeter, 1994 [1942]) and disruption (Christensen, 1997). In this rapidly evolving sector, organizational structures that were previously cutting edge may quickly be taken over or appropriated. These social, cultural and economic structures manifest within the rules of the domain and are acted upon by the field and, in turn, shape the creative practices and convergences that interconnect advertising, PR and graphic design agencies.

Agencies in this sector have been split into two basic categories. Many creative agencies include full-service, boutique, digital, in-house or media specialist agencies while promotion agencies include direct marketing, sales promotion, event planning, PR and design agencies (Mills, 2017, online) many of which have been combined into what are called full-service agencies:

> Full-service agencies provide clients with all the services they need for the entire advertising function. This includes planning, creating, producing, and placing the ads, as well as research before the campaign and evaluation after it to assess the campaign's effectiveness. Full-service agencies have expanded in recent years through consolidation—larger agencies buy them when they want to provide a one-stop shop for their global clients. In the process, the types of services that agencies provide has expanded to include PR, design, and event planning. (Saylor, 2017, online)

Some agencies focus on one aspect of the creative process such as creative production work or media buying. They refer to themselves as 'specialized agencies' (Saylor, 2017, online). For example, some companies will specialize in media planning and buying. Some interactive agencies, gaming agencies and search agencies may partner with other agencies 'to provide services for the full campaign as determined by the client or the lead agency' (Saylor, 2017, online). However, some companies prefer to retain control over advertising and 'may set up in-house agencies within the corporation. An advertising director typically runs the in-house agency; she [sic] chooses which services to buy and which to perform internally' (Saylor, 2017, online).

This in-house agency may keep 'creative services in house, create advertisements itself, and then purchase media-buying services from the outside. The inside agency may buy services from a specialized service agency or buy services à la carte from a full-service agency' (Saylor, 2017, online). In-house agencies are generally cost-effective and 'give the company greater control over the entire process' (Saylor, 2017, online). This strategy also provides other benefits: a deep understanding by those who work for the agency of both the customers and the company; and, better coordination between the marketing program of the company and what it does (e.g., the timing of product manufacturing and delivery) (Saylor, 2017, online).

> In addition to the types of agencies, there is also the role that the agency plays in the client's business. The most common and secure relationship is the agency of record, or lead agency. As clients may work with many different agencies for their various needs, the agency of record is the lead agency partner and usually has the majority of the client's business (Saylor, 2017, online).

Business Models Used by Creative Agencies

Advertising, marketing and public relations campaigns run out of creative agencies are conducted for a fee, usually negotiated upfront or calculated on hourly rates paid when a campaign is completed. Revenue within creative agencies may be generated from a number of sources—commissions, contracts, negotiated fees and media buying. Commissions, for example, may be 15% for broadcast or outdoor media while those for digital media are often negotiable. Mark-up charges are placed against content creation and production and fixed costs such as wages. The buying of media spots is another typical revenue stream, where the media bills the agency for the cost of a spot, and the agency then bills the client, adding commission to cover production costs, copywriting, art direction, and account service charges with a profit margin added. Contemporary media business models may have different drivers; no longer is their sole purpose to raise revenue, but they are 'increasingly about relationships with consumers, value creation and continual product and service improvements' (Villi & Picard, 2019, p. 129).

Traditional business models are increasingly challenged by the availability of freelance designers and other related creatives through global service groups such as Freelancer.com. This service allows anyone to "post a project", and those who have the skills to undertake the project can connect and offer their services; information and quotes are provided and work is commissioned. While internet-based access to global markets opens up new opportunities for those creative businesses able to compete, the tendency is to undercut pricing and create price-based competition.

Operational Methods Used in the Field

At the operational level, creative agencies may offer a complete range of services or they may offer boutique, digital, in-house or media specialist creative services. Marketing and promotional agencies will include direct marketing, sales promotion, event planning, PR and design services (Mills, 2017, online). In recent years, full-service agencies have expanded to include PR, design and event planning (Saylor, 2017, online).

The creative services required to deliver on a campaign are written into the creative brief. The creative brief details all the work to be undertaken to meet the client's aims and objectives and the content creation methods and strategies that an agency may employ to achieve the brief and inspire the creative idea (Solomon et al., 2009, p. 248). Traditionally, a client provided the agency with a brief of the scope of works to be completed. This generally included information on the product or service, the competition, the proposed target market, the consumer needs or problem to be addressed, consumer perceptions of the brand, what people need to believe about the product, how to achieve this, and some idea of the tone of the communication.

Traditionally, graphic design has occurred late in the production process, when the need has been to promote or package finished goods or services for sale, but co-design practices have elevated the creative process of design in contemporary practices. The drawing up of a creative brief will now include design thinking processes, which take a co-design or collaborative approach, allowing the client an opportunity to workshop ideas that may be useful for the delivery of their campaign. The five stages of design thinking were originally proposed by the Hasso-Plattner Institute of Design at Stanford, known informally as d.school. These include empathizing with the user, defining the problem, ideating or generating ideas, prototyping and testing. Design thinking is increasingly seen as useful where innovation is called for, and once the brief is agreed, the agency will respond with a novel campaign, product or service. This is now an important part of many agencies' operational methods to deliver on a creative brief, translated through the client's contract. Some agencies will specialize in one aspect of the creative process such as creative production work, app development, media planning or buying while some agencies may form partnerships 'to provide services for the full campaign' (Saylor, 2017, online). Serving all the client needs, described in the creative brief, allows agencies to hire in specialized services when required (Fig. 10.1).

Bringing in specialized services through sub-contracts or hiring freelancers is now common practice and these were often sourced networks and a field of peers. More recently, however, digital platforms where freelance services can be obtained, like HubSpot, have offered new ways to meet a client's brief if the creative services are not available in the agency.

However, some companies prefer to implement their own controls and 'may set up in-house agencies … which an advertising director typically runs, choosing which services to buy and which to perform internally' (Saylor, 2017, online). In-house agencies are generally cost-effective and

Fig. 10.1 Design typical full-service agency organization. (Original in Saylor, 2017, online)

internal employees may have a deeper understanding of the company and its customers. Insiders can also coordinate the promotion better with the company's overall marketing program and other functions, such as manufacturing and delivery. Other communication channels, overseen by public relations specialists, such as social media, partnerships with "influencers" or product placements in film or TV shows, are becoming increasingly important strategies.

Personnel from the Field: Important Choice Making Agents

A creative agency may employ a creative director, account executive, copywriter, media buyer and traffic controller as well as a graphic designer, PR specialist, brand manager, social strategist, developer and User Experience (UX) designer. Other freelancers may also be required and include filmmakers, web designers, photographers, illustrators, interior designers, set decorators and stylists. The accounts planner and team work collaboratively with the client and the creative director to draw up the creative brief (Solomon et al., 2009, p. 248). A traditional agency structure is organized around client, creative and marketing services running in parallel with management and human resources. Agencies provide many career possibilities for people who are 'artistic, good at writing, analytical and creative' (Saylor, 2017, online).

A creative director is a crucial visionary working in the agency. They are responsible for the quality of the work and allocation of the tasks as described in the creative brief. They decide which services will remain in house and which freelancers or subcontractors will be brought in to complete other components of the campaign. For example, an "app" may be developed by a specialized agency. Many agencies are known because of their creative directors, and their expertise and scope of their duties enable them to sensitively manage a creative team within the organizational climate to foster 'creativity and innovation, tolerate failure and encourage enterprising behavior' (Mazzarol & Reboud, 2020, p. 96).

Within agencies, some staff functions are generally retained in-house. These personnel include account managers who work with clients to ensure the brand is served well, the focus is on the target audience, positioning is competitive and there is an appropriate promotion plan. For market research, account planners 'obtain or conduct research that will help clients understand their markets and audiences' (Saylor, 2017, online). Art directors or copywriters 'develop concepts and messages that will catch consumers' interest and attention' (Saylor, 2017, online). The creative department will generate the ideas, images and words of the message. The agency will also typically employ a media buyer to 'evaluate the multitude of options available for ad placement—now greatly expanded by the internet. In doing this they can allocate budget to effectively reach the target audience' (Saylor, 2017, online).

A design agency is very similar in its structure and personnel and may also employ graphic, logo and website designers, for example, to fulfill work contracted from advertising agencies. Designers may also work as embedded creatives, employed internally in a government department or social media unit of a large corporation.

A number of other specialized companies with their own personnel service the many creative agencies (advertising, PR and design) and these include art studios, printers, and film and video companies who may produce vision and sound for screen-based media content using skilled operatives. Photographers are also in demand as images have become a crucial visual used in web design or specialized media strategies delivered on internet-based media platforms.

Promotion agents may also work within specialized sectors such as the music industry, while other PR agents will assist in marketing strategies, event planning and overall strategic communication. Various research companies, employing experienced researchers have also sprung up to service the advertising and design sector.

Advertising, Marketing, PR and Graphic Design: Hunter "Creatives"

Interviews with Hunter creatives confirm it is a sector of rapid change, with roles being blurred, and many people moving easily across boundaries in an interconnected (eco)system. The design field, in particular, has claimed an increasingly wide array of activities and Australian research confirms that 123,000 businesses engage in this work, most of which turn over less than $200,000 per year. These are small businesses in a highly competitive environment (CIIC, 2013). It is significant to note that while the CIIC Report (2013) identifies that 83.4% of creatives doing this work are actually embedded in other industries, this research focuses on the 2870 who work in advertising, marketing, public relations and graphic design in the Hunter, as they represent a significant number and are the largest sector in this region's creative industries.

Along with in-house staff, these advertising, PR and design agencies engage various freelance video makers and their crews, photographers and graphic designers, jingle writers and web designers. Many freelancers make up a network of creative services professionals who are highly educated and work in collaborative workspaces.

These varied employment possibilities are well represented in the Hunter. People develop their skills through formal study, although some do learn “on the job”. Digital skills are fundamentally important but traditional skills are still needed and, in a similar way to other creative industry sectors, newer forms of communication such as social media are increasingly part of the requirements for successful outcomes. Hunter agencies offer services across both the physical and digital economy applications and, while locally based, several have national and international clients and projects. It is also important to note that the networks developed by those working in the sector are a crucial part of how these industries operate.

Advertising Agencies: Creative Agencies

Many successful creative individuals began their careers in advertising. Philip Adams, filmmaker, author, globally appreciated radio presenter, public intellectual and long-term resident of the Upper Hunter, began his creative career in this sector. He found himself ‘[i]n the company of people like Bruce Petty, Fred Schepisi, Peter Carey, et al. … We didn’t know each other necessarily at the time, nor had we confessed our creative ambitions, but advertising gave us a home (Adams, i/v April 2016).

The unique demographic profile of Newcastle has traditionally been important to its advertising sector. Peter de Jong, a former musician, songwriter and creative director with Peach Advertising, explained: ‘If companies have a new product to launch, they’ll test it in Newcastle or Adelaide … They are good test markets and product release points … because they have a broad demographic make-up of socioeconomic factors’ (De Jong in Supersonic, 2003, p. 17). Peach Advertising ran many successful campaigns providing work for a diverse set of creative practitioners. It was, therefore, a target for takeover and it merged with its major competitor, Enigma. This merger allowed Enigma 'to expand its capabilities in digital media and government social marketing' (Lynchy, 2011, online). Enigma's Founder, CEO and Managing Director, Lisa Sutton Gardner, stated: 'For two decades Enigma and Peach have spear-headed Newcastle's ability to compete with Sydney and Melbourne … We're now harnessing that energy … to compete with multinational companies' (Lynchy, 2011, online).

Two Enigma employees are former musicians Matt Plummer and Brian Daly. Plummer worked as a musician with Supersonic before moving to the UK as a designer. There he 'created art for significant brands' (Plummer, 2017, online). He returned to Newcastle to take up the role of art director with Enigma, working with government and automobile campaigns. Daly took a different path and as a composer, director, writer, creative director and musician works across agencies including Enigma, Kent Woodcock, Sticky and Eluminate, making ads, videos and jingles (Daly, 2017, online).

A number of specialist creative people also move between firms. Jamie Lewis is a case in point.

Lewis graduated with a Bachelor of Arts (Communication Studies) from the University of Newcastle and was a member of Footlice Theatre Company. He began work in a media unit and then started as a copywriter/production assistant at Enigma where he learned to produce commercials. After nine years with Enigma, Lewis moved to Out Of The Square Media (OOTS) as creative director:

> In Newcastle, we often have many hats. I do a lot of copywriting and direct commercials, corporate videos and different forms of content as well as presenting to clients. But as a creative practitioner I call myself a writer and director and love creating fantasy stories with a twist on reality. (Lewis, i/v May 2015)

Lewis has treated his time in the advertising world as a learning experience, especially in regard to collaboration:

> I was terrible at this … always 'it's my idea, I have to make it'. The collaborative, to me, was quite wrong in that it was really just having people to

> help fulfill your vision. Which isn't collaboration it's ... "I've got this bloody big idea and you will do this, this and this". Then, working with Ian Hamilton (Limelight Creative Media) … collaboration was very intense and I saw the benefit. (Lewis, i/v May 2015)

OOTS was founded by Martin Adnum, formerly from NBN Television, and has grown from television and video production into a full-service creative agency (OOTS, 2017, online) in a merging of advertising, design and PR functions. Kara Sullivan, on the other hand, heads up Guts Creative, a small agency focusing on strategy, a direction based on her qualifications in marketing, organizational behavior and psychology. Her reasons for beginning her own business were personal: 'I didn't just want to sell stuff but wanted to work with brands that make a positive difference' (Sullivan, i/v March 2017). As Sullivan says:

> I think sometimes in agencies it's like a box model, you take the brief and go away and try to come up with all the answers yourself ... But I think that clients like to be involved in the planning and they have lots of ideas … I started Guts to focus on brand strategy—helping clients to understand who they are and what they stand for. What I really like, is turning that strategy into something creative and communicating it. (Sullivan, i/v March 2017)

While firms such as John Church, StickyAds, The Village of Useful, MAD Media Group, Artbeat and Level 7 construct complex digital environments for their clients, the use of highly interactive social media is not overt in their own digital environments. It appears that the "desire for intimacy" with the public, as Weinman (2013) argues, is deployed by advertising businesses but is not something they apply for themselves.

Design Agencies: Creative Convergence Across Interconnected Networks

Advertising and design often overlap, feeding off and informing each other in an increasingly important digital environment. The design sector offers not only graphic design services but also web and social media design, search engine optimization (SEO) and associated techniques. Competition has increased, with large media companies now offering services to small businesses in competition with design agencies. For example, the entry of Fairfax Marketing into the local creative business mix offers clients an integrated approach to their use of social media. The Fairfax presence is influencing smaller businesses to enter digital marketing in a new way with creative agencies such as Graphika, Redback Solutions, Nodding Dog Design, Suckerpunch Design and Glue Digital now outsourcing many services locally and, at times, internationally. Shannon Roman from Crackler expressed concerns about market saturation and struggling smaller companies. Kent Woodcock decries the fact that with the advent of modern software, people without training and experience in brand creativity offer services that are well tooled in the superficial but without the depth that informs traditional branding and marketing.

Headjam, ostensibly a design agency, describes itself as a "creative" agency. They offer graphic design, photography, branding, advertising, marketing, print media, project management, video production and 'web+digital' (Headjam, 2017, online). Headjam are digitally connected via sites such as Facebook, Twitter, Instagram, LinkedIn, Vimeo, YouTube, Pinterest and The Loop and use a blog for "spreading the word". Founder of the company, Luke Kellett:

> Worked in London creating media for music labels … and his photography has attracted to Headjam a portfolio that includes Boy and Bear, Hiatus Kaiyote and The Waifs, and won him prizes at the Melbourne Design Awards and the Woodford Folk Festival. Thousands of his ethnographic photographs of the bohemian community in Melbourne … form part of the permanent collection of the Victorian State Library. (Headjam, 2017, online)

Principals of the agency are notable for having worked overseas or interstate bringing their varied experiences "home to Newcastle". These include Sarah Cook, head of the design team, Helen Simmons, their broadcast designer who is a motion graphics expert, and Mike Preston, who spent 30 years with renowned advertising agencies: 'Directing the launch of major brands such as Optus and Hahn and working on two of Australia's longest running campaigns, one for Johnson & Johnson and the other for Colgate' (Headjam, 2017, online).

Kent Woodcock is founder of a respected small creative agency with a blue-chip clientele, local and national. His work history began with the practical training available through TAFE and with generous mentoring from his early employers, an experience he has taken forward in his own business model:

> I started off in window dressing, as a junior display person. I couldn't get into the advertising industry (which is what I wanted to do) coming from a country town. It was difficult but the display manager must have liked the smile on my face. He knew I eventually wanted to get into the advertising department and window dressing was a pathway ... I then did a marketing course at TAFE. I did a whole lot of practical skills.
>
> Then I moved into a junior art direction role and was mentored well … worked my way up from suburban newspapers into mainstream advertising. After that I set up my own little design business and began supplying shops with screen printed clothing … Then I ran into a telegraph pole and nearly killed myself so it was time to get out. That's when I came to Newcastle. (Woodcock, i/v Mar 2016)

Kent has some clear ideas on the current state of the industry:

> There are a lot of independent people out there. There are agencies trying to provide everything—it's just become so sporadic it's difficult to figure out where it's heading. I think that with going to the digital space, it's going so quickly not everyone knows how to keep up with it. I keep playing in the traditional areas. (Woodcock, i/v Mar 2016)

Kent Woodcock has been a mentor for new talent, and one of his mentees was Shannon Roman. Shannon is now director of his own branding and digital marketing agency Crackler, working true to Kent's prediction that he would need to move away from Woodcock's own focus on the traditional approach. Roman, too, is a graduate of the TAFE system: 'Initially I worked and trained in print—I did a trade in graphic arts and printing. Then I completed a TAFE Design Diploma' (Roman, i/v September 2016).

Crackler's staff have all completed formal training—in the domains of design, print, architecture and marketing communications:

> Our work is becoming more and more digital—digital set-ups. And not just a website but optimizing the whole digital environment for the client ... We are getting more and more work from Government agencies now. A couple of big e-commerce sites for retail corporates, stuff like that ... We have clients from Canada and Bermuda and New Zealand. There are not really any problems working globally. A key factor is definitely clear scoping. Having a clearly defined brief/proposal is essential, especially when you get into the bigger projects. (Roman, i/v September 2016)

Adding anecdotal confirmation to the bald statistics, Roman reflected some concerns about the number of agencies in this smaller, regional market: 'Oversaturation is a potential problem. There are definitely lots of creatives and small businesses offering creative services popping up. A lot are really struggling' (Roman, i/v September 2016).

Public Relations (PR) Agencies: Sole Operators, Specialists and Embedded Workers

The Hunter's PR professionals work for agencies, in their own businesses, within the corporate or public sector, and as freelancers. They are generally graduate trained. Typically, PR practitioners specialize in particular industries, for example sport, music, or government advice. Kath Elliott is one example who specializes in stakeholder engagement for large infrastructure projects (kathelliott, online). Christina Gerakiteys is another. Gerakiteys works as a sole operator contracting in additional services as well as operating as a freelancer:

> I contract myself out to other people and I contract other people to work with me. So, if I'm making a video for example, then I might be contracted in as the producer and then I will contract other people in as I need ... This is in contrast with an agency where they might have all the skills in-house ... it depends on budget. (Gerakiteys, i/v Jan 2015)

Alexandra Joy (AJ), previously known as Heidi Alexandra Pollard, started her PR practice in health promotions. AJ is now a successful entrepreneur offering international company cultural coaching services along with a suite of other services (McIntyre et al., 2023). When AJ was working in PR she argued that anything that did not fit neatly into finance, accounts or human resources within an organization was given to PR to 'sort something out' (Pollard, i/v May 2016) demonstrating the creative flexibility required of PR practitioners.

Kristie Ferguson, working as an embedded PR operative in a small not-for-profit organization explains how creativity is applied in her role: 'For me the creativity of it falls into when I'm developing a brief or an agency plan and how that is going to roll out. And then choosing the channels I'm going to roll it out through. And then probably writing the content side of it as well' (Ferguson, i/v Sept 2016).

Paula Jones, on the other hand, is a specialist with 30 years' experience in the music industry. Now Director of JonesPR and operating out of her premises in Merewether, she started work in retail 'followed by publicity, promotions and marketing with various record companies' (Jones, 2018, online). Her company undertakes 'publicity campaigns for clients with new release albums and tours within the Australian music industry' (Jones, 2018, online). As well as her hectic work schedule, Jones has mentored others through her teaching in the Music Industry course at TAFE, taken interns into her business from the Communication degree at the University of Newcastle, been a regular industry panel participant, and worked pro bono for Music NT as part of their Bush Bands Business project which assists Indigenous bands living in remote communities (Jones, 2018, online).

Collaborative Workspaces

In recent years, collaborative workspaces for creatives have been a fast-growing real estate phenomenon, both in Australia and overseas. While there is some debate about their impact on productivity, the opportunity to move out of home offices and into a supportive and often social environment was a consistent theme among our interviewees. In 2017, the

INNX Hub housed design and design-related businesses including Mezzanine Media, White Magazine and Headjam. The Roost Creative is 'a community of independent creatives sharing space and ideas' which hosts 'a mix of emerging creative and established industry mentors' (The Roost, 2017, online). The Creator Incubator is a collaborative workspace for artists and designers in the light industrial area of suburban Hamilton and The Soap Factory in Mayfield was established by glass and jewelry designer Sophia Emmett and her partner, furniture designer Jono Everett. For collaborative working spaces it is important that businesses are not in direct competition. Jono Everett explains their ethos for The Soap Factory:

> We had a collective ethos about acknowledging where Newcastle is at the moment and possibilities that, as it grew—even though everyone would be running their own individual businesses—we might be able to promote each business as a collective, tapping into what's happening in terms of the changes to the Newcastle scene. (Everett, i/v Sept 2014).

This collaborative approach allows strong networks to develop and it removes highly competitive situations that can become toxic in a regional network of creatives.

Summary

The advertising, PR and graphic design sub-sectors offering creative services are located primarily in the urban centers of the Hunter. This analysis does not focus on people embedded in other industries, estimated to be around 80% of the sector's employment (CIIC, 2013). Rather, it focuses on those who identify as working in this sector. It is the largest sector in this study with 2870 practicing creatives. Tellingly, and in line with other creative industries in the Hunter, these creative practitioners, those we are calling choice making agents operating within the creative (eco)system, work at various scales across the system, that is at the global, national and local level, often at the same time, and use digital tools and platforms that enable this endeavor, providing their clients wherever they are located, with the best possible service.

This sector provides a variety of employment possibilities and most are represented here. Many workers develop their skills, necessary parts of the shared knowledge of the domain, through study although there are still some that are self-taught or learn "on the job" by immersing themselves in those shared knowledges of the domain until the knowledge they have acquired becomes tacit. And, echoing Negus and Pickering's (2004) emphasis on the complementarity of tradition and innovation, both playing a key role in the creative process, digital skills are fundamentally important as are traditional skills. In fact, it is rare that one operates without the other. Most creative operatives, choice making agents, work primarily in full-service creative agencies, that is, organizations that offer a broad spectrum of services that intersect with advertising, design and PR agencies. These agencies offer services across the range of physical and digital economy applications with many doing national and international work.

Many people, the choice making agents within the (eco)system, who work within and for these agencies also operate across areas such as music, film and the art world. Roles across these interconnected networks are becoming increasingly blurred across sectors with many moving easily across boundaries. The design field in particular has claimed an increasingly wide array of activities. The advertising world gave birth to design agencies and PR agencies and both have modeled themselves similarly. The art collectives from an earlier time have now become collaborative workspaces, production hubs and co-working spaces for many designers and others and are run as enterprises for those who fund and constitute them.

The variety of forms we found in these businesses, the convergence of sub-sectors and the project-based collaboration people reported, confirm McLuhan's claim of an evolution of 'new shapes and positions' (McLuhan in Gordon, 2003 p. 237) and, again, demonstrates a creative and highly dynamic (eco)system in action.

References

AGDA. (2017). *About/history*. Australian Graphic Design Association. Retrieved August 16, 2017, from http://www.agda.com.au/about/history/

Baird, L. (Ed.). (1992). *Guide to radio production*. AFTRS.

Bogle, M. (1998). *Design in Australia: 1880–1970*. Craftsman House.

Christensen, C. (1997). *The innovator's dilemma: When new technologies cause great firms to fail*. Harvard Business School Press.

CIIC. (2013). *Valuing Australia's creative industries: Final report*. Prepared by SGS Economics and Planning for the Creative Industries Innovation Centre.

Crawford, R. (2008). Advertising. *Sydney Journal, 1*(2), 24–32. https://doi.org/10.5130/sj.v1i2.629

Dahlen, M., & Rosengren, S. (2016). If advertising won't die, what will it be? Towards a working definition of advertising. *Journal of Advertising, 45*(3), 334–345. https://doi.org/10.1080/00913367.2016.1172387

Daly, B. (2017). *Brian Daly*. Retrieved August 22, 2017, from http://www.briandaly.com.au/

Davies, R., & Sigthorsson, G. (2013). *Introducing the creative industries: From theory to practice*. Sage.

Design Council. (2013). *The power of branding*. Design Council. Retrieved April 4, 2023, from https://www.designcouncil.org.uk/our-work/news-opinion/the-power-of-branding/

DIA. (2017). *History of design in Australia: 1789–2002*. Design Institute of Australia. Retrieved August 16, 2017, from https://www.design.org.au/documents/item/136

Dickenson, J. (2016). *Australian women in advertising in the twentieth century*. Palgrave Macmillan.

Fry, T. (1988). *Design history Australia*. Hale & Iremonger.

Grunig, J., & Hunt, T. (1984). *Managing public relations*. Holt, Rinehart and Winston.

Headjam. (2017). *What we do*. Headjam. Retrieved August 26, 2017, from http://www.headjam.com.au/

Jones, P. (2018). *Paula Jones*. LinkedIn. Retrieved February 24, 2018, from https://www.linkedin.com/in/paula-jones-4174577a/?originalSubdomain=au

Knights, K. (2001). *Strategic planning in public relations*. Stylus Publishing.

Lynchy. (2011). *Enigma and Peach join forces in Newcastle*. Campaign brief. Retrieved April 19, 2023, from https://campaignbrief.com/

Mattelart, A., & Mattelart, M. (1998). *Theories of communication: A short introduction*. Sage.

Mazzarol, T., & Reboud, S. (2020). *Entrepreneurship and innovation: Theory, practice and context* (4th ed.). Springer.

McIntyre, P., Fulton, J. M., Kerrigan, S. M., & Meany, M. M. (2023). *Entrepreneurship in the creative industries: How innovative agents, skills and networks interact*. Palgrave Macmillan.

McLuhan, M. (2003). *Understanding media: The extension of man* (T. Gordon, Ed.). Gingko Press.

Mills, H. (2017). *The structure of advertising agencies*. Slideshare. Retrieved August 16, 2017, from https://www.slideshare.net/heleenmills/hoofstuk-22-ad-agencies-slide-share

Naiman, L. (2017). *Design thinking as a strategy for innovation*. Creativity at Work. Retrieved June 11, 2017, from https://www.creativityatwork.com/design-thinking-strategy-for-innovation/

Negus, K., & Pickering, M. (2004). *Creativity, communication and cultural value*. Sage.

OOTS. (2017). *About*. Out of the Square Media. Retrieved August 22, 2017, from https://www.outofthesquare.com/who-we-are/

Plummer, M. (2017). *Matt Plummer*. LinkedIn. Retrieved August 23, 2017, from https://au.linkedin.com/in/matt-plummer-193a3b3a

Rosengren, S. (2019). Redefining advertising in a changing media landscape. In M. Deuze & M. Prenger (Eds.), *Making media: Production, practices and professions* (pp. 389–398). Amsterdam University Press. https://doi.org/10.5117/9789462988118

Saylor. (2017). *Advertising industry structure*. Saylor.org Academy. Retrieved August 16, 2017, from https://saylordotorg.github.io/text_launch-advertising-and-promotion-in-real-time/s05-03-advertising-industry-structure.html

Schumpeter, J. (1994 [1942]). *Capitalism, socialism and democracy*. Routledge.

Sheehan, M. (2014). A brief history of public relations in Australia and New Zealand. In J. Johnston & M. Sheehan (Eds.), *Public relations: Theory and practice* (4th ed., pp. 20–46). Allen & Unwin.

Sinclair, J. (2014). Advertising and marketing. In S. Cunningham & S. Turnbull (Eds.), *The media and communications in Australia* (4th ed.). Allen & Unwin. Retrieved from https://www.amazon.com.au/Media-Communications-Australia-Stuart-Cunningham-ebook/dp/B08D2NCYRW/ref=sr_1_3?crid=1GRL2L9LM7LQ7&keywords=The+Media+and+Communications+in+Australia+%284th+ed.&qid=1682123905&sprefix=%2Caps%2C235&sr=8-3

Solomon, M. R., Duke Cornell, L., & Nizan, A. (2009). *Launch! Advertising and promotion in real time*. Flatworld Knowledge.

Supersonic. (2003). *Unpublished business plan*. Supersonic.

The Roost. (2017). *Home*. The Roost Creative. Retrieved November 7, 2017, from http://theroostcreative.com.au/

Tungate, M. (2007). *Adland: A global history of advertising*. Kogan Page.

Villi, M., & Picard, R. (2019). Transformation and innovation of media business models. In M. Deuze & M. Prenger (Eds.), *Making media — Production, practices and professions* (pp. 121–132). Amsterdam University Press. https://doi.org/10.5117/9789462988118

Vujnovic, M., & Kruckeberg, D. (2020). Global advertising and public relations. In Y. H. Kamalipour (Ed.), *Global communication: A multicultural perspective* (3rd ed., pp. 325–343). Rowan and Littlefield.

Weinman, J. (2013, June 4). How customer intimacy is evolving to collective intimacy, thanks to big data. *Forbes*. Retrieved April 20, 2014, from https://www.forbes.com/sites/joeweinman/2013/06/04/how-customer-intimacy-is-evolving-to-collective-intimacy-thanks-to-big-data/?sh=4303fb505dbc

Williams, R. (1981). *Culture*. Fontana.

Young, A. (2015). Commercial art to graphic design: The rise and decline of commercial art in Australia. *Journal of Design History, 28*(3), 219–234. https://doi.org/10.1093/jdh/epv021

Zawawi, C. (2009). A history of public relations in Australia. In J. Johnston & C. Zawawi (Eds.), *Public relations theory and practice* (3rd ed., pp. 26–46). Allen & Unwin.

11

Publishing

Introduction

As discussed in other chapters, the domain is the 'creativity language' (Sawyer, 2012), the shared knowledge, that an individual must learn in order to be able to produce a variation within it and, if an individual choice making agent does not engage with and use the domain 'it would be impossible for an individual to produce an innovation or for an audience to understand it' (Fulton & Paton, 2016, p. 29). In the domains of writing and publishing, examples of domain rules include 'style, technique, character, rhythm and genre conventions' (Paton, 2016, p. 119) as well as language and other written works. Paton (2016) also notes how the publishing industry, as a large component of the interconnected networks of the field, adds another layer of conventions on writers with deadlines, physical layout of the book and editing. In journalism, domain "rules" can include style of writing, story structure, news values, how to use technological tools, ethical obligations and legal requirements (Fulton, 2016). These domains of knowledge which a journalist learns provide the preconditions for agency as well as a structure for journalistic

P. McIntyre et al., *Creativity and Creative Industries in Regional Australia*, Palgrave Studies in Creativity and Culture, https://doi.org/10.1007/978-3-031-45972-6_11

practices. The various fields associated with these domains share similarities and, at the same time, diverge into their own social structures or interconnected networks. For example, in writing, publishing and journalism, an editor is a field member, although they work in slightly different ways in each field. In publishing and writing, other field members include publishers, agents, other writers, reviewers, and prize and funding judges (Paton, 2016) while in the subset of writers who are journalists, other journalists, sub-editors, media owners, chiefs of staff and cadets (Fulton, 2016) are examples of that field's members. These field members are tasked with understanding the shared domain knowledge and judging the creative contributions presented by the choice making agents working within these systems of production.

A Brief History of Publishing in Australia: A Heritage in Writing, Printing and Change

Publishing, as currently understood in the West, began after the invention of paper in China and the copying services that became important in Greece, Rome and China. These copied publications were laboriously reproduced by hand. The innovation in 1445 that was Gutenberg's press (Straubhaar et al., 2022) led to a rapid spread of printing and literacy with printed works being regarded as a convenient 'store or repository of wisdom' (McQuail & Deuze, 2020, p. 33). The first newspapers, as one arm of the publishing industry, began in the early 1600s but it was in the late seventeenth century that 'the transition from sporadic to regular publication occurred' (Watson, 2005, p. 310). By the eighteenth century, newspapers were established and 'between 1753 and 1775 the average daily sale of newspapers practically doubled' (Watson, 2005, p. 531) in England.

Publishing became a substantial industry in the nineteenth century with the introduction of inexpensive paper, steam power and typesetting (EB, 1994). An increase in education of the middle and working classes also led to a growth in the industry (Conley & Lamble, 2006) and what Blanning called a 'reading revolution' (in Watson, 2005, p. 509). And from the first incursion of Europeans into Australia, publishing has been part of this culture.

A printing press arrived in Australia on the first fleet (Conley & Lamble, 2006). One of Australia's early convicts, George Howe, came with a good education and printing skills and was put to work printing government documents (Blair, 2014). He printed the very first book to be made in Australia, *New South Wales General Standing Orders*, which was a very dry compendium of 'Government and General Orders issued between 1791 and 1802' (SLNSW, 2019, online). He then published Australia's first newspaper in March 1803—*The Sydney Gazette and New South Wales Advertiser*—as a weekly offering with four portfolio pages of official material and a small number of private notices (SLNSW, 2019, online).

Australian literature, newspapers and magazines have told the stories of this country. Bookshops and publishing houses came and went, giving rise to an industry that supported authors, printers, compositors, editors, journalists, newspaper editors, publishers and proprietors who established printing presses. This industry stood alongside a culture of reading soirees, poetry recitals and public lectures which were eventually supported and encouraged by various lending libraries, literary societies, Schools of Art and Mechanics Institutes. By the early twentieth century, the daily newspaper 'dominated the sphere of information' (Smith in Tiffen, 2014, p. 87). It is also important to acknowledge the vibrant Indigenous news industry, which has been published in Australia since 1838 (for a summary, see Burrows, 2014, pp. 215–217).

However, by the 1950s and 1960s, the press was competing with radio, movies and television and 'to say that the press was the most important of the mass media would no longer have been a very sensible proposition' (Tiffen, 2014, p. 97). Throughout the 1960s, 1970s and 1980s, the newspaper and magazine industry in Australia was dominated by Fairfax and News Corp and the Packer family's Australian Consolidated Press, a company that published iconic Australian magazines such as the *Australian Womens Weekly*, a magazine read by more than a million women in 1991 (Bonner, 2014, p. 195). By the 1990s, ownership concentration of news publishing had 'radically increased' (Tiffen, 2014, p. 101). A recent report on press ownership in Australia has found that

Murdoch's News Corp and Nine Entertainment, which is a merger of Nine Television and Fairfax, own more than 80% of the metropolitan and national print media markets (Brevini & Ward, 2021).

At around the same time as this consolidation was going on, between 1980 and 2007 sales of newspapers dropped by almost 50% in Australia (Tiffen, 2014, p. 97) with scores of mastheads closing. The disruption of the internet and "free" news has been blamed. Advertising, once the mainstay of newspapers, also declined and/or migrated online. Into this environment, zines and e-zines and so-called independent publishers began online news services often using traditional media as primary news sources. Currently, one in five Australians get their news via social media while 42% get their news via television (Park et al., 2020). According to the latest data, only 6% six of Australians access their news via print, although almost a quarter access news via online sources (Park et al., 2022). Nationally focused news outlets also have to compete with mastheads whose main news service is located elsewhere, such as *The New York Times* and *The Guardian.*

In regards to book publishing, Australia was linked to British publishing houses and, in the early nineteenth century, maintained close ties to Britain as their monopoly was maintained. For colonial Australia, printed publications were mainly restricted to newspapers and journals and it wasn't until the period between World War I and World War II that the Australian book trade started to flourish and acquire an identity of its own (Tian, 2008).

In 1948, the Australian Book Publishers Association was established (APA, 2017, online). Australian publishing houses like Allen & Unwin became the mainstay of book publishing in the 1970s. Firms like Angus & Robertson and Dymocks also flourished as booksellers. Indigenous publishing emerged in 1964 with the Aboriginal Studies Press, which focused on academic publications, and continued with publishing houses such as IAD Press and Jukurrpa Books, Magabala Books and Batchelor Press, all of which focused on Indigenous knowledge and stories. In the 1990s, one of the main drivers of the continuing development 'of the Australian book industry were the 1991 changes to the Copyright Act which enshrined the parallel import restrictions' (Coronel, 2017, online). With the creation of 'a solid, protected market for local editions of overseas-originated books, a "portfolio" model for publishing companies became the norm. The negative aspect of this story is that the larger companies became 'reliant on sales of overseas-derived titles for up to 55% of their revenue' (Coronel, 2017, online). With a growing proportion of readers buying online and offshore, this business model was destined to become self-defeating.

During the 1990s and 2000s, 'independent bookshops maintained a substantial market share; chain stores served the mass-market well; and the massive discounting wars that distorted the UK and US book trades … were largely averted' (Coronel, 2017, online). However, a downturn occurred, stimulated by online shopping, eBooks and the Australian dollar. When Amazon entered the book market in 2007, bricks and mortar retail stores began to disappear at an alarming rate. As pointed out in 2017:

> Various subscription services proliferate, print-on-demand increasingly takes the place of bulk hard copy printing, serialization again becomes the norm, companies experiment with diverse payment models, fan-fiction numbers grow and traditional distinctions between producers and consumers become increasingly untenable (Matulionyte et al., 2017, p. 192).

Apple has now successfully integrated eBooks into its iTunes catalog and as Tim Coronel explains 'eBooks are currently about 10% of publishers' revenue, but in the US eBooks now make up a quarter of mainstream publishers' revenues and [many titles] … are eBook-dominant or eBook-only' (Coronel, 2017, online). According to Watson (2021), revenue from eBooks in the US in 2020 was over a billion dollars.

The Structure of the Publishing Industry: The Shape of Things

The publishing industry can be divided into two broad sectors: those that produce periodicals and those that produce non-periodicals. Non-periodical publishing is the one-off printing and sale of such things as books and reports while periodicals appear at regular intervals and include magazines and newspapers. While these were paper-based at one time, it is expected that periodicals have an online presence. There are now digitally based publishing and self-publishing options that threaten to disrupt the traditional industry structure (Figs. 11.1 and 11.2).

Business Models in Flux

Book publishing, as Greco et al. (2014) indicate, generally derives income from direct sales and residual licensing deals. Publishers sell bulk purchases to retailers or directly to individuals in competition with the large book distributors. The revenue structure is that retailers generally take 55% of the listed price; the publisher 17.5% and the author 10%. As both distributor and retailer, Amazon takes 30–60%. Production, distribution and promotion account for 17.5%. Licensing deals and fees for eBooks are also made directly with institutions. The eBook market usually operates on a pay-per-use basis with online delivery attracting an advertising revenue stream (Fig. 11.3).

As Matulionyte et al. point out:

> Some of the newer business models which resulted from this dynamic system at work included the deployment of print-on-demand amenities, the adoption of subscription services, serialization, bundling, pay-per-view, pay-what-you-want, freemium content as well as the exploitation of embedded advertising, crowdfunding and patronage. At the same time publishing had to face not only dual distribution streams involving both hard copies and e-books, the shifts in the system also highlighted predica-

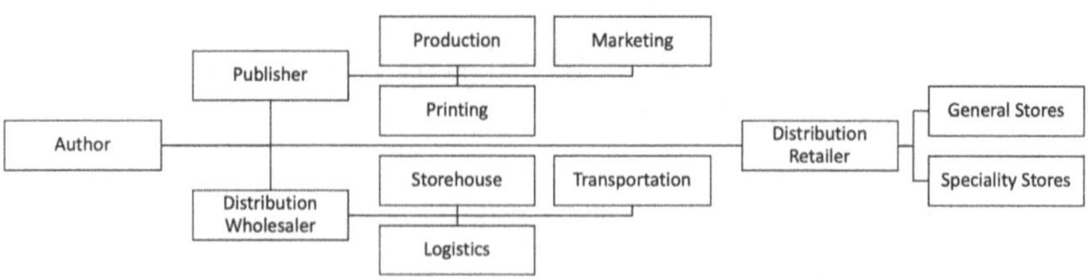

Fig. 11.1 Traditional publishing structure. (Original in Fernández-Pacheco: online)

Fig. 11.2 Digital publishing structure. (Original in Fernández-Pacheco: online)

> ments around a number of other factors including pricing, new payment systems employed in a digitized world, sharing and customized publishing, and the increasing ability of anyone to become involved in self-publishing and make these self published works available online themselves (2017, p. 205).

For magazines, as Hogarth (2019, online) tells us, the key to a successful business model is multiple revenue streams: brand extensions, including digital editions, events and books; advertising; sponsorships, particularly for events; sales, both subscription and off-the-rack, but also back issues; membership schemes; paywalled content with a micropayment system; and licensing. For newspapers, the business model is similar. Newspapers have long depended on the so-called rivers of gold, advertising generated from classifieds (Fulton & Balnaves, 2013; Tiffen,

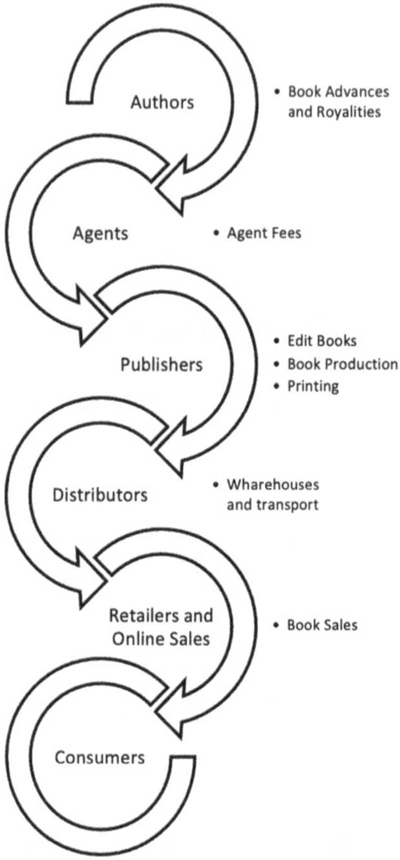

Fig. 11.3 Traditional publishing revenue structure. (Original from Publishing Revenue Structure: Online)

2010) as well as traditional advertising (Sinclair, 2014). The rise of the internet, particularly Google, and social media has meant audiences have fragmented, leaving the advertising industry scrambling for the attention of audiences. Since the 1990s, there has been 'a desperate casting about for new business models by means of which the traditional media can achieve a transition to the online world' (Sinclair, 2014, p. 5). For example, in 2015, global newspaper circulation revenues became greater than advertising revenues. According to the annual World Press Trends survey

(WAN-IFRA), 'the basic assumption of the news business model—the subsidy that advertisers have long provided to news content—is gone' (Kilman, 2015, online). News organizations have also employed such measures as paywalls, subscriptions, premium content, cross-subsidization and sponsorship (for more discussion on different payment models, see Benson, 2019; Hesmondhalgh, 2019; Olsen et al., 2021; Villi & Picard, 2019). Social news outlets such as *Junkee* and *Buzzfeed* are often supported by native advertising, 'a form of paid content marketing, where the commercial content is delivered adopting the form and function of editorial content, with the attempt to recreate the user experience of reading news instead of advertising content' (Ferrer-Conill, 2016, p. 905). And as noted above, both magazines and newspapers must now have an online presence with apps providing another revenue stream. Furthermore, in 2019 Australia became the first country in the world to pass a law that ensured Google and Facebook pay for news on their sites: 'the News Media Bargaining Code, has enabled Australian news organizations to extract more than $200 million (almost $150 million US) in the year since it went into effect' (Grueskin, 2022, online), thus providing publishers with funds to employ journalists.

Operational Methods of the Field

Publishing houses, as Greco et al. (2014) spell out, perform discrete but connected functions when producing books. First there is content acquisition, whereby an editor evaluates the author's skills, the content and its fit with expected consumer demand. Once commissioned, the book proceeds to content development and then to design and production, calling for a collaborative effort across finances, production and content. For production there is prepress, printing and paper binding or preparation of an eBook to be undertaken. The book is then finalized as hard copy and/or eBook. Once it exists in a material form, marketing and sales take over to complete the process through 'managing the warehouse and distribution of books, supervising book returns; and responding to unexpected demand' (Greco et al., 2014). Greco et al. also point out that publishing houses have multiple revenue streams which are largely associated with rights related to licensing, foreign sales, special sales and so on, and that their accounting processes rigidly apply contracts language since authors rely on this revenue stream.

The magazine and newspaper publishing sectors operate in similar ways. Both must go through comparable procedures to ensure they have content, which can be sourced from freelance writers, staff journalists, contributing editors, columnist or feature writers, overseen by an editor and copy editing either in-house or freelanced, although newer, online-only publications, such as social news outlets *BuzzFeed*, *Pedestrian.tv* and *Junkee* typically don't have the middle step of sub editing. The writing team will work with designers, generally a creative director, art director, photo editor and photographers. A sales team engages with advertisers and subscribers. These operations are necessary for both hard copy and digital distribution but differ at the point of going to press—printing hard copies or producing files for uploading. If printing hard copies then, apart from design, significant costs include typesetting, paper stock, printing, binding and distribution costs. If creating an online magazine, software such as Flipping Book Publisher allows the build of the online magazine for uploading to a website.

Blogging is another matter. Once content is developed and posted, the blogger must engage in SEO and use social media to drive audiences to the site—a highly active process (for further information on how bloggers and other entrepreneurs use social media, see Fulton, 2017). Once there is an established audience, money can be made from advertising, sponsorship, an e-store for affiliated merchandise or by donations from readers via sources such as Patreon and Kickstarter (McIntyre et al., 2023).

Important Personnel in the Interconnected Networks of the Field of Publishing: Choice Making Agents at Work

Writers are, of course, central members of the field in publishing. They may be freelancers, staff writers such as a news journalist, feature writer or columnist, or an author or blogger. Some may be most or all of these.

Their roles vary but the main task is to produce engaging content. Authors also undertake a variety of promotional activities. For book authors, a writer's agent is important to place their work with publishing houses, usually through a commissioning editor. Publishers generally employ editors to ensure the book is market ready.

For newspapers and magazines, editors are responsible for the overall output and tone of a publication. They ensure the written material is newsworthy and readable. The art director, designer and creative director, who may be one person, work closely with the editor to ensure the output is appealing. The photo editor sources suitable images from stock companies, archives or freelance photographers as well as specific images taken for a story by a photographer or a journalist. Typesetters and printers are necessary in the physical production phase as are distributors whereas for digital sales, online distribution platforms are necessary. Marketers work with the sales team who ensure all copies are supported by advertisers for magazines and newspapers while for book publishing, they make sure the book is sold through retailers or institutional buyers (Fig. 11.4).

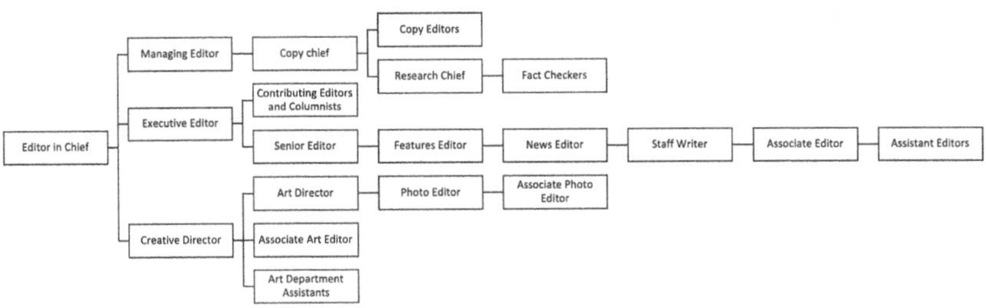

Fig. 11.4 Publishing personnel generic structure. (Original from Querimit: online Editorial Department Consumer Magazine)

Publishing in the Hunter Region: A Dynamic (Eco)System in Action

Publishing in the Hunter Region is diverse and well-established encompassing books, newspapers, magazines and newer forms such as zines and blogs. With storytelling deeply embedded in our social and cultural world, opportunities still exist for entrepreneurial publishers but locally some traditional forms of publishing struggle with the global digital changes.

Books in the Hunter: Authors and Publishers as Choice Making Creative Agents

An examination of the system of book publishing in the Hunter shows an intricate interweaving of structure and agency. The Hunter has a long history of producing internationally renowned authors who write fiction and non-fiction in a broad range of genres from poetry through to thrillers, anthologies and children's books. Located close to Scone in the Upper Hunter, Phillip Adams, public intellectual, columnist, broadcaster and author, claims that the Hunter Region has produced a high number of authors:

> Of course the Hunter is a strange place. As you would know, it must be something in the water apart from coal dust, because … tonight I'm launching a book at Gleebooks for Ian Lowe, and it's his update on *The Lucky Country*. Donald Horne was the most famous son in Muswellbrook. Patrick White, next door to my farm on Belltrees. [Henry] Havelock Ellis, people don't realize, who came up with the Narcissus complex which Freud knocked off, he taught in a school not far from where I live. There's Barbara Baynton who was regarded in her time as one of the great writers, you know, HG Wells comparing her to Tolstoy, lived in Murrurundi. (Adams, i/v April 2016)

Another successful author of note is Marion Halligan, born in Newcastle, who was a teacher and journalist before writing the prize-winning *Lover's Knots: A Hundred-Year Novel*, which put her on the literary map. Halligan has written short stories, a children's book and non-fiction books and, in a demonstration of her symbolic capital, has been nominated for most major book prizes for her ongoing work in fiction books. Tellingly, Halligan was on the Literature Board of the Australian Council as the chair in the early 90s (UQP, 2017, online), an example of her immersion in the domain of book publishing as a key member of the field.

Other authors include Barry Maitland, a trained architect who turned to writing after the Newcastle earthquake in 1989 led to a change in careers, and Jaye Ford, a journalist and public relations consultant whose first novel, a thriller called *Beyond Fear*, won Davitt Awards for Best Debut and Readers' Choice and became the 'highest selling debut crime novel in Australia in 2011' (Ford, 2022, online). Ford's writing career is covered in detail elsewhere (McIntyre et al., 2023) but, needless to say, the individual skills developed as a journalist played a large part in the success of her writing. A further key skill is Ford's engagement with the field where she attends writing events, festivals, conferences and teaching workshops. Audrey Pflugrath, who writes under the nom de plume Audrey J. Cole, is another Hunter author who understands the value of engaging with the field. Pflugrath promotes her books via local news outlets but also writes a regular blog called *Aspire*, which contains a wealth of advice for aspiring independent writers.

The local university has provided an ongoing support network for Hunter authors by offering a creative writing program taught by established award-winning authors. Associate Professor Keri Glastonbury is a successful poet who supervises Masters and PhD students and Dr. David Musgrave is another academic at the University of Newcastle who has authored books and won prizes in poetry while mentoring and supervising students. Academics at the university have written a multitude of non-fiction books as part of their core activity including the edited collection *Radical Newcastle* published by Newsouth Press and put together by James Bennett, Nancy Cushing and Erik Eklund. The book is a collection of short stories and poetry by Hunter-based and Hunter-affiliated writers and luminaries such as Marion Halligan, Philip Adams, Moya Farrell, John Bell, Nick Enright, the Biggins family, Les Murray, Norman

Talbot, John Doyle, Bruce Wilson, Barry Maitland, John O'Donoghue, John Ramsland, Betty Capper, David Rowe, Madeleine Randall, Mikey Robins, Donna Meehan and Cardiff's wild film-making son, Yahoo Serious.

The creative (eco)system is strong in the Hunter with publishing houses like Hunter Press, boutique press such as Catchfire Press, booksellers and writing centers supporting local writers. The Hunter Writers Centre, for example, provides guidance and mentoring to aspiring writers, generates publishing opportunities, administers writing competitions, offers resources, and acts as a liaison between authors and organizations and businesses.

Catchfire Press was established by Lisbet de Castro Lopo in 1996 as 'an independent boutique press to publish local writers of merit' (Catchfire Press, 2017, online). This press is located in Newcastle and they continue to 'publish writers from the Hunter area, in books wholly designed and illustrated here, and we have deliberately set a slow pace to maintain standards in book design and editing, as well as literary quality, comparable with anywhere in Australia' (Catchfire Press, 2017, online). Another notable example of a local publisher is Mark MacLean, the former owner and founder, along with his partner Christine Bruderlin, of MacLean Books in Hamilton, a suburb in Newcastle. MacLean is from the UK and, after the oft-taken round-the-world working holiday, met Bruderlin in Alice Springs in Central Australia. It was here he learned to write and edit while working for the Institute for Aboriginal Development, an Aboriginal-controlled adult education college in Alice Springs. After further travel, they moved to Newcastle, starting MacLean's Book store where they learned about book publishing, promotion, distribution, retail and the audiences for books. There was some rigorous competition in the city at that time. As McLean explains, 'there was, I think, three—Angus & Robertsons, a Collins and Dymocks, as well as all the independents such as Pepperina. I think there were about nine bookshops, nine places selling new books at the time. And we thought "this is a big deal", but we decided to do it. We just decided, we put the life savings on the line and said, "we'll do it"' (MacLean, i/v April 2016).

They sold the business in 2003 and set up Hunter Press, a small online publishing house which publishes books and stories with 'relevance and connection to the Newcastle and Hunter region of New South Wales, Australia' (Hunter Press, 2017, online). Books about Newcastle, such as Ruth Cotton's *Hidden Hamilton*, Howard Bridgman and Nancy Cushing's *Smoky City: A History of Air Pollution in Newcastle, NSW* and Gaye Sheather's *Rock This City: Live Music in Newcastle, 1970s and 1980s*, have done well for Hunter Press. In an example of diversification, they also offer editing and self-publishing services for a fee. MacLean realized early that they needed to diversify in order to gain a comfortable income:

> I think it's very difficult to work just as an editor and for Christine just to work as a designer, but we have a range of skills. And a lot of those skills we learnt when we had a bookshop. (MacLean, i/v April 2016).

MacLean learnt quickly about the value of networks and engaging with the field. As Davies and Sigthorsson note, 'it's important not just to network but network strategically ... to regard certain types of socializing as part and parcel of one's work and professional development' (2013, p. 109). MacLean also realized what was required in leveraging those networks and that moving the networking process online was imperative. They were one of the first to build and use a website. In comparison to their time in Alice Springs, where launches 'had been done by posting invitations out and putting an advert in the Centralian Advocate', in Newcastle 'it was all Twitter, Facebook, Instagram, and it was a completely different crowd. We looked at that and said "Wow". It was a real lights-on moment when you realize that this is how modern connections are made' (MacLean, i/v April 2016).

Newspapers in the Region: Dynamic Change in the (Eco)System

The Hunter is served by national and state-based metropolitan newspapers such as those produced by News Corporation (including *The Newcastle News*, a digital-only publication under the *Daily Telegraph* banner) and Nine Entertainment mastheads but it also has access to a variety of locally oriented newspapers, particularly those owned by Australian

Community Media (ACM). ACM provides community-based papers in many of the towns in the Hunter with each having an online version as well as a paper-based version. The main news publication in the Hunter is ACM's *The Newcastle Herald*, which has very deep connections to the region. The *Herald* had its origins in two early newspapers, *The Newcastle Chronicle and Hunter River District News* (established in 1858) and *The Miners Advocate and Northumberland Recorder* (established in 1873). In 1876, the two merged and the first copies of *The Newcastle Morning Herald and Miners Advocate* hit the streets and, in 1980, the "Morning" and "Miners Advocate" was dropped from the title (The Herald, 2017, online). In 2019, the *Herald* was acquired by the ACM stable. Another local newspaper, the *Newcastle Weekly*, is offered via print and online as a free weekly publication. Established in 2015, it focuses on 'trusted, community-focused editorial' (Newcastle Weekly, 2022, online). The *Weekly* is privately owned by a local couple, changing ownership in 2022 after the previous owner closed the publication due to COVID related lockdowns and an increase in costs. Journalists working at all these newspapers have helped create the news where their methods have been identified as part of a system at work (Fulton, 2011, 2013, 2016) with changes in technology, platforms and practices leading to an evolving domain.

Rosemarie Milsom is one of those journalists. Milsom is an award winning journalist who worked in the industry for 21 years (including at the *Herald*), seeing changes in technology and practices such as social media use, the reliance on the internet, a broadening skill set, and writing for an online audience: 'media outlets have obviously got websites, and there's information on the websites, and it's all now about SEO and clickbait and all those sorts of clichés that don't sit next to the printed-out newspaper, but we're in a really dramatic transition' (Milsom, i/v Sept 2015).

Milsom's story is illustrative of the disruptive changes that have beset the newspaper sector of the publishing industry and how writers have been made to change their approach. Milsom took the skills and networks learnt from her journalism role and, in 2013, started the Newcastle Writers' Festival, an annual festival that has become increasingly successful. After receiving a redundancy from the *Herald* in the wave of redundancies that hit Australian newsrooms (see Zion et al., 2016, 2018), Milsom took on a role as a radio presenter at the local public broadcasting station while continuing to write and organize the annual writers' festival. Milsom's employment trajectory demonstrates the shift from full time ongoing employment to a more freelance oriented and heavily casualized workforce. As Hesmondhalgh (2019) indicated, creative work is increasingly irregular, contracts are short-term with little job protection, career prospects have become uncertain and earnings are minimal and often unequally distributed.

With the longstanding *Newcastle Herald* facing competition at a local level, they are also being squeezed from the other direction as competition arrives from within the global arena. Successful foreign mastheads have now made significant inroads into Australian markets. As one example, *The Guardian Australian Edition*, since launching in 2013, has an Australian readership of 11.6 million (Meade, 2020, online). Furthermore, an increasingly fragmented and available media landscape means consumers can access news via international publications such as BBC World News, *The Guardian* and *The New York Times*.

Hunter Magazines: Telling Local Stories in a Global World

There are several magazines operating out of the Hunter Region, all of which are considered "niche" rather than mainstream publications, and not owned by large publishers such as Are Media. These include *Façon Australia*, *Hunter Lifestyle* and several others, particularly in the music sector.

Façon Australia is an ambitious and high-quality luxury fashion magazine published out of an inner-city suburb of Newcastle. It is a locally produced fashion magazine that features 'Hunter- based models wearing the brands of local designers and established national designers, as well as global fashion juggernauts including Versace, Ferragamo, Armani, Burberry and Escada' (Green, 2015, online). Its founder is Lara Lupish, the magazine's editor-in-chief and its creative director, and Lupish took extensive international experience and applied it to magazine publishing, launching *Façon* in 2015. Lupish noticed a lack of fashion coverage while working on another Hunter magazine, *Hunter Lifestyle*, and used her contacts in the fashion industry to produce the new magazine.

Façon is free, published biannually and available online and in retail and tourist areas. Hunter designers, such as Jean Bas, High Tea with Mrs Woo and Abicus, have been highlighted in the magazine alongside national and global brands. The Façon company emerged from the popularity of Instagram posts and has more than 12,000 followers on Instagram and 2000 on Facebook (as at January 2023): 'We started an Instagram page and started shooting material for the Instagram page and I guess from there we spruiked the magazine because I thought that we should turn it into a hard copy' (Lupish, i/v Oct 2016).

As noted, Lupish had been working briefly for *Hunter and Coastal Lifestyle Magazine.* This magazine was established in 2003 by Mary and Phil Collins before being sold in 2018 (due to ill health). It is published quarterly as both a glossy, hard copy print version and online with a Facebook following of more than 3000 followers and a similar number on Instagram. The Collins' have had varied careers and owned local newspapers, run home shows and done promotional work across the region. For the Collins', the magazine was inspired by *High Life Magazine* which Phil had seen in Bowral. He asserted that 'this area needs a high-profile presence like this magazine. I think we'll start one' (Marilyn and Phil Collins, i/v Nov 2015). For the first five years or so, Marilyn wrote all the articles although this changed to freelancers as the magazine grew. Phil's role was in advertising and marketing, including selling the advertising, getting the copy and getting the approvals. The magazine is designed to appeal to a broad audience, but, when interviewed, Marilyn agreed that 'it's very hard for magazines at the present moment. We're all having a bit of a downtime at the moment' (Marilyn and Phil Collins, i/v Nov 2015).

Other magazines include *intouch*, a monthly online and print publication which, according to its website, 'showcases what's hot, what's on and who's who with a dynamic blend of inspirational articles, lifestyle features, fashion, events, food and travel' (intouch, 2023, online) and *Swell Magazine*, a quarterly, print publication designed 'as a collectors item' to 'showcase the best that Newcastle and its surrounds has to offer' (Swell Magazine, 2023, online). The local university also has two magazines that are run by students: *Yak*, an online publication that covers 'student news, comment and lifestyle at the University of Newcastle' (Yak Magazine, 2023, online); and, *Opus*, a magazine that covers 'student life to politics, welfare, arts and entertainment' (Opus Magazine, 2023, online).

The music scene in the Hunter has also been well catered to by the publishing sector of the creative industries. For example, Steve Dunkley, a musician who also occasionally writes for *Hunter Lifestyle* magazine, was the publisher and creative director for *Social Life Magazine* (Issuu, 2015, online) which ran for 19 issues across 2011 to 2013. It was published exclusively online through the Issuu website. Sydney-based *On the Street* music magazine had a Newcastle page and local correspondent in Julie Williams prior to her moving to the news desk at radio station NEW FM when it was first established. Locally based *Concrete Press* followed and was edited by Mark Hughes for a number of years. This music magazine was succeeded by *U-Turn* run by Catherine Hart and her team from the Black Box space in Newcastle West. Under her editorship *U-Turn* was run efficiently and appeared regularly but ran into cash flow problems when a number of her high profile out-of-town advertisers began to pay irregularly. *Reverb Street Press* started as a hard copy print edition run in the manner of its predecessors *Concrete Press* and *U-Turn* but soon became an exclusively online only proposition. *Reverb Online* still features music news, reviews, interviews, giveaways and a comprehensive gig guide on its website and now also runs what it calls *Reverb Radio*. *Reverb Radio* has taken the *Reverb* archives and converted these to radio "shows".

Zines and Blogs and Active Choice Making Entrepreneurs

Zines are 'self-published, small-circulation magazines that allow people to share thoughts and disseminate ideas while unfettered by the constraints of mainstream media' (van Egmond, 2021, online) and, while most zines would typically now be classified as blogs (Straubhaar et al., 2022), there has been a small zine industry in the Hunter. The zines examined here provide an example of the intertwining of different creative industry sectors. *The Follower*, which ran briefly during 2015, claimed to be Newcastle's only 'Arts independent newspaper and events guide' (The Follower Newspaper, 2017, online) and had 'a circulation of over 50,000 copies' (The Follower Newspaper, 2017, online). This large circulation figure was likely due to its distribution within *The Leader* newspaper which was run out of Hamilton. *The Follower* was largely the brainchild of Zackari Watt, a long-term member of Newcastle's performing arts scene who dabbled in music and was a co-director of The Follower Studios, a 'multi-faceted "creative industries" focused studio HQ with a strong focus on performing & visual arts' (Renew, 2017, online). *Newcastle Mirage* was another self-published zine that ran pieces on music, art and culture in Newcastle. It was established in 2013 by Kian West and Ryan Williams and was produced out of Sawtooth Recording Studios and Burst Media Studios in Tighes Hill. Its editions regularly ran stories and photography by locals on local art exhibitions, restaurants, writers, bands and musicians, and artists. Its main source of income was advertising from local hotels, retail businesses, and music and art shops.

As to blogging, it has been a vital part of the publishing scene in the Hunter. When this study was done, there were many examples including, amongst others, Coal River Working Party, Newcastle Appearances, Hidden Hamilton, Icyclenewcastle, East End Footprints, Pink Patent Mary Janes, Showbag, The View From King Street, This Untidy, Smoky City, West End Adventures, Found In Newcastle, Little Eco Footprints, The New Industrial, Little House in a Tsunami, Newcastle Now & Then and Swamp Life. A few cases will serve to illustrate the various activities and styles of these writers. As identifiable by the names noted here, topics are broad, niche and local.

HUNTERhunter, for example, was started in 2013 by 'Fiona and Alissa a couple of frustrated Novocastrians who were sick of Googling and trawling the internet trying to discover where to go, what to do and what was new in the Newcastle and Hunter region' (HUNTERhunter, 2017, online). Their site has active Facebook (54 k followers) and Instagram (62.6 k followers) accounts and, while content is written by the team, they encourage writers, photographers, social media experts and local businesses to contribute. Another blog that showcased Newcastle and its gems was *The Novocastrian Files*, set up by Siobhan Curran a few months after moving to Newcastle. Curran began blogging partly as a way to find out 'more about some of the interesting and talented locals I was discovering and secondly as a means of identifying where the good coffee/lunch/dinner spots are via their recommendations' (NF, 2013, online).

Summary

The publishing sector of the creative industries in the Hunter Region is in a healthy cultural state despite, and possibly because of, the disruptions the digital revolution has wrought, and is an excellent example of a creative (eco)system in action. The region is well serviced for its size with non-periodical publishing that includes the one-off printing and sale of such things as books and reports while periodicals such as magazines and newspapers appear at regular intervals. While many of these were originally paper-based, increasingly there are now a number of digitally based publishing and self-publishing options that have, to an extent, disrupted the structure of this industry. In terms of freely circulated publications, ads and subscriptions are the primary revenue stream. With the advent of online publications, acquiring an ongoing and significant consumer base via digital hits has become important. In this case social media, with very little to no investment, has become critical.

The region has had several local and regional mastheads as well as the national newspapers. All of them compete with international mastheads that operate online, some with Australian editions. Journalists have survived the transition to digital by moving across and between other creative industries' sectors. This also seems to be a trait of those engaged in the magazine business who are all generally skilled in multiple professional roles. Writers, of course, remain important in the publishing sector. With the demise of hard copy newspapers in particular, they have taken on freelance work, working to a brief or on spec for various outlets. There are still a limited number of staff writers operating as news journalists, feature writers or columnists. Authors, and now bloggers, are ever present with some writers, of necessity, performing both functions. Their roles may vary but the prime function is to produce engaging content for their audience.

Overall, the publishing sector in the Hunter encompasses books, newspapers, magazines and newer forms such as zines and blogs. They have, in large part, survived the transition to digital, while being impacted in that transition by restructures, job losses and closures. At the same time journalists have acquired multiple skills and many have moving across and between other sectors. Writers per se remain important. Magazines and books remain strong as cultural forms. As elsewhere, this chapter on publishing is framed within the elements of the system model (Fulton, 2022). To illustrate this we first examined the domain knowledge of its history, structure, variety of business models and operational methods. These are parts of its shared knowledge. We moved on to looking at the important field members, the choice making agents within the system. The we scaled down our approach to allow professionals to tell the story of publishing in the Hunter, while we supplied evidence of how the structures of the domain and the interconnected networks of the field have been internalized by these writers and how, as individual choice making agents, these creative operatives engaged actively with the creative (eco)system of the publishing sector. What became evident from these case studies is that this area of the creative industries provides a good example of a dynamic and evolving creative (eco)system in action.

References

APA. (2017). *Australian Book Publishers Association*. Retrieved February 25, 2018, from https://www.publishers.asn.au//

Benson, R. (2019). Paywalls and public knowledge: How can journalism provide quality news for everyone? *Journalism, 20*(1), 146–149. https://doi.org/10.1177/1464884918806733

Blair, S. (2014). Howe family. In B. Griffen-Foley (Ed.), *A companion to Australian media* (p. 210). Australian Scholarly Press.

Bonner, F. (2014). Magazines. In S. Cunningham & S. Turnbull (Eds.), *The media and communications in Australia* (4th ed., pp. 193–208). Allen & Unwin.

Brevini, B., & Ward, M. (2021). *Who controls our media*. GetUp! Retrieved February 3, 2022, from https://d68ej2dhhub09.cloudfront.net/2810-GetUp_-_Who_Controls_Our_Media_.pdf

Burrows, E. (2014). Indigenous newspapers. In B. Griffen-Foley (Ed.), *A companion to Australian media* (pp. 215–217). Australian Scholarly Press.

Catchfire Press. (2017). *About*. Catchfire Press. Retrieved August 14, 2017, from http://www.catchfirepress.com.au/about/

Conley, D. P., & Lamble, S. (2006). *The daily miracle: An introduction to journalism* (3rd ed.). Oxford University Press.

Coronel, T. (2017). *What next for the Australian publishing industry?* The Wheeler Centre. Retrieved June 24, 2017, from https://www.wheelercentre.com/notes/a648df15d92e

Davies, R., & Sigthorsson, G. (2013). *Introducing the creative industries: From theory to practice*. Sage.

EB. (1994). Publishing. In *The new Encyclopedia Britannica* (Vol. 26, pp. 415–416). Encyclopedia Britannica Inc.

Ferrer-Conill, R. (2016). Camouflaging church as state: An exploratory study of journalism's native advertising. *Journalism Studies, 17*(7), 904–914. https://doi.org/10.1080/1461670X.2016.1165138

Ford. J. (2022). *About Jaye Ford*. Jaye Ford. Retrieved January 14, 2022, from https://www.jayefordauthor.com/about-bio

Fulton, J. (2011). *Making the news: Print journalism and the creative process*. PhD thesis. University of Newcastle. Retrieved from http://hdl.handle.net/1959.13/927269

Fulton, J. (2013). Communication joy: Print journalists and the experience of flow. In M. Pitts & T. Socha (Eds.), *Positive communication in health and wellness* (pp. 238–251). Peter Lang.

Fulton, J. M. (2016). Print journalism and the system of creativity. In P. McIntyre, J. M. Fulton, & E. Paton (Eds.), *The creative system in action: Understanding cultural production and practice* (pp. 87–99). Palgrave Macmillan.

Fulton, J. M. (2017). Media entrepreneurship: Social networking sites, the audience and new media professionals. In J. M. Fulton & P. McIntyre (Eds.), *Creating space in the fifth estate* (pp. 47–60). Cambridge Scholars Publishing.

Fulton, J. M. (2022). Investigative journalism: A system of creativity. In C. Coatney (Ed.), *Investigative journalism in changing times: Australian and Anglo-American reporting* (pp. 46–62). Routledge.

Fulton, J. M., & Balnaves, M. (2013, July). Australia and changes in Western media. In T. Lee, K. Trees, & R. Desai (Eds.), *Refereed proceedings of the Australian and New Zealand communication association conference: Global networks-global divides: Bridging new and traditional communication challenges*. ISSN 1448-4331, Fremantle, WA.

Fulton, J. M., & Paton, E. (2016). The systems model of creativity. In P. McIntyre, J. M. Fulton, & E. Paton (Eds.), *The creative system in action: Understanding cultural production and practice* (pp. 27–43). Palgrave Macmillan.

Greco, A., Milliot, J., & Wharton, R. (2014). *The book publishing industry*. Routledge.

Green, P. (2015, October 19). Pressing style on the runway. *The Newcastle Herald*. Retrieved August 12, 2017, from http://www.theherald.com.au/story/3433153/pressing-style-on-the-runway/

Grueskin, B (2022). Australia pressured Google and Facebook to pay for journalism. Is America next? *Columbia Journalism Review*. Retrieved September 16, 2022, from https://www.cjr.org/business_of_news/australia-pressured-google-and-facebook-to-pay-for-journalism-is-america-next.php

Hesmondhalgh, D. (2019). *The cultural industries* (4th ed.). Sage.

Hogarth, M. (2019). *Successful business models for magazine media*. What's New in Publishing. Retrieved September 16, 2022, from https://whatsnewinpublishing.com/successful-business-models-for-magazines/

HUNTERhunter. (2017). *HUNTERhunter*. Retrieved August 12, 2017, from http://www.hunterhunter.com.au/

Hunter Press. (2017). *About us*. Hunter Press. Retrieved August 29, 2017, from https://hunterpress.com.au/aboutus.html

intouch. (2023). *Intouch*. Retrieved January 24, 2023, from https://www.intouchmagazine.com.au/intouchmagazine

Issuu. (2015). *Steve Dunkley*. Issuu. Retrieved August 12, 2017, from https://issuu.com/stevedunkley5

Kilman, L. (2015). *World press trends: Newspaper revenues shift to new sources*. WAN-IFRA World Association of Newspapers and News Publishers. Retrieved March 15, 2017, from http://m.wan-ifra.org/press-releases/2015/06/01/world-press-trends-newspaper-revenues-shift-to-new-sources

Matulionyte, R., Paton, E., McIntyre, P., & Gleadhill, D. (2017). The system of book creation: Intellectual property and the self-publishing sector of the creative industries. *Creative Industries Journal, 10*(3), 191–210. https://doi.org/10.2139/ssrn.3083281

McIntyre, P., Fulton, J. M., Kerrigan, S. M., & Meany, M. M. (2023). *Entrepreneurship in the creative industries: How innovative agents, skills and networks interact*. Palgrave Macmillan.

McQuail, D., & Deuze, M. (2020). *McQuail's media and mass communication theory*. Sage.

Meade, A. (2020, April 14). Guardian Australia doubles audience to become fourth most popular news site in the country. *Guardian Australia*. Retrieved December 20, 2022, from https://www.theguardian.com/media/2020/apr/14/guardian-australia-doubles-audience-to-become-fourth-most-popular-news-site-in-the-country

Newcastle Weekly. (2022). *About us*. Retrieved December 20, 2022, from https://newcastleweekly.com.au/about-us/

NF. (2013). *About*. The Novocastrian Files. Retrieved August 12, 2017, from http://www.thenovocastrianfiles.com/about/#.WY_NiEdpX-U

Olsen, R. K., Kalsnes, B., & Barland, J. (2021). Do small streams make a big river? Detailing the diversification of revenue streams in newspapers' transition to digital journalism businesses. *Digital Journalism*, online. https://doi.org/10.1080/21670811.2021.1973905

Opus Magazine. (2023). *UNSA*. Retrieved January 24, 2023 from https://unsa.org.au/opus

Park, S., Fisher, C., Lee, J.Y., McGuinness, K., Sang, Y., O'Neil, M., Jensen, M., McCallum, K., & Fuller, G. (2020). *Digital news report: Australia 2020*. News & Media Research Centre, University of Canberra. Retrieved February 3, 2022, from https://apo.org.au/sites/default/files/resource-files/2020-06/apo-nid305057_0.pdf

Park, S., McGuinness, K., Fisher, C., Lee, J.Y., McCallum, K., & Nolan, D. (2022). *Digital news report: Australia 2022*. News & Media Research Centre, University of Canberra. Retrieved February 3, 2022, from https://apo.org.au/sites/default/files/resource-files/2022-06/apo-nid317946_0.pdf

Paton, E. (2016). The dynamic system of fiction writing. In P. McIntyre, J. M. Fulton, & E. Paton (Eds.), *The creative system in action: Understanding cultural production and practice* (pp. 113–124). Palgrave Macmillan.

Renew. (2017). *The follower studios*. Renew Newcastle. Retrieved August 11, 2017, from http://renewnewcastle.org/projects/project/the-follower-studios/

Sawyer, K. (2012). *Explaining creativity: The science of human innovation* (2nd ed.). Oxford University Press.

Sinclair, J. (2014). Advertising. In B. Griffen-Foley (Ed.), *A companion to Australian media* (pp. 3–6). Australian Scholarly Press.

SLNSW. (2019). *Australia's first newspaper, the Sydney gazette and New South Wales*. State Library of NSW. Retrieved January 21, 2023, from https://statelibrarynsw.tumblr.com/post/171541248239/australias-first-newspaper-the-sydney-gazette

Straubhaar, J., LaRose, R., & Davenport, L. (2022). *Media now: Understanding media, culture and technology* (10th ed.). Wadsworth.

Swell Magazine. (2023). *About*. Swell Magazine. Retrieved January 24, 2023 from https://swellmag.com.au/about/

The Follower Newspaper. (2017). *Home* [Facebook page]. Retrieved August 8, 2017, from https://www.facebook.com/pg/thefollowernewspaper/about/?ref=page_internal

The Herald. (2017). *About us*. The Herald. Retrieved August 9, 2017, from http://www.theherald.com.au/about-us/

Tian, X. (2008). *Book publishing in Australia: The potential impact of digital technologies on business models*. Unpublished PhD Thesis. RMIT, Melbourne.

Tiffen, R. (2010). Changes in Australian newspapers 1956-2006. *Journalism Practice, 4*(3), 345–359.

Tiffen, R. (2014). The press. In S. Cunningham & S. Turnbull (Eds.), *The media and communications in Australia* (4th ed., pp. 95–110). Allen & Unwin.

UQP. (2017). *Author: Marion Halligan*. University of Queensland Press. Retrieved August 6, 2017, from http://www.uqp.uq.edu.au/Author.aspx/926/Halligan,%20Marion

van Egmond, S. (2021). *Zines: An independent platform for expression*. Museum of Australian Democracy. Retrieved January 24, 2023, from https://www.moadoph.gov.au/blog/zines-an-independent-platform-for-self-expression/#

Villi, M., & Picard, R. G. (2019). Transformation and innovation of media business models. In M. Deuze & M. Prenger (Eds.), *Making media. Production, practices, and professions* (pp. 121–131). Amsterdam University Press. https://doi.org/10.1515/9789048540150-009

Watson, A. (2021). *E-books in the U.S.—Statistics & facts*. Statista. Retrieved September 16, 2022, from https://www.statista.com/topics/1474/e-books/#topicHeader__wrapper

Watson, P. (2005). *Ideas: A history from fire to Freud*. Weidenfeld & Nicolson.

Yak Magazine. (2023). *About Yak Magazine*. Retrieved January 24, 2023 from https://yakatuon.com/about-yak/magazine/

Zion, L., Dodd, A., Sherwood, M., O'Donnell, P., Marjoribanks, T., & Ricketson, M. (2016). Working for less: The aftermath for journalists made redundant in Australia between 2012 and 2014. *Communication Research and Practice, 2*(2), 117–136. https://doi.org/10.1080/22041451.2016.1185924

Zion, L., Sherwood, M., O'Donnell, P., Marjoribanks, T., Ricketson, M., Dodd, A., & Winarnita, M. (2018). *New beats report: Mass redundancies and career change in Australian journalism*. New Beats Project.

12

Radio

Antecedent Conditions: The History of Radio in Australia

The field of radio in Australia has developed over a lengthy period. Its history (Criticos, 2016; Holloway, 1975; Lane, 1994; Potts, 1989; Tebbutt, 1989; Walkington, 2000) is indicative of a mature creative industries sector and can be divided into a number of distinct but overlapping eras. Initially, radio developed as a 'new technology and means of two-way communication in the 1920s' (Miller, 1993, p. 41). After the early experimental years, listeners could purchase "sealed sets" but this control method proved unworkable as listeners 'simply opened the sets up and adjusted them' (Walkington, 2000). The licensing authority, the Post Master General's office, then divided broadcasting stations into those financed by listeners' licence fees ("A" Class stations) and those financed by advertising ("B" Class stations), and abolished sealed sets (Holloway, 1975, p. 13). After some stations developed financial difficulties, the Federal Government nationalized the "A" class stations. The Australian Broadcasting Company (ABC) was formed from this and was

P. McIntyre et al., *Creativity and Creative Industries in Regional Australia*, Palgrave Studies in Creativity and Culture, https://doi.org/10.1007/978-3-031-45972-6_12

contracted to supply programs for a national broadcasting service, resuming expired Class "A" licenses. It was difficult to satisfy all audiences given distance and scattered population, so the government established a service similar to the BBC. The Australian Broadcasting Commission Act was passed in 1932 'ensuring that national and commercial stations operated in the public interest' (Holloway, 1975, p. 15). The Australian Federation of Commercial Broadcasting Stations was formed at a similar time to protect the interests of the "B" Class stations.

With these broad and nascent structures in place, radio entered its "Golden Age" in the 1930s (Lane, 1994). The medium was now the country's primary one and its success saw the 'emergence of a diverse production sector and debates over Australian content and wartime censorship in the 1940s' (Miller, 1993, p. 41). Radio set the scene for much of the social and cultural activity in the country as well as being a forerunner of what was to come.

Television was introduced in 1956, heralding changes in radio listening habits. It was during this third phase that many advertisers transferred their money to television and doomsayers predicted radio's death. However, while the large-scale, show business aspects of radio of the 1940s and early 1950s were no longer viable, commercial radio quickly fashioned a new identity (Potts, 1989, p. 168) through specialization (Keith, 1990, p. 163). Radio became linked to popular music and formats such as the Top Forty, borrowed from the USA, were put to commercial use.

In another development, community broadcasting began in the Seventies following perceived listener dissatisfaction with existing media services. The FM broadcasting band had become available and people wanted more access and participation in the media: 'Australia was one of the first countries to legislate for independent, non-government, non-commercial broadcasting' (Letch, 1997, online). The catalyst for the introduction of community radio was the Music Broadcasting Societies (MBS) and the Public Broadcasting Association of Australia was established. The Department of the Media understood the call for access to public radio as a desire for inclusion by educational bodies, disadvantaged minorities, various individuals and the musically deprived (Tebbutt, 1989, pp. 128–129). Two pirate stations are said to have made the first non-core broadcasts, but they were short-lived with the police smashing and jamming equipment. It's generally accepted that 'Adelaide University station 5UV was the first public broadcaster, commencing in 1972 on a restricted and experimental basis' (Letch, 1997, online).

The 1970s also saw a rigid approach to formatting for commercial radio, as well as the advent of 2JJ (or Double J as it came to be known) on the ABC and the inception of public or community radio, alongside the introduction of FM (Letch, 1997). The early 1970s also saw the rise of what became known as media mercenaries, such as Rod Muir, with its effect on the reorganization of commercial radio. From 1974 onward, the Australian content quota ensured a vibrant music industry. While music depended on radio for promotion, at the same time radio, conversely, depended on music for much of its content (Marlow, 1995). By the 1990s, the structure of radio in Australia reflected nationally oriented commercial and government radio networks, increased talk radio, niche broadcasting and now the arrival of narrowcasting.

As Steve Ahern asserts, 'the convergence of radio receiver technology, the further specialization of niche formats, increased competition from other media and changing consumer habits' (2006, p. 14) can be seen in the birth of the Digital Audio Broadcasting (DAB) digital radio standard, upgraded to DAB+, which is used to broadcast digital radio (DITRDCA, 2023a, online). More typically, it can be seen in the advent of internet radio and podcasting. In more recent times, competition from streaming services has challenged 'radio to keep adapting and reinventing itself' (Ahern, 2006, p. 14). Many radio operatives 'now also live-stream their programs and use their websites to provide program and personality information, conduct promotions and interact with listeners' (Griffin-Foley, 2014, p. 149). Despite all of the increased competition and rapid technological change, radio still remains 'the world's most ubiquitous medium, certainly the one with the widest reach and greatest penetration' (Pease & Hendy quoted in Hendy, 2000, p. 2). It has 'survived challenges and threats due to constant adaptation' (Griffin-Foley, 2014, p. 150) and its ongoing resilience is reflected in the 2022 Infinite Dial Australia study which shows that:

> Radio is the leading audio choice, and podcasts continue to capture the imagination and ears of Australian listeners with a staggering level of individual weekly listening of over seven hours every week. With increases in the key drivers of growth such as smart speaker ownership, connected cars, use of radio station apps and great podcast content, we can expect to see this level of digital audio growth to be sustained … Podcast listening through in-dash systems took a jump as 13% of podcast listeners in Australia age 12+ say they listen through an in-dash system, up from 8% in 2021 … Eighty percent of Australians 12+ are reached by AM/FM/DAB+ radio in the last week, both live and on-demand. Online listening to radio via a radio station's app is up six percentage points year over year as 50% of online radio listeners use the station's app v. 44% in 2021. (Edison Research, 2022, online)

The Structure of Radio in Australia

Radio in Australia operates across four sectors. Side by side, it has a commercial (free-enterprise) sector and a national, government-funded system centered on the ABC. The former was based on the American model and the latter on the BBC (Webb, 1981, p. 159). Community radio came later with the 1970s introduction of FM. Now there are independent internet-based radio services that rely on streaming, podcasting and other digital operations. Based on the Broadcasting Services Act, the Federal Government's Department of Infrastructure, Transport, Regional Development, Communication and the Arts has oversight of the industry (DITRDCA, 2023b, online). Within its purview sits the Australian Communications and Media Authority (ACMA), which is the organization that oversees ownership and control rules. At the next level down, 'most aspects of program content are governed by codes of practice developed by industry groups' (ACMA, 2023, online). Commercial radio is represented by Commercial Radio Australia (CRA) and community radio by the Community Broadcasters Association of Australia (CBAA) while independent and/or net-based operators are partially represented by The Independent Australian Radio Broadcasters Association (IARBA).

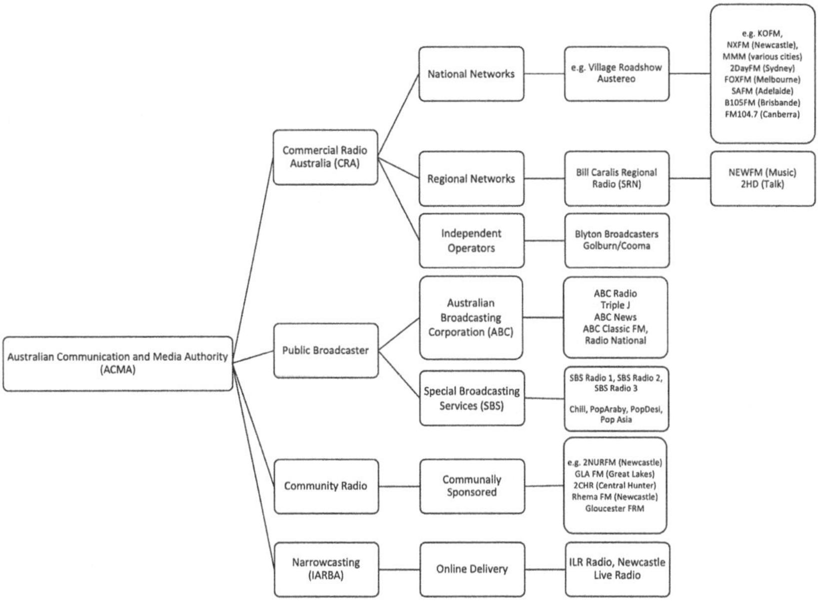

Fig. 12.1 The structure of radio in Australia

The ABC is responsible to Parliament through the ABC Charter (Fig. 12.1).

Business Models: Part of the Shared Domain Knowledge for Radio

Various business models, ways of earning an income, are important constituents of domain knowledge and are necessary to understand in order to operate within the radio industry. For example, commercial radio's income depends on aggregating audiences around content and on-selling this audience to advertisers: 'Under their licence conditions, commercial radio stations … charge fees for broadcasting commercials' (CRA, 2002, online). Ratings services such as Neilson determine audience share. Expenditures include infrastructure, licences (ACMA), fees for playing music (Australasian Performing Rights Association known as APRA), wages, operations and studio production costs.

On the other hand, government radio is funded by public monies through Parliament and augmented through sales of merchandise. For example, the ABC's Charter is to 'provide innovative and comprehensive broadcasting services of a high standard … and to transmit news, current affairs and entertainment programs outside Australia' (APH, 2017, online). The ABC delivers broadcasting services: over four national radio networks (Radio National, ABC Classic FM, Triple J and ABC NewsRadio); local radio through nine metropolitan radio stations in capital cities and Newcastle, and 51 regional stations throughout Australia; three internet-music-based services; and Radio Australia, an international service run by the ABC that broadcasts via shortwave, online, satellite and local rebroadcasts to the Asia-Pacific region in five local languages—Indonesian, Tok Pisin (Pidgin), Chinese, Vietnamese and Khmer (Cambodian)—as well as English (APH, 2017, online).

The community sector (CBAA, 2006) earns income from sponsorship, donations and grants. It runs on a shoestring budget using volunteers and minimizes costs by pooling resources. For example, CRN is the national Community Radio (Satellite) Network that enables community stations to share news, talk, music and entertainment programs. The CRN service offers stable, cost-effective, broadcast quality audio, accessible via either the Digital Delivery Network (DDN) or live satellite audio feed (CBAA, 2017, online).

Independent radio is where diverse business models operate and a number of innovative entrepreneurial approaches occur. Ison Live Radio (ILR), for example, syndicates weekly programs to terrestrial stations around the globe. These are produced in multiple formats with 'over a million free to air radio listeners each week' (Ison, i/v May 2015). ILR also delivers non-stop music programming in nine formats via the internet or satellite. Ison claims that 'although web casting is a somewhat minor concern with us, we also have a substantial share in online radio in Australia' (Ison, i/v May 2015). Income is primarily derived from the sale of syndicated programs and aggregated audiences to advertisers.

Operational Methods: Field Actions

Most stations in Australia, including the ABC, now belong to networks managed and programmed from centrally run administrative centers (Criticos, 2016).

The Australian Broadcasting Corporation (ABC) is a federal agency that works within the ABC Act 1983 and its Charter (ABC, 2023b, online). Its functions are to provide creative, innovative and comprehensive broadcasting services, contribute to a sense of national identity, and inform and entertain, reflecting cultural diversity and providing educational content. Transmission outside Australia broadcasts news, current affairs, entertainment and cultural enrichment to encourage awareness of Australia and its attitudes while informing Australian citizens overseas (ABC, 2023b, online).

Proprietors of commercial networks may be larger companies, but the network structures and operational methods have remained reasonably consistent for three decades. How workers operate within a station depends on its size: 'Generally, a metropolitan radio station employs more staff than a provincial or regional station. Sometimes, in smaller stations, team members may have multiple responsibilities' (CRA, 2017a, online). However, each station has a similar set of positions covering administration, programming (including news) and production, traffic and scheduling as well as various technical roles and functions. The commercial sector includes sales and audience research.

The administration sector of a station 'includes the general manager and staff who generally ensure the station operates in a businesslike way' (CRA, 2017a, online). The sales section is critically important as it produces the station's revenue by selling the audience acquired by the programs. Advertising is sold on the basis of airtime cost which is related to daypart and ratings/share. Advertising may also be handled by local and national representatives and agencies. National accounts can have a dedicated account executive but are more usually handled by the sales director, who deals directly with an advertising agency or media buyer. Sales people most often work on a retainer supplemented by a commission, delivering against a target budget.

The programming section (Romaro & Wheatley, 1992) puts together:

> a coherent and profitable program schedule. They make all program choices and decide on scheduling and on-air matters ... Programming is overseen by a program director (PD) … The whole economic and psychological direction of the radio station is in the program director's hands. They must not only be seen to have flair, but also must be rational, analytical and verbal … they need to develop excellent antennae for the nuances of programming and understand the economics and budget of their department. (CRA, 2017a, online).

The music director (MD) works closely with the program director and they are the link between the music industry (suppliers of content) and the radio industry. The on-air announcers, who may be disk jockeys or news journalists, are the celebrity voices that the station uses to ensure the program material is linked together and presented cohesively.

> Radio listeners tune-in to hear music, news, announcers and journalists. Meanwhile journalists … compile and report the news … The closer the relationship announcers and journalists build with listeners, the higher the loyalty and the longer the audience listens … The success of this team effort is measured by independent radio audience surveys. (CRA, 2002, online)

All these positions are supported by the technical department: 'Putting radio to air is … a team effort' (CRA, 2002, online).

Important Personnel: Choice Making Members of the Field of Radio

Personnel and the jobs they enact are typically much the same across all sectors of radio, with slight variations, but for now we will assume the commercial sector as the basis for our description here.

> The job of Station Manager requires commercial acumen, creativity and the ability to lead and direct a team. Responsibilities include handling the

> daily problems of station operations in consultation with the Program Director, Sales Manager and Chief Engineer. The manager oversees policies and handles relations with the Australian Broadcasting Authority (ABA) and other government bodies, also usually participating in community activities. (CRA, 2002, online).

The Sales Director and salespeople produce the station's revenue by maintaining existing sales levels and generating new accounts, researching new angles and compiling advertising packages for clients. In doing this, they are supported by, and work with, the Creative Director who comes up with concepts while a 'copywriter [then] aims to write exciting and fresh radio commercials that observe a client's advertising objectives and appeal to listeners' (CRA, 2002, online). When the Creative Director has a script, requirements are passed onto production where '[a] producer will use audio and technical equipment … and might also: use music; historical tapes from news archives; original and pre-recorded sound effects; and voice talent' (CRA, 2002, online). The Traffic Scheduler coordinates the timing of ads and spots with programming and sales. Program Directors (PD) oversee the on-air sound, manage staff, conduct checks to improve on-air performance, promotions and production and adhere to license requirements. They check all logs before distribution to on-air staff, coordinate station research and review new music. They are the liaison figure between sales and programming, overseeing production of commercials and promotions and must understand all station sections. The PD works closely with the Music Director (MD), whose main function is to select music that is appropriate for the station's format. On-air announcers or disk jockeys are the voice of the station and present and link the program material compiled by the team. The news team compiles and reports the news—the news director's direct responsibility. The technical department is responsible for maintenance of the broadcast equipment (Fig. 12.2).

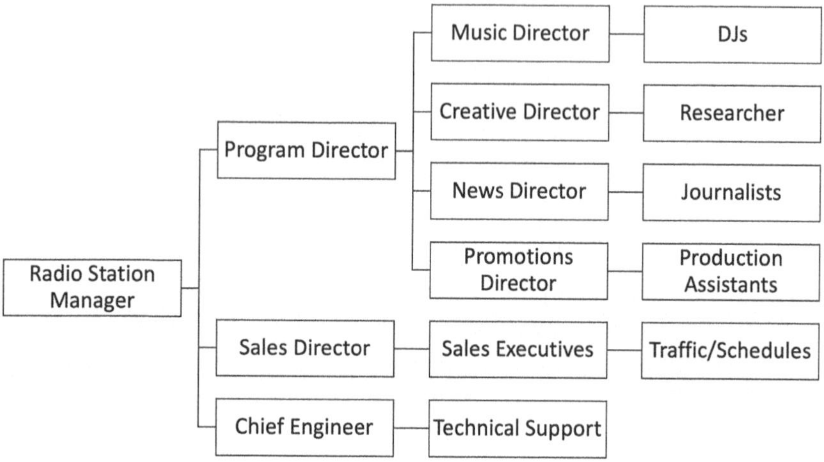

Fig. 12.2 Radio personnel involved in a typical radio station

Hunter Region Radio: Field, Domain and Agency at Work

Radio is 'constantly reinventing itself broadcasting in both analogue and digital' (CRA, 2017c, online). This is certainly the case for radio in the Hunter, itself a reflection of and a constituent part of broader national structures. Radio is ubiquitous. It can be heard in most households, in cars, via apps on mobile phones, and often in many retail outlets and workshops in the valley. It is claimed to be 'the original interactive media—live on-air, via sms, email and online opportunities to interact and express a view' (CRA, 2017c, online). Importantly, as demonstrated by the actions taken by 1233 ABC during emergencies in this region, radio is seen as 'reliable when access to other media breaks down such as when natural disasters strike and mobile phone networks go down' (CRA, 2017c, online). Like all regional radio, radio in the Hunter is perceived to be 'live and local, reflecting the community of listeners' (Criticos, 2016).

Community Radio: An Important Part of the Interconnected (Eco)System

Since licenses became available in the 1970s, community stations have flourished in the Hunter. Great Lakes FM broadcasts adult contemporary music and news on satellite relay from commercial radio station 2UE while other community stations in the Valley include Gloucester FM, Rhema FM, 2NURFM and 2CHR which:

> serves as voice media for the community of the Central Hunter area. It is operated completely by volunteers … Programs include a wide variety of musical tastes interspersed with hourly News and Weather. There is also pertinent local information and bulletins, regular community notices and many specialty shows of cultural and social interest. (2CHR, 2023, online).

Gloucester Broadcasters Association Inc. was formed in 2005 and, after taking three years to acquire a temporary license (TCBL), has 'been broadcasting on 104.1FM since 1 June 2009' (Bucketts Radio, 2023, online) as Bucketts Radio. Their transmitter is on loan and they are staffed by volunteers and 'sponsorship advertising from mainly local businesses, as well as memberships and donations' (Bucketts Radio, 2023, online). Rhema FM Newcastle, a Christian community station, 'has been established for over 35 years and has been on air full-time for over 20' (Rhema FM, 2023, online). Meanwhile, 2NURFM at the University of Newcastle began broadcasting in March of 1978. Wayne Stamm, having begun his radio career in the Seventies, was station manager from 2005 until 2018:

> Everything that I've picked up about the industry is by working in the industry. I was lucky enough to start in those days where you could run off and work at a commercial station in the bush somewhere and learn your trade … We're seeing more people come out of Communication courses now. (Stamm, i/v Apr 2016)

Having worked in news, in sales, on air and now in management, Stamm understands what makes a radio station work. Given its nature as a creative medium 'there has to be an awful lot of collaboration' (Stamm, i/v Apr 2016). There are similarities but also radical differences between the commercial and community sectors. Stamm notes that community radio has to give on-air access to the community and is limited to five minutes per hour of sponsorship. Commercial radio has more freedom to play what they like on air and they 'of course are in it for the money' (Stamm, i/v Apr 2016). While the commercials' business model relies on advertising, some community stations are affiliated with a University and raise their funds from sponsorship with fundraising underwriting much of the work. It was thought that streaming services such as Pandora and Spotify would have a large impact but Stamm feels there is evidence that Pandora and Spotify 'have well and truly peaked' (Stamm, i/v Apr 2016) with podcasting growing.

> We thought that was going to have a huge impact on what we were doing but we've changed the way we do radio so it's become more of an interactive medium … The gen Ys and Millennials are the ones dropping off things like Pandora and Spotify … Facebook and Twitter and Instagram are ways we now communicate with the audience. (Stamm, i/v Apr 2016)

Competition is broader than sponsorship or listeners alone, but while the radio world has opened up through digitization, many stations, constrained by regulation, don't find it feasible to move too much activity online. The station Stamm manages has moved into the social media sphere and towards podcasting: 'We're posting interviews … It allows you to do more than you can on air' (Stamm, i/v Apr 2016). But audience growth has not expanded in a commensurate way. As Stamm says,

> the amount of money we're paying for our online stream per listener is significantly higher than we're paying for our terrestrial signal … Networked terrestrial radio remains significant … but there is also talk of hybrid radio superseding the push for digital audio broadcasting … Hybrid radio would work on your smart phone so you would get the metadata which will give you the album cover notes, an opportunity to download the song, and maybe even give you concert information. That would come up as part of your data feed. (Stamm, i/v Apr 2016)

Hybrid radio may therefore overcome one of the major problems of digital radio: 'The problem with digital radio is it's restricted to the capital cities. The biggest drama is that digital, unlike FM, doesn't fade. Digital stops ... then there is a substantial cost for community broadcasters to be part of digital' (Stamm, i/v Apr 2016).

If the FM chips in smartphones are activated, 'hybrid radio is the right way to go' (Stamm, i/v Apr 2016) but Stamm also suggests but FM is not 'going to be turned off for a long time' (Stamm, i/v Apr 2016) adding that 'people listen to radio … because they like it' (Stamm, i/v Apr 2016).

The ABC: A Creative and Innovative Organization That Has Embraced the Digital

The ABC has a strong presence in the region. Along with Triple J, Classic FM is nationally networked into the Hunter, as is ABC News. Radio National broadcasts programs that explore ideas in science, arts and books, the mind and human behavior and is also broadcast into the Hunter on the AM band as well as being available on the ABC Listen app. Radio Australia, broadcasting internationally into Asia, has a large online presence while, at the other end of the scale, ABC Local Radio has mutated into ABC Regional: 'In 2014, the Corporation created two new divisions: Digital Network … and ABC Regional. New investment in digital platforms and better streaming facilities … to meet audience expectations' (ABC, 2023a, online). For example, the Triple J is the youth network that both broadcasts and narrowcasts into the Hunter. Richard Kingsmill, a long-standing PD at Triple J until recently, was well aware of what music suited the demographic he was servicing. He stated that:

> We certainly listen to our audience. I do as much field work as I can by going to record stores … We use the overseas press as a guide, but we need to stay ahead … If there's a vibe on a band … this is important. (Kingsmill, i/v Jul 2014)

Content, available as podcasts and iView first-release productions, has become an important audience contact point. ABC Radio has now integrated its digital and broadcast platforms better and taken on audience-centric approaches, allowing audiences to listen live, go to station websites or listen on the ABC Listen app. This means ABC radio employees now need to be multi-skilled.

To demonstrate, Phil Ashley-Brown's story is typical. He completed a degree at Newcastle but then, being unemployed, he volunteered for a local member of Parliament, eventually working as a speechwriter. Radio 'had always interested me. I was inspired by what you could do with radio, with the intimacy [its] scope, where you can go' (Ashley-Brown, i/v Sep 2015). In his holidays, he did 'work experience in different ABC stations around the country' (Ashley-Brown, i/v Sep 2015) until he secured work. He became the Station Manager at 1233 ABC in Newcastle and is now Manager of Broadcast Content Quality for the ABC's Regional Division network. His skill set includes interviewing, editing and writing which also consists of multi-track editing and mixing but he notes that 'everyone here has to be able to take a photo ... shoot some basic video ... to post onto Facebook' (Ashley-Brown, i/v Sep 2015). *River Stories*, available as a podcast, is one of his projects:

> *River Stories* is about the Hunter River from its beginning in the Barrington Tops all the way down to Newcastle Harbour ... As someone who'd grown up in Muswellbrook, I'd experienced the river in floods, I'd seen fires rage [and] I'd met farmers who'd worked on the river, and so I came up with this idea of doing a radio series ... And then 10 years later ... I went back, but this time with a film crew, and we filmed the river ... we're not just a radio station any more, we were a multimedia centre. (Ashley-Brown, i/v Sep 2015)

These radical changes in the modes of delivery are still coupled with traditionally important functions:

> During emergencies, stations like this [1233 ABC Newcastle] are the hub of the community, and we work really hard to make sure that what we're doing here reflects truly what's going on. We use every single element of the radio station ... But the skills of our audience are really where the power is. Those people have more information than any of the emergency services ... They're the people on the ground. So, it's almost like we've got 100,000 people out there reporting in. (Ashley-Brown, i/v Sep 2015)

The Upper Hunter has its share of storytellers working for the ABC. One of these is the nationally iconic Philip Adams. Adams lives in the Upper Hunter and often uses the ABC Upper Hunter radio studio to do his long running *Late Night Live* radio series for Radio National. His program is heard and followed worldwide. Adams has been awarded a number of honorary doctorates and other prestigious honors. The National Trust cites him as a National Living Treasure. He began his radio career on commercial station 2UE, working the late shift in the 1980s and 1990s before moving to take over the *Late-Night Live* program on Radio National. It now goes global via the internet. This move into the digital realm has been successful for Adams. He suggests that this success, where he now attracts a sizable international audience with many authors and public intellectuals from around the world clamoring to be part of his radio program, is attributable to one important factor: 'I've always taken the view, whether you're making a film or writing a column, that in a sense this is cultural specificity. Being local is probably the best way to have a hope of being international' (Adams, i/v April 2016).

Adams also realizes how important his team is to him and at the same time understands the difficulties his style of conversational, locally rooted but globally oriented broadcasting presents to them. He knows he is not the only person from the creative industries, to reside in, or come from, the Upper Hunter. Murrurundi in the Upper Hunter is a case in point: 'And there, in itself, is this little festering hot spot of all sorts of very eccentric creative people living in a town which is almost ruined by poverty, and which is now being recycled as a cheap and interesting place to live by artists' (Adams, i/v April 2016).

Commercial Radio: The Interconnections of Art and Commerce

Commercial radio, with its imperative to make money, broadcasts in the Hunter primarily from Newcastle and Lake Macquarie with some stations in the Upper Hunter Valley (CRA, 2017b, online). Triple M Newcastle (previously KOFM and, originally, 2KO) has a targeted demographic profile of 30 to 54-year-olds, running an "adult variety" format while its sister station, HITFM, is a "hot adult contemporary" format for 18- to 39-year-olds. These formats are directed at specific forms of music, indicating a symbiotic relationship between radio and the music industry. As Mike Byrne, former program director for the stations, said:

> Music is art and it is commerce and when the music industry treats itself like a business, they sell more records. When what we are able to play intersects with what the music industry delivers to us both industries benefit. (Byrne, i/v 2003)

Both HITFM and Triple M Newcastle belong to the Southern Cross Austereo (SCA) network. This network 'has the largest regional commercial radio footprint in Australia with stations … separated into two targeted brands' (SCA, 2017, online). These brands include the HIT and Triple M networks but SCA also owns the Fox, 2 Day and SeaFM brands (SCA, 2017, online). Out of all the commercial stations in Australia, SCA operates the most digital radio spectrum with stations such as Buddha Radio, Easy Radio, Old Skool Radio and Kinderling Kids Radio all available to the Hunter audience. The group is also involved in regional free-to-air TV networks as well as online, mobile and various one-off events, giving it a large media footprint.

Hunter stations, 2HD and NEWFM, on the other hand, are part of the Super Radio Network (SRN). As Harry Criticos (2016) writes, SRN is a subsidiary of the privately owned company BOL, which owns 40 radio stations across Northern NSW and South East Queensland. SRN is the largest regional network in NSW with two formats operating: music (contemporary hit radio/adult oriented radio) on FM and DAB+ (digital radio) and talk/music (adult oriented radio) on AM. Apart from the regional stations that have a window to broadcast locally from 5:30 a.m. or 6:00 a.m. to 6:00 p.m., SRN stations receive networked programs from 9:00 am until 5:30 a.m. the following day. Supplying and distributing networked programs is shared between three SRN stations in NSW so there is no central control point for the distribution of AM program content when compared to the FM network on SRN, which is heavily centralized (Criticos, 2016, pp. 115–116).

John McGahan, former station manager at 2KO (the station that is now Triple M Newcastle) and community station 2NURFM, gave examples of how Newcastle radio audiences have been categorized. 2HD audiences were typified by a '40+ blue collar bloke who enjoys 2–3 schooners after work at the pub … He lives on "Struggle Street" but gets by' (McGahan, i/v 2003). 2KO audiences were best envisaged as 'white collar workers, female aged 30–49 … "grocery buyers"' (McGahan, i/v 2003). NEW FM 'aimed at the 13–34 demographic, skewed to males … employed blue collar workers who spend money on cars and entertainment. They have little loyalty and are hard to keep as listeners' (McGahan, i/v 2003). NXFM (now HITFM) was aimed at 'females whose average age is 26. They like dance music [and] to be in the know in terms of gossip' (McGahan, i/v 2003). The ABC's audience is 'conservative. They don't listen to commercial radio and they also don't listen for a great length of time' (McGahan, i/v 2003).

The Upper Hunter area, Singleton, Muswellbrook and Scone, is serviced by two commercial stations. 2NM targets a 40+ demographic with an "adult contemporary" format while Power FM targets 18 to 35-year-olds with a "contemporary hit radio" format. Both are part of the Grant Broadcasters network, a family owned business that owns stations in the Northern Territory, Queensland, South Australia, Tasmania, Victoria and, of course, the Upper Hunter in New South Wales.

The Independent Sector: Disruptors and Innovators Within the Creative (Eco) System of Radio

Radio has continued to be resilient and adaptable. This willingness to try new things is a hallmark of radio's continuing survival. As well as the national broadcaster, commercial networks and the community sectors, it also has room for small independents such as Bay FM in Port Stephens, which is local, and family owned and operated. However, an example of an innovative approach taken in the independent radio sector is that of Sean Ison's Live Radio (now Australian Broadcast Media).

Ison began his career 25 years ago as a "cart boy" and working as a producer for commercial stations. He then went on-air in community radio and from there to narrowcast programming. He is now President of The Independent Australian Radio Broadcasters Association and co-owner of a small media business that successfully syndicates narrowcast programming internationally and delivers streaming services. Ison asserts that 'every product that's created has to be saleable, it has to have a dollar value attached to it. It has to be something we can either fly with advertising or something we can sell as a package to other radio or TV stations' (Ison, i/v May 2015).

Unlike the region's free-to-air commercial radio stations, Ison's Live Radio (ILR) has fully leveraged the internet and its affordances. This wasn't always the case. Ison admits that initially 'I had no real use for the internet, no experience of it until I went back to university in Newcastle, and it opened up a whole world for me' (Ison, i/v May 2015). He realized he could use the platform well, but the programs he made needed content, domain material from the space of works, and they needed buyers, or member of the field: 'We were working with a lot of musicians and a lot of them actually put us on to stations' (Ison, i/v May 2015). Ison then:

> Set up an industry website called ausradiosearch.com and offered all kinds of free services and content as a package. This attracted a lot of Australian and overseas traffic from radio stations (about 800 visitors a day at its peak). We then hitched onto this and offered them shows. (Ison, i/v May 2015)

It was this free service that demonstrated the actions of the gift economy and why reciprocity is so valuable. This interchange enabled Ison to make the international contacts he needed. This, in turn, enabled ILR to deliver programs to just about every continent on the planet. As Ison also reveals, 'although webcasting is a somewhat minor concern with us, we also have a substantial share in online radio in Australia with our daily web casts' (ILR, 2016, online). Furthermore, Ison too further entrepreneurial risks and established Australian Broadcasting Media (ABM). ILR and a business partner:

> …got investors from Israel to set it up and we bought a stack of stations—they're all country music stations—down the Hume Highway and in towards the Riverina, [all] narrow casts; they're low power FM. But if you chain it together you end up with one big sort of radio station. Our business is sort of two tiered now; we're still doing syndicated programming but we're also able to put the same resources into radio stations of our own, and we play quite a lot of syndicated shows as well … The way those [stations] are set up they go into independent mode where it's all computerized. They basically play, do their own thing at certain times of the day and then at particular times we have a nationally syndicated morning show. (Ison, i/v May 2015)

These shows use music as their main form of aggregated content. As such, there is a legal requirement for remuneration to the musicians who originate the content. ILR pays fees to the Australasian Performing Rights Association (APRA) which remits the fees to songwriters nationally and, with its partner organizations, internationally as per the Berne Convention. Ison states that his company negotiated an arrangement with APRA. Once he moved into streaming, these practices became complex. As Ison explains 'we started a thing called Radio Sydney which is 250-odd streams of internet radio, and we had to negotiate a special arrangement for that' (Ison, i/v May 2015). Ison readily admits that 'the whole industry legally is in a state of flux' (Ison, i/v May 2015). A court case based on the legalities around simulcasting, made possible by certain technological innovations was a test case for radio overall. CRA had argued that an internet simulcast was not a broadcast and, on appeal to the Full Federal Court it lost that case. Radio broadcasters could now no longer employ their existing PPCA licenses to stream audio recordings over the internet: 'The decision meant that rather than having one PPCA licence covering both radio and internet broadcast, radio stations are obliged to have a second, separate PPCA licence to broadcast their programming online' (ACC, 2016, online).

As Ison argued, there were 'several concepts that were simply outdated that just didn't really apply' (Ison, i/v May 2015). His lawyers argued, as they were negotiating with APRA that 'the wording of the legislation didn't cover what was being said, or it may have covered it, but it didn't cover it accurately' (Ison, i/v May 2015). Despite this, both ABM and APRA negotiated a suitable arrangement that was amenable to both parties and, as Ison continues his business in a dynamic context continually in a state of flux, he keeps on scanning the horizon for other possibilities. He realizes that 'you have these different models overseas. I think we just need to catch up' (Ison, i/v May 2015).

Summary

Radio, as we have seen above, has a long and deep history within the region and is an important and mature sector within the Hunter's creative industries. This entire sector is populated by a group of dedicated and idiosyncratic choice making agents, that is those possessing decision making agency, who are connected locally, nationally and globally. They exist with the structures of an industry that is largely thanks to the digital world it now exists in, at one and the same time, local, national and global. These structures include highly interconnected and networked commercial businesses, government-funded stations with a strong online presence, a well-established community sector and a set of independent operators usually working online and outside the prior categories. Podcasting has become important within the radio sector not apart from it. As a cultural form and also as an economic concern, radio has continued to be resilient and adaptable inside a complex, interactive and scalable creative (eco)system. This creative system in action is central to the creation of novelty and value in the sort of changing marketplaces that typify the radio sector and certainly typify the broader, loosely coupled system of production that is the creative industries.

References

2CHR. (2023). *About 2CHR*. Retrieved March 15, 2023, from https://www.2chr.org/aboutus.html

ABC. (2023a). *ABC history*. ABC. Retrieved March 15, 2023, from http://about.abc.net.au/abc-history/#2010s

ABC. (2023b). *Legislative framework*. ABC. Retrieved March 15, 2023, from http://about.abc.net.au/how-the-abc-is-run/what-guides-us/legislative-framework/

ACC. (2016). *Navigating the content streams*. Australian Copyright Council. Retrieved June 25, 2017, from https://www.copyright.org.au/acc_prod/ACC/News_items/2016/WINv9_-_PPCA.aspx

ACMA. (2023). *Industry codes of practice*. Australian Communications and Media Authority. Retrieved March 15, 2023, from https://www.acma.gov.au/industry-codes-practice

Ahern, S. (2006). *Making radio: A practical guide to working in radio* (2nd ed.). Allen & Unwin.

APH. (2017). *Funding of the Australian broadcasting corporation* (e-brief: Online only issued November 2006, revised and updated version of august 2003 brief by Dr Kim Jackson). Parliament of Australia. Retrieved March 7, 2017, from http://www.aph.gov.au/About_Parliament/Parliamentary_Departments/Parliamentary_Library/Publications_Archive/archive/fundingabc

Bucketts Radio. (2023). *Bucketts Radio 104.1FM*. Retrieved March 15, 2023, from http://buckettsradio.com.au/

CBAA. (2006). *Content*. Communication broadcasting Association of Australia. Retrieved July 20, 2006, from http://www.cbaa.org.au/content.php/2.html

CBAA. (2017). *Community radio network*. Communication Broadcasting Association of Australia. Retrieved June 26, 2017, from https://www.cbaa.org.au/crn

CRA. (2002). *Careers in commercial radio*. Federation of Australian Radio Broadcasters. Retrieved June 20, 2017, from http://www.commercialradio.com.au/ssl/documents/Careers_in_Commercial_Radio.pdf

CRA. (2017a). *Careers in radio booklet*. Commercial Radio Australia. Retrieved March 7, 2017, from www.commercialradio.com.au/.../Human.../Careers-in-Radio-Booklet-2014-(1).doc

CRA. (2017b). *Commercial radio market profiles—Upper Hunter*. Retrieved June 26, 2017, from http://radioitsalovething.com.au/RIALT/media/RIALT/Audio/NSW-ACT_Hunter-Valley.pdf

CRA. (2017c). *Why radio?* Retrieved June 26, 2017, from http://www.radioitsalovething.com.au/Why-Radio.aspx

Criticos, H. (2016). *The effect of centralisation on regional radio: A case study of the Super Radio Network in Northern New South Wales and south East Queensland*. Unpublished PhD Thesis, University of Newcastle.

DITRDCA. (2023a). *Digital radio*. Department of Infrastructure, Transport, Regional Development, Communication and the Arts. Retrieved March 15, 2023, from https://www.infrastructure.gov.au/media-technology-communications/radio/digital-radio

DITRDCA. (2023b). *Media, communication and arts*. Department of Infrastructure, Transport, Regional Development, Communication and the Arts. Retrieved March 15, 2023, from https://www.infrastructure.gov.au/media-communications-arts

Edison. (2022). *The infinite dial 2022 Australia*. Edison Research. Retrieved March 15, 2023, from https://www.edisonresearch.com/the-infinite-dial-2022-australia/

Griffin-Foley, B. (2014). Radio. In S. Cunningham & S. Turnbull (Eds.), *The media and communications in Australia* (4th ed., pp. 133–150). Allen & Unwin.

Hendy, D. (2000). *Radio in the global age*. Polity Press.

Holloway, J. (1975). *Radio in Australia*. Reed Education Publications.

ILR. (2016). *Home*. Ison live Radio. Retrieved July 19, 2016, from http://www.isonliveradio.com/index.html

Keith, M. (1990). *Radio production: Art and science*. Focal Press.

Lane, R. (1994). *The golden age of Australian radio drama: 1923–1960*. Melbourne University Press.

Letch, K. (1997). *Just what is community broadcasting anyway?* Retrieved August 15, 1997, from http://rrr.apana.org.au/triprad/community.html

Marlow, K. (1995). *The crucial role of radio in the music industry*. AUSMUSIC.

McGahan, J. (2003, May 17). *Notes for guest lecture to CMNS2050 radio industry studies*. Personal Collection of J. McGahan, University of Newcastle, Newcastle, Australia.

Miller, T. (1993). Radio. In S. Cunningham & G. Turner (Eds.), *The media in Australia: Industries, text, audiences* (pp. 41–58). Allen & Unwin.

Potts, J. (1989). *Radio in Australia*. NSW University Press.

Rhema FM. (2023). *Who we are*. Rhema FM. Retrieved June 26, 2017, from https://www.rhemafm.com.au/about/

Romaro, C., & Wheatley, A. (1992). Programming. In L. Baird (Ed.), *Guide to radio production* (pp. 83–89). Allen and Unwin.

SCA. (2017). *Southern Cross Austereo*. Retrieved June 26, 2017, from http://www.southerncrossaustereo.com.au/radio/

Tebbutt, J. (1989). Constructing broadcasting for the public. In H. Wilson (Ed.), *Australian communication and the public sphere* (pp. 128–146). Macmillan.

Walkington, R. (2000). *History of professional radio broadcasting*. Radioscholl. Retrieved February 16, 2000, from http://radioscholl.com.au/web6e.htm

Webb, M. (1981). Radio on: Music in the air. In P. Beilby & M. Roberts (Eds.), *The Australian music directory 1981–82*. Australian Music Directory Pty Ltd.

13

Film and Television

A Brief History of Global Film and Television

Celluloid filmmaking has been around for over a century and it has 'straddled national boundaries and crossed continents' (Dawson & Holmes, 2012, p. 1). Cinema genres include 'comedies, westerns, thrillers, science fiction, drama, melodrama, documentaries, historical dramas, raw footage, compilation films, actuality footage, costume dramas, spoofs and remakes (Treacey, 2016, p. 2). In Western cultures, Hollywood cinema dominates. In non-Western cinema, the Indian and Nigerian film industries have greater outputs but earn less at the box office (Dawson & Holmes, 2012). The electronic medium of television, developed throughout the twentieth century, brought screen content into living rooms (Collie, 2007; Shimpach, 2020) and, in more recent decades, into consumers' hands, via social and digital platforms existing on smartphones (Schleser & Xu, 2021). Television encompasses other screen forms apart from drama, comedy and documentaries such as live events and sports, 24/7 news and current affairs, reality TV, infotainment, games and panel shows as well as all forms of children's content. It has merged with the

P. McIntyre et al., *Creativity and Creative Industries in Regional Australia*, Palgrave Studies in Creativity and Culture, https://doi.org/10.1007/978-3-031-45972-6_13

processes involved with unrestricted access to digital multi-channels, web series, and platforms like YouTube (Brown & Duthie, 2019). Commercially, both film and television have had complex business structures coupled with the ownership over content creation through copyright and the means of exhibition, distribution or broadcasting of that content. Recent innovations for both film and television are focused on the capture and exhibition end of the production chain, although these innovations do present interesting challenges for screen creatives who need to earn an income whilst responding to changing practices and commercial structures.

Cinema began in 1895 when the Lumiere brothers patented the *cinematographe*, a lightweight film camera and projector. The first commercial film screening took place in Paris in that year too (Lule, 2016, pp. 374–378). In 1906, the first commercially successful feature film, *The Story of the Kelly Gang* was made in Australia. However, many of the films in the very early years were non-fiction works such as travel films and documentaries. An example is the 1922 documentary *Nanook of the North* by Robert Flaherty. The silent film industry was well established in Hollywood by 1915 and the *talkies* followed with *The Jazz Singer* in 1927. In Australia there was a boom occurring too, with the production of 150 local films before the Great Depression (Weaving, 2014). Cinema was originally black and white, with color film stock appearing in the late 1940s. Cinema's "Golden Age" began in the 1930s with unparalleled social, cultural and economic success—two-thirds of Americans were attending cinema once a week (Lule, 2016, p. 385). What underpinned this success was the establishment of US Motion Picture Studios like Warner Bros., Metro-Goldwyn-Mayer and 20th Century Fox. These were vertically integrated businesses controlling every part of the system, from production to distribution and exhibition, with complex contracts preventing all film personnel like directors, actors, writers and technical assistants from moving between studios (Lule, 2016, p. 384). The rapid growth was not sustained, however, due to several factors including significant inflation issues following World War II, a temporary loss of key foreign markets, the beginning of television and changes to the vertical integration practices. In 1948, the Paramount Decree prevented film production companies from owning exhibition companies, and hence ended the domination of the Hollywood studio system (Gil, 2015). While the cinema industry adjusted to the implications of the Paramount Decree, the implications enabled television to thrive.

The development of television, which began early in the first decade of the twentieth century, was interrupted by World War II and that allowed the US to take the lead. By 1951, many US stations were transmitting in color (Collie, 2007, p. 12), while other nations were waiting for television to arrive. Australia was one of those, with television first broadcast in 1956 to coincide with the Melbourne Olympic Games and color broadcast arriving in 1973 (Collie, 2007). To improve the viability of television, the US developed networks and moved from a single sponsorship format to a multiple advertising model (Lotz, 2014, p. 23). This was the basis of the Free-To-Air (FTA) commercial model that allowed television networks to expand and to dominate as a mass communication medium across the latter half of the twentieth century (Shimpach, 2020).

As global television audiences grew and technology advanced, the US networks began selling content globally, initially between countries with the same technical system and common languages, while foreign language programs were subtitled or dubbed to increase profitability (Shimpach, 2020). News syndication services allowed both local and global news to be accessible. Other television genres emerged, and included current affairs, drama, sport, children's, light entertainment, quiz, panels and games shows with reality TV emerging in the 1990s. The industry transitioned to a multi-channel system hungry for content, which gave the networks a superior financial position with producers unable to cover the cost of production; they 'received license fees that were often 20 percent less than costs' (Lotz, 2014, p. 23).

While television was growing, the cinema industry was adjusting its content, markets and global business structures. The global rise of television throughout the 1960s and 1970s forced cinema to develop new genres and markets by targeting younger and untapped demographics. Smaller nations like Australia were competing with Canada and Ireland to build a reputation as an offshore Hollywood production hub. The concept of a 'local Hollywood' (Goldsmith et al., 2010) was coined for the Australian Gold Coast studio facilities with US blockbusters also being attracted to Melbourne and Sydney's Fox Studios. Blockbuster films made in Australia include *Moulin Rouge* (2001), *The Great Gatsby* (2013), *The Lego Movie* (2014), *Pirates of the Caribbean: Dead Men Tell No Tales* (2017) and, more recently, *Aquaman* (2018), Marvel's *Shang-chi and the Legend of the Ten Rings* (2021) and *Thor: Love and Thunder* (2022), and *Elvis* (2022). A favorable US exchange rate and federal and state government schemes and incentives have been critical in attracting blockbusters to Australia (Kerrigan et al., 2020). Unfortunately, the production of Australian feature films has been in a slow decline for some time. In the decade from 2010 to 2020, there has been an average of 38 Australian films produced per year with an average budget per film of $8.8 million (Screen Australia, 2022, online) and these have not had any impact at the global box office (Verhoeven et al., 2015).

The Australian film production sector operates on two-speeds, the local Hollywood model attracting US films and the cottage industry production of Australian features filmed mostly on modest and subsidized budgets (Maher et al., 2016). At the same time, the future of television is now connected to live events' coverage and the concept of 'appointment television' (Maxcy, 2013, pp. 18–35), which dominates genres like sports, spectacles, concerts and reality TV (Brown & Duthie, 2019). What television is defined as is also responding to changing viewing habits, the impact of COVID and the next generation of viewers, the Millennials, who are able to access screen content on any device, seemingly anywhere, anytime (Maxcy, 2013, p. 12; Shimpach, 2020). This ongoing digital revolution continues to reshape screen industry structures and the types of screen content being produced and hence production opportunities and practices.

Screen Industry Structures: Interconnected Global and Local Networks

The global screen industry is an import/export industry and, as screen products and practices converge, is structured to support the creation of content for a variety of large, small and handheld screens. There are three major and related sectors: local screen production; foreign screen production; and, distribution and exhibition, which separate into cinemas with box office revenues and digital online platforms, formerly known as television. The screen production sectors are volatile and often responsive to currency variations which impacts on the volume of foreign and local productions, skilled film crews and studio facilities in Australia (Kerrigan et al., 2020). Foreign film productions bring in income that contributes to local economies and enhances international recognition and access to global networks for local filmmakers.

The screen industries provide a clear example of a creative (eco)system in action with individual agents, private organizations, government entities and support services all playing a key role in the production and distribution of stories on the screen. The creation of screen ideas (Macdonald, 2012) is the first phase of creative activity where unique, innovative and novel screen content is developed. This is an expensive process that requires investment from commercial as well as, in the Australian case, government funding agencies, often requiring support from multiple global organizations to assess and invest in the best possible ideas. The production and post-production phases involve infrastructure, facilities, and high-end specialist equipment obtained through hire or rental services. This is where filmmaking creative processes occur in a staged and task specific process which is 'dependent on filmmaker's working collaboratively and creatively, in small and large teams, to complete discrete tasks that are frequently iterative and recursive' (Kerrigan, 2019, p. 335). In fact, this system of production includes all screen practitioners from key creatives, actors and booking agents through to crew members and support services. Many of these people operate as sole traders or are employed by film production studios such as, for example, Kennedy Miller Mitchell or Icon Pictures (McIntyre et al., 2023). The screen production sector also stimulates activity across the promotion and distribution arms (See Fig. 13.1).

The promotion arm of the industry focuses on industry events as well as traditional and social media, and is serviced by dedicated public relations (PR) agencies. The distribution arm is currently built around cinema exhibition, retail, rental and, increasingly, online subscription and streaming services. In Australia, most of this latter sector is foreign-owned or controlled. While US companies still dominate, there 'are also

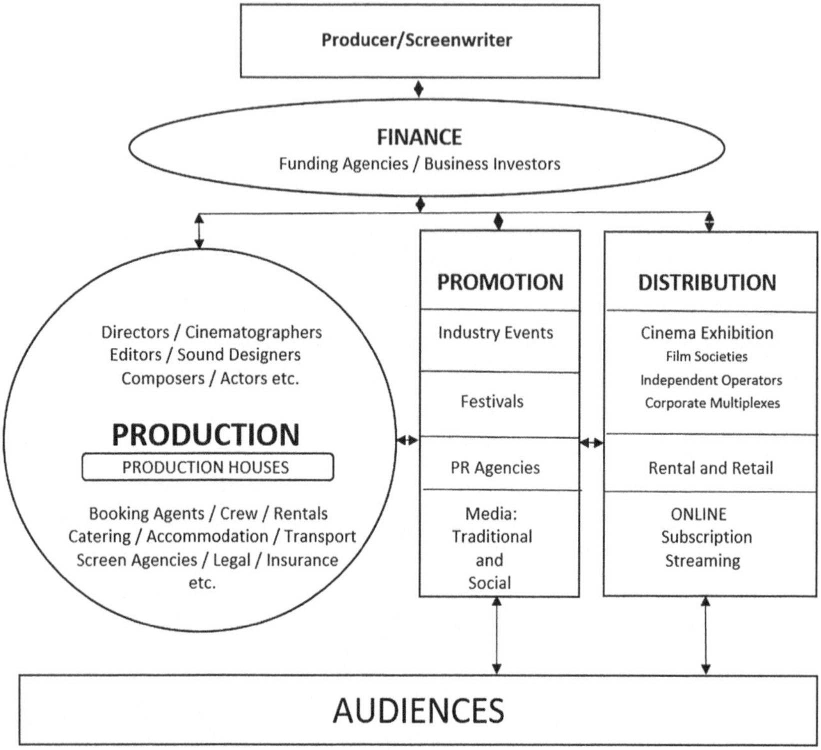

Fig. 13.1 Screen industry generalized structure

numerous smaller independent distributors in film such as Studiocanal, Rialto Distribution, Icon Film Distribution' (DAE, 2016, p. 3). The exhibition subsector includes businesses that operate cinemas as independents or as franchises for single-screen and multi-screen multiplexes (DAE, 2016, p. 3).

Associated with each of these structures are training institutions, hire companies, funding agencies, legal firms, regulators and affiliated media. All the people engaged in the film-making (eco)system rely on the success of distributors in engaging with audiences who judge, support and appreciate the filmmakers' work.

Television media ownership and control in most nations is structured through government regulations with the aim of supporting local content production and avoiding the domination of larger markets such as the US. Typically, television is comprised of four major, related sectors: commercial Free-To-Air (FTA) networks; community not-for-profit stations; government-funded public television; and, subscription services including PayTV and video-on-demand platforms (SVOD) such as Netflix, Stan and AppleTV. In Australia, these sectors are regulated by the Australian Communications and Media Authority (ACMA). ACMA enforces the Federal Government Act called the *Australian Broadcasting Services Act 1992* and also houses the codes of television practice for the commercial, community and subscription sectors, and for narrowcast television and subscription broadcast television (Pay TV). Australian television also has to comply with censorship regulations and content quotas, enforcing the creation of locally made content to be broadcast, and government policies and charters describe content commissioning, purchasing and broadcasting procedures that permit funding, and, in the case of public television, protects the service from editorial influences from the government of the day (Fig. 13.2).

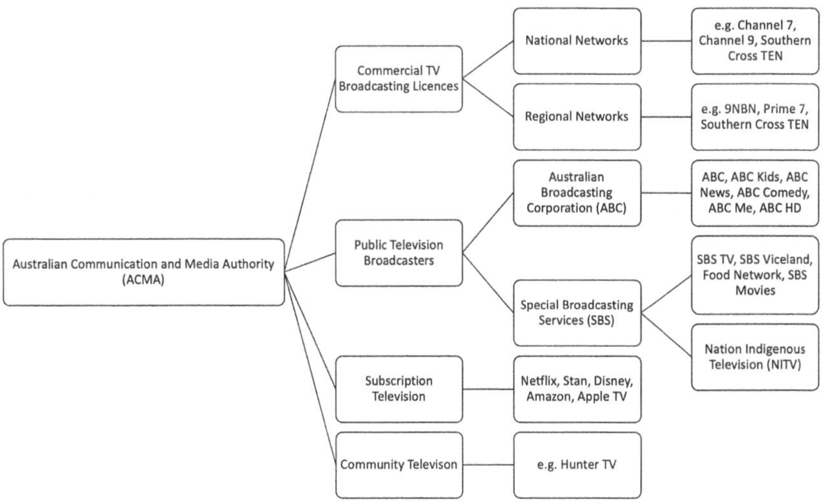

Fig. 13.2 The structure of television in Australia

Screen Business Models: Part of the Shared Domain Knowledge for Screen Industries

Screen business is focused on the production and distribution of original screen content, allowing creative agents to turn a profit by drawing on shared domain knowledges through their creative teams. These sectors use various business models while operational methods are both formal (e.g. use of contracts, government funding) and informal (e.g. sharing of labor and equipment within a gift economy). The screen industry is a marketplace where these exchanges are brokered between organizations who want to commission screen content and those who offer their screen production and filmmaking services to create that content. It is a business-to-business (B2B) model. A screen business aims to commission the best films or programs so they will deliver a Return-On-Investment (ROI) by recouping production costs and returning a profit to the film investors (Velikovsky, 2016). Given this situation, a film producer must manage and reduce the financial risk of a film's production while also maximizing the marketing and distribution opportunities. Reducing financial risk can be achieved by restructuring companies specifically for production or development operations or as a single-picture producing company (Lee & Gillen, 2011, p. 158). This business arrangement moves away from specific screen projects, instead supporting the companies that develop the screen projects, which allows the system to improve the financial viability and longevity of screen businesses. This model functions on a contractual or sub-contractual basis, with contracts used to secure production work and also used to secure the services of the people who do the work (Hesmondhalgh & Baker, 2011). Many filmmakers operate as freelancers, often represented through intermediaries such as talent and booking agents.

Multi-national television networks are focused on raising revenue either through advertising or through viewer-based subscription services. The advertising sales generate a profit, covering the commissioning or purchasing costs of television content/programs, although this model is being superseded by subscription services. Formatting rights are another source of income; networks can also make a profit from formatting original TV programs and selling those rights to other global networks (Collie, 2007). A format is a template of how to make a program, which is sold so a program can be made in another country using the original branding and production designs. Games, quiz and reality TV shows are usually formatted (Brown & Duthie, 2019) and examples include *Master Chef* or *Australia's Got Talent.* Once produced, the programs can also be sold to other global networks.

There are some differences between the cinema, television and online sectors that should be considered. In the cinema and online sector where feature films, documentaries and web series are produced, there is, in the case of Australia, usually some type of national, state, regional or local government agency offering financial support for screen projects (Kerrigan et al., 2020). The type of funding available often reflects the genres being made (e.g. fiction or documentary) or the stage of production (development, production, post-production, distribution, festivals, marketing and awards categories) (Maher et al., 2016). For example, film producers in Australia can receive a 40% refundable tax offset for feature film production (Olsberg SPI, 2016). On the other hand, cinema exhibition businesses use the brokerage model, generally operating as a franchisee on a business to consumer model (B2C). Exhibitors are supplied with a slate of films by the franchise, who decide what films will be available in their multiplex cinemas and the entry prices. Box office receipts are a crucial form of income.

Streaming platforms carrying both films and television series use a B2C model to secure user-pays subscriptions with consumers. Viewers pay an ongoing subscription, usually monthly, for unbridled and advertising-free access to all the content available on the service. These services are also called Video on Demand (VOD) or Subscription Video on Demand (SVOD) and provide time-shifting options on platforms like Netflix and Stan. Film and television producers enter into contracts with SVOD services to sell their back catalogs on a royalty basis. Other subscription services like iTunes, Apple TV, Google Play or Kayo, allow viewers to pay through an application to access the service on their own electronic device, described as a pay-per-click model. These SVOD and app-based services have become so successful that they now are able to commission content for production, a return to the B2B production model. One other model is that used by YouTube, an ad-supported VOD (AVOD). Pre-COVID television advertising was also under threat from user-pays subscription models but during the pandemic, Broadcast Video on Demand (BVOD) grew as audiences used Smart TVs connected to the internet to access content via platforms such as YouTube. This shift in domestic technology has meant advertisers can continue to create campaigns for mass audiences (PWC, 2022, pp. 5–6), meaning advertising models remain a viable way to raise revenues while, at the same time, audiences have free access to innovative and emerging technologies and screen content.

Two final models are *community-based television* and *public television*, which also operate on the B2C model. Public television is completely or partially funded by government and was designed to provide a universal service with diverse programming for minority and cultural groups (Collie, 2007, p. 14). In Australia it covers the ABC (the Australian national broadcaster) and SBS (Special Broadcasting Services), Australia's multicultural broadcaster. The ABC is exclusively funded through its charter while some profits have been generated through television merchandising and SBS has an additional revenue option through limited advertising. Community-based television, also called the not-for-profit sector, was once cost prohibitive but, with current technology, pricing can function in a more sustainable way, so there may be growth in this sector in the future.

Filmmaking as an Operational Method: Fields in Action

Filmmaking is the operational method used to make screen content. Filmmaking is used to create feature films, short films, documentaries, television programs and online content, all of which form part of the screen industries domain. Studio and field productions are the two primary operational methods and frequently both methods are used to create screen content. These operational methods are experienced across a staged production process of project development, pre-production,

production, post-production and distribution (Cohen et al., 2009). Filmmaking production stages simultaneously enable and constrain filmmakers through financial, technological, procedural, editorial, aesthetic and creative practices (Kerrigan, 2013; Kerrigan & McIntyre, 2010). Ideally the stages of production are linear although sometimes a non-linear path or an iterative process occurs. Examples of this are documentaries where filming a time-sensitive event may occur before the project development is completed. A *fast-turnaround production* is the term used to describe long form television series where the production stages are frequently intertwined, with pre-production, production and post-production occurring in parallel, requiring large teams of highly skilled crew to effectively complete the production for tight distribution schedules.

There are three filming techniques used in the production stage—single camera, multiple cameras or multi-cam—and each has its benefits or limitations, and the choice of which one to use is made against economic effectiveness, timeframes, skill of crew and production genres (Collie, 2007, p. 311). Broadly speaking, single camera is typically used for fiction filmmaking, multiple cameras are used for documentaries to capture the same action from multiple angles, and multi-cam is suitable for studio recordings or live events, sports broadcasting, games, sit-coms, news breakfast or panel shows. For example, a reality television show will use both single and multi-camera production methods (Collie, 2007, p. 227) while sporting events like the Olympics Games are broadcast "live" using outside broadcast multi-cam techniques that also record an event and make that recording available to view "as-live" with minimal post-production requirements (Collie, 2007, p. 311). Recent technological advances have streamlined the live and as-live production workflow substantially.

The green light process used in the screen industry indicates that a project is ready to proceed into production. A "green-lit" script is given a financial commitment from investors for the personnel, equipment and facilities to be committed to produce the film. Part of the green light process is to confirm which filmmaking techniques will be used to determine the scale of the production that will be enabled or constrained by genre, script length, budget and logistics. The green lighting process for a television serial is where the investors commit the money for the first episode to be shot as a pilot. A pilot episode demonstrates proof of concept. If the pilot is well received by the investors then the series may be funded for production, providing the green light to contract cast and crew over a longer production time frame.

Distribution is where the film or television show is marketed and delivered to audiences through cinemas, film festivals, television broadcast or online. Online distribution platforms (SVOD) have been an area of significant innovation over the last decade and have weakened the mass broadcasting methods that have previously dominated the distribution sector.

Creative Screen Production Personnel: Choice Making Agents and Field Members

Creativity and collaboration are the basis of filmmaking (Petrie, 1991, p. 204) and the interpersonal relationships that occur between a film's key collaborators demonstrate the social aspects that allow a screen idea to be made. Key creative collaborators, often called Heads of Department include the screenwriter, producer, director, cinematographer, sound designer, production designer and editor, with actors or presenters drawn in through a separate casting process. Technological advancements have significantly improved operational choices around filming and editing, also making it possible to use smaller film crews to make a film that may have previously required a highly skilled, much larger crew (Collie, 2007, p. 310) but large production crews are still required to service high quality big budget productions in both film and television. Regardless of the size of the crew, screen production personnel are engaged in socially distributed creative acts (de Zutter, 2011; Glăveanu, 2014) that involve multiple creative agents working across all stages of the creative and collaborative process (Kerrigan, 2019).

Other film roles are organized across the stages of film production (See Fig. 13.3) and include crew roles like assistant directors, production runner, script supervisor, camera operator, gaffer, key grip, sound recordist,

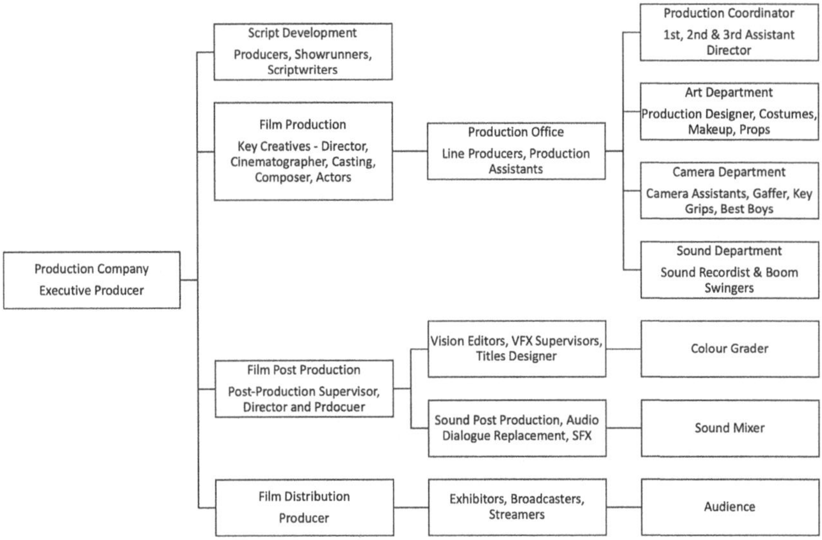

Fig. 13.3 Feature film personnel organizational structure

boom swinger, locations manager, costume and set designer, makeup artist and hair designer. In post-production there are managers who supervise the facilities and technology as well as those who edit the film. There is an ever-expanding team of visual effects supervisors (VFX), computer-generated imagery (CGI) teams and virtual production teams who digitally enhance the story worlds and add real world effects to scenes. Color grading, composing, Foley, sound FX and ADR producers also work on the sound tracks and mix, coordinating with the editor, director and producer to finish the film.

In television production, the key personnel involved are broader because the business models are more complex as purchasing and or creating screen content to fill a broadcasters schedule means more genres are being produced. For example, there are news presenters, journalists, researchers, program schedulers, program buyers, closed captions, PR, marketing staff, celebrity presenters, production designers, make-up, wardrobe, staging, musicians as well as television production crews. Serial television production also involves a range of executives and commissioning editors in the green light process. These executives are powerful gatekeepers in the field who decide what will be commissioned as a television program (Brown & Duthie, 2019).

In summary, it can be argued that 'screen ideas will be socially judged for novelty by the creative field, which determines the scale and scope of the film's production' (Kerrigan, 2019, p. 350) and that 'the execution of the screen idea will be constrained or enabled by the creative practices of the filmmakers as leaders and practitioners' (Kerrigan, 2019, p. 350). To see how these concepts manifest in actuality, we turn to the Hunter Region as an example.

Hunter Region Screen Industries: Field, Doman and Agency at Work in Film

The Hunter's film industry sits within its national context and also in relation to the US industries, positioning it within a global perspective. Several films, including Hollywood productions, have been made in the Hunter and the region has small film and TV production houses, small distribution outlets, and film societies and festivals. The industry is well supported by Screen Hunter, the longest-serving regional film agency in NSW, which brings $8 million to the region annually. The region is home to highly successful freelancers but ABS statistics record full-time work in the Hunter film sector as minimal, with only 1% of people employed in the Creative Industries citing film as their primary occupation. This number, though, is not indicative of the hundreds of unpaid hours of those who make films while supporting themselves with other work. Nor does it capture those who create films and other screen projects through amateur clubs and student programs.

Our snapshot of the Hunter screen industries revealed a busy sector of dedicated creatives and our interviews confirmed that the region's appeal as a filmmaking location subsists in its natural beauty and, in terms of production, its accessibility to Sydney and lower overheads. Productions that have filmed in the Hunter include features, TV shows, ads and video clips, including *Tomorrow when the War Began* (2010), *Air Rescue*, *Baggage Handlers*, *My Kitchen Rules* (Channel 7) and *Farmer Wants a Wife*

(Channel 9). Local beaches such as Stockton, with its picturesque sand dunes, is an impressive location that has attracted Hollywood films like *Wolverine*, *Matrix Reloaded* and *Superman Returns*. Bollywood has also filmed in the region, with Indian companies like Sri Laxmi Productions and Template Productions using Hunter locations for their productions.

Generally, local film productions are based on local history, contemporary stories or lifestyle insights. While all these films may not be financially successful, they showcase filmmakers with the tenacity and dedication to complete large productions. A standout exception is the internationally successful feature *Young Einstein* (1988), a comedy in which writer, director and producer Yahoo Serious also starred. It grossed $13 million in Australia and $11 million in the US and was funded by the Australian Film Commission and private investment. A number of real-life local stories have also become feature films. *Blackrock* (1997) retold the story of the rape and murder of local teenager Leigh Leigh. *Newcastle* (2008) was the cinematic story of a group of surfers and featured actors Shane Jacobson and Barry Otto with cameos by sporting heroes Andrew Johns, Layne Beachley and Mark Richards. *Aftershocks* was based on the 1989 Newcastle earthquake. Four internationally award-winning indie features, *Mikey's Extreme Romance* (2008), *Bathing Frankie* (2012), *Love is Now* (2014), and *Pop-Up* (2015) were filmed across the region on nano-budgets working with local crews. Locally made documentary films include *Lockout* (2008), that retold the local story of Australia's most violent industrial conflict, and *Honeymoon in Kabul* (2009), filmed in Afghanistan, that told the story of a Newcastle couple who delivered medical aid to Afghan communities (Ronin Films, 2018, online). A community-based documentary, *Using Fort Scratchley* (2008), had a budget of $39,000 and utilized oral histories to tell the historical, military, maritime, coal mining and Awabakal stories of an iconic Newcastle headland (Kerrigan, 2013). While these films may not have been financially successful, demonstrating in some cases a lack of experience or expertise in the art of promotion and distribution, they do indicate a vibrant local screen industry.

Film and Television Production Houses at Work in the Hunter

The Hunter's film and television production houses have built their reputations while remaining in Newcastle, frequently soliciting work from outside the region. They are owned and run by multi-skilled, talented individuals who have created diverse media content and received industry awards. While the main source of income may be generated through advertising and corporate film work, they also nurture passion film projects. These standout production houses are Limelight Creative Media, Good Eye Deer and Storyhaus.

Storyhaus is a Newcastle-based production company owned by Karl Brandstater. Brandstater was born in Sydney, lived in Europe and the US and moved to Newcastle in 2000. His deep immersion in the film domain and field—he has worked with Universal Music, Disney, Village Roadshow, Sony Music and Warner Brothers—enables his understanding of what works. He says, 'Newcastle brings that wonderful balance of authentic art and creativity and processes ... It's easy to live here [and] It's not difficult to work internationally' (Brandstater, i/v Oct 2016). Brandstater's eight-part documentary series *Barinia* (2015) was filmed on a yacht, sailing the Italian, Greek, Turkish and French coastlines (Barinia Tales, 2017, online). It has been screened in France, Italy, Poland, Russia and Brazil. However, and demonstrating the talent and accessibility of creative professionals in the Hunter, Brandstater worked with an all-Newcastle team including design agency Headjam, musician Tim McPhee, creative support and writer Mike Preston, and sound mixer Rob Preston.

Limelight Creative Media is a boutique communication studio that offers a fully integrated service including film production, writing, photography, time lapse and design. Company directors Dr. Anna Kelly and Ian Hamilton have a shared passion for producing content that makes a positive difference with a strong focus on health and education. Limelight wins national tenders to produce documentary, educational, health, corporate and training videos against national competitors (Hamilton, i/v May 2015). Their past television work includes making four broadcast documentaries for the ABC Series *Australian Story* and their *Pain Management Network* films won a national ATOM award in 2014 for Best Instruction/Training Resource (Kelly, i/v Sept 2015). Another award-winning production company is Good Eye Deer. Owned by Gavin Banks and Olivia Olley, the company has won 12 national and international awards for brand films, corporate videos, educational series and TV commercials (GED, 2018, online). In 2022 their documentary *Everybody's Oma* (2022) was nominated for an Australian Academy of Cinema and Television Arts (ACCTA) award.

The region also hosts several post-production companies that provide film-finishing services of high quality, often within co-working clusters that engender a creative buzz. Final Post offers a high-end film finishing service that uses DaVinci Resolve to color grade and complete the look of a film (Kerrigan & Hutchinson, 2016). Final Post has graded a number of Australian features including *Love is Now* (2014). Owner Shane Burrell feels that Newcastle is an accessible location and is 'coupled with lower regional overheads' (Kerrigan & Hutchinson, 2016, p. 7). One80 is an independent production arm of the local television station, Nine Entertainment Co. that offers production, facilities provision, and outside broadcast (OB) for external clients. It has 13 full-time producers, editors and directors.

The Television Arm of the Screen Industry System: Creative Innovation at Work in the Region

The Hunter's television sector does not reflect the post-networked television era that exists in the US although the transition to a multi-channel system is partially underway as digital terrestrial television and SVOD offers non-linear viewing for some genres in the region. Furthermore, free-to-air advertising still appears viable in the Hunter, whereas nationally it is under threat of collapse. In this region, there are 122 full-time television workers: 37% are females and 63% are males. The industry's personnel are similar to the film industry with experienced people working interchangeably across both sectors. The ABS measure used in this study revealed that these people work as directors, artistic directors and media producers, or identify simply as media professionals. These statistics, however, do not capture the wider set of occupations involved in TV production and management. In line with film production, there are screenwriters, producers, directors, cinematographers, art directors, editors, color graders, VFX supervisors, sound designers, recordists and audio mixers all working in television in the Hunter.

As elsewhere, the Hunter's television industry has two primary and overlapping sectors—production and distribution. News and advertising are the types of content produced locally. The ABC Newcastle office employs their journalists as cameraperson/editors to create regional content for the national network. The local commercial FTA networks are Prime 7, Southern Cross Austereo and Channel 9-affiliated NBN. Originally independent, NBN (Newcastle Broadcasting NSW) has been operating in the Hunter since 1962. NBN offers starting positions for journalists and production staff but regional journalism is not well paid and people frequently move into public relations. However, NBN employs some very experienced staff who have chosen to stay in the region. At the time of the study, it was the fourth largest market in Australia with a broadcasting footprint of 1.9 million people in NSW and southern Queensland.

The most valuable innovation in the Hunter is that of NBN News, a regional news service which has found a way to broadcast a non-linear news model that offers the viewer a viable mix of local, national and global news. This innovation in news delivery is evidence that the production of local content can work within a global sphere but still operate as a self-sustaining system. In 2016, NBN News produced a nightly, one-hour news bulletin, and its 60 employees produced 20,000 stories annually. News production for this service is sophisticated and complex and ensures regional audiences receive local, regional, state, national and international content through "windows" for its six markets. The technical mastery required to create six slightly different, simultaneously broadcast news bulletins from one location, demonstrates the creativity needed to deliver collective and localized news to regional areas simultaneously.

NBN was so successful at it that this news model was replicated by Austereo across 15 regional areas across Australia.

Other TV stations in the area include community broadcaster Hunter TV, which provides a live streaming and VOD service, and the highly innovative Bar TV Sports, which specializes in filming high-definition sporting games for mid-tier and grassroots competitions, sub-contracts to Foxtel and uses social media platforms to stream sporting games from over 900 sporting fixtures across Australia, the UK and Europe.

In terms of online content distribution there are digital and social media offerings with Hunter TV and Bar TV both using social media platforms as the primary way to distribute their content. NBN has an integrated digital strategy and uses its website and social media as an adjunct to their broadcast service. NBN's social media drives traffic to their website with more than 280,000 Facebook "friends" (as at March 2023), 20,000 twitter followers and 8000 Instagram followers. NBN has also started podcasting where reporters share their opinions and thoughts on news, current affairs and sport.

Support Organizations and Collaborative Spaces in the Hunter Region

Screen Hunter is a crucial organization facilitating the connection between film industry productions and regional communities, organizing accommodation, catering, hire cars and employment for local filmmakers and crews. Managed by Annette Hubber for more than a decade, Screen Hunter developed national and international networks by servicing filming enquiries, thus bringing a global aspect to screen production in the Hunter. Hubber suggested that the region is popular because of its 'proximity to Sydney' and 'stunning locations' (Hubber, i/v Aug 2015). Screen Hunter processes more than 200 filming permits annually with each production bringing income into the region (Screen Hunter, online). Hubber also notes, though, that the state of the Australian dollar affects 'the opportunity of pitching on … overseas work' (Hubber i/v Aug 2015): 'We quoted an American job when the Aussie dollar was trading low and then it bounced back, and we lost it. It was a huge blockbuster' (Hubber, i/v Aug 2015).

In a similar fashion to other creative industry ecosystems, other affiliated businesses, festivals and societies offer support such as networking opportunities, events to showcase films and co-working spaces. The Production Hub, for example, provides office space for digital production companies. Innx provides co-working hot and permanent desks, meeting spaces and private studios for 20 businesses including Mezzanine, Headjam, Final Post and Fisheye Creative. The Roost Creative is another that 'is a coworking space for creatives building community and sharing ideas' (The Roost, 2023, online). Many filmmakers begin their businesses in their bedrooms and garages and co-working spaces such as these offer a degree of professionalism for filmmakers but, importantly, networking opportunities as well.

Film Distributors, Societies and Festivals in the Region: The Interconnected Field and Consumers

Film Distributors, Societies and Festivals are the final link in the chain to ensure that Hunter films and documentaries reach their local and global audiences. The distribution outlets that were active in the Hunter during the study include mainstream cinema distributors, film societies, film festivals, summertime Cinema under the Stars and independent cinemas. Larger chains like Hoyts, Event Cinemas and Reading cater to the general consumer looking to view the latest Hollywood blockbuster in the bigger centers. Smaller towns are catered for by independent cinema venues like Scotties at Raymond Terrace, The Regal in Birmingham Gardens and Lake Cinema at Boolaroo, which all show a varied selection including specialized and arthouse movies. And, nostalgically, Heddon Greta Drive-In 'is the only drive-in theater in the Hunter Valley' (HGDI, 2018, online) and regularly shows the latest blockbusters.

Film societies and festivals have long been present in the Hunter. The Newcastle Film Society was established in 1984 (NFS, 2018, online).

The Real Film Festival began in 2012, and was an annual event showcasing films 'by independent international, national and local storytellers' (Real Film Festival, 2020, online), while also offering a short film competition, workshops and master classes for local filmmakers. Italian films are screened at the Newcastle Italian Film Festival (Gregory, 2017, online) and the Dino Cesta Memorial Scholarship is awarded annually to a local film student. Newcastle also regularly hosts traveling film festivals like Flickerfest and Sydney's Travelling Film Festival.

The Shoot Out was a 24-hour filmmaking festival that began in Newcastle in 1999 and ran for a decade. The Shootout was unique for its time as contestants had to include local locations and specific items in their films and shoot within 24 hours. The Shoot Out Festival was also held in two other regional locations and two international cities. Newcastle's Shoot Out launched the career of Jason Van Genderen who has also won Tropfest in New York (Street, 2014). There are also amateur and professional film clubs operating in Newcastle—Video Moviemaker, Newcastle Filmmaker and Film Republic—as well as student film programs offered by TAFE and the University of Newcastle.

Summary

The production of film and television can be viewed as a socially distributed creative act where screen ideas are socially validated as being novel and that assessment allows those screen ideas to be made into films and television shows (Kerrigan, 2019). While the Hunter's census statistics appear modest, that does not mean that filmic activity itself is minimal; the extent of the gift economy and those making films by earning a primary income in another sector, reflects the larger story and structure of the national industry (Kerrigan et al., 2020).

Structurally all sectors of the film industry are represented in the Hunter and are deeply interconnected through traditional business relationships with creative workers willing to work on low-, nano-, or no-budget films to tell their culturally located stories. The Hunter provides opportunities for smaller businesses to establish themselves as regional production houses that offer services locally, nationally and globally.

Lower costs, proximity to Sydney and the natural beauty of the region makes the Hunter attractive to international filmmakers, providing local creatives with the skills to produce their passion projects.

The local television network, NBN, continues to have a viable advertising-based business model while national and international networks experience hardship. NBN's news production model permitted multiple broadcasts of regionally specific news simultaneously and can be seen as a significant business innovation, one that signals the longevity of the advertising-supported broadcasting models which deliver free content via a digital network. This example embraces the non-linear functions offered through an expertly curated, multi-channel system while simultaneously endorsing the principals of legacy broadcasting. NBN also combined traditional news platforms. Social media has allowed them to continue to experience a strong audience share, regardless of threats such as SVOD. While the FTA models and production of advertising are viable in an Australian region such as the Hunter, it is difficult for new players to enter the market although independent operator Bar TV has remained viable by finding new markets with community sporting associations who pay a reduced fee for sports coverage.

Screen production and filmmaking in the Hunter Region represents, in large part, the workings of the gift economy that is endemic in the creative industries. While there are Hollywood blockbusters that generate huge box office revenues, some filmed in the Hunter, there will also be the other end of the spectrum where Australians want to tell their own stories for themselves. It is both cultural success and the economic profitability that allows this sector to keep generating new content be that at the global or the regional level.

What we can say by way of conclusion is that the global screen industry, comprised of film, cinema, television, film festivals, short films, web series, animation and digital games, is a mature sector of the creative industries worldwide(Dawson & Holmes, 2012). In narrowing our focus to Hunter we, firstly, took an historical approach to the shared knowledge of the domain that constitutes this sector as well as the business structures and operational methods that comprise important constituent parts of the interconnected networks of the field. All film and television workers are members of this field, choice making agents who enact those operational methods and earn income through selling their services, skills and film products through the business structures set up to connect with and to profit from local and global audiences. We detailed this activity in the last few sections of this chapter revealing how these choice making agents' creativity has emerged from internalizing the opinions of the field and immersing themselves in the shared knowledge of the domain, enabling them to creatively contribute to the (eco)system of film and television centered on the Hunter.

References

Barinia Tales. (2017). *Barinia*. Retrieved February 24, 2018, from http://www.foodsaillove.com/

Brown, L., & Duthie, L. (2019). *The TV studio production handbook*. Bloomsbury Academic.

Cohen, H., Salazar, J., & Barkat, I. (2009). *Screen media arts*. Oxford University Press.

Collie, C. (2007). *The business of TV production*. Cambridge University Press.

DAE. (2016). *Analysis of the Victorian screen industry*. Deloitte Access Economics. Retrieved March 21, 2023, from https://vicscreen.vic.gov.au/images/uploads/FV-DAE_Analysis_of_the_Victorian_screen_industry_Key_Findings_2016.pdf

Dawson, A., & Holmes, S. (2012). *Working in the global film and television industries: Creativity, systems, space, patronage* (1st ed.). Hart Publishing. https://doi.org/10.5040/9781780930220

De Zutter, S. (2011). Distributed creativity in performing groups: A case study. In C. Lobman & B. O'Neill (Eds.), *Play and culture series Vol II: Play and performance* (pp. 237–260). University Press of America.

GED. (2018). *Good Eye Deer*. Retrieved February 24, 2018, from http://goodeyedeer.com.au/

Gil, R. (2015). Does vertical integration decrease prices? Evidence from the paramount antitrust case of 1948. *American Economic Journal: Economic Policy, 7*(2), 162–191. https://doi.org/10.1257/pol.20120245

Glăveanu, V. (2014). *Distributed creativity: Thinking outside the box of the creative individual*. Springer.

Goldsmith, B., Ward, S., & O'Regan, T. (2010). *Local Hollywood: Global film production and the Gold Coast*. University of Queensland Press.

Gregory, H. (2017, October 27). Newcastle Italian film Festival 2017: Seven films spanning romantic comedy, drama and classics. *The Herald*. Retrieved February 1, 2018, from http://www.theherald.com.au/story/5016647/slice-of-italy-on-screen/

Hesmondhalgh, D., & Baker, S. (2011). *Creative labor: Media work in three cultural industries*. Routledge.

HGDI. (2018). *Home*. Heddon Greta drive-in. Retrieved February 1, 2018, from http://www.drive-in.com.au/

Kerrigan, S. (2013). Accommodating creative documentary practice within a revised systems model of creativity. *Journal of Media Practice, 14*(2), 111–127. https://doi.org/10.1386/jmpr.14.2.111_1

Kerrigan, S. (2019). Innovation in the arts: Collaborative and creative filmmaking processes. In P. B. Paulus & B. A. Nijstad (Eds.), *The Oxford handbook of group creativity and innovation* (pp. 335–352). Oxford University Press. https://doi.org/10.1093/oxfordhb/9780190648077.013.20

Kerrigan, S., & Hutchinson, S. (2016). Regional creative industries: Transforming the Steel City into a creative city in Newcastle, Australia. *Creative Industries Journal, 9*(2), 1–14. https://doi.org/10.1080/17510694.2016.1206357

Kerrigan, S., & McIntyre, P. (2010). The "creative treatment of actuality": Rationalizing and reconceptualizing the notion of creativity for documentary practice. *Journal of Media Practice, 11*, 111–130. https://doi.org/10.1386/jmpr.11.2.111_1

Kerrigan, S., Ryan, M. D., McIntyre, P., Cunningham, S., & McCutcheon, M. (2020). The creative sustainability of screen business in the Australian regions. *Studies in Australasian Cinema, 14*(2), 111–129. https://doi.org/10.1080/17503175.2020.1811486

Lee, J., & Gillen, A. M. (2011). *The producers business handbook: The roadmap for the balanced film producer*. Focal Press.

Lotz, A. D. (2014). *The television will be revolutionized*. New York University Press.

Lule, J. (2016). *Understanding media and culture: An introduction to mass communication*. FlatWorld/University of Minnesota Libraries Publishing.

Macdonald, I. (2012). *Screenwriting poetics and the screen idea*. Palgrave Macmillan.

Maher, S., Silver, J., & Kerrigan, S. (2016). Australian feature films and distribution: Industry or cottage industry? *Studies in Australasian Cinema, 10*(1), 79–96. https://doi.org/10.1080/17503175.2016.1140462

Maxcy, J. (2013). Rapidly advancing technology and policy choices: Transforming the economic landscape of the sport media. In P. Pedersen (Ed.), *Routledge handbook of sport communication* (pp. 471–481). Taylor and Francis.

McIntyre, P., Fulton, J., Kerrigan, S., & Meany, M. (2023). *Entrepreneurship in the creative industries: How innovative agents, skills and networks interact*. Springer. https://doi.org/10.1007/978-3-031-19455-9

Olsberg SPI. (2016). *Measuring the cultural value of the Australian screen sector*. Retrieved February 24, 2018, from https://www.screenaustralia.gov.au/getmedia/1dce395e-a482-42d1-b5a9-47bb6307f868/Screen-Currency-Olsberg-SPI-Nov2016.pdf

Petrie, D. (1991). *Creativity and constraint in the British film industry*. Macmillan.

PWC. (2022). *Australian entertainment media outlook report*. Retrieved October 29, 2022, from https://www.pwc.com.au/entertainment-and-media/2022/australian-outlook-2022-report.pdf?sfmid=eyJzZm1jaWQiOiJza2VycmlnYW5Ac3dpbi5lZHUuYXUifQ==

Real Film Festival. (2020). *Home*. Real Film Festival. Retrieved April 22, 2023, from https://realfilmfestival.com.au

Ronin Films. (2018). *Honeymoon in Kabul*. Ronin Films. Retrieved May 3, 2018, from https://www.roninfilms.com.au/feature/2819/honeymoon-in-kabul.html

Schleser, M., & Xu, X. (2021). *Mobile storytelling in an age of smartphones*. Palgrave Macmillan. https://doi.org/10.1007/978-3-030-87247-2

Screen Australia. (2022). *Australian feature film production activity*. Screen Australia. Retrieved April 23, 2023, from https://www.screenaustralia.gov.au/fact-finders/production-trends/theatrical-feature-production/australian-feature-films

Shimpach, S. (2020). *The Routledge companion to global television* (1st ed.). Routledge.

Street, K. (2014, June 17–19). Researching "the shoot out filmmaking Festival" by targeting creativity. *Refereed proceedings of ASPERA screen explosion: Expanding practices, narratives and education for the creative screen industries*. University of Newcastle, Newcastle, Australia. Retrieved March 15, 2018, from https://www.aspera.org.au/_files/ugd/cac777_8a23c72e19704a469ff8789bac52afd6.pdf

The Roost (2023). *Homepage*. The roost creative. Retrieved April 22, 2023, from https://theroostcreative.com.au/

Treacey, M. (2016). *Reframing the past: History, film and television*. Routledge. https://doi.org/10.4324/9781315639161

Velikovsky, J. (2016). *Communication, creativity and consilience in cinema: A comparative study of the top 20 return-on-investment (RoI) movies and the doxa of screenwriting*. Unpublished PhD, University of Newcastle.

Verhoeven, D., Davidson, A., & Coate, B. (2015). Australian films at large: Expanding the evidence about Australian cinema performance. *Studies in Australasian Cinema, 9*(1), 7–20. https://doi.org/10.1080/17503175.2014.998098

Weaving, S. (2014). *Writing an Australian film noir*. Unpublished PhD Exegesis. University of Canberra.

14

Electronic Games and Interactive Content

Introduction

The Australian Government's Digital Economy Strategy claims that overall digital activity in 2019–20 was approximately $109b with increases in online ecommerce, business tech, employment and IT graduates. The global gaming industry alone is estimated to be worth more than US$100b (Keogh, 2021) and, according to claims by Strabhaar et al. (2022), the industry's revenues are greater than the music, television and movie industries. It was believed that revenue for the industry overtook the movie industry in 2008 (Velikovsky, 2013, p. 15) and, in 2010, it was estimated that the global games industry was worth $105b. According to the latest figures from the Interactive Games and Entertainment Association (IGEA, 2021, online), the total value of video game sales in 2021 was $AUS396 million. However, a word of caution needs to be added here. As David Hesmondhalgh (2019) revealed:

> the digital games industry achieved high rates of growth in the early twenty-first century, whereas revenues from recorded music stagnated or declined. However, claims about how games were outstripping other industries were

P. McIntyre et al., *Creativity and Creative Industries in Regional Australia*, Palgrave Studies in Creativity and Culture, https://doi.org/10.1007/978-3-031-45972-6_14

> based on dubious data. For example, the sales of hardware (consoles, hand-held devices) were usually included alongside games software. This was like including figures for the sale of DVD players and recorders in the figures for film, or iPods in the figures for music. These figures were then compared to the box office figures for industries such as film or sales figures for music … When sales of games (as opposed to devices such as consoles) were compared with revenues from cinema box office and DVD sales and rentals, it was apparent that the games industry had not yet reached the size of television or even film. (Hesmondhalgh, 2019, p. 316)

Nonetheless, Deloitte's latest Digital Pulse report states that '[d]igital technology has become fundamental to Australian businesses, the workforce and the economy' (2022, p. 6). The workforce in technology represents 6.7% of the overall Australian workforce and, while growth in the sector dropped slightly in 2020–21 (likely due to COVID), the five previous years showed an annual growth of 5% per annum. The demand for technology workers has increased by 8% each year since 2016 and, while the majority of workers are in ICT related work, 55% were employed in other industries (Deloitte, 2022). Of note here is also the fact that in 2016 Deloitte predicted 'existing technologies will see growing uses in new industries, sectors and occupations; and new forms of technology will also emerge over the coming years' (2016, pp. 10–11), a prophecy that came to pass. While Deloitte was, in 2016, interested in cloud computing, social media, mobile and analytics as disruptors, in 2022, artificial intelligence and an AI ecosystem was seen as 'a significant opportunity with benefit for individuals, businesses and the Australian economy' (Deloitte, 2022, online).

While multinational corporations such as Nintendo comprise a major proportion of the gaming industry, according to Brendan Keogh (2021), as well as successful "indie" producers, many game producers are not making a living from developing their craft. There is also a tension between commerce and creativity, as seen in other forms of cultural production, in that the requirement for "freedom" to create games independent of the large traditional gaming structure still holds sway (Keogh, 2021; McIntyre et al., 2023). Language such as "indie" is prevalent in the industry, a term that rose in the mid-2000s to 'give cultural credibility to a range of independent modes of production that were explicitly *not* the dominant blockbuster industry' [italics in the original] (Keogh, 2021, p. 121). Keogh also claims that the indie studios are now the backbone of the Australian industry and there is no so-called mainstream industry or at least a studio willing to identify itself as such.

A Brief History of Electronic Games and Interactive Content: Building a Tradition of Innovation

The history of the IT sector with all of its moving parts, would be difficult to summarize in this chapter. Others have done a thorough history of the trajectory of computers, software, the internet, smartphones, apps, gaming, virtual reality (VR), augmented reality (AR) and artificial intelligence (AI) (see, for example, Goggin, 2014; Goldsmith, 2014; Hjorth, 2014; Okunev, 2023; Rajaraman, 2022a, 2022b; Straubhaar et al., 2022; Sunita & Sharma, 2021). The software industries started in the 1950s/1960s with the concept of a "stored program" attributed to John von Neumann (Grad, 2015, online). This advance grew out of the technology of punch cards and manual electrical relays, and the massive mainframe calculating machines of IBM through magnetic tape technology, transistorized circuits and random-access storage (Random History, 2008, p. 1). From there, further differentiation developed between the programs and instructions that run a computer, the software, and the physical machinery or hardware that carries that software. The coming of the digital age and exponential growth and innovation through ubiquitous access to the World Wide Web consolidated what had become the distribution and sales of software as a significant and fast-moving industry sector (Random History, 2008, p. 1). Other related industries were growing. In Australia, the development of video games has been traced to 1980, when Beam Software was established (Environment and Communications References Committee, 2016) and, as Sahil Sharma points out, 'the first handheld mobile phone was created by Motorola in 1973' (2015, p. 12). Its full potential wasn't released until the 1990s when portability and connectivity became available. By 2021, the World Economic Forum claimed that there were around 8.6 billion active mobile device subscriptions in use (Alvarez, 2022, online). This gave the software "apps" industry a chance to grow 'phenomenally quickly on the back of the popularity of smartphones and tablet computers' (Goldsmith, 2014, p. 339) but its commercial history is a relatively short one. Goldsmith notes that 'the first recorded use of "app" as shorthand for "application"—meaning a computer software program—was in 1985 when Apple released the MacApp programming tool' (2014, p. 339). The term is now commonly understood in reference to 'software programs designed to run on mobile platforms and devices, although apps have now been developed for a range of devices from televisions to cars' (Goldsmith, 2014, p. 339). With the proliferation of the mobile web, smartphones and, to a lesser extent, tablets, app development has been boosted by the realization that they, in league with the mobile web and smartphones, facilitate 'innovation in market development and work practices, as well as being conduits to investment and new revenue streams' (Goldsmith, 2014, p. 339).

While the story of mobile phones and apps is relatively recent, the idea of a virtual world has appeared in writings and film for a very long time. In the 1930s, Stanley Weinbaum's book *Pygmalian's Spectacles* had a 'pair of goggles which enabled the user to navigate in a fictional world and included the senses of smell, taste and touch' (DeWitt, 2018, online). Commercial flight simulators were invented in 1929 although the first head-mounted mask was developed in 1960. This technology continued to develop, including in the 1980s where VR was increasingly used in education and training (DeWitt, 2018, online). In the 1990s, VR headsets began to make their way into arcade games and then into homes and, in 2010, Oculus Rift was created, which made VR popular again. Today, VR applications are widespread in industry, training, personal information, translation services, navigation, TV broadcasts, advertising and, increasingly, complex gaming (Hollerer & Schmalstieg, 2016, p. 1).

The creation of video games, according to Larissa Hjorth (2014), was connected in the 1950s and 1960s to the development of computer science as a discipline at MIT. In 1962, the Tech Model Railway Club (TMRC), a research group operating at MIT, created *Spacewar*, a game designed around the PDP-1 computer at MIT but it had no facility for simultaneous player interaction. This changed in 1971 when this game was developed enough to become the first digital arcade game. In 1972, a US defense contractor developed this game technology for television, which enabled the transition of electronic games from the arcade to the domestic sphere. The stand-alone games console appeared soon after. *Space Invaders* was released by Atari in 1979 and 'the early 1980s saw the introduction of many home consoles from Atari, Nintendo, Sega, Microsoft and Sony' (Hjorth, 2014, p. 273).

Concurrently, mobile handheld gaming developed but for video games, 'after the software and hardware peak of 1982, the boom was over—suddenly production dwindled and declined' (Hjorth, 2014, p. 274). In the 1990s, 'arcades declined dramatically in the face of the rise of handheld gaming and MMOGs' (Hjorth, 2014, p. 274). Following a disastrous move from CD-ROMS to cartridges, which held less data at a time when more complex graphics were needing more memory, Nintendo lost tremendous market share to the new PlayStation platforms. There was now a 'growing significance of the portable (mobile) game systems (Sony PlayStation Portable [PSP], Nintendo DS) and the rise of the online, networked UCC in the form of game "modding" (whereby players could remodel games environments and gameplay)' (Hjorth, 2014, p. 274).

At this point, Sega exited the business, Sony gained a larger share of the market and the games industry became very attractive to Microsoft. Social and locative games were now possible and it wasn't long before mobile technology became the central entertainment medium for players with the launch of Apple's iPhone in 2007. In 2016, the Pokémon Go app became a worldwide phenomenon when it superimposed gaming elements onto the real world via a smartphone screen, and thus 'introduced millions to augmented reality' (Straubhaar et al., 2022, n.p.).

Structure of a Dynamic Sector

Electronic games and interactive content, compared to other sectors, is a relatively new, dynamic, and constantly changing sector in the creative industries and it is difficult to get a solid grasp of its overall structure. For example, mobile software applications and interactive media in the form of VR, AR and games are increasingly important elements of the digital economy. This economy's general structural backbone has been described by the government as 'the global network of economic and social activities that are enabled by information and communications technologies such as the internet, mobile and sensor networks' (Clarke, 2009, online).

Within this global network, serious games have become as significant as leisure games. Serious games are those that have at their heart something other than entertainment—real learning. They move on from simulations through the addition of gamification. They are also linked to VR and AR simulations and there is a growing application for both in areas such as military, safety, mining, medical and pharmaceutical training, and for sales and heritage presentations. As Pease and Zistl argue, 'from research and development to planning and production, products and processes are increasingly taking shape in the virtual world' (2014, online). These environments are 'overwhelmingly virtual, such as buildings, trains, and models of wind turbines or drilling platforms, which are supplemented by real-time images taken by technicians in the real-world' (2014, online). This is where serious games, using these VR and AR approaches, have come into their own.

App developers, on the other hand, cater primarily to the mobile phone industry supplying applications that cover a vast range of uses. Marcus (2005) notes that in areas dominated by software applications there are both large conglomerates concerned with production and distribution of creative goods as well as small firms seeking and promoting talent. Some of these companies develop applications in-house from creation to development to engineering while others outsource each aspect using freelancers from across the world. Some work to a specific brief, planning and documenting meticulously while others use a more agile and iterative process; the first gives control to the financier and costs less overall while the second method tends to be costlier and take longer but its reliance on feedback makes it solid when it enters the market.

Business Models in a Diverse Environment

It should be noted that games come in a variety of forms such as massive multiplayer games (MMOs), core PC/MAC games, casual web games, mobile phone games, tablet games, handheld games and TV/console games and the following is a broad brushstroke.

In a paper that examined gaming within Bourdieu's cultural production model, Keogh claims that videogames are 'both project-driven and hit-driven' (2021, p. 120) and, in Australia, gamemakers are typically entrepreneurs or (more rarely) sign up with "indie" publishers. While Keogh's research found that many of those that work in the industry are dependent on a range of 'precarious and contingent means' (2021, p. 120) to survive, demonstrating the pernicious effect of neoliberalism, business models can include a generous tax offset provided by the Australian government for games and app developers as well as State-based incentives (ATIC, 2022, online).

According to Pelipaja (2015), making money with games occurs in a number of ways. While the cost structures include advertising the game, as well as the cost of development and, depending on type, cost of server space plus app store commissions (for example, from Apple App Store, Google Play, Windows Store or Steam), the revenue stream often comes primarily from direct sales, selling virtual goods or selling ad space. As far as online games go, in-app advertising appears to be increasing in relation to direct sale of games via app stores. Direct sale or paid games give an immediate return when people purchase and/or download it with a usual 30% commission going to the store. The Freemium model is a variant of this with free-to-play games largely relying on advertising. Subscription services, on the other hand, work primarily for MMOs or serialized games and, of course, merchandising also features heavily with many games and apps. Other revenue generating models include trading virtual items between players and pay-per-tap where 'people download your app for free and every time they tap on one of the advertisements scrolling across the screen, you get paid' (Pelipaja, 2015 in McIntyre et al., 2019, p. 448).

Revenue is earnt from apps in very similar ways to games. These include:

> Freemium where the app is free to download but it contains in-app purchases; Paid, where there is a direct purchase with no in-app purchases; Paidmium, where the download comes with in-app purchases; In-App Advertising which contains ads (banner ads, video ads, etc.); and the Dynamic Business model which shifts depending on certain factors (app shifts to an ad-supported model if the user does not make in-app purchases, etc.). (Pelipaja, 2015 in McIntyre et al., 2019, p. 448)

Revenues are also generated by 'creating an online store within the app itself' (Rakestraw et al., 2013, p. 11). Some games companies offer a free-to-play game with the additional feature of offering paraphernalia associated with the game for purchase. Services may be sold directly from an app that acts as an e-store, for example selling tickets to films by attracting customers with dense information such as reviews and trailers of the movie.

Operational Methods of the Field

As far as operational methods for the mobile apps development industry goes, there are generally four stages involved after entrepreneurs have sourced finance from venture capitalists: identifying the type of app required; bringing the idea into the tangible realm; design; and launch. For the games industry, its operational methods tend to follow a more detailed linear process. When the developer delivers the game, the publisher markets, launches and manufactures the product. This publishing sector has moved toward a concentrated oligopoly where there are 'fewer and fewer publishers, which tends to mean less competition—and a tougher life for developers' (Williams & Srivastava, 2014, p. 1). While self-publishing has begun to develop as a force in the market, a lot of power is still in the hands of the big publishers (Williams & Srivastava, 2014, p. 1). For Williams and Srivastava:

> production takes place at the development stage in which games are conceived, created and programmed—the content. Games designed for one platform are often recoded at lower costs for another, a process known as "porting" and recently made easier with the rise of Unity as a platform. (2014, p. 1)

As lukefollows11 (2013) explains, development occurs in three or four ways. *First party developers* generally confine themselves to one platform. Nintendo is a good example as most of their games are made internal to the company. *Second party developers* are generally owned separately from the platform but games are made for the platform owners. In other words, the platform owners outsource the development of the game to an independent studio who then makes the game exclusively for the platform or other company who funds the game. *Third party developers* make games for multiple systems or platforms. *Independent (indie) developers* typically self-publish.

As Velikovsky sets out, a game development company will bid, in competition with others, for a contract with a game publisher. Once a contract is secured, a "Milestone Delivery Schedule Contract" will be drawn up 'between the Game Publisher and Game Developer, and the Publisher will pay a pre-agreed monthly amount to the Developer (e.g. say $500,000 per month) based on whether the Milestone each month has been delivered on time and to the Publisher's satisfaction' (Velikovsky, 2013, p. 5). The game developer might construct their 'own proprietary game engine—or more often, will license a commercial game engine, for a fee' (Velikovsky, 2013, p. 5). The game gets built using the art and sound assets the team has created and 'the game engine makes it all "work" on the relevant game platform, in each case (e.g., on a PS3, an Xbox360, or a PC, the web, a smartphone, etc.)' (Velikovsky, 2013, p. 5). Once the game is completed by the developer, it goes through what is called:

> the Playable Demo, and then Alpha, then Beta, and finally Gold Master stages (say, from 2 to 4 years, for a AAA game) and the Gold Master (disc) is finally delivered by the Developer to the Publisher—then a Distributor (which, may also be the Publisher) markets it, and places it in various Retail

outlets. A Consumer (5) then buys it, from the store (or online) and plays it. (Velikovsky, 2013, p. 5)

With this background in mind, operational methods need to be adaptable as do the roles people in these industries take on, especially as shifts in the workforce through outsourcing and casualization take hold.

Important Personnel in the Field: Choice Making Agents Within the (Eco)System

A mobile app development team tends to be limited. It still consists of a number of players but the central ones are the project manager, the UI/UX designer, the coder and the QA engineer (Quora, 2018, online). On the other hand, the games industry tends to be similar in some respects to the film industry; the credits are extensive. Broadly speaking, developers make the game, publishers market and promote the game and they 'are the rights-holders for the games' (Williams & Srivastava, 2014, p. 1). Distributors are involved in the logistics of delivering the game to retailers or direct to consumers, the platform is the machinery, the console or format, the game is played on, retailers sell the game to consumers and, of course, there are the consumers themselves.

To give some more detail, third party developers generally work for publishers who supply the finance. Both have input to the development of the game but, as elsewhere, whoever finances a production is the party who makes the final decisions. Independent developers are typically small firms who self-publish. They generally do not have the budgets of the prior categories. They do, however, get to make all the creative decisions with no financier establishing input.

As Velikovsky (2013) indicates, a typical games development studio employs around 50 people across the two years it often takes to develop a game. These will include producers, a project manager, a game designer, who is like a director on a film, and assistant game designer, around five level designers or builders, a dozen programmers and a dozen artists, one or two sound engineers, a music composer, an interface designer, an animation team of around four people, one voice over artist or, as is most often the case, two dozen v/o artists working across two years, which is the equivalent of employing one person to do this for two years, and of course a writer (Velikovsky, 2013, p. 6).

The field in gaming and interactive software also includes programmers, software developers, IT practitioners, content developers, 3D modelers, animators, artists, coders, engineers, educators, IP experts, investors, producers, testers and writers (ATIC, 2022). The Australian Government characterizes the Australian games industry as creative, tech-savvy, cutting edge led by 'bright, dynamic and multicultural entrepreneurs' (ATIC, 2022, p. 1) that is backed up by a strong base of complementary creative industries, including film and television, design, advertising and new media (Austrade, 2014, p. 1). There are 3228 FTE employees working across the digital games industry in 405 companies ranging from large through to micro, including 1327 FTE employees working in game development studios (ATIC, 2022, p. 12).

It should be noted here that workers in this industry are increasingly embedded in convergent projects and across traditional industries. Non-ICT sectors such as finance and insurance, construction, health and community services and cultural, recreational and personal services (Martinez-Fernandez et al., 2005) employ ICT workers. A key concern in the industry, however, is diversity and inclusion with less than a third of ICT workers in the technology sector women. Older Australians, First Nations peoples, those with a disability and regional Australians are also under-represented (Deloitte, 2022, online).

The Hunter and the Electronic Games and Interactive Content Sector of the Creative Industries

While the relevance of the digital economy for the creative industries and its future is clearly laid out in both State and Federal Government agendas, the opportunities provided by the exponential growth of the games and apps industries have not been taken up in the Hunter in any significant way. In assessing the Hunter's participation in these industries, the numbers were confounded by overlapping sectors and employment definitions, signaling the convergence and complexity that exists in this fast-moving sector and its relationship to other areas such as design, visual and performing arts, and music. While the production of apps and leisure games is small, with limited opportunities for graduates, there is a strong games retail and hobby sector in the Hunter. VR and AR elements are also well represented in the Hunter.

Virtual and Augmented Reality Simulations in the Hunter: Innovation Within the Field

The VR and AR sector of the games industry is represented in the Hunter, in part, as arcade games. For example, in Newcastle, Virtual Reality Studio (VXRP) provided a small space where customers could 'explore underwater worlds, create 360° interactive paintings and defend your castle as a medieval archer' (VRXP, 2018, online). This room scale virtual reality business was run by Andy Gallagher. Gallagher's experience consisted of making videos. He made the region's first 3D virtual reality video project, *360 Reasons to be in Newcastle*, which was 'produced in collaboration with Enigma, The Newcastle City Council, Newcastle Now and The Business Centre' (Gallagher, 2018, online). These forays into video making demonstrate his immersion in the creative industries, increasing his domain knowledge for application in a different but related domain of virtual reality. Another VR business in Newcastle, Slice Virtual Golf, allowed customers to experience 110 of the world's most famous golf courses (SVG, 2018, online). Both of these businesses are now closed but Unreal VR, in Lake Macquarie, still offers games such as Batman, The Blu, Space Pirate, Tilt Brush, Google Earth, Elven Assassin and a treasure trove of other VR Games (UVR, 2018, online).

Jet Flight Simulator Newcastle is another VR/AR experience that is locally based and offers an immersive 'flight experience to suit the complete novice right up to highly experienced commercial pilots wishing to pass the Air Line Candidate Recruitment Assessment Check Flight' (JFSN, 2023, online). Customers/pilots manage airspeed, altitude, headings and so on while monitoring other air traffic. As with the real world, this virtual one provides multiple screens, indicators and monitors to simulate the real experience. Customers are invited to '[e]scape into a virtual world of aviation, where you will captain one of the most popular commercial airliners in the world' (JFSN, 2023, online).

While these commercial establishments provided entertainment-focused VR, facilities such as those at The Virtual Reality Technologies (VRT) center located at the Newcastle Mines Rescue Station have a serious intent. This service is a training center used by hazardous industries like the coal industry and it relies on virtual reality, augmented reality and mobile applications to train underground workers and reduce the risk to workers in the initial stages of their training.

VRT shows something of how the creative industries can function in a region with a base in heavy industry where creative inputs have made a regional industry the global leader in safety. This business deploys desk-based training as well as physical training in an artificial "mine" where physical scenarios are implemented via interactive dome-based presentations for small groups and within large hemispherical spaces where interactive virtual reality scenarios are designed for teams to deal with a wide range of potential incidents. As Matt Farrelly explains, it looks and feels like a mine 'because you need the muscle memory, to know what smoke smells like, to know the heat from the fire, what it feels like to pull out an extinguisher and put the fire out. It's resource intensive but essential' (Farrelly, i/v April 2016). These options offer high-level visual inputs, sophisticated programming, training and practical applications that have now been developed to the point where their expertise can be deployed for other industries where people are at risk—transport, fire-fighting, police work and other emergency services.

Karen Blackmore, an Associate Professor in IT at the University of Newcastle and a former cartographer, believes simulation rather than gaming will be more beneficial to the Hunter, since:

> The world is full of unemployed game developers ... So, not in gaming but in simulation—absolutely. Totally. It's ongoing so it ties in many of the skills. It encapsulates many of the skills we see in game development, particularly in asset generation—that kind of thing. (Blackmore, i/v Sept 2016)

The defense industry, for example, is an area where simulation is a key training strategy for a range of scenarios:

> What you've got with Defence, for example, is a digital training environment … So you have a library of digital assets and a world that you can compile that in, so you can establish scenarios around which you can develop training—e.g. U.N. peace keeping or it may be other scenarios. (Blackmore, i/v Sept 2016)

Government provides support for these initiatives in the form of funding and the University of Newcastle received such funding from the New South Wales government to establish four innovation hubs, including at the Aerospace Centre, to 'allow the university—with strengths in cyberspace, control systems, autonomous vehicles, simulation modeling, propulsion and energy storage—to work with defence companies to develop commercial opportunities' (Investment NSW, 2019, online).

One of these companies is Bohemia Interactive Simulations (BISim), which is most likely the best representative case of a serious game environment to be found in the Hunter Region. It uses game-based technology, much of it derived from their commercial games arm, as well as a significant and highly skilled in-house group of engineers to develop 'high-fidelity, cost- effective training and simulation software products and components for defence applications' (BISim, 2018, online). BISim incorporates virtual reality hardware with its own software for training and their round-earth visualization technologies allow military exercises to be conducted on an epic scale across all sort of terrain and urban locations. Another business is Applied Virtual Simulator (AVS), a smaller simulation business associated with the defense forces. Founder Martin Carr, a former army officer, claimed that he 'used my knowledge as a trained officer to design simulators to achieve training outcomes that I would have wanted and saw were required' (Green, 2017b, online). The company develops and upgrades simulation-based training systems such as simulators for heavy vehicles.

Apart from this activity in the region with major industries, there are also smaller companies operating in the Hunter who are not associated with the major industries. For example, Tim Davidson and Ivan Demidov are the principals of Virtual Perspective, an agency that specializes in creating customized software for VR and AR technology across a broad range of industries. Davidson explained how they started working together:

> Ivan was working on 3D technology from a programming perspective and I was working on 3D scenes—that's what I do, I build scenes. We were a perfect match—so we started working together. I build scenes and then Ivan works with them for the VR. (Davidson, i/v July 2016)

As Demidov adds, 'I work to build the engine and Tim makes them look really good' (Demidov, i/v July 2016). They also explained how they engage with other specialists in the field to provide their customers with the best possible product:

> We work mainly on our own with external collaborators or use others who have specialist skills … We work with others to increase our capabilities—we work with a guy in Sydney who does 3D scanning and photogrammetry. We also have contacts who do drone flyover footage. What one of my other businesses does is to take that drone footage and I superimpose a 3D object building on drone footage. That allows real estate companies to show their investors what the building will look like when it is finished, when it is that location but with the existing cityscape around it. (Davidson & Demidov, i/v July 2016)

The Games World in the Hunter: A Developing Field

Linked to both the role and future of VR and AR, the related games world in the Hunter, in terms of production, is quite small; nobody from the Hunter Region was listed as a member of the Games Developers Association of Australia as at 7 October 2017 (GDAA, 2017, online). There is still, nonetheless, a small enclave of traditional and digital games related activity. Hunters for Collectors, a comic and pop culture shop run by Deitmar Leiderwasch, provides, in small part, access to board games that pre-existed the digital world. Good Games is part of an international franchise which gives customers access to fantasy games such as *Dungeons and Dragons*, *Warhammer* and *Rune Wars*. These fantasy games have acted as precursors and models for what are called massive multiplayer online role-playing games or MMOs for short. They in turn have spawned the phenomenon of e-sports with businesses such as Gomaz Vs Pedro.

Tom Cupitt and Josh Freinberger have used the names Gomaz and Pedro since they were teenagers playing electronic games. Gomaz Vs Pedro, an e-sports center located in an old cinema in Tighes Hill that changed its name to GVP esports, grew out of their interest in gaming. The location functioned as a games center and internet café and used multiple Nintendos and Playstations as well as PCs. Significantly, the business hosted live tournaments that were streamed via Twitch 'the world's biggest video platform and community for gamers, creating advertising revenue in the process' (Green, 2017a, online). These niche games are big business in the United States with tournaments filling stadiums where contestants, mainly teenagers, can earn seven figure incomes. After starting out, Cupitt and Frienberger had ambitions to franchise their business nationally and 'create a gaming circuit where the best of the best compete … we want to build it to the point that you can watch a tournament in the same way you can watch a professional sport' (Cupitt in Green, 2017a, online) but, due to several factors, including COVID, they closed in April 2022. Outlets such as this have been a major nexus point for gamers in the region but there are also retailers ranging from independent stores through to franchised chains accessible throughout the region.

Consumers are well serviced across the region by retailers. These include DownForwardPunch, Highway Entertainment and Games Workshop as well as JB Hi Fi and Jaycar Electronics in Newcastle. In Lake Macquarie there is, once again, JB Hi-Fi, TimeZone, The Games Shop, Electronics Boutique, Unreal VR, Gamer Collect and NewXpress in Swansea. Maitland has Playhard Gaming, Sanity and Good Games. EB Games has outlets across the region. This multinational company which is headquartered in Texas in the USA, has 370 locations with 4000 employees in Australia, is located in the region at malls such as those in Kotara, Charlestown, Jesmond, Maitland, Singleton, Muswellbrook, Forster, Raymond Terrace and Salamander Bay. As well as supplying games for PS4, Xbox One, Nintendo, Phones and PC, they also retail a wide variety of consoles and accessories. They trade games, refurbish and on-sell second-hand consoles and phones while maintaining a large community of gamers through their various events and promotions aimed at the consumers of games (EB Games, 2018, online).

Cameron Baker is one of those in the region who has moved beyond the consumption end of games. He works in game development but Australia's gaming industry, to him, means a variety of things: 'It generally means any interactive technology. That can encompass anything from traditional games to mobile games and apps, to installations at museums and exhibitions—anything like that' (Baker, i/v Nov 2016). While Baker works full time in the gaming field, clients that he works with are not gamers, per se. These clients include a major bank, a national museum and a range of American automotive shows but there is employment uncertainty:

> The industry in Australia isn't there for big-budget games. So, I'm trying to push getting as much experience as I can—building up my portfolio and skill set to make me a more attractive recruit for an overseas company … there's no support for game development in Sydney or here—some in Melbourne but not in NSW. (Baker, i/v Nov 2016)

Emma Leggett studied interactive entertainment but when she found work it was in a digital agency with multi-media marketing material. She knows people who are without work in the field some years after graduating: 'I was lucky, I got my job. I have been holding onto this one. However, I don't think that there are very many games opportunities' (Leggett, i/v Nov 2016). Since the interview, Leggett has taken up a job working as a multi-media specialist with a major television network but has also worked in the United Kingdom as an assistant producer at Supermassive Games and as an Associate Producer at Sledgehammer Games in Melbourne.

Software Applications in the Hunter: Convergence Across Fields

Technology convergence and digitization, renders it increasingly difficult to analyze, differentiate and report on the integration and separation of the digital economy and the creative industries, especially in the related sub-sectors of software applications and interactive media. However, while the 'apps industry has grown phenomenally quickly on the back of the popularity of smartphones and tablet computers' (Goldsmith, 2014, p. 344), there is not a great deal of activity with apps in the Hunter Region. Development is sporadic and there isn't a critical mass of developers.

One such business is CIBIS International, which has been 'designing, coding and managing business software solutions and digital platforms for more than two decades' (CIBIS, 2023, online). They are 'a leading Australian developer of custom business software, web and mobile applications' (CIBIS, 2023, online). Another is Headjam Creative Agency, which, among many other services it offers, has 'the ability to complete high-end mobile app development, and specialize in the latest software solutions to be used across all types of mobile devices, from mobile phones to tablets' (Headjam, 2018, online).

Summary

Modeling by PriceWaterhouseCoopers (PWC, 2015) on economic opportunities created through digital change, identified that the small businesses in the Hunter and Newcastle Federal electorates could unlock $897 m of increased private sector output across the coming decade through improved access and use of mobile and internet technologies. The electronic games and interactive software sector is integrally linked to such opportunities. What has emerged out of this relatively new sector is the distinctive and possibly unique characteristics of the scene in the Hunter, with significant elements reflecting the region's industrial history and collaborative culture. Links, for example, with traditional Hunter sectors such as defense and mining demonstrate the versatile applications of gaming and interactive design. Simulations, in particular, play a crucial role in ensuring safety and education in highly dangerous industries.

While the region demonstrates the popularity of the electronic games industry primarily through its retail outlets, there was little evidence of commercial game development for the leisure market or any considerable commercial development of software application. In contrast to the optimistic lauding of the industry by the Australian government (see, for example, *Level Up: A guide to the Australian games industry*, published by the Australian Trade and Investment Commission), the Hunter is an example of how regional areas do not enjoy a booming game and interactive content industry. We do, however, note that such activity may be "hidden" from general statistical or public domain information.

It is of note that Newcastle City Council has taken on the notion of being a smart city. Smart cities are generally accepted as cities that use technology to improve community life which means a reliance on ICT. Smart cities strategies broadly aim to enhance livability, wellness, sustainability and efficiency and to support initiatives in the areas of community engagement, information sharing, environmental monitoring and personal welfare. This will open up opportunities in software development and interactivity in the future. Growth in the electronic games and interactive software sectors is expected to continue, but in assessing the Hunter's participation, the numbers were confounded by overlapping sectors and employment definitions, signaling the convergence and complexity that exists in this fast-moving sector and its relationship to other areas. As such, the electronic games and interactive content industries in the Hunter provide an exemplary case study of the horizontal and vertical integration of the creative industries demonstrating that this creative (eco)system is broadly interconnected. Some software development, the exploitation of serious gaming and the use of virtual reality characterize it in the Hunter Region. Its practices are dynamic, in a state of flux and open to change.

This chapter drew on interviews with those choice making agents who work in the field of IT and gaming in the leisure and retail sector as well as those who make use of gaming and IT in serious applications such as work health and safety, smart cities, defense and health. These confirmed that critical opportunities in the Hunter seem to lie in interconnections with the region's traditional strengths. We explored the domain structures of the sector by looking at a brief history, followed by how it works and its significance to the Australian economy, and what business models are typically used. We then identified key members of the field before asking those choice making agents how they engage with the shared knowledges of the domain and the interconnected structures of the field as each constitutes this rapidly developing and highly dynamic creative (eco)system.

References

Alvarez, P. (2022, October 27). *This infographic shows the rise of mobile device subscriptions worldwide*. World Economic Forum. Retrieved February 13, 2023, from https://www.weforum.org/agenda/2022/10/mobile-device-subscription-rise-technology/

ATIC. (2022). *Level up: A guide to the Australian games industry*. Retrieved October 5, 2022, from https://www.globalaustralia.gov.au/sites/default/files/2022-08/level_up_agttagi_a4_booklet_lowres.pdf

Austrade. (2014). *Digital games*. Austrade. Retrieved April 18, 2017, from https://www.austrade.gov.au/ArticleDocuments/1358/Digital-Games-ICR.pdf.aspx

BISim. (2018). *Home*. Bohemia interactive simulations. Retrieved April 14, 2018, from https://bisimulations.com/

CIBIS. (2023). *About us*. CIBIS International. Retrieved February 15, 2023, from https://www.cibis.com.au/about-us

Clarke, T. (2009). *Digital economy report: What's in it?* ARN. Retrieved January 9, 2023, from https://www.arnnet.com.au/article/311201/digital_economy_report_what_it_/

Deloitte. (2016). *Australia's digital pulse: Developing the digital workforce to drive growth in the future*. Deloitte Access Economics Australian Computer Society. Retrieved August 2, 2017, from https://www.acs.org.au/content/dam/acs/acs-publications/Australia's%20Digital%20Pulse%202017.pdf

Deloitte. (2022). *ACS Australia's digital pulse | Unlocking the tech sector: Beyond one million*. Retrieved January 9, 2023, from https://www.acs.org.au/content/dam/acs/acs-publications/AustraliasDigitalPulse_2022F.pdf

DeWitt, D. (2018). *Virtual reality history*. Retrieved February 13, 2023, from https://wiki.mq.edu.au/display/vr/Virtual+Reality+History

EB Games. (2018). *Home*. EB Games. Retrieved April 4, 2018, from https://ebgames.com.au/

Environment and Communications References Committee. (2016). *Game on: More than playing around (Chapter 2)*. Retrieved January 5, 2023, from https://www.aph.gov.au/Parliamentary_Business/Committees/Senate/Environment_and_Communications/Video_game_industry/Report/c02

Gallagher A. (2018). *Andrew Gallagher*. LinkedIn. Retrieved April 8, 2018, from https://www.linkedin.com/in/andrew-gallagher-3215688b/

GDAA. (2017). *Members*. Games Developers Association of Australia. Retrieved October 7, 2019, from http://www.gdaa.com.au/members

Goggin, G. (2014). The internet, online and mobile communication. In S. Cunningham & S. Turner (Eds.), *The media and communications in Australia* (4th ed., pp. 247–268). Allen & Unwin.

Goldsmith, B. (2014). The apps industry. In S. Cunningham & S. Turner (Eds.), *The media and communications in Australia* (4th ed., pp. 339–344). Allen & Unwin.

Grad, B. (2015). *Software industry*. ethw.org. Retrieved July 25, 2017, from http://ethw.org/Software_Industry

Green, P. (2017a, March 20). Gomaz vs Pedro brings e-sports tournaments to Newcastle. *Newcastle Herald*. Retrieved March 25, 2017, from https://www.theherald.com.au/story/4513316/game-on-for-mates-in-tournament-venture/

Green, P. (2017b, June 26). Applied virtual simulation among elite companies to showcase simulator technologies at Australian open army day. *Newcastle Herald*. Retrieved July 3, 2017, from https://www.theherald.com.au/story/4729866/defence-a-ripe-frontier-for-virtual-innovators/

Headjam. (2018). *Mobile app development*. Headjam. Retrieved April 18, 2018, from https://www.headjam.com.au/what-we-do/mobile-app-development

Hesmondhalgh, D. (2019). *The cultural industries* (4th ed.). Sage.

Hjorth, L. (2014). Games: Mobile, locative and social. In S. Cunningham & S. Turnbull (Eds.), *The media and communications in Australia* (4th ed., pp. 269–283). Allen & Unwin.

Hollerer, T., & Schmalstieg, D. (2016). *A brief history of augmented reality: Introduction to augmented reality*. Informit. Retrieved October 17, 2017, from http://www.informit.com/articles/article.aspx?p=2516729&seqNum=2

IGEA. (2021). *Australian consumer video game sales: 2021 snapshot* [infographic]. Retrieved January 5, 2023, from https://igea.net/wp-content/uploads/2022/05/ACVGS-2021-Infographic-scaled.jpg

Investment NSW. (2019). *Hunter defence targets innovation and growth*. NSW Government. Retrieved February 16, 2023, from https://www.business.nsw.gov.au/innovation-and-research/programs/boosting-business-innovation-program/news/hunter-defence-targets-innovation-and-growth

JFSN. (2023). *Jet flight simulator Newcastle*. Retrieved February 15, 2023, from https://jetflightsimulatornewcastle.com.au/

Keogh, B. (2021). The cultural field of video game production in Australia. *Games and Culture, 16*(1), 116–135. https://doi.org/10.1177/1555412019873746

lukefollows11. (2013, September 20). Organisational structures in the games industry. *lukefollows11*. Retrieved April 23, 2023, from https://lukefollows11.wordpress.com/2013/09/20/organisational-structures-in-the-games-industry/

Marcus, C. (2005). *Future of creative industries: Implications for research policy*. Foresight Working Documents Series, European Commission. Retrieved October 9, 2017, from https://meakultura.pl/cdn/docs/1326303611.pdf

Martinez-Fernandez, M.C., Soosay, C., Venkata, K.V., Turpin, T., & Bjorkli, M. (2005). *Knowledge intensive service activities in the software industry in Australia*. AEGIS, Western Sydney University. Retrieved February 15, 2023, from https://www.westernsydney.edu.au/__data/assets/pdf_file/0014/33431/KISA_-_Innovation_of_the_Software_Industy_in_Australia.pdf

McIntyre, P., Balnaves, M., Kerrigan, S., King, E., & Williams, C. (2019). *Creativity and cultural production in the hunter: An applied ethnographic study of new entrepreneurial systems in the creative industries*. University of Newcastle and Australia Research Council, School of Creative Industries. Newcastle. Retrieved October 15, 2021, from https://soci.newcastle.edu.au/hci/2019/02/27/final-report/

McIntyre, P., Fulton, J. M., Kerrigan, S. M., & Meany, M. M. (2023). *Entrepreneurship in the creative industries: How innovative agents, skills and networks interact*. Palgrave Macmillan.

Okunev, R. (2023). *The psychology of evolving technology*. Apress. https://doi.org/10.1007/978-1-4842-8686-9_3

Quora. (2018). *How much does mobile application development cost in general for a business app?* Quora.com. Retrieved March 29, 2018, from https://www.quora.com/How-much-does-mobile-application-development-cost-in-general-for-a-business-app

Pease, A., & Zistl, S. (2014). *Simulation: Bringing reality to the virtual world*. Siemens. Retrieved October 9, 2017, from https://www.siemens.com/innovation/en/home/pictures-of-the-future/digitalization-and-software/simulation-and-virtual-reality-trends.html

Pelipaja. (2015). Business Models In Video Game Industry, thelatestbook.com https://thelatestbook.com/download/4677769-business-models-in-video-game-industry-pelipaja (accessed 14/11/2023).

PWC. (2015). *Small business digital growth: The potential for internet and mobile technologies to transform small business—Summary findings*. PriceWaterhouseCooper. Retrieved April 14, 2016, from www.digitalinnovation.pwc.com.au/small-bsuiness-digital-growth

Rajaraman, V. A. (2022a). Concise history of the internet—I. *Resonance, 27*, 1841–1856. https://doi.org/10.1007/s12045-022-1483-2

Rajaraman, V. A. (2022b). Concise history of the internet—II. *Resonance, 27*, 2045–2068. https://doi.org/10.1007/s12045-022-1505-0

Rakestraw, T., Rangamohan, E., & Rammohan, K. (2013). The mobile apps industry: A case study. *Journal of Business Cases & Applications, 9*, 1–26. Retrieved from https://www.aabri.com/manuscripts/131583.pdf

Random History. (2008). *Programming code from punch cards to HTML—A history of software*. Random History. Retrieved October 10, 2017, from www.randomhistory.com

Sharma, S. (2015). *Market structure of the global mobile industry and the Indian market*. Retrieved February 15, 2023, from https://doi.org/10.2139/ssrn.2684253

Straubhaar, J., LaRose, R., & Davenport, L. (2022). *Media now: Understanding media, culture and technology* (10th ed.). Wadsworth.

Sunita, J. T., & Sharma, S. K. (2021). Gaming: Around the world geography. In R. Kumar, B. K. Mishra, & P. K. Pattnaik (Eds.), *Next generation of internet of things. Vol. 21: Lecture notes in networks and systems*. Springer. https://doi.org/10.1007/978-981-16-0666-3_1

SVG. (2018). *Home*. Slice Virtual Golf. Retrieved April 4, 2018, from http://www.slicevirtualgolf.com/

UVR. (2018). *Home*. UnReal VR. Retrieved April 14, 2018, from https://www.unrealvr.com.au/

Velikovsky, J. (2013). *On sound and music in games*. Unpublished paper, University of Newcastle.

VRXP. (2018). *About*. Virtual Reality Experience. Retrieved October 9, 2018, from http://www.vrxp.com.au/

Williams, D., & Srivastava, J. (2014). *History and structure of the video game industry*. ninjametrics. Retrieved October 8, 2017, from https://www.ninjametrics.com/tag/history-and-structure-of-video-game-industry/

15

Support Organizations, Education and Training

Introduction

As demonstrated in previous chapters, creative industry systems are multifactorial in origin and in effect. Gone are the days when individuals alone could do all that is necessary to be innovative and bring complex creative works into being, if that was indeed ever the case (Becker, 1982; Csikszentmihalyi, 1997; Sawyer, 2012). All practitioners need support of some sort, whether it be financial, technological, administrative, legal, political, social, cultural or educational, in order to bring new and innovative products to market. The creative industries do not exist in a vacuum; structures are provided within the system that help support the core activities. Reminiscent of Howard Becker's (1982) concept of an Art World, a creative (eco)system is that 'network of people whose cooperative activity, organized via their joint knowledge of conventional means of doing things, produces the kind of art works that art world is noted for' (Becker, 1982, p. x). The "artist" (in this case the journalist, designer, musician, filmmaker, broadcaster, etc.) performs the core activity but this would not be possible without the other participants performing support activities.

P. McIntyre et al., *Creativity and Creative Industries in Regional Australia*, Palgrave Studies in Creativity and Culture, https://doi.org/10.1007/978-3-031-45972-6_15

Education and Training: Domain Acquisition

In order to adopt an entrepreneurial approach to the creative industries, anyone wishing to do this must be socialized or enculturated into the system they will eventually take an active part in. In this regard, Csikszentmihalyi contends that:

> a person who wants to make a creative contribution not only must work within a creative system but must also reproduce that system within his or her mind. In other words, the person must learn the rules and the content of the domain, as well as the criteria of selection, the preferences of the field. (1997, p. 47)

Thus, learning to be part of the creative industries is most often a process of being educated into it. Education, according to Haralambos and Holborn (2013), is simply one particular aspect of socialization that is specifically concerned with the acquisition of knowledge and the learning of skills. This process of acquisition may take many forms but, for our purposes, we can supply two categories, that is, either formal or informal. While informal socialization into the field and enculturation into the domain may take the form of mentoring, familial immersion or various degrees of autodidacticism, this chapter is focused primarily on the formal process and that includes state- and federal-funded institutions as well as private providers and specialty schools.

University Education and Shared Knowledge: Formal Acquisition of the Domain in the Creative Industries

Formal education and training in the creative industries fields at the University level is concentrated in the lower Hunter and is primarily on offer within the regional hub in Newcastle. The Hunter is considered to be a one-university town and the University of Newcastle (UON) prides itself on being a 'university of our regions and for our regions' (UON,

2022, p. 4). Since its inception, UON has been best known for its strengths in engineering, medicine, science and architecture but in recent years has given a greater recognition to the role and potential of the creative industries.

There are well over 3000 students undertaking courses at the UON in fields that are classified as part of the creative industries. These fields include Drama, Visual and Performing Arts, Film, Media and Cultural Studies, Creative Writing, Architecture and Industrial Design, Graphic Design, Animation, Journalism, Public Relations, Television, Radio, Sound Production, Multimedia, Web Design, IT, Software Application and Interactive Content Development. Many of the programs that focus on these areas are taught by creative industry professionals and are guided by a number of established External Advisory Boards comprised of current, highly successful creative industries operatives.

The University provides a set of institutional structures aimed at nurturing the creative industries. Creativity and innovation in the creative industries was specifically targeted as an emerging research strength at UON. The University, two Faculties, the former Hunter Creative Industries and Technology (HCIT) research center and the recently formed Future Arts Science Technology Lab (FASTLab), have all been focused on that aim.

Vocational Education and Training: Industry Linked Domain Acquisition

TAFE NSW Hunter and Central Coast is the primary vocational education and training institution in the Hunter. TAFE (Technical and Further Education) has a strong record in education in the creative arts and media providing programs at Certificate, Diploma and Advanced Diploma level and, in its online communications, characterizes the region as a "hotbed of creative talent". At the time of writing, TAFE offered courses in Creative Industries, Fashion and Media including acting, digital media and communications, fashion, interior design and decoration, graphic arts and design, the music industry, product design and photography. For those engaged in fine art, TAFE also houses Newcastle Art School, an intensive training facility that 'is well known for its studio-based fine arts training for professional artists' (Australian Ceramics Community, 2023, online). Another important part of TAFE's creative industries offerings is Design Centre Hunter, a 'connected, collaborative hub to inspire and support students, teachers and industry in design related disciplines, [it]encourages students across disciplines to work together in new and innovative ways' (HunterTAFE, 2018, online). The exhibition space attached to the Design Centre opened in 2016, giving design students a dedicated venue to present their work. Practical experience is also highlighted through other vocational providers such as the Regional Institute of Performing Arts and the Regional Music Institute.

Specialty Schools: Shared Knowledge of Specific Domains

Secondary schooling in the Hunter has a sporadic approach to education in the creative industries. In the public school system, Callaghan College offers high school students a chance to move beyond their traditional education and take up, among many other offerings, classes in Computing and IT. Also in public schooling, the Hunter School of the Performing Arts (HSPA) is a performing arts school with students ranging from years 3 to 12 (approximately aged 8 to 18). It is the only fully selective performing arts school in NSW and enrolment is via auditions. It should be noted that the NSW school curriculum for public schools offers teaching in dance, drama, music and visual arts. The Hunter Valley Grammar School, a private school in the Maitland area, also highlights its achievements in the creative arts. Located inside the regional Catholic education system, St. Francis Xavier's College in Hamilton is one of the few schools that offer a media studies option to their students.

Other Training and Learning Centers: Acquiring Field Skills and Domain Knowledge

The region is rich in private training options. This includes both the development of the "content" skills and the business skills needed to join the creative industries and earn a living (for a detailed discussion on how to acquire business skills in the creative industries see McIntyre et al., 2023). The Business Centre, Hunter is perhaps the largest of these. Headquartered in Newcastle, but with outreach centers on the Central Coast and Mid North Coast, and with a Business Innovation Centre in Newcastle, it is a business assistance organization providing professional services to micro, small and medium businesses. It is closely involved with local projects for innovation and the creative industries. Similarly, the Hunter Region Business Hub is a Business Enterprise Centre providing practical assistance in business planning, advice on marketing, budgeting and cash flow and provides those services to the creative industries practitioners in its areas as does Lake Macquarie's Business Growth Centre. These centers are partly funded by government contracts but provide other services on a fee-for-service basis.

Atwea College (formerly WEA Hunter) also provides business courses but in addition delivers qualifications in subject areas such as the music industry and working in the theater. There are also "Learn for Fun" courses, which include, of interest to those who enjoy the creative industries offerings, photography, music, fine art, computing, and other lifestyle and community courses in a range of special interests.

Other private training options are widely available. Art Mania Studio at Wallsend, for example, provides community-learning opportunities in a wide variety of creative arts. Hunter Design School is a registered training organization, providing training in graphic design, interior design and color consultancy for design stylists. The Pump House School in Newcastle provides training in design, commercial software, media production, digital photography and social media. And, similar to many educational institutions, offerings from these providers are often available online.

Support Organizations, Groups and Businesses: The Interconnected Networks of the Field at Work

The creative industries consist of a series of contextual factors that impact and affect all operatives in these industries. Some of these factors are well beyond the control of individual creatives. As a result, various organizations have been established in the region to advise, encourage and support the actions of creative industries personnel and to help catalyze the generation of business opportunities for these industries. These organizations range from smaller cases of what could be called self-help collective processes through to larger, usually government-funded, agencies and organizations. There are also industry-specific support organizations. A key observation from this examination is how deeply embedded and integrated these support organizations, groups and businesses are with each other, with the educational institutions discussed earlier, and with the broader ecosystem.

Industry Development Organizations: The Field Supporting Creatives and Industry

Key industry development organizations range from those that support individual agents through to others that take a more macro view of the Hunter. These include the UON-led Integrated Innovation Network (I2N) that conducts skill development training, hosts community workshops, provides support for SMEs and links to research where relevant. Another is Hunter iF Limited, a project-based peak support organization established in 2018 with more than 300 people from industry, government and research developing the key objective of turning the Hunter's growing innovation ecosystem 'into a world-class, sustainable model attracting entrepreneurs, investors and industry to the region and diversifying its economy' (Hunter iF, 2023, online). By the very nature of Hunter iF Limited views on innovation, enterprises within the creative industries are being drawn into its broad strategies.

Renew Newcastle, on the other hand, focused on stimulating the activity of individual choice making agents from the creative industries operating within smaller communities. During its tenure (2008–2019), it aimed to find artists, cultural projects and community groups to use and maintain empty buildings in the Central Business District until they became commercially viable or the buildings were redeveloped. Artists, designers, photographers and craftspeople were invited to set up temporary galleries, studios and offices in empty buildings in collaboration with the owners. Co-founder Marcus Westbury's primary interest was in:

> Small-scale creativity basically like whether that's record labels, computer game designers or makers or craftspeople. I'm really interested in that really small-scale layer, the layer that doesn't really figure on the radar of sort of policymakers and big institutions. (Westbury, i/v June 2015)

Christopher Saunders was general manager of Renew from 2014 to 2019. Saunders' background in acting and theater, story-telling, project management and his role as Chair of Tantrum Youth Arts prepared him for the GM role. Saunders believes that 'there's an enormous opportunity for creative people to play a part in shaping the future of this city' (Saunders, i/v June 2015) and that Renew is playing an important role in this as "an enabler". He says 'there's a history in the world of creatives coming in when a place has fallen into disrepair … I think that creatives are very good at taking advantage of opportunities and bringing something new to a place and I think that's what's happened in Newcastle' (Saunders, i/v June 2015).

HunterNet, on the other hand, is a long-standing organization established to support the manufacturing industry at a time of regional downturn. HunterNet provides programs for businesses 'active in national and international infrastructure and asset management, energy and resources, defence and advanced manufacturing supply chains' (HunterNet, 2018, online) in areas such as 'business development, business systems and processes, WHS and training, marketing and communications, innovation, business improvement; and government advocacy' (HunterNet, 2018, online). The group recognizes the role of the creative industries in the manufacturing and engineering sectors and supports their further development. HunterNet aims to bring together smaller business collaboration and networking so that their skills and expertise can be combined to secure larger contracts.

Business Enablers, Consultants and Other Support Organizations: Building the Creative (Eco)System

Gunilla Burrowes is deeply embedded in the creative industries space as a founding member of Rights House, a Hunter angel investment organization, and as Chair of Eighteen04, an industry incubator focused on clean tech and smart city innovations. Burrowes is actively involved in interconnected networks across the Hunter. She insists that 'community networks are also important for the innovative ecosystem to grow and this is where the contribution of the creative industries is so important for technical based start-ups' (Burrowes, i/v Jan 2017). A similar enabler is Steph Hinds, the Director of Growthwise Business Consultants. Hinds is the Joint Convenor of Digifest, is a member of the Lunaticks Society, and sits on a number of global and national advisory panels for organizations. Hinds trained in accounting and business and 'liked reading about technology and start-ups and that developed as an interest' (Hinds, i/v March 2017).

Hinds noted how those who work in the creative industries are good at what they do but often their business sense is lacking:

> they were all exceptionally talented at what they did, but most of them had no want or desire or hadn't done any training in relation to business … Our question became "how could we help what we do to be a continuation of their business and get them to make profit at the same time?" (Hinds, i/v March 2017)

A further observation from Hinds, and in line with others working to support the creative industries, is collaboration and networking is a key component to success as is understanding the region: 'People need to collaborate in partnership with other businesses—that could really make sure they are sustainable for the long term' (Hinds, i/v March 2017).

Seeking the same ends, RDA Hunter (Regional Development Australia Hunter) is a key regional body which has recognized the creative industries as one of seven areas of "smart specialization" for the region. They have noted the role they can play in sustainable economic diversification. For example, in their submission to the NSW Government's proposed Creative Industries Taskforce in 2013, they claimed that the 'creative industries will drive economic growth, exports, productivity, innovation and competitiveness for the Nation, the State of NSW and the Hunter region' (RDA Hunter, 2018, online). In the meantime, CEO Todd Williams suggests that there are other connections to be made:

> In a perfect world I would like to build better links between manufacturing and creative industries certainly. And I think, medicine and education—from the perspective of economic development—high value jobs and growth. The creative industries really put the after-burners on something like that. Defence. Agriculture. (Williams, i/v March 2017)

On a more localized scale, Newcastle Now, the Business Improvement Association for inner city Newcastle, has taken a long-standing focus on the role of the creative industries in city and economic revitalization, supporting through sponsorships and grants a range of organizations, events and projects that link the creative industries to skill development, business activation and placemaking. CEO Michael Neilson, like many others, was aware that the city was populated with a significant number of artists and musicians with limited incomes but admits his view was:

> a pretty ignorant view—the basket-weaving model so to speak. So, I probably didn't give it the respect that it deserved. But then my eyes were opened to what the creative industries were, and are—a new understanding of the sector. And I realized that it is big. (Neilson, i/v Nov 2016)

Newcastle Now worked with local councils and government agencies, invested in research and projects such as Hunter Innovations and iF Projects, and collaborated to support Smart City infrastructure and focused specifically on the creative industries by providing funding for research. One example of their approach is Night Time Spaces, a collaborative project of Newcastle Now, Newcastle Council, University of Newcastle, Hamilton Chamber of Commerce and Hunter Development Corporation, which uses interactive design in public spaces to counter problems in high-crime hot spots while newer projects use sensor-based technology to drive "smart-play" interactive areas in the public domain. Neilson asserted that Newcastle Now's 'primary purpose is that things do the job they are designed to do. Creativity and innovation are often a key element' (Neilson, i/v Nov 2016).

While organizations such as Newcastle Now, and the projects they stimulated, have been enablers of the broader creative industries, there are other organizations that focus at enabling specific sectors and there are examples of these right across the Hunter. In the Upper Hunter, Arts Upper Hunter is supported by the local councils of the Upper Hunter Region and it supports projects, promotes artists and galleries, museums and historical societies, coordinates creative workshops and maintains a directory of art and cultural groups. It is also a strong supporter of Indigenous arts and culture. Other arts support organizations in the Upper Hunter such as Scone Arts and Crafts Inc. also aim to enthuse, practice and demonstrate all branches of the arts. The Singleton Arts and Music Society present orchestral concerts, chamber recitals, opera concerts and plays. Further down the valley, the Newcastle Community Arts Centre supports the development of community-focused arts activities by individuals, groups and organizations, providing space and skills development and promoting events, while the Octapod Association aims to inspire new ideas in arts and media and support a creative and diverse arts sector. Octapod has supported the development of artists through programs such as the culturehunter.org, Podspace Gallery and This Is Not Art (TINA) Festival. TINA is an annual festival of experimental and emerging arts. It attracts artists and visits from across the country. One of its highlights is a Young Writers Award. The Dungog Festival is an arts festival that highlights art in many genres and includes film, workshops, Sculpture on the Farm, music in a street party and lots of family entertainment.

In architecture, the Newcastle Division of the Australian Institute of Architects (AIA) services the Greater Hunter Region, coordinating and delivering professional development, awards and prizes, events, policy and advocacy and noting significant architecture. It also provides a range of services to members including HR assistance, benchmarking, Australian Standards, insurance and a "Find an Architect" service.

For the film world, Screen Hunter, the regional film office, supports production in the Hunter Region. This office is funded by Hunter Councils and its aim is to capitalize on the unique qualities of the region by increasing film production and fostering and driving the development of a creative and sustainable film industry in the region. As discussed previously, it has been successful in attracting film projects to the region and, with them, the flow-on jobs to local film workers and actors.

The visual arts community is supported and enabled in its activities right across the region. As an economic booster for micro enterprise, it is strongly evident through opportunities such as the Gloucester Arts Trail and the highly successful markets such as Olive Tree, Hand Made in the Hunter, Singleton Farmers and Craft, Wollombi Village, Maitland, Laguna, Wine Country and Hunt and Gather Markets as well as the many smaller markets that present throughout the region. Similarly, it seems that almost every town across the region has a small gallery, arts-based retail outlet or annual art show where local creatives are given the promotion and support they need. Several societies are actively engaged in providing a broad creative impetus. These include: the Artisan Collective Port Stephens; the Australian Decorative and Fine Arts Society Scone, which promotes education in the study of the decorative and fine arts; the Gloucester Arts and Cultural Council, a not-for-profit that operates a gallery and provides workshops and activities; Dungog Arts Society, which aims to provides a focal point for fostering creative activities in their community; the Lake Macquarie Art Gallery Society; and the Newcastle Art Society. Delivering a broad approach, Murrurundi Arts and Crafts Council is a not-for-profit volunteer-based arts council which runs workshops and ArtStart lessons and hosts the annual Murrurundi Art Prize, photographic Prize and biennial Opera Murrurundi, while the Hunter Arts Network is a non-profit group of artisans that strives to facilitate opportunities of promotion of members and their work through an art bazaar and promotional activities. Port Stephens Community Arts Centre provides facilities for community arts and craft activities and a gallery as does the Muswellbrook Regional Arts Centre, while Newcastle

Printmakers Workshop is a dedicated space run by volunteers and available to artists. Ceramics is a strong interest with groups such as Newcastle Studio Potters, Scone Ceramic Group and the Pot House at Muswellbrook all having active ceramics groups, with shared studio spaces for creating ceramics and there are also private teaching studios. Textiles and fiber arts are a consistent interest with an apparently growing commercial market, locally moving out of functional items and into fine arts. From more traditional crafts, such as those represented by the Knitters Guild, Fibreholics Clarence Town focuses on spinning and knitting crafts and Daughters on Dowling is a networking and skill development group working with textiles in Dungog. In Newcastle, Creative Embroiderers and Textile Artists work with fibers, textiles, quilting and jewelry while Timeless Textiles is a gallery store and open studio featuring textile arts and providing workshops and visiting artists programs.

All Councils in the Hunter Region also actively support Indigenous cultural programs through their gallery spaces and events programs. Indigenous art is represented in many galleries including the dedicated Free Spirit Aboriginal Gallery, Outback Art and Red Ochre Workshops, all in Newcastle. The Wollombi Valley Arts Council supports an Aboriginal arts and culture group while the Hunter Valley Visitors Centre and Cessnock Art Gallery also highlight Indigenous arts. Tobwabba Art, based a little to the north in Forster, represents 22 artists but is an internet-based business, successfully linking the traditional to contemporary markets and crossing regional boundaries. Speaking in Colour is a business delivering Aboriginal art workshops and education resources across the region.

For the literary-minded, writers' support groups are evident throughout the region that focus on both appreciation and skills development. Gloucester Writers Centre, for example, delivers readings, classes, lectures, films, writers-in-residence and community events. The Hunter Writers Centre is a not-for-profit organization devoted to both aspiring and established writers and delivers courses, conducts competitions and awards, and (differently from other groups) provides writing services. The Lake Macquarie Branch of the Fellowship of Australian Writers meets monthly as do the Raymond Terrace, Maitland and Singleton Writers Groups, which provide a range of writing workshops and meetups.

Writers Festivals are very popular. The National Young Writers Festival is the country's largest gathering of young and innovative writers working in both traditional and new forms including zines, comics, blogging, screenwriting, poetry, journalism, comedy and prose. It presents panels, discussions, workshops, performances and many forms. The Newcastle Writers Festival, established in 2013, has quickly become a well-established event attracting a broad audience and successful writers. The Scone Literary Festival aims to "maintain the page" in this digital age, promoting books and a love of literature.

For the performing arts sector of the creative industries, individual facilitators like Shane Bransdon are essential. His interest in the performing arts is broad and active but he sees himself primarily as a facilitator and is immersed in the domain as a key field member of the sector. Bransdon has long been involved in the performing arts sector but worked as an educator until 2018 when he began a drama business with Daniel Stoddart called OzTheatre. Bransdon has also lectured in drama at the University of Newcastle. Importantly he devotes a great deal of his time to the theater. He is a judge of the City of Newcastle Drama Awards (CONDAS) which entailed, for example, seeing 60 shows in 2013. He was Chair of the Newcastle Performing Arts Taskforce from 2012 until 2015 and is the drama representative on the arts funding body for the NSW Department of Education. He also researched performing arts for his PhD at the University of Newcastle. For Bransdon, collaboration remains central and this sentiment can be extrapolated across all the creative industries: 'It's really important because a lot of us are individuals who look after our own craft, whether it's development or seeking employment, creating work for ourselves, collaboration has to happen' (Bransdon, i/v Dec 2014).

Part of that collaboration involves social media. Theater companies in Newcastle, according to Bransdon, are using social media, and whatever form of communication that entails embedding into their posts, to promote their shows:

> We do have a wonderful community in Newcastle theater [and] everybody is linked into social media, regardless of age ... Being able to tag people, share the experience. People are able to instantly access five or six

> hundred of their friends by making a single post. I am the coordinator of the CONDA Facebook page and I am able to see, using data, how many people are exposed to our posts. When I posted about the CONDA winners it was in the vicinity of 900 people that that post reached, just by typing in a sentence and adding an attachment and clicking post. Stooged Theatre have in particular—and I'm not sure if it is entirely social media but I believe that is a significant factor—been able to access an entirely new young audience that nobody else has been able to capture. (Bransdon, i/v Dec 2014)

Apart from a focus on the arts, performing arts, publishing and film communities, the digital sector also has its supporters and enablers. Hunter Digit, for example, is a non-profit organization committed to establishing the Hunter Region as a leading digital economy with a global reputation. Leaders of the group have been closely involved with the Hunter Innovation and iF Projects which are delivering these outcomes. Closely linked to Hunter DiGiT is Eighteen04, which provides an incubator and co-working space for smart cities and green technology. It runs start-up events and hackathons and provides mentoring and skills development.

The Lunaticks Society is a not-for-profit association of digital and creative enthusiasts and related professionals and entrepreneurs who are engaged in the digital economy and want to network and promote their ideas and achievements to others. Gordon Whitehead, who has a background in IT services, business development and a Masters in marketing, is its Chair and founder. As Whitehead explains:

> I helped form the Lunaticks Society—named after the Lunar Society of Birmingham—which is dedicated to digital innovation and new ideas in Regional Australia. One program is the annual Newie Awards for digital creativity based on a whole range of technologies—social media, new technology solutions, agency work, start-ups, solutions for government and tourism … We've run Coffee Mornings and evening sessions where we talk about creative topics. We are trying out a more TV-style program approach with our goal to do more consumable programs. It's all about collaboration—agencies, suppliers, clients. At Lunaticks—it's everyone who is involved. Stop the competitive stuff. Collectively we can lift the bar … My

> goal is to generate optimism. It's an exciting time. We are in an age of experimentation and innovation we have never seen before. The big issue is the transition from traditional businesses on the street corner to the new services, as well as the new industries and the businesses that support them. (Whitehead, i/v Sept 2016)

A further group of support organizations for the creative industries are organizations that provide co-working spaces that specialize in clusters of related creatives. Among the growing complex of privately run co-working spaces are the INNX Hub, which provides co-working space, studios, meeting spaces and hot desks for creatives such as filmmakers, architects, designers and photographers. The Production Hub is another that is a co-working space in Newcastle for filmmakers, 3D artists, animators, graphic designers, UX designers and web developers. Harry Balding is the Community Manager for the DASH co-working space. After studying Communication at the University of Newcastle, he worked in marketing, sales and business development for a manufacturer before taking up his role with DASH:

> Here, we've got media producers, website designers, graphic designers—quite a few working in the creative sector … Dantia, the vehicle for Lake Macquarie's economic development strategy, is DASH's parent company. We thought to set up a place for people in the knowledge economy to thrive and to meet, and to collaborate and connect. We also feature in Council's smart cities and ecosystem management strategies … Newie Start-ups is a meet-up group that has just grown. For each event we have held, there have been more attendees. We did a pitch event last October and had 85 people come and 8 start-ups pitched. The University provided the prizes. It's one of a whole lot of innovative meet-up groups in Newcastle—Agile Newcastle, Newcastle Intracoders, Newcastle Ruby Developers, Hunter Young Professionals, UON Bizcom, UON Computing Society and others. Within Newie Start-ups and DASH there is now lots of informal and social mentoring around. (Balding, i/v Jan 2017)

Balding's comments about the informal and social mentoring confirms again the importance of networking, collaboration and field engagement in this dynamic and well supported creative (eco)system in action.

Summary

The creative industries, like all others, do not exist in a vacuum. Once operatives within these industries acquire enough knowledge to become contributors to help complete the jigsaw puzzle, they become part of the field for their own sector (and, increasingly, across sectors) and need support to access shared knowledge and information, finance and advice as they make their way through an increasingly complex and interconnected creative world. Educational opportunities at all levels are available in the Hunter Region with many courses on offer focused specifically at the creative industries. In addition to formal approaches to education, which are predominantly the function of state-based institutions or professional associations with mandatory training options, creative workers also seek training and learning opportunities through informal pathways such as mentoring, classes, and various degrees of self-education as they immerse himself in the shared knowledge of the domain.

It is these structures, and the interconnected networks they service, that help enable creatives, choice making agents, to go about their business and they range from private enterprises through to support from the public purse via government agencies. Local, state and federal instrumentalities have been set up to ensure that the viability of these and other industries serves to benefit the region. The private sector also recognizes the need to help budding entrepreneurs realize their objectives and, at the same time, provide research and project support where possible. A number of businesses are focused at this exact task by training, advising, consulting, encouraging and, at times, financing those willing to take risks in the creative industries.

There is also a rich creative (eco)system of family connections, community music and arts organizations, private training colleges and teachers, theater groups, festivals and masterclasses, accountants and lawyers, professional and service networks and even co-working spaces. And there is a deep recognition of the value of these connections and how they support creative workers as they go about their business of writing and performing music, putting on plays, making films, television, podcasts and radio shows, designing fashion, buildings or games, developing marketing and advertising campaigns, telling stories, and producing art. All of this enables the interconnected networks, defined by shared knowledges, and supports these choice making agents as they endeavor to be entrepreneurial within the creative industries (eco)system.

References

Australian Ceramics Community. (2023). *TAFE NSW Hunter street | Newcastle art school.* Australian Ceramics Community. Retrieved April 23, 2023, from https://www.australianceramicscommunity.com/listing/tafe-nsw-hunter-street-newcastle-art-school/

Becker, H. (1982). *Art worlds.* University of California Press.

Csikszentmihalyi, M. (1997). *Creativity: Flow and the psychology of discovery and invention.* Harper Collins.

Haralambos, M., & Holborn, M. (2013). *Sociology: Themes and perspectives* (8th ed.). Harper Collins.

Hunter iF. (2023). *About us.* Hunter iF. Retrieved January 13, 2023, from https://hunterif.com.au/about-hif/

HunterNet. (2018). *About us.* HunterNet. Retrieved August 15, 2018, from https://hunternet.com.au/about-us/

HunterTAFE. (2018). *Design Centre Hunter.* TAFENSW Hunter & Central Coast. Retrieved May 7, 2018, from http://www.hunter.tafensw.edu.au/careerareas/cifm/pages/design-centre-hunter.aspx

McIntyre, P., Fulton, J. M., Kerrigan, S. M., & Meany, M. M. (2023). *Entrepreneurship in the creative industries: How innovative agents, skills and networks interact.* Palgrave Macmillan.

RDA Hunter. (2018). *Initiatives.* Regional Development Australia—Hunter. Retrieved August 15, 2018, from http://rdahunter.org.au/initiatives/initiatives

Sawyer, K. (2012). *Explaining creativity: The science of human innovation* (2nd ed.). Oxford University Press.

UON. (2022). *2021 Annual report.* The University of Newcastle. Retrieved April 27, 2022, from https://www.newcastle.edu.au/__data/assets/pdf_file/0004/819490/2021-2025-Annual-Report-2021_Part01-REP-3.1-Complete-WEB.pdf

16
Conclusion

From all of the above, from the literature review, statistical analysis and the qualitative work derived from each of the sectors—music, performing arts, visual arts, architecture, fashion, advertising and design, publishing, radio, television, film, and electronic games and software development—we can say that creative practitioners, choice making agents, constitute an important part of a diverse and continually dynamic creative system focused on disseminating, profiting from and valorizing the signifying practices used to produce symbolic messages. These symbolic messages emerge from a creative system in action. This system, set out by Csikszentmihalyi (1988, 1997, 1999, 2014), was reconceptualized by Kerrigan (2013) and detailed in McIntyre et al. (2016). It works in combination with Bourdieu's research into cultural production (1993, 1996).

The effect of Bourdieu's thinking, in toto, is to take the creative agent out of the center of thinking and emphasize their interrelationships with the social and cultural structures they are embedded in and, at the same time, act upon. For Bourdieu, the idea of the space of works, the

P. McIntyre et al., *Creativity and Creative Industries in Regional Australia*, Palgrave Studies in Creativity and Culture, https://doi.org/10.1007/978-3-031-45972-6_16

accumulated heritage of all possible works produced in a cultural field to this point:

> presents possibilities of action to an individual who possesses the necessary habitus, partially composed of personal levels of social, cultural, symbolic and economic capital that then inclines them to act and react within particular structured and dynamic spaces called fields. These fields are arenas of production and circulation of goods, ideas and knowledges. They are populated by other agents who compete using various levels of the forms of capital pertinent to that field. Bourdieu suggests that it is the interplay between these various spheres of cultural production that makes practice possible. (McIntyre, 2009, p. 7)

The important thing to consider about all of this is to recognize that if we are to understand the way culture comes into being, especially in the creative industries, we need to be examining each of these things 'all at the same time' (Johnson in Bourdieu, 1993, p. 9).

Laying this thinking against Csikszentmihalyi's ideas on creativity, themselves an amalgam of both psychological and sociological thinking, we can see, again, that the system of creativity consists:

> of three interlocking and interactive subsystems. These include a structured knowledge system manifest in all the collected works pertinent to that symbol system. This is called a domain. It also consists of a field, that is, a structured social organization that operates using domain knowledge in a process of coopetition. This field is populated by all those who can act upon and affect the symbol system, that is those with varying expertise including other produsers, gatekeepers, cultural intermediaries and audiences. The third subsystem we will call an agent. This agent is an active choice making entity which may be scaled outward from individuals to dyads, groups and other collective entities such as institutions who make "changes to the stored information that pre-exists them" (Csikszentmihalyi, 1988, p. 329). These agents necessarily have a unique but shared background and bring their distinctive characteristics to bear on the entire system. (McIntyre, 2021, pp. 8–9)

Each of the elements of the system operates through 'dynamic links of circular causality' (Csikszentmihalyi, 1988, p. 329), where the starting point of emergence is not attributable to a single causal factor but to many, 'indicating the systems essential nonlinearity' (McIntyre, 2009, p. 7). It can be represented graphically in a number of ways (Csikszentmihalyi, 1988, 1999; McIntyre, 2021; Sawyer, 2006, 2012) but Kerrigan's reconceptualization of this system is more than apt for our purposes here (Fig. 16.1).

We note that this system is not singular or static. It is dynamic and scalable and can be used to represent holarchies, that is, systems operating above and below the one being observed. From this perspective, holarchies are comprised of a hierarchy of holons. Holons are themselves complete systems and, at the same time, are parts or partons, of a larger

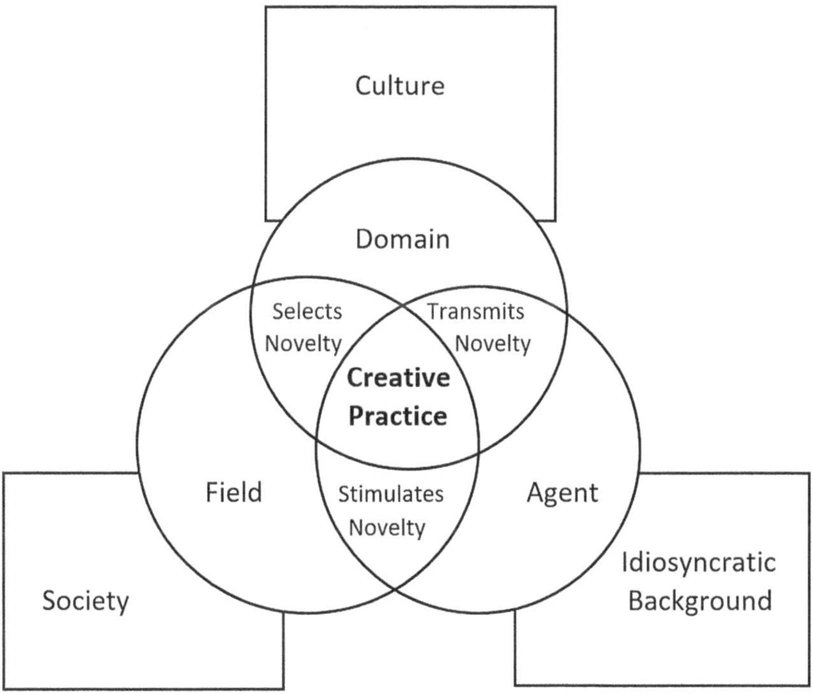

Fig. 16.1 Systems model of creativity reconceptualized by Kerrigan

system, one nested inside the other. None of these nested systems 'can be regarded as more primary than the other' (Skyttner, 2006, p. 34). With this complexity in mind, we can also say that, coming from the research we have set out in this book, a portion of this overall system, that is the field, the interconnected networks of action defined by a set of shared domain knowledges, can also be represented in the following way (Fig. 16.2):

This representation of the field, itself a system—or "ecosystem" if the notion of systems appears unpalatable—is not only comprised of specialist, support and embedded persons, who make the most obvious statistically measurable set of operatives within the creative industries, that is, the recognized professionals, but also those members of the industry who are counted elsewhere in other industries such as in education, retail, or manufacturing. This perspective also recognizes that the education, retail and manufacturing arms are very much a part of this creative (eco)system. For example, those working at Musos Corner in Newcastle West

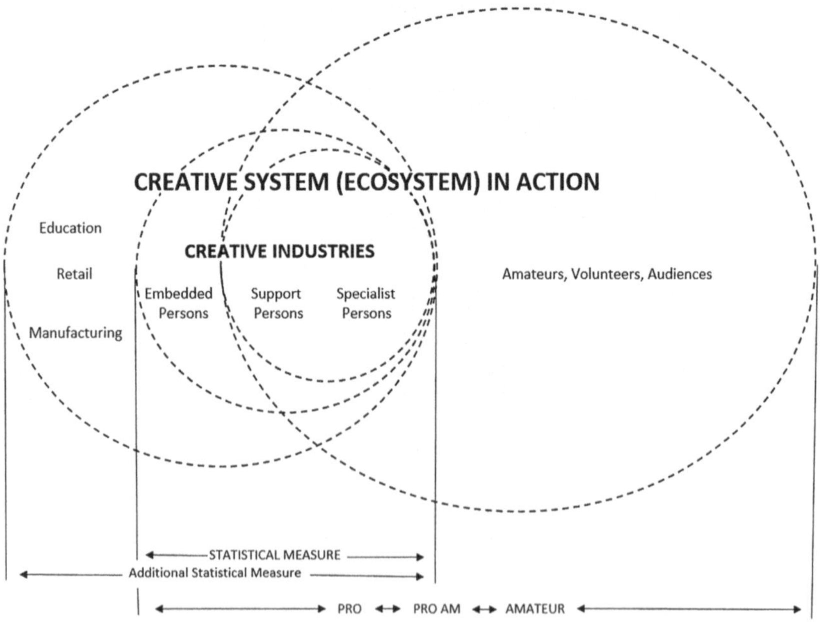

Fig. 16.2 The creative (eco)system of the field in action

and at Eckersley's in Hamilton see themselves as very much part of the music industries and art worlds respectively. Looking at the creative activity in this region in this way also accounts for the all-important pro-ams, as well as the numerous amateurs, volunteers and audiences who comprise a very important set of contributors to this entrepreneurial system. This system of the field, the social organization that coalesces around certain shared domains of knowledge, produces economic, social, cultural and symbolic value for the economy and the broader community.

Some sectors of the creative industries system that have developed in the Hunter Region, and continue to do so, are mature while others are still emerging. Radio, architecture, television, and advertising and design, for example, are well established in the commercial sphere in the Hunter valley while publishing, the performing and visual arts, and music have maintained a long and deep sociocultural tradition in the region. Local communities have sustained them for a long time. Unsurprisingly, electronic games and software development are emergent sectors which could, if encouraged and financed adequately, stimulate further creative activity in nearly all of the other sectors. Many operatives from other sectors are already in demand within this sector nationally, particularly for the production of games.

There have also been ongoing and, at times, remarkable changes in this (eco)system. This dynamism has certainly occurred across the lifespan of this research project. Apart from the variations in the way people, choice making agents within the system, have been deriving income and the means by which they have been producing a variety of symbolic messages, it needs to be noted that one of the significant changes is in that of attitudes within the region to the notion of the creative industries itself. From the beginning of the study it was observed that culturally specific beliefs and assumptions, particularly about creativity and the way it is believed to work, played a major part in actions taken by many significant institutions and active decision-making entities. Many of these exhibited little understanding of what the creative industries actually are. A number, relying on what could be called a well-worn set of Romantic myths, beliefs and assumptions, would either want to divorce creativity completely from the notion of an industry altogether, or have little real cognizance of the social, cultural, symbolic or indeed economic input the creative industries are contributing to the region. Towards the latter part of the project it was noticeable from observation and interviews that the term "creative industries" had grown, if not in acceptability, certainly in recognition, within the region. For example, the Newcastle City Council in their *Newcastle's Economic Development Strategy 2016–2019* document not only reinforced the importance of innovation and creativity (NCC, 2016, p. 5) but directly recognized the creative industries as a strategic growth sector (NCC, 2016, p. 34). Prior to actions such as this, there tended to be an understanding of the creative industries, certainly from within the business community, as primarily "basket weaving", as one respondent put it. It has come as a surprise to some that the creative industries are indeed strong contributors to the regional economy just as many of the more traditionally focused industries are. Coupled with the recognition of the creative industries' contribution, it was observed that there is also now a tendency on the part of financial donors, patrons and investors, to expect more than "art for art's sake" from the recipients of these funds. Economic indicators are increasingly part of the selection criteria for many involved in sponsorships and grants from these sectors, with the notable exception being for what has been called "straight arts funding".

It was also observed that many participants inside the creative industries themselves tended to view these industries, again unsurprisingly, from within their own specific sectoral lens. It was not uncommon, as one example only, to hear people working within the design community to refer to themselves as the "creatives" within the region, neglecting to observe the possibility that creativity was occurring across all the other sectors, including not only the arts but also the media and IT, as well. Similarly, regional understandings have tended to be focused at the urban center. It was difficult for many, including for the researchers on this project, to look beyond the urban hub and not just focus on Newcastle in particular. Scalability, as a property of systems, is nonetheless still deeply operative in this regional system. The hinterland remains deeply interconnected with the urban center, just as this regional hub is still deeply connected to the state capital, and, significantly, with the rest of the world. The movement of people, ideas, projects, goods and services between and within this scaled system, from the local to the global, was one of the characteristics found to be true of this creative system in action.

Observations and in-depth interviews revealed that quite a number of operatives are "glocally" oriented, that is, many of them are locally rooted but globally active. Each sector revealed at least one story, and often many more, where particular people developed their skills within the regional system to the point where they could trade on them internationally and move out into the wider world. This creative drain, from the regional to the global, was often reversed as, after approximately a decade of this activity on the international stage, many have moved back to the region to live and raise a family, bringing a global level of expertise, and a desire to continue to operate at that level, to the region. This situation was coupled with those who found their way to the Hunter in an attempt to escape the overcrowding and real estate pressures felt in larger urban agglomerations. Many of this latter group have been surprised by what they found in this region and have generally relished the lifestyle opportunities it affords. Either way it was observed that the region gained a net benefit in terms of the input of the global expertise that has become part of the fabric of the region.

Commensurate with these migratory patterns often associated with the creative industries, are the affordances provided by the digital technologies they now have at their disposal. As well as the increasing use of these tools in the creative production process, there is a growing concern over the necessity for extensive storage and fast broadband speeds. Apart from diminishing the isolation of regional centers, the internet in particular has presented commercial opportunities not apparent to earlier incarnations of the creative sector. Whether they engage with the NBN or wait for the far faster 5G network, many practitioners employ newer digital technologies, applications and platforms to varying degrees in the creation, distribution and promotion of their products and services. In short, internet access is now *de rigueur* for the creative industries to connect them with their global customers.

While some more traditional and established creative industry businesses are ambivalent in their engagement with the digital environment (simply having a website, for example), a number of innovative and emerging players are much more *au fait* with the digital economy and adept at using the tools it offers. Further, they engage with other creatives locally, nationally and internationally to extend their knowledge bases, communication networks and markets. Many creative businesses do also deploy social media and many, especially those in the design and advertising field, appear to understand its benefits. However, based on an examination of these companies' websites, a number still engage with social media only as a form of mass communication. For example, all the key advertising agencies in Newcastle emphasize the importance of an aesthetic "look" and use a form of engagement in their websites through the use of video clips, but a number do not use social media as a form of conversation. In this case, it can be claimed that social media is primarily treated as a mass communication channel in the region which is designed to send out information with little expectation of reply or desire for comment as part of a genuinely encouraged conversational interaction. There are, of course, many exceptions since many of the cooperatives and collaborative spaces are much more dynamic in terms of blogging and open creative expression. What is common to each sector is an increasingly necessary presence on social media, some businesses operating solely online and others using a mix of traditional and more innovative entrepreneurial approaches (for details see McIntyre et al., 2023, pp. 90–104). These entrepreneurial strategies are, of course, linked to the way they gain income for their businesses and the finances available to them (McIntyre et al., 2023).

Apart from the general issues surrounding finance for creative industry professionals and small business owners, choice making agents who depend on a certain level of income to stay afloat, there is also the question of the effect of the gift economy. There is little doubt that the gift economy is a significant part of the creative system at work. The gifts exchanged in these processes, many of which go unaccounted for in many business models, are both tangible and intangible. Exchange in the gift economy is not only an economic transaction, it is also good in itself, resulting in social capital or the strengthening of personal relationships. This personal interaction is fundamental to the establishment of networks since social capital can be converted into economic capital. Additionally, the use of social, cultural or symbolic capital will often supersede financial capital as the basis of the gift economy. The actions of gifts in the Hunter Region are not only linked to the formal and thus more measurable economy, as seen in the figures in Chap. 4 indicating Gross Regional Product, but this informal gift economy is highly operative and one where not only professionals exchange the gift but volunteers, amateurs and pro-amateurs dominate in its operation. It was observed that many sectors, whether they are mature or emergent, have come to rely on these amateurs and pro-amateurs to support their industrial structures.

The creative industries rely on this army of volunteers, amateurs and pro-amateurs to underpin much of the activity in each of the sectors. This idea reinforces the point that we are looking at not just an industry measure via ABS statistics, seemingly complete in itself, but a creative system, or (eco)system, that encompasses all of those individuals—core, support and embedded workers as well as all the volunteers, amateurs and pro-amateurs—involved in each sector and the vital contribution they make. There is a deep connection, as one example, between the 16 FTE positions available in the theater world and the approximately 11,000 volunteer positions that undergird the 41 active theater companies in the region. Businesses like Musos Corner do not cater solely to fully professional musicians; they would go out of business if they did. It is the amateur and pro-amateur musicians—the weekend warriors—that support them. The economic contribution to the regional economy of the multiplier effect, as seen in the film sector, is also applicable here. In short, it is readily apparent from the observational and interview components of this ethnographic study that the gift economy is enormous in comparison to what the analyses from both statistical measures have revealed.

In the face of these interconnections as well as the rapid changes associated with digitization and globalization, a variety of business models, that is, a specific method or procedure for generating revenue, are being used by the creative industries in the region. While internet commerce has generated a slew of supposedly new ways of doing business it needs to be stressed that many of these apparently new methods of gaining revenue are simply reinventions of "tried-and-true models" (Rappa, 2010, online) indicating, yet again, that an immersion in a set of antecedent conditions is still vital to the introduction of any novelty. While it can be observed from all of the above that there is a complex and variable set of income streams operating across most creative industries, as noted, many of these models are extensions, sometimes radical, sometimes not, of pre-existing revenue earning opportunities (McIntyre et al., 2023, pp. 91–94).

What can be said with certainty from analysis, observation and interview, is that, in an effort to maintain their productive output and competitive edge, companies and individuals working within this dynamic creative ecosystem in the region, all of them being choice making agents constrabled by the structures they are part of (Criticos, 2021), have become increasingly and excessively diversified in generating income streams. Discerning the difference between what a recording studio like Tommirock currently offers, as one example, and what advertising agencies do for income, is becoming increasingly difficult. At the same time, and interconnected with the prior situation, we have observed a rapidly growing trend toward outsourcing, freelancing and the casualization of the workforce. As a result many creative industries operatives have been forced to work cross-sectorally in order to gain an income; for many of them there is a need to undertake multiple tasks in order to gain one income, with a commensurate set of core skills needing to be maintained by most of them. In this case, we can claim that most operatives in the creative industries need to be specialized vertically as well as multi-skilled horizontally. This way of working has become known as having a necessarily T-shaped profile. As a result, it was observed that there is an increasing degree of mobility between occupations. This necessity to be multi-skilled, while maintaining a specialization, is coupled with an increasing set of difficulties for many casuals and freelancers to gain finance, particularly from banking institutions, to facilitate business expansion, finance a home or partake of what used to be called a "normal" life.

Related to these difficulties is the idea that the tangible structures of production that typify traditional industries, that is, 'firms, labor, production network, industrial districts, and markets—that is the normal stock in trade of industrial investigation' (Hutton, 2009, p. 139) are mutating. There are, as this research has identified, 'shifting boundaries of function, evolving technical divisions of labor, and emergent product sectors' (Hutton, 2009, p. 139). While the term "industry", once used to describe evolving and organizational structures, arose at the same time as the advent of the industrial revolution, its conception continues to change. For example, in 1972 G.B. Richardson pointed out that industries are not islands. Instead 'there is a dense network of cooperation and affiliation by which firms are inter-related' (1972, p. 883) where 'industry and market boundaries are porous and "fuzzy" especially where globalization is taking place' (McGee et al., 1995, p. 261). Todeva, Knoke & Keskinova also indicate researchers have periodically noted an 'imprecision of industry definition and the "fuzziness" of industry boundaries in economic environments' (2007, p. 2). As our own research here confirms, in the twenty-first century there is an increasing tendency to recognize industries as loosely coupled systems of production (e.g., Dubois & Gadde, 2002). We claim the creative industries in the Hunter Region of Australia exhibit these tendencies.

In observing what we see as increasing changes from creative industries to creative systems, or (eco)systems, we also claim that current entrepreneurial approaches in the region are not only primarily employing extensions of more traditional business models but are, by necessity, adapting to pressures of globalization and digitization. Pointing to these contextual features, Schulz asserted 'the technological advances made in the last decade have been breathtaking, but it is likely still just the beginning … It is the kind of sea change that can only be compared with 19th century industrialization, but it is happening much faster this time' (2015, online).

To reiterate, the creative industries, like all others, do not exist in a contextual vacuum. The same idea can be applied to this study. As we outlined in Chap. 3 there were many creative industries reports and studies that preceded and fed into this one (e.g., ACG, 2013; CIIC, 2013; Essential, 2013; Grace, 2009; Lhermitte et al., 2015; NR Arts, 2012). Similarly, this study was not the last word to be had on this matter. As we had signaled earlier, out of this regional study came a national-level study that took the overall methodological approach and applied it to regional creative industries across the country. Adding to and leaping off from the Hunter project, we undertook what eventually became known as the Creative Hotspots Study, this time led by Distinguished Professor Stuart Cunningham from the Queensland University of Technology (QUT) in partnership with our team from the University of Newcastle. We expanded our range of industry partners which went on to include Arts

Queensland, Create NSW, Creative Victoria, Arts South Australia and the Western Australian Department of Local Government, Sport and Cultural Industries.

The identified creative hotspots located in regional Australia, apart from Newcastle and the Hunter Region, included: Cairns, the Sunshine Coast, the Gold Coast and the Central West in Queensland; Coffs Harbour/Bellingen, Marrickville, Wollongong and Albury in NSW; Wodonga, Ballarat, Bendigo and Geelong/Surf Coast in Victoria; and Geraldton, Fremantle, Busselton and Albany/Denmark in Western Australia. The South Australia research took place in Adelaide using one precinct. There were 455 fieldwork interviews conducted across the entire project with an analysis of these revealing a set of key insights from the regional hotspots. These themes were centered around: the creative ecosystem; allied industries; the role of government and local councils; digital skills, and Indigenous creative enterprise. All of the fieldwork for the Creative Hotspots Study was conducted in 2019 prior to COVID.

As set out in our White Paper (Cunningham et al., 2022), we saw from our statistical analysis and qualitative fieldwork that there was, as was the case with the Hunter, a set of systemic, interconnected and dynamic relationships at work within the creative sector that included the commercial and the non-commercial sectors within what was a complete creative ecosystem. The regional emphasis indicated that the 'interconnections between sectors are more common and there is less opportunity for siloisation and division of labor as in the more complex ecosystems of larger metros' (Cunningham et al., 2022, p. 5). It was noted that media institutions in the regions were vitally important, far more so than in metropolitan areas. We saw that 'the role of broadcast advertising, community-oriented and tourism related programming constitute a major-scale contribution to popular perceptions of sense of place, community belonging and cultural identity' (Cunningham et al., 2022, p. 5) and the loss of commercial broadcasting and print media, in particular, had an obvious and major impact on the regions. It was also noted that creative industry operatives, choice making agents working in the regions had 'little option but to be entrepreneurial, with creatives forging portfolio career paths as they incorporate commercial work alongside their non-commercial practice' (Cunningham et al., 2022, p. 6). Similar to the

Hunter study, 'prominent brokers, often people making, or having made, decent livings in commercial roles, act as intermediaries, giving back as mentors and through leadership of community organizations' (Cunningham et al., 2022, p. 6) and the 'power and potential of digital innovation is clear' (Cunningham et al., 2022, p. 7).

The national Creative Hotspots Study also revealed that the demand for creative and cultural outputs was not just a factor of end-user's engagement. Key allied industries were also identified as underwriting a sustainable regional creative economy. Education, health, tourism and strong social enterprises, for example, all helped to drive demand for the creative industries' output in those regions. As noted in the project's White Paper, many creative operatives, choice making agents within the system, also engaged with the education sector as they offered tailored education programs aligned with their expertise allowing many people to 'stay to practice their profession, join businesses in the regions and to become educators themselves' (Cunningham et al., 2022, p. 8).

What also marked these Creative Hotspots out was the 'role of government and council and the importance of vision and effective planning at the council level' (Cunningham et al., 2022, p. 11). While most federal, state and territory governments have cultural plans in place it is not common for local governments to do so. The local government in each hotspot were an exception, as was the case in the Hunter Region. Those:

> with a vision for developing cultural infrastructure and delivering cultural services bring a vital demand-side perspective, crucially supplementing federal, state and territory governments' supply-side arts grant programs. Furthermore, where there is aligned vision and political heft brought to bear across three levels of government, there is often outstanding resource alignment allowing significant infrastructure investments. (Cunningham et al., 2022, p. 11)

Interestingly, and unlike the Hunter Region, a lack of digital skills was evident in each regional creative hotspot studied. This deficit was built on an 'inability to train, attract and retain talent with advanced levels of digital literacy' and was commensurate with the 'size of the hotspot and its proximity to a capital city and a university' (Cunningham et al., 2022,

p. 14). Without a large enough base, 'a lack of training opportunities and a perceived lack of work' (Cunningham et al., 2022, p. 14) meant many who did want to engage digitally were faced with leaving the region. Not so for many Indigenous communities. It was a highlight of the study that we encountered a number of Indigenous-controlled businesses, as well as festivals, that provided not only cultural tourism experiences but also 'important employment and training opportunities for their First Nations staff' (Cunningham et al., 2022, p. 17).

While the timeframe for the research was a snapshot of a particular time and place, the impact of COVID-19, coming as it did at the tail end of the fieldwork, could not be dismissed too rapidly. A preliminary and limited indicative survey was conducted at this time with creative industries business owners and self-employed creatives by members of the Creative Hotspot Analysis' research team (Flew & Kirkwood, 2020). The survey indicated that 75% of the respondents were living in regional or rural NSW, Victoria and Western Australia with 60.87% of respondents female and 39.13% male. None of the respondents were First Nations. The respondents were employed across the gamut of creative industries occupations with those working in Festivals and Events (44%) and Visual Arts and Crafts (44%) being heavily represented, as was Music and Performing Arts (30%), Advertising and Marketing (26%) and Architecture and Design (21%). Those working in Writing and Publishing stood at 13.04% with Film, TV and Radio represented by 8.7% of respondents. The main type of employment was within an SME with less than 20 paid staff (22%) with Sole Traders, Creative Entrepreneurs and Not for Profit Organizations represented by 8.7% of respondents each for these categories. In terms of results, the majority of respondents declared that their Industry (or CI sub-sector) had been adversely affected by COVID-19 (74%), but surprisingly a quarter of respondents confirmed that their sector was not affected. Reduced cash flow (82%) was listed as a major concern for these CI workers and 57% confirmed that COVID-19 had adversely affected their livelihood, while some indicated that it did not (35%) with a small number (9%) being "unsure". An overwhelming majority (70%) said they were required to work from home in relatively adverse circumstances. Other issues associated with these circumstances were reduced hours of work (38%), having to do "home duties" such as home-educating children (31%), and a number unable to travel for work (23%). For this latter group, they were unable to operate due to government restrictions on travel (53%). A third of respondents indicated that the economic impact of COVID-19 on their profession/industry meant they were significantly impacted with between 50% and 99% indicating they were worse off.

There were, however, some positive responses. A minority (17%) indicated their income was greater than it was prior to March 2020. Nearly all of the respondents overwhelmingly adopted online strategies to distribute their content (94%) in an attempt to reach out to their primary audiences (70%). When asked if these were successful measures to take, the majority (60%) were positive with some indicating it was not yet clear (20%) how successful this strategy was.

In terms of the outlook for the future, COVID-19 has meant that more of the respondents (48%) felt less optimistic about the future of cultural and creative industries in their regional area than they did 12 months ago. The respondents had mixed views about how quickly their sectors would return to normal, with most feeling it would take at least two years (35%) to return to normal, while others thought six months (26%) and a limited number feeling it could be immediate (17%) once a vaccine became widely available.

It is of note that the overwhelming number of people involved in the creative industries adopted online strategies very quickly, using these to distribute a wide variety of content in an attempt to reach out to and maintain their primary audiences as the COVID-19 pandemic set in (McIntyre & Kerrigan, 2020). At the same time, many of those who were locked down in their homes turned in overwhelming numbers to the outputs of the creative industries—films, podcasts, social media content, news subscription services, streaming platforms, kindle books, and games and apps of all types—which helped them to maintain a sense of equilibrium and social connection through the trying times COVID presented. Educators, for example, turned to their overseas and national colleagues to find out methods for immediately delivering material in an online world. They did this through social media, with videos posted on YouTube and much information being exchanged through Zoom. Musicians began recording their daily activities in song on their laptops, amusing many as they did so. Facebook pages showing photographs of "views from my window" from countries all over the world began to circulate rapidly. All of this creative industries' output was watched, listened to and read avidly online and all of this was provided for them by the operatives, amateur through to professional, from the creative industries (McIntyre & Kerrigan, 2020).

In the midst of the uncertainty created by COVID-19, the creative industries were increasingly central actors in what can be called a global signifying system. All of the sectors in the creative industries were used not only to represent corporate, political and economic activity, which had an effect on the public sphere, but it remained the case that all other industries depended on the creative industries to get their messages out and mediate their ideas through a variety of audio-, visual- and text-based cultural forms (McIntyre & Kerrigan, 2020). When asked if the online tactics ramped up during COVID-19 by those working in the creative industries were successful measures to take in the face of that pandemic, the majority of creatives were positive with some indicating it was not yet clear how successful this strategy would be economically. Many gave away their products, and the hours, days and months involved in making them, for free. The difficulty, as always, had been how to monetize this gold rush of attention and awareness in a purely online world.

The risks inherent in introducing novelty into a society, despite COVID, remain fundamental to developing valued products and services for the creative industries. These industries have had to become even more entrepreneurial, continue to generate motivated risk takers and learn to be, as they have had to do in good times and bad, highly resilient, especially given the competitive and complex global environment in which all of this has occurred. Those who depend on the creative industries to mediate their world through a variety of audio-, visual- and text-based cultural forms may often be unaware that these bellwether industries exist in a set of structural conditions that include international legal frameworks, industrial settings, trade agreements, public and private sector investment, as well as the second and third legs of the triple bottom line (Elkington, 1999), that is, a veritable host of financial, sociocultural and environmental entanglements. In the face of these dynamics, new occupations such as social media manager, transmedia storyteller, technopreneur or digital strategist are emerging at an exponential rate. However, focusing solely on the economic implications also belies the community building and social cohesion that emanates from such things as telling one's own stories, singing one's own songs or relying on each other to build successful teams whose sole aim is not simply to gain an income. If culture is about a whole way of life (Williams, 1981), the creative industries are particularly adept at symbolizing this aspect of ourselves for ourselves and in succeeding in carrying these signifying practices to the rest of the world. It is, in fact, these activities, these signifying practices, that differentiate the creative industries from most other industries. That said, the social and cultural value of these industries at the local, national and global levels has not always equated to financial value, although in many cases here in the Hunter it has. In this case, we can claim that the Hunter Region houses a set of complex and dynamic creative (eco)systems, that is, creative industries sectors which operate as subsystems of a broader creative system in action, where active, creative choice making agents are both constrained and enabled by the social, cultural, technological, economic, environmental, political and legal structures that afford their innovative activity. Creative industries agents, those choice making entities who employ creativity on an almost daily basis, do so within highly interconnected networks that form the subsectors of the creative industries and, at the same time, they cooperate and compete with each other while exploiting their expertise in the form of hard-won domain knowledge, shared by the fields they work in, as they attempt to profit from this regional creative system in action.

References

ACG. (2013). *Scoping a research and innovation cluster in the creative industries in Newcastle and the Hunter Region: Report to the University of Newcastle*. Allen Consulting Group.

Bourdieu, P. (1993). *Field of cultural production* (R. Johnson, Ed.). Columbia University Press.

Bourdieu, P. (1996). *The rules of art: Genesis and structure of the literary field*. Polity Press.

CIIC. (2013). *Valuing Australia's creative industries: Final report*. Prepared by SGS Economics and Planning for the Creative Industries Innovation Centre. Retrieved March 21, 2023, from https://sgsep.com.au/assets/main/Valuing-Australias-Creative-Industries-Final-Report-December-2013_Email.pdf

Csikszentmihalyi, M. (1988). Society, culture and person: A systems view of creativity. In R. Sternberg (Ed.), *The nature of creativity: Contemporary psychological perspectives* (pp. 325–329). Cambridge University Press.

Csikszentmihalyi, M. (1997). *Creativity: Flow and the psychology of discovery and invention*. Harper Collins.

Csikszentmihalyi, M. (1999). Implications of a systems perspective for the study of creativity. In R. Sternberg (Ed.), *Handbook of creativity* (pp. 313–335). Cambridge University Press.

Csikszentmihalyi, M. (2014). *The systems model of creativity*. Springer.

Cunningham, S., McCutcheon, M., Ryan, M., Kerrigan, S., McIntyre, P., & Hearn, G. (2022). *Creative hotspots in the regions: Key thematic insights and findings from across Australia*. Australian Research Council/Digital Media Research Centre. QUT.

Dubois, A., & Gadde, L. (2002). The construction industry as a loosely coupled system: Implications for productivity and innovation. *Construction Management and Economics, 20*(7), 621–631. https://doi.org/10.1080/01446190210163543

Elkington, J. (1999). *Cannibals with forks: Triple bottom line of 21st century business*. Capstone Publishing.

Essential. (2013). *Creative industry in rural Victoria: Economic analysis*. [Essential Economics P/L for Rural Councils Victoria]. Municipal Association of Victoria.

Flew, T., & Kirkwood, K. (2020). *Submission to the parliamentary inquiry into Australia's creative and cultural industries and institutions*. House of Representatives Standing Committee on Communication and the Arts, Parliament of Australia.

Grace K. (2009). *Mid north coast creative industries research project*. Evolve Network Australia. Arts Mid North Coast.

Hutton, T. (2009). Cultural production in the transnational city. In A. Pratt & P. Jeffcutt (Eds.), *Creativity, innovation and the cultural economy* (pp. 139–160). Routledge.

Kerrigan, S. (2013). Accommodating creative documentary practice within a revised systems model of creativity. *Journal of Media Practice, 14*(2), 111–127. https://doi.org/10.1386/jmpr.14.2.111_1

Lhermitte, M., Blanc, S., & Perrin, B. (2015). *Cultural times: The first global map of cultural and creative industries.* Ernst & Young Report for the Confederation of Authors and Composers Societies. EYGM Ltd.

McGee, J., Thomas, H., & Pruett, M. (1995). Strategic groups and the analysis of market structure and industry dynamics. *British Journal of Management, 6*, 257–270. Retrieved from https://markwpruett.com/wp-content/uploads/2019/01/1995BJM.pdf

McIntyre, P. (2009, July 8–10). Rethinking communication, creativity and cultural production: Outlining issues for media practice. In T. Flew (Ed.), *Communication, creativity and global citizenship: Refereed proceedings of the Australian and New Zealand communications association annual conference, Brisbane, Australia.* ISBN 987-1-74107-275-4.

McIntyre, P. (2021). Songwriting practice and production: The past, present and future. *Songwriting Studies Journal, 1*, 5–26.

McIntyre, P., Fulton, J. M., Kerrigan, S. M., & Meany, M. M. (2023). *Entrepreneurship in the creative industries: How innovative agents, skills and networks interact.* Palgrave Macmillan.

McIntyre, P., Fulton, J., & Paton, E. (Eds.). (2016). *The creative system in action: Understanding cultural production and practice.* Palgrave Macmillan.

McIntyre, P., & Kerrigan, S. (2020). *Submission to the parliamentary inquiry into Australia's creative and cultural industries and institutions.* House of Representatives Standing Committee on Communication and the Arts, Parliament of Australia.

NCC. (2016). *Economic development strategy 2016-2019.* Newcastle City Council. Retrieved February 18, 2018, from www.newcastle.nsw.gov.au.

NR Arts. (2012). *Northern Rivers arts and creative industries strategy 2009–2012: Mapping report.* Arts Northern Rivers.

Rappa, M. (2010). *Business models on the web.* Retrieved June 26, 2017, from http://digitalenterprise.org/models/models.html

Richardson, G. (1972). The organization of industry. *The Economic Journal, 82*(327), 883–896. https://doi.org/10.2307/2230256

Sawyer, K. (2006). *Explaining creativity: The science of human innovation* (1st ed.). Oxford University Press.

Sawyer, K. (2012). *Explaining creativity: The science of human innovation* (2nd ed.). Oxford University Press.

Schulz, T. (2015, March 4). Tomorrowland: How Silicon Valley shapes our future. *Speigel Online: International.* Retrieved April 21, 2015, from http://www.spiegel.de/international/germany/spiegel-cover-story-how-silicon-valley-shapes-our-future-a-1021557.html

Skyttner, L. (2006). *General systems theory: Problems, perspectives, practice* (2nd ed.). World Scientific.

Todeva, E., Knoke, D., & Keskinova, D. (2007). *Porous and fuzzy boundaries: A network approach to corporate diversification*. Retrieved April 10, 2023, from http://assets.csom.umn.edu/assets/101202.pdf

Williams, R. (1981). *Culture*. Fontana.

Correction to: Introduction

Correction to:

Chapter 1 in: P. McIntyre et al., *Creativity and Creative Industries in Regional Australia*, Palgrave Studies in Creativity and Culture, https://doi.org/10.1007/978-3-031-45972-6_1

The original version of this chapter has been revised; the book title mentioned in the content of the introduction chapter in the fourth para (in the middle of p.3) has been updated. The correction can be now found at https://doi.org/10.1007/978-3-031-45972-6_1

The updated version of this chapter can be found at https://doi.org/10.1007/978-3-031-45972-6_1

P. McIntyre et al., *Creativity and Creative Industries in Regional Australia*, Palgrave Studies in Creativity and Culture, https://doi.org/10.1007/978-3-031-45972-6_17

Index[1]

[1] Note: Page numbers followed by 'n' refer to notes.

P. McIntyre et al., *Creativity and Creative Industries in Regional Australia*, Palgrave Studies in Creativity and Culture, https://doi.org/10.1007/978-3-031-45972-6

H

Q

The manufacturer's authorised representative in the EU is Springer Nature Customer Service Centre GmbH, Europaplatz 3, 69115 Heidelberg, Germany. If you have any concerns regarding our products, please contact ProductSafety@springernature.com

Printed and bound by CPI Group (UK) Ltd, Croydon, CR0 4YY
30/09/2026
02225439-0012